DEGREES *of* GIVENNESS

INDIANA SERIES IN THE PHILOSOPHY OF RELIGION

Merold Westphal, *editor*

DEGREES
of
GIVENNESS

On Saturation in Jean-Luc Marion

CHRISTINA M. GSCHWANDTNER

INDIANA UNIVERSITY PRESS
Bloomington and Indianapolis

This book is a publication of

Indiana University Press
Office of Scholarly Publishing
Herman B Wells Library 350
1320 East 10th Street
Bloomington, Indiana 47405 USA

iupress.indiana.edu

Telephone   800-842-6796
Fax   812-855-7931

Manufactured in the United States of America

Cataloging information is available from the Library of Congress.

ISBN 978-0-253-01419-1 (cloth)
ISBN 978-0-253-01428-3 (ebook)

1 2 3 4 5   19 18 17 16 15 14

für Dorli

CONTENTS

PREFACE

In this book I consider Jean-Luc Marion's proposal for a phenomenology of givenness and saturated phenomena, asserting a greater need for "degrees" of givenness and saturation. I discuss a variety of phenomena that Marion identifies as saturated, but also argue for other phenomena as saturated that Marion does not consider in his proposal, especially phenomena of nature. I move from some of the phenomena Marion identifies as "simply" saturated (event, idol, flesh, icon) to those he sees as "doubly" saturated, namely the phenomenon of revelation or religious phenomena. Throughout I contend that all these phenomena require an account of degrees of saturation, of degrees of "negative certainties," and especially a stronger role for hermeneutic preparation than Marion so far admits. The introduction sets the context by briefly laying out Marion's phenomenological project of givenness, explaining its most important terminology, such as those of the saturated phenomenon and negative certainty, and highlighting some of its central difficulties, especially those surrounding the role of hermeneutics. It discusses the ways in which Marion does or does not allow for degrees of givenness and considers why he focuses so strongly on the most excessive manifestations of phenomena. The introduction hence provides the background for understanding Marion's phenomenology but also articulates the contribution this particular study will make to that project. Although this book is critical of various aspects of Marion's thought, it certainly does not constitute a rejection of Marion's project per se; rather, it works within his phenomenology of givenness by suggesting important aspects that have not been explicitly considered by Marion himself but are not therefore incompatible with his project.

Chapter 1 focuses on historical events. Marion presents historical events as overwhelming encounters to which no historical account can ever do justice. They are excessive in quantity, so overwhelming that they cannot be "counted." He includes cultural and more personal events, such as a public lecture or a friendship. Marion admits that an "endless hermeneutics" is necessary in their regard because no account ever gives the full picture. Yet Marion says little about how distinguishing between accounts is possible, occasionally giving the impression that critical historical research is meaningless and futile. I show that he does not acknowledge that we might come to understand an event better after researching it carefully, that knowledge about it might increase, and that some accounts may well be more accurate than others and argue that these are essential aspects of a full account of historical phenomena as given both in saturated and less saturated form.

Chapter 2 considers Marion's discussion of art. Marion defines the artist as the one who has had a vision of the unseen and is able to communicate this vision in the painting, which gives what was previously unseen to full visibility. Great art always has to be seen again and again and continually reveals new dimensions on the viewer. Instead of being an object we impartially observe, it is instead a given phenomenon that overwhelms us with the impact it has on us. While some great paintings may indeed be given in such overwhelming fashion, I suggest that degrees of givenness are also required for taking account of the fact that we are not always completely overwhelmed by every work of art we view and that this is not merely a "fault" of the observer who cannot bear the bedazzling weight of the painting's glory. In this context I also contend that Marion's account of the artist comes dangerously close to Kantian versions of the "genius" and is thus subject to Gadamer's critique of this account.

In chapter 3 I propose natural phenomena as candidates for saturated phenomena. Marion's account so far has no place for nature. Animals and plants seem reduced to "technical objects" or are ignored entirely. This is deeply problematic both for ecological reasons and for what it means to be human. I suggest that natural phenomena can indeed be given as "saturated" phenomena in Marion's sense, but that hermeneutics and degrees of saturation are necessary for such an account. In this chapter I also provide an analysis of Marion's account of the flesh and suggest that a more "natural" account of the flesh and its sensations as rooted in our experience of nature might well prove necessary and illuminating.

In chapter 4 I examine Marion's troubling comparisons of love with war and argue that it highlights the "absolute" nature he attributes to love in his account. Love is utterly kenotic, totally overwhelming, inexpressible. I suggest that it must be possible to speak of a response to love and that it is problematic to speak of a lover who loves completely without any such response, that somehow the "phenomenon of love" can exist without a beloved. I also critique Marion's contention that an account of love must be "univocal" (that God loves in the same way as humans do) as inconsistent with his account in *Théologie blanche* that there can be no univocity in language applied to divine and human. Instead, I suggest that there are many different kinds and degrees of love and that even Marion's excessive account requires previous hermeneutic commitments.

Chapter 5 focuses on the phenomena of the gift and of sacrifice. Marion has extensively examined the topic of the gift and some of his more recent accounts qualify his earlier statements. I depict this trajectory and show that the more recent account in *Certitudes négatives* relieves many of the earlier difficulties, but is still too excessive. I join to this an analysis of Marion's descriptions of sacrifice and forgiveness, which he closely associates with the gift. I argue that these accounts disregard normal human experience in order to focus entirely on extremely exceptional instances which are rare if not nonexistent. Again I argue that hermeneutics is necessary to recognize gifts as such and that gifts also come in degrees.

Chapter 6 examines Marion's accounts of prayer in *The Crossing of the Visible* and other places in his work and suggests that it is too extreme and solitary. Marion consistently speaks of prayer in the singular and does not consider communal dimensions of religious experience, such as liturgical prayer. This points to a more general problem in Marion's account in that religious experience is almost exclusively thought in terms of the mystic at the heights of solitary contemplation. Such accounts are difficult to "verify" or even to describe phenomenologically. The chapter also reflects on Marion's discussion of sanctity as completely invisible and suggests important parallels to his accounts of prayer. I show that the larger tradition, on which Marion draws, considers degrees an essential aspect of growth in prayer.

Marion has repeatedly provided analyses of the Eucharist, beginning in *God without Being* and continuing in several later articles. Chapter 7 examines these various accounts and shows how the more recent ones resolve problems in the earlier descriptions. At the same time, I point to places where difficulties remain in this work and that these difficulties are consistent with the issues perceived in Marion's work overall: the emphasis on absolute excess, the disregard for communal or corporate experience—particularly troubling for an account of the Eucharist—and the dismissal of hermeneutics, especially in light of the fact that Marion talks about a "eucharistic hermeneutics" in the early account in *God without Being*.

The conclusion brings these various critiques together in a more general consideration of Marion's account of "saturated" experience as a whole. I show how it is conceived primarily in very excessive terms and argue that this is not representative of experience more generally and indeed not even of religious experience more specifically. I also wonder about Marion's habit of employing religious experience as paradigmatic for all other experience and suggest that this might not be the best way to talk about other saturated phenomena or indeed about religion and its role in human life. Throughout, I contend that even saturated phenomena require degrees of saturation, that they cannot always be given as "absolute" in the pure sense Marion suggests. I argue that saturated phenomena must differ not only in "kind" but also in "degree" and that this requires a fuller account of what might constitute less saturated phenomenality—a topic largely unexamined in Marion's work. Similarly, "negative certainties" must admit of degrees of increase; negative "knowledge" cannot be as pure and total as Marion suggests. There are "better" and "worse" ways of knowing or comprehending something about a work of art, a historical event, another person, and so forth. Increase in knowledge must be possible, even if it can never be total.

Finally, I contend throughout for the necessity of a more significant place for hermeneutics in an account of givenness and suggest that this brings together and maybe resolves to some extent many of the other difficulties (i.e., of excess and pure individuality and thus incommunicability and unverifiability). I argue that a hermeneutic dimension is necessary to contextualize experience and to make it possible to be "experience" even in a mode of "counter-experience," that it is necessary to speak about degrees both in terms of experience and in terms of knowledge about and account for experience, and that it is necessary for a more communal and less individualized account. Hermeneutics then emerges as maybe the most significant lacuna in Marion's thought, but also the issue with the most potential for resolving some of the difficulties of his phenomenology.

ACKNOWLEDGMENTS

Earlier versions of several of the chapters in this book have appeared elsewhere. All have been significantly revised, but I thank the editors of the following journals and books for allowing me to reuse aspects of previously published material:

An earlier version of parts of the introduction appeared as "Marion and Negative Certainty: Epistemological Dimensions of the Phenomenology of Givenness" in *Philosophy Today* 56.3 (2012): 363–70.

An earlier version of chapter 3 appeared as "Might Nature Be Interpreted as Saturated Phenomenon?," in *Interpreting Nature: The Emerging Field of Environmental Hermeneutics,* edited by Forrest Clingerman, Brian Treanor, Martin Drenthen, and David Utsler (New York: Fordham University Press, 2013), 82–101. The present version of chapter 3 is quite different but originated in this earlier piece. Some aspects of the arguments in that paper also appear in the introduction to this book.

An earlier version of chapter 4 appeared as "Love as a Declaration of War? On the Absolute Character of Love in Jean-Luc Marion's Phenomenology of Eros," in *Transforming Philosophy and Religion: Love's Wisdom,* edited by Norman Wirzba and Bruce Ellis Benson (Bloomington: Indiana University Press, 2008), 185–98.

An earlier version of chapter 5 appeared as "The Excess of the Gift in Jean-Luc Marion," in *Gift and Economy: Ethics, Hospitality, and the Market,* edited by Eric R. Severson (Newcastle upon Tyne: Cambridge Scholars Publishing, 2012), 20–32. Some ideas in that chapter also appeared in my response to Marion's "Sketch of a Phenomenological Concept of Sacrifice" on the Martin Marty Center's Religion and Culture Web Forum of the University of Chicago (Nov. 2008).

An earlier version of chapter 6 appeared as "Praise—Pure and Personal? Jean-Luc Marion's Phenomenologies of Prayer," in *The Phenomenology of Prayer,* edited by Bruce Ellis Benson and Norman Wirzba (New York: Fordham University Press, 2005), 168–81.

In this context I also wish to thank the many other people who have made this work possible and have provided much encouragement and assistance along the way: Donald A. Yerxa, my first philosophy teacher, who awakened a love for philosophy in me as an undergraduate, gave generously of his time to mentor me in countless ways, and also provided important pointers to sources for the first chapter. Stuart Martin at Boston College continually encouraged me to stick with philosophy and shaped me as a scholar not only by challenging me but by believing in me and investing in me on all kinds of levels. I also especially thank Richard Kearney, Merold Westphal, and Jack Caputo, for their support, mentoring, friendship, and stimulating exchanges at many conferences. I am grateful to my former colleagues in the philosophy department at the University of Scranton (especially Matthew Meyer) and also to the many grants and other kinds of support I received from the university in my ten years of teaching there, including the tireless assistance and kindness of our fabulous secretary, Mary Rafter. My gratitude goes also to my new colleagues (especially Samir Haddad) and students at Fordham University, who have made teaching there a genuine pleasure. The interlibrary loan staff at the Fordham University library, Charlotte Labbé and Christine Campbell, were immensely helpful in locating several foreign language sources at the last minute.

As indicated above, several of these essays had a first life in other publications, often in the context of presentations at the Society for Continental Philosophy and Theology. The stimulating conversations at these conferences contributed much to my thinking, and I particularly want to thank the organizers, especially Bruce Ellis Benson and Norman Wirzba, as well as the group of colleagues who over years of interactions have become friends: Brian Treanor, Eric Severson, Jeffrey Hanson, Sharon L. Baker, and B. Keith Putt. Tamsin Jones and Merold Westphal read an earlier draft of the manuscript and made many valuable suggestions. Jean-Luc Marion, whose work provided the main inspiration for this book, has always been most generous and kind. I am also very grateful to the fabulous staff at Indiana University Press, with whom it is always a pleasure to work, especially Dee Mortensen, Sarah Jacobi, and June Silay. Thank you also to Deborah Oliver for her excellent copyediting and patience with my many questions, to Father Calinic Berger for help in finding the cover image, and to Dan Baditoiu for allowing us to use his photo of the icon at Sucevița monastery. Much of this book was written in Boston at the home of my generous and hospitable friends, Esther Bowen and Keith Hemmings. Their unfailing friendship sustained me, as did that of the many other friends and colleagues too numerous to mention who listened and talked and commiserated and inspired my thinking and writing along the way.

This book is dedicated to my sister, Dorli, who has put up with me far more and far longer than anyone else, listened to more of my complaints, seen more of my many faults, and yet remains one of my very best friends. For your kindness and generosity, your endless patience, marvelous sense of humor, profound insight, continual encouragement, and just for listening again and again and again—thank you.

ABBREVIATIONS OF WORKS BY JEAN-LUC MARION

The abbreviations in this list refer to the actual editions cited in this book, but date of first publication appears in brackets. For further information, see the full listings in the bibliography.

BG/ED   *Being Given: Toward a Phenomenology of Givenness.* Translated by Jeffrey L. Kosky. Stanford, Calif.: Stanford University Press, 2002. *Étant donné. Essai d'une phénoménologie de la donation.* Paris: Presses Universitaires de France, 1998 [1997].

CN   *Certitudes négatives.* Paris: Grasset, 2010.

CpV   *Le croire pour le voir. Réflexions diverses sur la rationalité de la révélation et l'irrationalité de quelques croyants.* Paris: Parole et Silence, coll. Communio, 2010.

CQ/QCI   *Cartesian Questions: Method and Metaphysics.* Chicago: University of Chicago Press, 1999. *Questions cartésiennes. Méthode et métaphysique.* Paris: Presses Universitaires de France, 1991.

CV/CdV   *The Crossing of the Visible.* Translated by James K. A. Smith. Stanford, Calif.: Stanford University Press, 2004. *La croisée du visible.* Paris: Presses Universitaires de France, 1996 [1991].

EG/QCII   *On the Ego and on God: Further Cartesian Questions.* Translated by Christina M. Gschwandtner. New York: Fordham University Press, 2007. *Questions cartésiennes II. L'ego et Dieu.* Paris: Presses Universitaires de France, 2002 [1996].

EP/PE   *The Erotic Phenomenon.* Translated by Stephen E. Lewis. Chicago: University of Chicago Press, 2003. *Le phénomène érotique. Six méditations.* Paris: Grasset, 2003.

FP   *Figures de Phénoménologie. Husserl, Heidegger, Levinas, Henry, Derrida.* Paris: Vrin, 2012.

GH   *Givenness and Hermeneutics.* The Père Marquette Lecture in Theology 2013. Translated by Jean-Pierre Lafouge. Milwaukee, Wisc.: Marquette University Press, 2012. Includes French text of the lecture on facing pages.

GWB/DSL   *God without Being.* Translated by Thomas A. Carlson. Chicago: University of Chicago Press, 1991. *Dieu sans l'être.* Paris: Presses Universitaires de France, "Quadrige," 1991 [1982].

ID/IeD   *The Idol and Distance: Five Studies.* Translated and introduced by Thomas A. Carlson. New York: Fordham University Press, 2001. *L'idole et la distance.* Paris: Grasset, 1977.

IE/DS   *In Excess: Studies of Saturated Phenomena.* Translated by Robyn Horner and Vincent Berraud. New York: Fordham University Press, 2002. *De surcroît. Études sur les phénomènes saturés.* Paris: Presses Universitaires de France, 2001.

MP/PM   *On Descartes' Metaphysical Prism: The Constitution and the Limits of Onto-theo-logy in Cartesian Thought.* Translated by Jeffrey L. Kosky. Chicago: University of Chicago Press, 1999. *Sur le prisme métaphysique de Descartes.* Paris: Presses Universitaires de France, 1986.

OG   *Sur l'ontologie grise de Descartes.* Paris: Vrin, 2000 [1975].

PC/PaC   *Prolegomena to Charity.* Translated by Stephen E. Lewis. New York: Fordham University Press, 2002. *Prolégomènes à la charité.* Éd. de la Différence, 1986.

PPD   *Sur la pensée passive de Descartes.* Paris: Presses Universitaires de France, 2013.

RC   *La Rigueur des choses. Entretiens avec Dan Arbib.* Paris: Flammarion, 2012.

RG/RD   *Reduction and Givenness: Investigations of Husserl, Heidegger, and Phenomenology.* Translated by Thomas A. Carlson. Evanston: Northwestern University Press, 1998. *Réduction et donation. Recherches sur Husserl, Heidgger et la phénoménologie.* Paris: Presses Universitaires de France, 1989.

RoG   *The Reason of the Gift.* Translated by Stephen E. Lewis. Charlottesville: University of Virginia Press, 2011.

SP/LS   *In the Self's Place: The Approach of Saint Augustine.* Translated by Jeffrey L. Kosky. Stanford, Calif.: Stanford University Press, 2012. *Au lieu de soi. L'approche de Saint Augustin.* Paris: Presses Universitaires de France, 2008.

TB   *Sur la théologie blanche de Descartes.* Paris: Presses Universitaires de France, 1991 [1981].

VR/VeR   *The Visible and the Revealed.* New York: Fordham University Press, 2008. *Le visible et le révélé.* Paris: Éditions du CERF, coll. Philosophie & Théologie, 2005.

DEGREES *of* GIVENNESS

Givenness, Saturated Phenomena, Negative Certainties, and Hermeneutics

As the subtitle of *Being Given* indicates, Marion's philosophy can be defined as a "phenomenology of givenness." The term "givenness" featured already in his earlier preparatory work *Reduction and Givenness* where he first developed the notion of a "third reduction" to givenness. "Givenness" translates the French *donation,* which ostensibly translates the German term *Gegebenheit,* which is an important Husserlian term also used by Heidegger, as Marion contends in a more recent essay on that topic (RoG, 35–49; FP, 45–58). This translation of *Gegebenheit* with *donation* and givenness is not uncontroversial, and Marion has been challenged on this.[1] The piece on Heidegger collected with two other articles on Husserl in his book *Figures de phénoménologie* justifies his use and translation of this term in light of the criticism.[2] While givenness in general was the primary characteristic of Marion's first phenomenological proposals, the notion of the saturated phenomenon, which developed out of this phenomenology of givenness, has increasingly become not only the most well-known aspect of Marion's work but also the primary focus of Marion's later writings. Givenness is still central to the saturated phenomenon, as it is precisely a phenomenon that is given fully and certainly relies for its justification and description on a phenomenology of givenness, but this larger context of givenness has been somewhat overshadowed by the saturated phenomenon's specific mode of givenness.

This focus, however, also concentrates Marion's work and discussions of his philosophy almost exclusively on the most excessive aspect of givenness. In theory, at least as Marion first outlines his proposal in *Being Given* and also as he recapitulates it at the end of *Certitudes négatives,* givenness covers the entire range of phenomena in varying degrees: from "poor" phenomena or "technical objects" to ordinary or "common" phenomena to saturated ones. Saturated phenomena are only one particular instance or "degree" of phenomena, namely those most "saturated" or most "reduced." This almost exclusive focus on the most excessive instances of the given is somewhat unfortunate, as it covers over or even ignores *degrees* of phenomenality and makes Marion's phenomenology more excessive than it needs to be—and maybe more than is healthy for it. Jocelyn Benoist contends that Marion "absolutizes the phenomenon" and pushes it to an excessive extreme.[3] Similarly, François-David Sebbah chides Marion's phenomenology for hovering on the very limit of phenomenality, while remaining in a metaphysics of presence par excellence.[4] Vincent Holzer speaks of Marion's phenomenology as a "radical phenomenology," Martin Gagnon names it a "phenomenology at the limit," and Emmanuel Falque calls it a "phenomenology of the extraordinary."[5] This is exacerbated by Marion's fairly heavy use of superlative terminology in his descriptions. Yet even what Marion identifies as saturated phenomena might not always appear as excessive and extreme as he occasionally seems to indicate.

In light of this focus on excess, this book tries to develop the less saturated aspects of Marion's phenomenology or rather to argue that even the more saturated ones come in "degrees": that they are not the all-or-nothing experiences they are often presented or understood as. This discussion hence does not attempt to be a critique of Marion's project per se, but it tries to work within that project's overall framework in order to argue for greater attention to the "degrees" of phenomenality's givenness and for the importance of the hermeneutic dimension in interpreting and experiencing degrees of saturation or phenomenality more generally.[6] Although I am at times critical of various aspects of Marion's project, obviously it serves at the same time as the primary inspiration of my analysis. It is precisely because Marion's work is so rich and in many ways innovative that it gives rise to questions, requires qualifications, and occasions further discussion. In this introduction I briefly spell out Marion's proposal for a phenomenology of givenness, his notion of the saturated phenomenon, his more recent suggestion of "negative certainties" as an epistemological dimension of saturation, and the role hermeneutics has or has not played in this discussion. This is not necessarily an introduction to all of Marion's work, but it does try to provide enough context and information for what follows.[7]

Givenness

As indicated, givenness has been central to Marion's phenomenology from the beginning. In *Reduction and Givenness* he first tries to develop a phenomenology of givenness through a critique of Husserl and Heidegger. He suggests that their respective reductions to "objects" or "objectness" in the case of Husserl, and "beings" or "beingness in the case of Heidegger, have restricted the self-showing of the phenomenon or at least of certain phenomena that cannot be described as objects or beings and are not experienced in that fashion.[8] Their phenomenality does not "fit" the traditional descriptions, which are too reductive and limiting. The phenomenological reduction does not do justice to them because it makes too much dependent on the constituting ego that operates the reduction by constituting phenomena through its intentionality. This makes phenomena ultimately subject to the ego's constitution instead of allowing them to appear "from themselves" as they show themselves or give themselves to consciousness. This self-showing of the phenomenon is, of course, a central claim of phenomenology, which sets aside (via the epoché) all concerns with the phenomenon's existence "out there" or any other concerns that would "transcend" what is experienced by consciousness. Marion therefore capitalizes on one central phenomenological insight in order to criticize or even "overcome" another: we must allow phenomena to show or give themselves more freely than our "intentional" attempts at constitution have permitted them so far.

In *Reduction and Givenness,* Marion proposes this in terms of what he calls a third reduction that would operate on the principle "as much reduction, so much givenness." This means that if certain restrictions are set aside or "reduced," the phenomenon will show or give itself more fully. In this work Marion tries to develop the phenomenology of givenness naturally out of Husserl's and Heidegger's respective phenomenologies by showing their limitations and logical consequences. He argues that both open the field of given phenomena in certain ways but do not themselves proceed into it. Both Husserl and Heidegger insist that phenomena must show themselves from themselves; both acknowledge the importance of the given, but both ultimately draw back before its abundance. They open the possibility of moving beyond metaphysical constrictions, but they do not realize this possibility as fully as they should have. The given as such hence remains limited by objectity (or objectness) in the case of Husserl and by beingness (or the power wielded by Being) in the case of Heidegger. Marion instead seeks to uncover givenness in all its fullness and remove any restrictions whatsoever. He does so by exercising the reduction—as the fundamental phenomenological method—more rigorously and removing even the phenomenological horizon when it threatens to restrict the self-showing of phenomena to their form or to being (RG, 161; RD, 240). Beyond the "call of being," as Heidegger delineated it, a more originary call can be heard, the call or claim of the other (RG, 197; RD, 295). Henceforth I am summoned (as *interloqué*) by the unconditional and unconstrained call of the given as such (RG, 204; RD, 304).

Marion develops this proposal much more extensively in *Being Given.* The first part of that book spells out more fully the critique of Husserl and Heidegger as restricting the self-givenness of phenomena via a preoccupation with objectness and beingness, respectively, and justifies the ultimate principle linking radical reduction and full givenness in much more detail. Part 2 develops his earlier discussion of the gift and now uses it as a paradigm for the givenness of the phenomenon more generally.[9] Parts 3 and 4 concern the "determinations" and "degrees" of the given. The final part examines the recipient of the given: *l'adonné,* the one "given over" or "devoted to" (or "gifted by") the given. Parts 3 and 4 specifically concern aspects of phenomenality that are appropriately described as "degrees" of givenness, and the saturated phenomenon is articulated only fairly briefly in the latter half of part 4 (BG, 199–247; ED, 280–342), where the poor phenomenon also still occupies part of the discussion. Yet Marion's subsequent work focuses almost exclusively on this notion of saturation and on the various types of saturated phenomena. The poor phenomenon and the possibility that there might be degrees of givenness disappear almost entirely from view.[10]

Yet this earlier discussion of "determinations" and "degrees" of the given is illuminating in various ways, besides raising some questions about Marion's phenomenology that have not been fully addressed. Part 3 of *Being Given* begins by stating that, based on the discussion of givenness and the gift in parts 1 and 2 respectively, *all* phenomena must appear as given; phenomenality and givenness are identical. Here clearly not only saturated phenomena are meant. Part 3 articulates this "given" in terms of what is called anamorphosis, sudden arrival (translated as "unpredictable landing"), fait accompli, incident, event and "being given." When they are first formulated, these aspects indicate aspects of givenness more generally and do not yet apply exclusively to saturated phenomena. Marion's examples speak of technical objects "with the mode of Being of technology," of "practical" and of "theoretical" objects, and range from the experience of a computer, over that of a shading tree in hot weather, to the hailing of a taxi cab or the experience of shopping (BG, 128–29; ED, 181). The latter are identified as "habitual phenomena," a term Marion never uses again in his subsequent work. The way in which they are introduced certainly seems to imply that they constitute an important category: "I call these phenomena *habitual phenomena*. Habit does not mean that they function longer than the others (some of them are signaled by their brevity and incessant changing), but essentially that we must habituate ourselves to them. Habituating ourselves to them sometimes implies taking the time to accustom *ourselves* to them . . . and always finding the right attitude, the correct disposition, the *hexis* or the *habitus* that helps resist them, behave in relation to them, use them, potentially understand them. When habitual phenomena are at issue, the question therefore consists only in knowing and being able to inhabit them" (BG, 130, trans. mod.; ED, 184; original emphasis). It is surprising that Marion neither returns to this issue nor mentions this category again, especially as the need to "habituate" oneself to a phenomenon has significant overlap with his later suggestion that some people might have a predisposition to "see" certain phenomena while others remain entirely blind to them.

At the end of this section on anamorphosis, Marion identifies these experiences of technology and habit as examples of "contingency" and ultimately of anamorphosis: These phenomena are "given" to me because I need to be in a certain place or position to experience them properly (BG, 131; ED, 185). They are surprising and unpredictable phenomena that limit our initiative to receptivity and make intentional constitution impossible. Similarly, Marion outlines the "facticity" and "incidental" nature of the given in a general fashion that applies not solely to saturated phenomena but to "phenomenality as such without exception" (BG, 143–50; ED, 202–212). In fact, he explicitly says that "facticity brings it about that phenomena are encountered, and therefore it also determines, *in a gradation* [à une dénivellation près], *all* phenomena—precisely because they give themselves" (BG, 147; ED, 208; emphasis added). He illustrates this with tools of various sorts, with a "simply subsisting being," and an "ideal" such as the "integral calculus" (BG, 148–49; ED, 209–210). In this section, Marion repeatedly stresses that his analyses apply to *all* phenomena, regardless of their level of saturation and most of his examples are in fact technical objects or mathematical truths or other clearly "nonsaturated" phenomena, although that terminology is not yet used here. Yet when Marion employs the terms of "anamorphosis," "fait accompli," or "incident" in his subsequent work, they are almost exclusively applied to saturated phenomena.[11]

There is also a curious tension between Marion's use of the term "degrees" here and his description of the saturated phenomenon as a "paradox."[12] Marion concludes part 3 by asking: "Couldn't we imagine, by contrast, that givenness admits variation by degrees [des variations de degrés]? On this hypothesis, the determinations of the given phenomenon, while remaining originary and definitively acquired, would modulate with variable intensity. As a result, thresholds of phenomenality in terms of givenness would define discontinuous strata of phenomena, which would then be distinguished by their level of givenness and no longer by their belonging to a region" (BG, 178; ED, 249–50). Part 4 is subtitled precisely "Degrees" (Degrés), and Marion proposes three degrees of givenness in this context: poor phenomena that lack intuition, common-law phenomena that "vary in terms of givenness" and could in principle receive adequate fulfillment, and saturated phenomena that are rich in intuition (BG, 221–26; ED, 309–316).

While the notion of degrees and indeed Marion's discussion of it, would seem to indicate a slow progression and infinite variation of degrees of givenness from poorer to richer phenomenality, the notion of the paradox and Marion's descriptions of the saturated phenomenon instead indicate far more absolute distinctions: a phenomenon is *either* "poor" *or* "saturated," intuition is *either* "empty" *or* "full," consciousness *either* controls and constitutes the phenomenon *or* it is overwhelmed by what is given and utterly unable to constitute it or impose its own parameters on it. This latter account has become the far more common description of Marion's project. Yet his discussion in these middle parts of *Being Given* would indicate that at least at one point in his work a less absolute articulation of givenness was still possible. And there are occasionally hints that this possibility of degrees of givenness or saturation has not been completely abandoned. Before we get to this later suggestion, however, a little more should be said of the saturated phenomenon.

The Saturated Phenomenon

Marion first develops the notion of the saturated phenomenon in an early article responding to Dominique Janicaud's criticism of his *Reduction and Givenness* as exercising a "theological turn."[13] This early articulation of the saturated phenomenon, which Marion later heavily qualifies, is hence primarily in religious terms. As mentioned above, Marion provides a somewhat fuller account in his work *Being Given*, which seeks to lay out a phenomenology of givenness more generally. Most fundamentally his project is to examine phenomena that do not appear as objects, which he reiterates in his important article "The Banality of Saturation": "Now, the entire question of the saturated phenomenon concerns solely and specifically the possibility that certain phenomena do not manifest themselves in the mode of objects and yet still do manifest themselves. The difficulty is to describe what would manifest itself without our being able to constitute (or synthesize) it as an object (by a concept or an intentionality adequate to its intuition)" (VR, 122; VeR, 148). This stress on the particular focus of his project goes a long way toward explaining why Marion says so little about lesser forms of phenomenality: It is his goal to show the possibility of the most intensely saturated ones. In *Being Given*, Marion describes the saturated phenomenon as a paradox, which flips Husserlian understandings of phenomena on its head. *Poor* phenomena (the ones he claims Husserl describes) are those constituted by consciousness, which employs intention in order to add to the little intuition given by the poor or "common" phenomenon. Such poor phenomena are perceived by an intentional subject who constitutes them as objects by providing whatever is lacking in the intuition received from them by consciousness. It is hence able to reach (and impose on the phenomenon) a clear signification.

Conversely, *rich* or *saturated* phenomena give abundant data to intuition yet any intention that might be directed at them or any attempt to impose signification upon such phenomena always fails or at least falls short: "Because it shows itself only inasmuch as it gives itself, the phenomenon appears to the extent [*à la mesure*] that it arises, ascends, arrives, comes forward, imposes itself, is accomplished factically and bursts forth—in short, it presses urgently on the gaze more than the gaze presses toward it. The gaze receives its impression from the phenomenon before any attempt at constituting it" (BG, 159, trans. mod.; ED, 225). These phenomena give "too much"; their intuitive excess cannot be contained. Marion depicts them as overwhelming and bedazzling. They cannot be grasped or controlled, but blind us with their excess. They defy our attempt to analyze them as deriving from a clear cause.[14] Saturated phenomena undo all our usual categories of experience and hence impose themselves via a "counter-experience" that reverses the usual direction of constitution.[15] Instead of consciousness constituting the phenomenon, the experience of such phenomena constitutes consciousness:

> We cannot have vision of these phenomena, because we cannot constitute them starting from a univocal signification, and even less produce them as objects. What we see of them, if we see anything of them that *is,* does not result from the constitution we would assign to them in the visible, but from the effect they produce on us. And, in fact, this happens in reverse so that our gaze is submerged in a kind of counter-intentionality. We are hence no longer the transcendental *I* but the witness, constituted by what happens to us. This makes for the para-dox, inverted *doxa.* In this way, the phenomenon that befalls and happens to us reverses the order of visibility in that it no longer results from my intention but from its own counter-intentionality. (IE, 113, trans. mod.; DS, 136; original emphasis)

Saturated phenomena are identified precisely through the effect they have on the one who witnesses them.

Marion employs the categories of experience, as they are articulated by Kant, in order to show all the ways in which saturated phenomena defy them.[16] There are four (or ultimately five) such ways: First, phenomena can saturate our sense of *quantity* by giving too much information, by overwhelming us with data, by providing an event of such richness and complexity that it cannot possibly be contained. Marion identifies historical or cultural events as such phenomena. Second, phenomena can bedazzle us with *quality,* blinding us in their overwhelming visibility. These are works of art for Marion, especially paintings.[17] Third, phenomena can be overwhelming in *relation* inasmuch as they can appear as so immediate that no relation or analogy can be established with them. Here Marion appropriates Henry's analysis of the human flesh. Fourth, the phenomenon of the human face is saturated in terms of its *modality.* Marion here draws on Lévinas's analysis of the face, although he chides Lévinas for what he deems his far too exclusive emphasis on ethics. *Any* encounter with the human face can become a saturated phenomenon. Marion's preferred example for this is an erotic rather than an ethical encounter with the other person. Finally, Marion suggests in *Being Given* that there might also be phenomena saturated to a second degree (what he calls the "paradox of paradoxa") inasmuch as they combine all four aspects of saturation. This is the phenomenon of revelation, which Marion posits as a possibility while making no claims about its historical actuality.[18] He insists that he is merely investigating a structural possibility. If there really were phenomena of revelation, they would appear as saturated in these four respects.[19] Marion also suggests that while the "simply saturated" phenomena push to the very edge of the phenomenal horizon, the phenomenon of revelation transcends any horizon whatsoever.[20]

Marion has also analyzed other phenomena in terms that would suggest that they are saturated or he has even explicitly identified them as such. Thus, the erotic phenomenon is clearly saturated in many respects and maybe ultimately the best instance of the fourth type of saturated phenomenon (the "icon").[21] A similar claim can certainly be made of the various religious depictions Marion provides throughout his work, especially his analyses of the Eucharist.[22] The experience of prayer, of the sacrament, of holiness, all are phenomena of revelation, hence saturated phenomena. This also seems to apply to his more recent explorations of the gift and of the phenomenon of sacrifice in *Certitudes négatives,* where he qualifies some of his earlier analysis in part 2 of *Being Given.*[23] In all these contexts, Marion no longer seems to employ the quasi-Kantian categories as strictly.[24] Thus he appears content now to speak of saturation as richness and then to qualify in the examination of the phenomenon the ways in which such richness overwhelms us. What matters to the saturated phenomenon is its bedazzling excess, its overwhelming splendor, its giving more than we can possibly bear, the impossibility (or at least inadequacy) of reducing it to a mere object. These are the characteristics shared by all saturated phenomena.[25]

Yet, these characteristics seem somewhat problematic if they are taken to depict all phenomena of this type (historical, cultural, aesthetic, interpersonal, religious, and so forth). Are really *all* historical events, *all* works of art, *all* encounters with other people, *all* religious phenomena experienced in this absolute and excessive fashion? The same questions may be raised in regard to Marion's other illustrations of the saturated phenomenon, put forth precisely in order to illustrate their "banality," namely their frequent nature and accessibility to all (see next section for more detail on this). Maybe some people can indeed lose themselves completely and utterly in the voice of a diva, but some think about the worries of daily life at the same time. There are surely some mortals who are utterly and completely overwhelmed by Mona Lisa's smile and must return to be seduced by her again and again, but many others are occasionally slightly distracted in museums (and surely this happens not just to people who have no artistic sensibility). Of course, some people are completely swept off their feet by a glance stolen across a crowded room, and there might possibly be some who are passionately and completely unselfishly devoted to their beloved all the days of their life. Yet it may also be the case that such an excessive picture of romantic infatuation has led to distorted expectations about love, which play at least some role in the breakdown of so many relationships today. While a kenotic and self-sacrificial love, a completely gratuitous and entirely unselfish gift, a devoted and pure appreciation of art, or a profound sense of the utter uniqueness of each historic and cultural event may be the *ideals,* surely they cannot describe the experience of *all* love, *all* gifts, *all* art, *all* events without thereby implying that all less extreme versions immediately collapse into objectivity and certainty.[26]

Marion acknowledges this difficulty in two ways. First, he does at times, albeit rarely, discuss phenomena of lesser saturation: the "habitual" phenomena mentioned above, some "common-law" phenomena, or other phenomena where intuition and intention are more evenly balanced. Unfortunately, as Anthony Steinbock has pointed out, these depictions are sparse.[27] They also do not seem to provide many intermediate positions, but tend to congregate at the "lower" end of the phenomenological spectrum, as Marion outlines it. Steinbock contends that Marion's description of the poor phenomenon is ambivalent, and he distinguishes four connotations of poverty in Marion's account: "the poor phenomenon proper," such as a perceptual object; the "humble" phenomenon, such as a common and everyday object revealing something larger or more significant; the "denigrated" phenomenon, such as a rich phenomenon misunderstood as a technical object or limited to a narrow sphere; and, finally, "pride as the poverty of the gifted," namely the recipient's inability or unwillingness to receive the given. He suggests that Marion's account of poverty actually makes the most sense of the "denigrated" phenomenon, not primarily, as one would expect, the perceptual object.[28] Marion has not fully elaborated the poor phenomenon in itself or the ways in which the saturated phenomenon determines or resituates poor or common phenomena.

What consequently still seems to be missing in Marion's work, though is not necessarily incompatible with it, is an account of the transition, the development, the degrees, the in-between: the range where a phenomenon is no longer poor and yet not as excessive and absolutely bedazzling as he presents, when there is some excess but maybe also some deficiency. If love *must* always be like a "declaration of war,"[29] if sacrifice can only follow the paradigm of the "holocaust" of one's only child, if only the likes of Cordelia, Clélia, and Christ can truly love and forgive,[30] if prayer is only possible when we find ourselves envisaged by the divine gaze that completely empties us of ourselves, we are in a scary position indeed. This is not to say that saturated phenomena do not appear or cannot be experienced or are incoherent or that their depiction and phenomenological analysis is unnecessary. Rather, it is to call for an account of the less than absolutely pure and excessive or the *somewhat* saturated: the instances and shadows of truth, beauty, and justice, which have not (yet?) reached the realm of the absolute and possibly never will.

As Steinbock points out, Marion also speaks of the possibility that the saturation of a phenomenon might not be recognized or sustained by a recipient. Marion discusses this possibility already in *Being Given* when he examines the devoted and the reception of the saturated phenomenon. Yet, this is only explored negatively. The recipient always falls short of the intuition of the phenomenon and only makes it visible to the extent to which he or she can bear its impact. Thus the phenomenon is able to appear to the extent to which its recipient is able to receive and phenomenalize it.[31] While the phenomenon does impose itself as saturated in this case, the reception of the phenomenon fails and hence the saturation is not recognized or only recognized to some extent. Here the problem is more epistemological. As Steinbock formulates it: "Essentially, the gifted cannot receive the given in the manner in which it gives itself . . . the gifted in the responsal may 'want' to receive the given, but essentially (because of our finitude) cannot do so." He formulates the central aporia as follows: "In this case, poverty does not belong to the structure of the object, but to our deficiency in being ready to receive the givenness, which is to say, to see it as saturated. We thus have two types of poverty: An essential poverty that is peculiar to every kind of seeing, and about which I think there is nothing we can do, and a poverty of self-imposition without reception, in which the saturated phenomenon as revelation, as call, is missed."[32] Steinbock contends that these types of poverty require further elucidation and elaboration. Indeed, Marion returns to the epistemological question more fully in *Certitudes négatives*.

Negative Certainties

The saturated phenomenon, as it has just been outlined according to Marion's most common depictions, appears as so overwhelming and bedazzling that it defies all attempts to comprehend, categorize, or even to see it. *Being Given* articulates it as a phenomenon that gives itself without any conditions being imposed on it. It is "saturated with intuition" to the point that intention cannot grasp it and no easy signification can be given (BG, 199; ED, 280). It cannot be constituted by the recipient because it overwhelms all categories that might be used to determine it and exceeds all horizons within which it might be contained: "In this way, by giving itself absolutely, the saturated phenomenon also gives itself as absolute—free from any analogy with already seen, objectified, comprehended experience. It is freed because it does not depend on any horizon. In all cases, it does not depend on this condition of possibility par excellence—a horizon, whatever it might be. I therefore call it an unconditioned phenomenon" (BG, 211–12; ED, 296). It is blinding in its excessive effect on the observer, barely distinguishable from total darkness.[33]

Thus, it seems that it cannot have any epistemological dimensions, and indeed, in this work Marion repeatedly emphasizes the essential anonymity of the phenomenon, which is only identified in the response of the witness or recipient to its impact. In response to the claim that such phenomena are rare or even nonexistent, figments of his own imagination, Marion explicates what he calls the "banality" of saturation in an article under that title, where he suggests that such phenomena are indeed quite common and experienced daily by many people. He illustrates this by giving examples for each sense (hearing, seeing, smelling, tasting, touching), in each case showing how a phenomenon might move from being "poor" in character and easily constituted in a concept to being "rich" or "saturated" in character and defying any attempts at constitution or comprehending in a concept. This essay in particular raises the epistemological question again more forcefully: How might we know when a phenomenon has moved from being "poor" to being "saturated"? How can a phenomenon be identified as one or the other? The concept of "negative certainty" may well be read as a response to precisely this question.

Marion's *Certitudes négatives* claims that the saturated phenomenon has become a commonly accepted phenomenological term and must now be supplemented with the notion of "negative certainty." He begins the work by apparently aligning knowledge with certainty and suggesting that on this reading only the hard sciences with their emphasis on evidence truly have knowledge in this sense (CN, 11). He immediately goes on to challenge this conception, which effectively excludes most of our knowledge and experience, especially anything treated by the social sciences or humanities. Only *objects* can be known with any sort of certainty derived from perception and its types of evidence. Any phenomena that appear to us in other ways (i.e., that cannot be reduced to objects) defy the attempt to provide evidence based on observation, which simply is not appropriate to what they are and how they appear. Marion suggests that, in these cases, knowledge of such phenomena not only must be disconnected from certainty, but in fact we can have a kind of "negative certainty" that they will remain unknowable, that is, that they cannot possibly be known in the sense in which objects are known. This negative certainty is a constitutive limit inherent within the phenomenon itself or within the way in which it is apprehended by us, but essentially so. It is not a lack of knowledge or evidence that could be alleviated by further research, but an aspect of the phenomenon and its appearing. These negative certainties hence do not depend only on our (mis)interpretations of the phenomena. In fact, in these cases it is not an issue of interpretation at all.[34]

Marion recalls the limits Kant places around our ability to know the *noumenon*, the thing as it is in itself, which are necessary and not arbitrary limits rooted in phenomenality and consciousness itself. This does not mean, of course, that these phenomena should not be researched as thoroughly as possible and be encountered fully. Negative certainty is not a warning sign to stay away and leave well enough alone. Rather, they are an acknowledgment that these phenomena include a dimension of unknowability in the very makeup of their phenomenal reality. Such phenomena, according to Marion, include the phenomenon of self, other, and God, but also the event, the gift, and sacrifice, all phenomena he investigates in great detail in *Certitudes négatives*. Saturated phenomena, although experienced frequently, have so far not been sufficiently examined, he suggests, precisely because the way in which they are known has been misunderstood (CN, 313). Because their abundance of intuition invalidates any concepts one might apply to them and because they do not appear as objects but overwhelm us with their bedazzling appearance in an "indirect" counter-experience, they are indubitable precisely through the impossibility of constituting their signification (CN, 314).

This "limitation" of knowledge in the case of saturated phenomena thus functions as a broadening of knowledge in the sense of a negative certainty about their inherent unknowability. The "certainties" that operate in these phenomena do not seek to relieve our finitude or lack of knowledge, but rather forbid any attempt to do so. To attempt to reduce the other to a number or a statistic is precisely to have negated and disregarded what it means to encounter another. (Marion gives the example of a hospital experience, of a stateless person, and of the market where the person becomes a mere "consumer statistic.") Indetermination is not merely "an aporia of intersubjectivity" but, in fact, the only way to have any sort of access to encounter with the other (CN, 315). The same is true for encounter with the divine and with any number of other rich phenomena. "Positive" certainty would be an obstacle to know these phenomena. Instead, negative certainty is a priori and constitutive of them. This, in Marion's view, is a "negative and real enlargement of the limits of knowledge" (CN, 315).

Yet, does this really fully resolve the difficulty of distinguishing between "poor" and "saturated" phenomena, especially if certain phenomena can move from being simple or poor to becoming saturated? Part of that move concerns precisely the inability to depict them fully, to say anything intelligible about them that would not reduce their excess. We cannot truly describe the song of a diva, the smell of a perfume, the effect of a painting. Instead of "knowing" them "certainly," as objects from which we are to extract information, they have an impact on us—we encounter them. This raises a number of questions: For example, what exactly is the "negative certainty" in regard to the song of the diva or the smell of the perfume? Is negative certainty in this context anything other than a refusal of the ability to describe perfectly or to reduce to pieces of information? Does the notion have a fuller function than merely to suspend judgment, to identify the phenomenon as one that overwhelms us? What kind of knowledge does one gain from being overwhelmed by the phenomenon and unable to describe its impact?

Furthermore, how does one know when a phenomenon has passed from "poverty" to "saturation"? Does it rely entirely on a personal, presumably subjective experience? Or is there something within the phenomenon itself (maybe something "eidetic") that would indicate the level of saturation? What is the point—to employ the language of *Being Given*—where the experience flips into paradox, where the Kantian categories are turned upside down? Does the epistemological negativity Marion posits for these phenomena somehow help identify them as saturated? Is it when one is unable to classify or enumerate that one is convinced that one has encountered a saturated phenomenon? Even more interestingly, can "negative certainties" help us decide when we move to the second degree of unknowing, the paradox of paradoxa, the phenomenon of revelation? Is God somehow *more* "negatively" uncertain than my experience of the human other or of my own flesh? What would be a paradoxically "doubled" negative certainty?

This also raises the question of whether there are not only degrees but also different *kinds* of certainty. Is the negative certainty that one cannot comprehend the divine different (not just in the level of intensity but in its very nature) from the negative certainty of the perfume's fragrance? If they are different, what enables one to make the distinction? If a distinction can be made, how might the difference of *degree* interact with and qualify the difference of *kind* in this particular case? Even the more simply saturated phenomena, according to Marion, are distinguished by which aspect of phenomenality they saturate or transgress: Historical events are excessive in quantity, paintings in respect to quality, the experience of one's flesh exceeds relation and the face of the other modality. Consequently, one might wonder whether their respective certainties are different, as well. Is the negative limitation of knowledge for historical events precisely one of quantity, of not being able to list all relevant data or an inability to grasp the magnitude of information? Is the negative limitation of knowledge in the case of the work of art one of quality, in regard to flesh of relation, and facing the other of modality? What would be a negative certainty of relation or modality? Marion says nothing about these issues in his first proposal of the idea, but they all seem to be interesting and important implications to pursue.[35]

Finally, one may wonder whether the negativity of this knowledge could be alleviated to some extent or whether it always remains absolute. In Marion's initial proposal here, it appears that knowledge is either entirely "positive" (the "clear and distinct" Cartesian certainty one can have about objects) or completely negative. Yet what happens when the saturated phenomenon is experienced more frequently or examined more fully? Does its certainty become increasingly more or less "negative," or does this "negativity" not admit of any degrees?[36] Can there be an increase of knowledge in the case of saturated phenomena? Can distinctions and judgments be made about historical or cultural events, quality of paintings or other works of art, authenticity of religious experience, and so forth? Does "negative certainty" give us any "positive" parameters for our experience of saturated phenomena? In *Being Given,* Marion suggests in the context of the "habitual phenomena" mentioned earlier that increase in knowledge or training might be necessary at least for some phenomena: "Even supposing there is a sense in claiming complete knowledge of the computer or television screen, this still would not dismiss us from training or habit. Contingency is not reducible to the uncertainty of knowledge; it is therefore not summed up by an extrinsic relation of the known to the knower" (BG, 134; ED, 189). What is the exact status of this "training or habit"?

One may also wonder whether such increase in training or habit should be limited to technical or poor phenomena. Surely historians' understanding of an event or period increases with further research, even if the past event is never captured fully. Does not love grow and increase as the lovers spend more time together and get to know each other more fully? Surely appreciation for art and music is something that is cultivated and developed over time and does not strike one *ex nihilo* the first time one encounters a great work of art. As I seek to show, for many of these phenomena, certainly for the cultural or historical event, for the work of art, and even for the encounter with the human person, knowledge can indeed increase even if it can never be final. One will appreciate a painting more fully if one knows something of the artist's work and history, of the context of the time, of its history of interpretation, and so forth. Indeed, the painting may well overwhelm us, and new interpretations will always be possible, even must continue, yet surely some interpretations are better than others (and some maybe entirely false). This brings us to the issue of interpretation, which is closely linked to the epistemological questions Marion raises in *Certitudes négatives*.[37]

Hermeneutic Dimensions

Early on, Marion's work was criticized for not being sufficiently hermeneutical. Jean Greisch first raised the question with regard to *Reduction and Givenness*.[38] He suggests that any phenomenology that deals with the "unapparent" must of necessity be hermeneutical. The "call" in particular requires the context of a hermeneutics of facticity in which it can be heard. Greisch shows how Heidegger parses phenomenological possibility in terms of an existential knowing, which requires the hermeneutic unveiling of phenomena as its primary research method. Greisch points to Ricoeur's hermeneutic of the self as a possible development of Marion's phenomenological analyses, especially the latter's insistence on a self that is outside of or beyond being. Greisch insists that the search for givenness requires a hermeneutic method. Jean Grondin carries this critique further in response to *Being Given*.[39] While he praises Marion's creative and ambitious project, he finds him still beholden to a Cartesian desire for absolute foundations, while also deeply influenced by Heideggerian notions of finitude, dispossession and dereliction, two tendencies he suggests might ultimately be irreconcilable. In Grondin's view, Marion ignores the advancement made by philosophy of language and hermeneutics, especially in regard to the linguistic dimension of the given, which can never present itself in the utterly pure sense Marion suggests.[40] After a fairly extensive summary of *Being Given*, in which he especially objects to the notion of the saturated phenomenon and the reintroduction of "Revelation," Grondin concludes that a firmer distinction between "receptivity" and "passivity" is required and that any receptivity of the meaning given in the phenomenon must of necessity be deeply hermeneutical. Givenness depends on language, and the given can only be received or identified hermeneutically.

Richard Kearney has also pressed Marion repeatedly on this issue. In several interviews he raises questions about the hermeneutic dimension of saturated phenomena.[41] He argues that there is no such thing as a pure or absolute phenomenon, but that phenomena are always already interpreted. A hermeneutic reading of the phenomenon is necessary especially in order to distinguish the incomprehensibility of the divine from the terror caused by other overwhelming and less benign events. He also wonders whether any type of religious experience presents itself as saturated and how one might distinguish between different religious traditions and their respective experiences of "revelation": "Do you think that the phenomenon of God can be experienced outside a specifically monotheistic context? Is there something in the notion of revelation as an absolute saturated phenomenon that requires a Judeo-Christian theology? It is not just any God that appears in revelation, is it? And how can we tell the difference?"[42] Kearney consistently pushes Marion to consider the possibility of other experiences of revelation and to think more fully about how such experiences might need to be interpreted.[43]

In response to this criticism, starting with his discussion of each of the saturated phenomena separately in his *In Excess,* Marion has admitted more fully that some of the saturated phenomena might include a hermeneutic dimension.[44] He briefly outlines such a possibility of an "endless" or "infinite" hermeneutics in the chapters on the event and that on the face of the other.[45] In contrast, he apparently sees little need for hermeneutics in the case of the phenomena of art, of the flesh, or of the divine, or at least does not discuss the issue in those contexts.[46] In chapter 2 on the event Marion engages in a close phenomenological analysis of the space in which he and his audience find themselves: the room (the Salle des actes in the Institut catholique in Paris) in which the lecture is conducted. Yet he goes on to show that this and other phenomena (his second example is the friendship between Montaigne and La Boétie, but he also speaks of the phenomena of human birth and death), if rightly considered, actually are saturated. In this context, Marion explicitly admits a hermeneutic dimension of the event. It must always be interpreted and interpretation can never come to a close, the phenomenon can never be fully grasped: "Such a hermeneutic would have to be deployed without end and in an infinite network. No constitution of an object, exhaustive and repeatable, would be able to take place" (IE, 33; DS, 39). Here infinite interpretation is required precisely because no single account could ever do justice to the phenomenon. He also emphasizes this point in response to Kearney in the interview mentioned above.[47]

Marion admits a similar need for interpretation in the chapter on the icon or the face of the other, which actually includes the idea of a "hermeneutics without end" in the chapter title itself (chapter 5):

> All that I would perceive of the other person as regards significations and intentions will remain always and by definition in the background and in deficit in relation to his or her face, a saturated phenomenon. And, therefore, I will only be able to bear this paradox and do it justice in consecrating myself to its infinite hermeneutic according to space, and especially time. For as I have already observed, even after the death of this face, hermeneutics must be pursued, in a memory no less demanding than the present vision. And it will be pursued— or at least should be—after my own death, this time entrusted to others. The face of the other person requires in this way an infinite hermeneutic, equivalent to the 'progress toward the infinite' of morality according to Kant. Thus, every face demands immortality—if not its own, at least that of the one who envisages it. (IE, 126; DS, 152.)

The face of the other requires infinite hermeneutics, because it is an "immortal" face and any depiction would always fall short of it. Depictions of the other's life therefore have to be multiplied endlessly. Interpretation, then, is necessary after the phenomenon has appeared and only because it imposes itself in this overwhelming and abundant manner.

Shane Mackinlay suggests that this is a distorted understanding of hermeneutics, namely one that limits it to interpretation of what has already occurred, and disregards other dimensions of hermeneutics, especially ones articulated by Heidegger in terms of the structural dimensions of human Dasein. He summarizes Heidegger's insight as follows: "Therefore, rather than hermeneutics being restricted to the interpretations of existence that arise when it is subsequently recounted, human existence is itself considered to be hermeneutic *in the very structure of its happening.* Consequently, phenomena are not only interpreted *after* they have appeared, but are *always already* interpreted in their very appearing" (original emphasis).[48] Mackinlay suggests that Romano's account achieves a more successful hermeneutic balance. He argues throughout that there is an essential hermeneutic dimension to the ways in which phenomena appear, which Marion misses to his detriment. This is closely linked for Mackinlay with a more active role for the receiving subject, whom he thinks Marion depicts as essentially passive.

Tamsin Jones agrees with Mackinlay that Marion's somewhat greater appeal to hermeneutics in his phenomenological work remains unsatisfying.[49] Like

Mackinlay, she suggests that "the radical passivity with which Marion character-izes receptivity seems to abandon the possibility of hermeneutics" and wonders whether Marion's insistence that interpretation comes after the event but does not precede it can be maintained.[50] She argues that Gregory of Nyssa's theory of inter-pretation might have helped Marion provide a more nuanced account, especially as Marion draws on Nyssa for other arguments, even when he does not fully ac-knowledge doing so. She concludes that "two related lacunae, in particular, trouble Marion's phenomenological project: a lack of attention to the role of preparatory practices in developing a capacity to receive phenomena as pure givens, and the absence of comment on how, or even whether, we might judge the relative benev-olence or malevolence of the phenomena that have such a powerful impact upon us." She worries about the fact that "this crucial ambiguity within the reception of saturated phenomena does not seem to concern Marion, or at least he never ex-plicitly addresses it as a concern. Marion never discusses how one might begin to establish a mode of judging such phenomena and their intent."[51] This is a similar concern to the one Kearney raises in his interview with Marion, especially in re-gard to the need for discernment.

In contrast to Jones, who for the most part agrees with Mackinlay on this point, Stephen Lewis thinks that Mackinlay confuses hermeneutic and epistemic dimensions in his criticism of Marion: "Mackinlay seeks to eliminate the possi-bility of willful blindness to the reception of saturated phenomena, and as a result he in many respects converts the hermeneutic issue involved in recognizing a phe-nomenon as saturated into" what he refers to as "an epistemological problematic of perception."[52] For Lewis, Mackinlay's confusion on this matter is due to his in-adequate account of the "gifted's affection for what appears" and of "the impor-tant place of affection, or love, in Marion's conception of givenness."[53] As emerges throughout this book, I believe Lewis correctly deems Marion's account of the reception of phenomena to be more nuanced and less exclusively passive than Mackinlay supposes. It is also not linked to the issue of hermeneutics in as linear of a fashion as Mackinlay suggests in some passages, although certainly it is not entirely disconnected from it. Nevertheless, Mackinlay is right that Marion focuses the role of hermeneutics almost exclusively on interpretation "after the fact." The "endless hermeneutic" that Marion espouses more frequently now always comes *after* one has encountered a saturated phenomenon and tries to make sense of it.

Marion himself does link the epistemic and the hermeneutic in some con-texts, such as in the proposal of negative certainties. We can be certain that we cannot reduce the other person to mere data because of a person's particular kind of phenomenality. In fact, in this context Marion speaks of this endless herme-neutics as "a need of reason" (*un besoin de la raison*): "The face of the other com-pels me to believe in my own eternity, as a need of reason or, what comes down to the same thing, as the condition of its infinite hermeneutic" (IE, 127, trans. mod.; DS, 153). Negative certainty and hermeneutics then emerge as connected at least on some level. Many interpretations are required, because reason always falls short and no objective certainty will ever be reached. Marion reiterates this conclusion in both his book on Augustine and his discussion of negative certainty. In his analysis of Augustine, Marion distinguishes between being aware of one's existence and knowing one's essence—a knowledge that remains hidden so that I remain unknown to myself (SP, 73; LS, 114). Cartesian certainty is replaced by desire for the infinite, a truth that remains undetermined and unknown as such and is discovered only in love (SP, 90–96; LS, 136–42). This creation of the self in love culminates in a hermeneutic of praise, an endless song of confession (SP, 243–45; LS, 332–34). The "indefinition of man" is a distinctive human privilege, rooted in creation in the divine image (SP, 260; LS, 352). The endless hermeneutics of love preserves this privilege of unknowing. The same point about the incomprehensibility of the human in light of its creation in the image of God is made in *Certitudes négatives* (CN, 69–71). An endless hermeneutic is required precisely because of this incomprehensibility, the impossibility ever to comprehend or define the human self (CN, 81–83).[54]

It appears, then, that Marion admits that saturated phenomena do require interpretation of some sort, albeit still in a fairly limited fashion. As both Mackinlay and Lewis acknowledge in different ways, this is closely linked to Marion's account of the recipient of the saturated phenomenon whom he describes as someone called, interlocuted, witnessing, or finally devoted, given over and even addicted to the phenomenon. Marion consistently attempts to maintain a fragile balance between the priority of the phenomenon (which he tends to emphasize more strongly) and the recipient's response to it, which alone makes the phenomenon visible, as a phenomenon is not a phenomenon if it is not experienced by someone. Marion contends that the devoted "remains in the end the sole master and servant of the given."[55] Both are necessary for the phenomenon to be given as saturated.

In this paradoxical balance, it is the phenomenon that has the initiative for Marion. It "gives itself" freely without any limits imposed upon it, especially in the case of the saturated phenomenon.[56] The saturated phenomenon is hence always anonymous. It does not announce its identity. Marion stresses this dimension of anonymity fairly strongly in *Being Given,* although he mentions it considerably less often in more recent work. In *Being Given,* he emphasizes consistently that we do not know the origin of the call: does it proceed from Being (Heidegger), the other (Lévinas), the flesh (Henry), or God? The phenomenon, Marion contends, is only identified in the response. The recipient serves as the screen upon which the phenomenon crashes and thereby makes it visible.[57] It is imagery like this that leads Mackinlay to conclude that "there is no sense of activity in the reception, not even of 'mediation'—the *adonné* seems to be simply passive" or Joeri

Schrijvers to claim that "Marion's givenness requires a powerless subject, at least a subject that does not distort with its own intentions the gift of phenomena. . . . the subject is stripped of its subjectivity, i.e. it is reduced to a mere receptiveness and passivity towards givenness."[58] Both claim that Marion simply reverses intentionality, turning the phenomenon into a Cartesian subject and the recipient into an entirely passive object.[59]

It is certainly true that Marion stresses the reversal of intentionality and the receptivity of the one devoted or given over to the phenomenon. Marion's analysis of Augustine's *Confessions* makes this point in a different tenor. Most of the book is devoted to an analysis of the self as "gifted," as recipient of divine love. He works out far more fully than in other works the receptive stance, the "place of the self," as it is open to the divine gift: "I am not when and each time that I decide to be by deciding to think. I am each time that, as lover and as devoted, I let the immemorial come over me, as a life that does not belong to me and that, for that very reason, inhabits me more intimately than myself" (SP, 100, trans. mod.; LS, 148). This life of the self, ultimately participation in the image and likeness of God, is incomprehensible and indescribable, always received as a gift (SP, 259, 260, 285; LS, 350, 351, 384). Marion makes a much stronger connection here between self, gift, and the given phenomenon. He insists that "it is necessary that the self receive itself as a gift. But, in this case, the ego discovers itself received like one of its other gifts, contemporaneous with, not anterior to, its other gifts, not preceding them, still less conditioning them. . . . The self comes over me like a given, which I receive at the same time as all the other givens" (SP, 286; LS, 384–85). Marion insists on the apophatic character of this reception in Augustine, but at the same time he consistently stresses the dimension of liturgical praise, in which the self actively responds to the gift.

The separation of the ego from the self, as it is pursued in this book on Augustine, does not imply that the self is lost or entirely passive. Rather, the self responds to and devotes itself fully to the divine gift of beatitude. Loving response is always required in a ceaseless and infinite movement: "There where I find God, all the more as I continue to seek him, I find myself all the more myself as I never cease to seek that of which I bear the image. In the self's place there is not a shape of consciousness, nor a type of *subjectum*, but that unto which the self is like and refers" (SP, 312; LS, 421). Although Marion does not say a word about hermeneutics in this context and reiterates his strong emphasis on the essential receptivity of the self, this self is far from entirely passive and continually responds in love to the divine call.

Marion addresses the same question again in a quite different context in his *Sur la pensée passive de Descartes,* which also treats the passivity of the self in the context of its flesh and its passions, but now as an analysis of the final Meditations and *The Passions of the Soul.* He shows an important dimension of passivity in Descartes's analysis of the self, including a passive (and passionate) dimension of thought. He contends that the distinction between activity and passivity is too simplistic and misses an important aspect of Descartes's argument (PPD, 230). Perceptions, feelings, and emotions are all "passions," or movements, of the soul. Yet, at the same time, the soul is affected and hence receptive to what comes to it. Even the Cartesian ego receives access to its phenomenality via sensing itself and its passions (PPD, 237), including identifying the will as a movement of the passions and hence characterized by an essential passivity and receptivity (PPD, 243). Marion identifies generosity in Descartes as a passion with an important active element (PPD, 246–50). Even the "activity of virtue" ultimately becomes part of the passivity of the Cartesian cogitatio that Marion examines in this book. In Marion's view, Descartes finally recognizes the importance of self-affectivity and an originary passivity of the self (PPD, 265), even if the subsequent tradition focuses solely on his earlier formulations of the ego.

If, however, it is indeed the recipient's role to identify the phenomenon or even to determine it, then intentionality and interpretation have not been completely suspended.[60] Indeed, Marlène Zarader claims that Marion smuggles subjectivity "paradigmatically" "in through the back door."[61] Marion is careful to insist that the recipient can never "grasp" the phenomenon fully, that it always gives too much, is always an overwhelming experience. And yet—as we see more fully in subsequent chapters—the recipient does identify and describe, makes choices in light of the phenomenon, possibly even creates a great work of art. Both Derek Morrow and Stephen Lewis rightly point to the important role of Marion's analysis of *capax/capacitas* for this discussion.[62] The recipient of the phenomenon is not entirely passive, but has a capacity to accept or reject and to respond to the phenomenon. Even if the *adonné* is not a Cartesian subject in total control of its world, it does have an important hermeneutic dimension. It tells the phenomenon's story.[63] While the story may well remain fragmented due to the incredible weight and overwhelming nature of the phenomenon, it is still a narration of some sort, even if it must not be verbal.[64] It is hence hermeneutic, at least on some level.

In the aforementioned "The Banality of Saturation," Marion qualifies his proposal even further in a way that appears to give much more space to hermeneutics, although even here his stance on hermeneutics ultimately remains ambivalent. In this context he responds precisely to the criticism (referring to Zarader) that his account of the saturated phenomenon posits "an experience without a subject." He clarifies in a footnote:

> Of course, the devoted was never defined in such a way, since it finds itself charged, at the very moment when it receives itself with what gives itself, with the visibility of the very thing that gives itself. Here there is nothing like a simple choice between "activity" and "pas-

sivity," with no other option. . . . The devoted operates according to
the call and response and manages the passage of what gives itself to
what shows itself: neither the one nor the other corresponds to these
categories. "Passivity" and "activity" intervene only once the characteristics of the devoted are misconstrued. (VR, 174, referring to VR,
123; VeR, 149)

Even more fully, he engages Benoist's claim that saturated phenomena are rare
and only seen by very few people, which might imply that they do not actually exist or that the saturated phenomenon is a purely manufactured or imagined experience. Marion quotes Benoist's question, "What will you say to me if I say to you
that where you see God, I see nothing?," and then responds: "Indeed, what should
I say? Yet the force of the argument can be turned against the one who uses it, for
the fact of not comprehending and seeing nothing should not always or even most
often disqualify what it is a question of comprehending or seeing, but rather the
one who understands nothing and sees only a ruse" (VR, 124; VeR, 151). As Kevin
Hart puts it: "Look again!"[65]

Drawing on the medieval term of the vassal (*ban*) Marion claims that saturated phenomena are "banal" and quite accessible to anyone. In this context he
suggests that a phenomenon might actually move from "poor" to "saturated" or
that the same phenomenon might be *interpreted* as either poor or saturated: "The
banality of the saturated phenomenon suggests that *the majority of phenomena, if
not all* can undergo saturation by the excess of intuition over the concept or signification in them. In other words, the majority of phenomena that appear at first
glance to be poor in intuition could be described not only as objects but also as phenomena that intuition saturates and therefore exceed any univocal concept" (VR,
126, original emphasis; VeR, 155). He goes on to appeal explicitly to the role of interpretation in this transition: "Before the majority of phenomena, even the most
simple (the majority of objects produced technically and reproduced industrially),
opens *the possibility of a doubled interpretation,* which depends upon the demands
of my ever-changing relation to them. Or rather, when the *description* demands
it, *I have the possibility of passing from one interpretation to the other,* from a poor or
common phenomenality to a saturated phenomenality" (VR, 126; VeR,156; emphasis added). Thus, here the difference between whether something appears as
a poor or a saturated phenomenon seems to depend on the recipient's *interpretation of it* as either common or rich. While that is a fairly strong hermeneutic claim,
it is not clear in the rest of "The Banality of Saturation" that Marion actually intends to go that far.

To show that saturated phenomena are "banal" or easily accessible he gives
examples of all five senses: seeing, hearing, smelling, tasting, touching, in each case
contrasting a poor with a saturated experience (VR, 127–33; VeR, 157–65). The

colors red, yellow, and green can refer to the concept of a traffic light that solely provides information, or it can refer to the colors on Rothko's painting *Number 212*, which cannot be reduced to a concept but is an overwhelming experience. The sound of a voice can refer both to the information provided over the loud-speaker at a train station or airport and also to the rich experience of hearing an opera diva. Someone's groping around in the dark to find the light switch is dif-ferent from the touch of loving caress. Taste can distinguish poison from sugar or refer to the rich flavor of a good wine. The odor of gas in my house provides im-portant information, while one inhales the fragrance of a famous perfume in a very different manner. Yet it is not really the *same* phenomenon that is experienced in one case as poor (e.g., the female voice over the loudspeaker at the airport or train station that only conveys information) in the other as rich (e.g., the voice of the diva to which no critic can do justice). The voice over the loudspeaker, even if it is pleasant, obviously *is not* the voice of the diva—even on the unlikely occasion that the same person were to do the speaking in both cases. It is hence not as clear as in the initial claim that it is the *interpretation* that matters here: to listen in rap-ture to the loudspeaker's voice or to critique the diva's performance is to identify the phenomena incorrectly, but not to move the *same* phenomenon from poverty to saturation through the interpretation.

Yet although this is not highlighted by Marion, it does appear that both phe-nomena require not only interpretation after the fact, but, even more importantly, a hermeneutic context or horizon. It is not only the voice (the phenomenon) that differs but also the context. It matters for our identification of the phenomenon whether we stand at a train station and the platform for our outgoing train has just been changed or whether we sit in the Met or the Lyric expecting to hear Renée Fleming or Anna Netrebko. Marion does not seem to acknowledge this context as much as appears required. Indeed, to push this a bit further, presumably one would have a more saturated experience if one had listened to many operas and many divas and were able to hear the particular nuances of the performance in a way not possible for the neophyte (or someone who is not an opera lover). Marion suggests as much when he speaks of the person who can distinguish the smell of Chanel from that of Guerlain or the vintner who "knows what he or she has tasted and can discuss it precisely with an equal, though without employing any concept, or else with an endless series of quasi-concepts, which take on meaning only after and only according to the intuition that is the sole and definitive authority," which requires endless discussion (VR, 131; VeR, 162).

Despite Marion's insistence that the intuition "is the sole and definitive au-thority," these cases indeed suggest that one could be "trained" to some extent to perceive and identify saturated phenomena, that a hermeneutic circle might be established in which greater understanding and appreciation is gained through further exposure and greater awareness of the larger context. Marion here also clarifies that he did not mean to suspend horizons entirely: "The hypothesis of saturated phenomena never consisted in annulling or overcoming the conditions for the possibility of experience, but rather sought to examine whether certain phenomena contradict or exceed those conditions yet nevertheless still appear, precisely by exceeding or contradicting them" (VR, 133; VeR, 166).[66] Later in the essay, he suggests again that it depends on the phenomenon whether it can be constituted as an object or has to be described as saturated, but then adds: "This affair is not decided abstractly or arbitrarily. In each case, attentiveness, discernment, time, and hermeneutics are necessary" (VR, 136; VeR, 170). This would suggest that not merely is "infinite hermeneutics" necessary after a rich phenomenon has been experienced, but it also prepares the conditions for experiencing such phenomena in some important fashion.

The hermeneutic dimension comes to the forefront again in the final section of the essay where Marion examines the role of the witness to the saturated phenomenon, who is no longer a subject. This witness "develops *his* vision of things, *his* story, *his* details, and *his* information—in short, he tells *his* story, which never achieves the rank of history" (VR, 143; VeR, 180; original emphasis). Here this clearly seems an admission of a hermeneutic dimension in the reception of the phenomenon (Marion actually calls it an "infinite hermeneutic"), even if (or maybe precisely because) it is never a definitive version because no final constitution is possible. The response of the witness is certainly a hermeneutic one, although in Marion's view it is not a hermeneutic horizon that contextualizes the event but rather an attempt to articulate its effect after the experience. Marion concludes by reiterating his conviction that "real" phenomenology has as its task the "making visible" of what is previously "unseen" (VR, 144; VeR, 182), which he implies is a much more worthwhile task than mere interpretation of what is already visible.[67] This idea that phenomenology "discovers" phenomena that did not previously exist and thus is not merely interpretive in character is reiterated in *Certitudes négatives:* "This enlargement here does not simply consist in a hermeneutics of already visible and received phenomena (moving them from objectivity to eventness), but in *discovering* saturated phenomena so far misunderstood by virtue of the very excess of their evidence" (CN, 313, original emphasis). In this admittedly brief statement, he portrays hermeneutics as a first enlargement of phenomenology whose role it is to move the phenomenon from the horizon of the object or being to that of givenness. The analysis of saturated phenomena goes far beyond this initial (hermeneutic) enlargement and finally culminates in a "third enlargement," that of "negative certainty."

Marion returns to the topic of hermeneutics the most explicitly in his Marquette lecture "Givenness and Hermeneutics." He argues that at first glance hermeneutics and givenness seem to contradict each other because givenness speaks on its own terms (GH, 18–19). This is a false assumption, however, and he goes on to show that the two are compatible in certain ways. He rejects any arbitrary authority of hermeneutics that would operate directly on the given, but insists instead that hermeneutics depends on the call and response structure (GH, 44–45). He calls for a phenomenological hermeneutics instead of a hermeneutic phenomenology (GH, 46–47, 62–63) and distinguishes between four senses of such a hermeneutics or four hermeneutic "moments" in givenness, which all help identifies the anonymous call of the given and hence bridge the gap between what gives itself and what is shown (GH, 54–55). First, as in *Being Given,* the call must be heard and identified as a call (GH, 56–57). Second, as in *In Excess,* the saturated phenomenon is so rich that it requires infinite interpretation (GH, 58–59). Third, as in "The Banality of Saturation," one must distinguish between poor and saturated phenomena (GH, 58–61). Finally, as in *Certitudes négatives,* hermeneutics distinguishes between objects and phenomena (GH, 60–63). This lecture, then, brings together the various senses of hermeneutics identified in Marion's other writings, although it does not resolve the conflicts outlined above, but to some extent merely restates the interpretive role of hermeneutics and the priority of the given. It does, however, go further than some of the other texts in assigning a more positive and significant role for hermeneutics in Marion's overall project.

What I argue, then, is that hermeneutics is not just an early phenomenological stage that henceforth must be overcome, as suggested in *Certitudes négatives,* but an essential aspect of the appearing of all phenomena, including and maybe especially excessive and saturated ones, as hinted at in "Givenness and Hermeneutics." This is one of the reasons why I focus in this book primarily on the phenomena Marion has already described and articulated instead of suggesting instead a range of "poorer" phenomena for consideration—which may well also be an important project. Rather, I want to show that the very phenomena Marion posits as saturated cannot appear exclusively in the excessive and utterly overwhelming sense he often suggests, but instead require both the possibility of "degrees" of phenomenality and an important hermeneutic dimension. And this is true not only of the more "banal" phenomena that Marion describes as "simply" saturated, but also of the religious phenomena that are "doubly" saturated and supposedly transcend all (especially hermeneutic) horizons altogether. Neither of these claims, I will suggest, is incompatible with Marion's overall project of a phenomenology of givenness. Givenness instead emerges much more fully as a possible paradigm for all phenomena, when it takes fuller account of degrees of phenomenality and their many and varied hermeneutic contexts.

ONE

Historical Events and Historical Research

Marion uses the term "event" in two different but closely connected senses in his work, especially in his presentation in *Being Given*. On the one hand, he speaks of the event as a characteristic of all given phenomena: phenomena give themselves as events, they are "being given." He develops this in §17 of *Being Given* as the fifth characteristic of *all* phenomena alongside anamorphosis, arrival, incident, and fait accompli. Most prominently, however, the event is *one type* of saturated phenomenon, namely the phenomenon saturated according to quantity. The phenomenon of the historical or cultural event gives "too much" information, it can never be quantified, never be recreated. The event is overwhelming in quantity. This "giving too much" is, of course, to some extent also a characteristic of all saturated phenomena. Thus, although Marion draws distinctions between the four different types of saturated phenomena, depending on whether they saturate our sense of quantity, of quality, of relation, or of modality, at the same time all saturated phenomena give too much and are events in some sense.

This becomes particularly obvious in his treatment of friendship in *In Excess* as an example of an event, although it could be depicted equally well as an encounter with the other, characterized as an icon. And, in fact, friendship does feature in his later treatment of the erotic phenomenon.[1] The discussion of the event in *In Excess* develops the brief preliminary account given in *Being Given*. *Certitudes négatives* also contains a chapter on the event as the unforeseeable—interestingly enough, this is the final chapter, preceded by discussions of the human, of God, and of the gift. One may certainly also speak of an *event* of sacrifice or forgiveness. There is hence significant overlap between the gift or sacrifice and the event. The categories between the four types here appear to be much more fluid and the terminology of quantity, quality, relation, modality is far less prominent, although Marion briefly reiterates the distinctions among the four types in the conclusion to the book.

Marion's discussions of phenomena of revelation blur the categories further. Do not prayer or the Eucharist constitute events of some type, maybe qualifying as "sacred events"? The event is hence not only one particular specified category of saturated phenomenon but a broader characteristic of saturated phenomena in particular and maybe all phenomena more generally. Mackinlay claims that "in its broad sense, *event* (referring to eventness) is a *characteristic* of phenomenality. When this eventness is assigned priority over other characteristics, *event* is *norma-*

tive for phenomenality."[2] While he is right that the event ends up applying to all saturated phenomena in certain ways, as we see in later chapters, the work of art and the icon or face of the other and ultimately the Eucharist also become paradigms for the other saturated phenomena or even for all of phenomenality. This subtle conflation of what characterizes or distinguishes different types of saturated phenomena with what characterizes all of them, or might even be paradigmatic for all of phenomenality, may well be linked in important ways to the absolute and excessive nature Marion wants to claim for such phenomena.

Another curious feature of Marion's discussion of the event is the fact that although Marion most often speaks of the first type of saturated phenomenon as a *historical* event, his examples for such historical events are almost exclusively taken from poetry and literature and not from historical writings. Thus, despite Marion's claims that any account of history would require an "endless hermeneutics," he does not actually engage historiography or historical writing. What I seek to argue in this chapter is that Marion's account of history so far is too total and absolute, that historical research instead requires approximations and degrees instead of an absolute either- or account. Although we can never know what happened completely or entirely, we certainly can give better or worse accounts and need to be able to distinguish between them. To conceive of all historical events as completely saturated phenomena in some sort of absolute sense seems to make any historical research impossible, which has serious repercussions not only for historical writing, but especially for a history of the oppressed, for justice for the victims of violence in history. The injunction not to forget requires at least an approximate account of what happened, an account that gives voice to the victims by providing some kind of witness to the events.

At the same time, the notion of the saturated phenomenon does express an important aspect of historical phenomena, one difficult to grasp when treating historical research as simply "scientific." The events of history are not identical to the "facts" of documents and archives. Historical events come in varying levels of complexity, some indeed so complex that speaking of them as "overwhelming" or "saturated" can provide important insight and remind of the dangers of oversimplification. Yet, we cannot stop there, but must go on to spell out more fully all the ways in which phenomena are more or less saturated. And while, in response to criticisms like those of Greisch, Grondin, and Kearney explored in the introduction, Marion increasingly recognizes that some element of hermeneutics may well be required for such phenomena, I want to argue much more strongly for the central and positive role of hermeneutics in the context of historical research. It matters profoundly to the victims of genocide and slaughter what sort of account we provide of what happened to them and their loved ones. The first section of this chapter discusses the more general event-like character of phenomena, and the second section focuses more specifically on the event as a saturated phenomenon. The third section turns to Marion's discussion of the event in the context of "negative certainties." The chapter concludes by drawing out the implications of this treatment for historical events and research, although I also comment on this throughout the chapter.

The Event as Characteristic of the Phenomenon

In his first discussion of the event, Marion distinguishes between the "in-itself" of the object (as described by Kant) and the "self" of the phenomenon, which gives itself but not as an object (BG, 159; ED, 225). The phenomenon imposes a weight on us that hinders us from mastering it. This "*self*" of the phenomenon is marked in its determination as event" (BG, 159; ED, 226; original emphasis). The event comes to surprise me, affects me, marks me, but cannot be produced, provoked, or controlled. The main characteristic of the event here is its lack of causality—which of course is neither a lack nor a deficiency, but a strength: it cannot be constituted in terms of cause and effect. The effect here actually precedes the cause, as we search for the cause only because of the effect—the impact the phenomenon has had on us. This event escapes metaphysics, inasmuch as it is not subject to a principle of sufficient reason, cannot be foreseen or made intelligible (BG, 160; ED, 226–27). "Event-ness" characterizes phenomena more profoundly than "object-ness" or "being-ness."

The discussion of causality frames Marion's account here in important ways. His goal in showing the event-character of all phenomena is primarily explicated in terms of their not being subject to causality. As causality is the most fundamental ground of the object, unforeseeability is the most fundamental characteristic of the given phenomenon. The concern about causality is firmly based on Marion's interpretation of Descartes, where he develops a careful definition of modern metaphysics via an analysis of the onto-theo-logical nature of Descartes's system and its various aspects. It should always be kept in mind that Marion's writings on Descartes prepare and ground many of his phenomenological claims and insights.[3] Marion repeatedly contrasts the phenomenon to the Cartesian object in terms of the principle of causality: "I suggest that phenomena as such, namely as given, not only do not satisfy this demand, but far from paying for their refusal with their unintelligibility, appear and let themselves be understood all the better as they slip from the sway of cause and the status of effect. The less they let themselves be inscribed in causality, the more they show themselves and render themselves intelligible as such. Such phenomena are named events" (BG, 162; ED, 229). Here Marion seems to indicate that intelligibility and even knowledge of such phenomena would indeed be possible. Describing them as given phenomena, as events, enables them to be understood and made intelligible—and apparently more successfully so than if they were described as objects. Yet Marion does not tell us what this understanding or intelligibility consists of, and in fact in *Certitudes négatives,* he seems to suggest precisely the opposite, namely that no knowledge can ever be possible and that we can be *certain* of this fact, certain about the continued (and infinite) incomprehensibility of such phenomena.

It is certainly true that establishing "causality" in any straightforward fashion is not the aim of historical research. Historian Ludmilla Jordanova points out the "loss of confidence in causal explanations" in historiography. Yet, while it is far from clear that historical research always aims to establish causality, it certainly does aim at providing increased understanding and intelligibility of events. Jordanova continues: "We no longer imagine that causes were *either* political *or* economic *or* social, but rather see all of these at work, and find them all dependent upon, or at the very least bound up with, cultural shifts, with changes in ways of understanding and feeling about the world. . . . Nor do we like the idea of invoking single causes or one type of cause, preferring to chart a wide range of factors" (original emphasis). While "confidence in causal explanation" has eroded and a variety of approaches are now pursued by historians, they still aim at "appropriate and satisfying historical explanations," even if the criteria of "appropriateness" and "satisfaction" have shifted.[4] One must ask, therefore, how describing the events the historian investigates as saturated phenomena might enable or at least aid such greater comprehensibility. How does this category illuminate the phenomena instead of obscuring them?

While a historical event may indeed "bedazzle" and even overwhelm us, we cannot stop there. Certainly to some extent historical research "objectifies" what it treats through the careful gathering of data and precisely by considering it as an "object" of research and investigation. Yet, a historian also recognizes that one does not come to the topic or the data without presuppositions or from a completely neutral stance. And the data and texts shape perception and comprehension of historical events in important ways. They certainly do impose themselves on the researcher in some fashion. Historians know that their investigation and depiction of historical events will never be total and will never lead to complete comprehensibility of a period, a person, or an occurrence.[5] Historical phenomena are far too complex for simple accounts of straightforward causality or complete transparency in regard to what might have occurred. Yet it is certainly possible and a significant aim of research to shed greater light on an event, to establish some connections of correlation, and to strive for greater coherence and intelligibility, even if it can never be total or absolute. For example, after warning about "simple formulae and blanket definitions" in historical research, Jordanova reminds the reader that "just because there is an element of taste does not mean that no general criteria of judgement exist."[6] I return to these issues later in the chapter.

Marion does not describe the move from poor to saturated phenomenality as a *process* of increase in complexity or decrease of objectification. Rather, he speaks of "paradox" and "reversal" (BG, 163). We do not have less causality or more complexity, but we have its total opposite: no causality at all (he calls this "negentropy" in this context). In terms of phenomenality, the effect is first and is what makes a phenomenon appear or show itself. It hence has temporal and spatial privilege (BG, 164; ED, 231–32). The cause becomes "effect of the effect" (BG, 165; ED, 232). This is an important insight. Indeed, historical scholarship does in a sense work "backward" from effects to the tentative establishment of or at least conjecture about possible causes. Because a phenomenon occurred as a historical "event," we are moved to try to understand it and investigate what brought it about, hence we move from effect to cause. Marion claims that effects trump causes and give them their rationality: "Causes offer reasons for effects, but solely in terms of intelligibility" (BG, 165; ED, 233). For this Marion first gives examples of technical objects, which are assessed as they "work" and not in terms of their causality.

He then illustrates this lack of causality further with an actual historical event: World War I had no clear cause, because there is an overabundance of information, an accumulation of a huge variety of facts and data (BG, 167; ED, 235). In fact, the causes for the war compete with each other and therefore no cause is adequate, nor does a combination of causality work: "The event therefore accepts all the causalities one would assign to it" (BG, 168; ED, 237). Yet, although it is certainly true that for many historical events no clear cause can be firmly established or that there are many causes that all work together in some fashion, does this really mean that there is actually *no* cause of any sort, that the event occurs without any causality at all? And does this imply that *any* cause whatsoever can be assigned to the event? That seems an arbitrary conclusion. Historical research on World War I certainly points to the complexity of this event and agrees that no single or simple cause can be assigned to the conflict. That does not mean, however, that it had no cause at all or that any cause can be given for it. Rather historians seek to illuminate the ways in which a variety of conditions, none of which are sufficient by themselves, came together and interacted with each other in manifold ways that culminated in the outbreak of war. New interpretations continually emerge that examine new aspects of the problem and may well change previous understandings and conceptions. Yet it is their goal to provide an increase in comprehension and intelligibility, not merely to confuse things further. Mere awe or bedazzlement in face of the event is not an acceptable response.[7] I return to this contention in the final section of the chapter.

Marion asserts that the event combines necessity and contingency. It is utterly contingent in that no satisfying account of it can be given—it arises in surprising, unforeseeable, and unpredictable ways, yet it is fully accomplished and in that sense it is necessary and nonarbitrary, the center around which everything else is organized (BG, 169; ED, 238–39). And this is not just due to the complexity of the event, as Marion tries to illustrate with the taste of a piece of cake as described by Proust, a miniature event that is not on the level of great historical complexity and yet gives rise, in Marion's view, to the same sort of surprise.[8] The event "sums up" all the other "determinations" of the given phenomenon, precisely in its lack of causality, its unrepeatability, its excessive character. Marion insists that the event-like character of the phenomenon shows it to be a sudden and paradoxical occurrence: "The event passes directly from impossibility (in the concept, according to essence) to the fait accompli (holding the place of existence and the effect) without passing through phenomenological possibility" (BG, 173; ED, 243). In this context, the description still applies to all given phenomena, that is, to *all* phenomena. Later it will apply primarily, if not exclusively, to saturated phenomena.

Most interestingly, Marion here claims that the event gives rise to a "world" or even to "the world" (BG, 170; ED, 240). So there is a sense in which the event initiates a completely new way of living and experiencing and a different way of making sense of the world. Marion puts this in rather excessive terms: "The event prompts . . . the total world of history" (BG, 170; ED, 240). The event therefore becomes the origin and maybe in some sense even the cause of what goes before it. The more excessive the event, the more fully is the past experienced in light of it: "The level of eventness—if one can speak thus—is measured by the amount of the phenomenon's excess over its antecedents" (BG, 171; ED, 241). The event is hence defined in terms of excess: it exceeds any cause or predictability and any quantity or measure. And this excess is seen to be working backward. It influences how we experience the past and interpret it in light of the event. And it is obviously the case that certain excessive or extreme events can indeed radically reshape the "world" and even profoundly influence how we view what comes before it.[9] The event of the Holocaust fundamentally altered how German history before Hitler is interpreted. Similarly, 9/11 has reshaped U.S. self-understanding and view of the world in a significant manner. Marion himself points to this in respect to 9/11 in an interview with Dan Arbib (RC, 145, 271).[10] His analysis might enable us to appreciate the profound impact of such apparently singular events in deeper ways. To call them "saturated phenomena" may well be an apt description of their "phenomenal" significance.

The Event as Saturated Phenomenon

"The saturated phenomenon is attested first in the figure of the historical phenomenon, or the event carried to its apex," Marion affirms. It is saturated precisely because "nobody can claim for himself a 'here and now' that would permit him to describe it exhaustively and constitute it as an object" (BG, 228; ED, 318). This contrast to the object is central also to Marion's later discussions of the event, including the account given in *Certitudes négatives*. The example he uses in both *Being Given* and *Certitudes négatives* (though not in the chapter on the event in *In Excess*) is the battle of Waterloo, especially as portrayed by Stendahl in *The Charterhouse of Parma* through the confused eyes of the central character, Fabrice. This literary depiction of the battle particularly illustrates the partial perspective that provides a personal but incomplete and insufficient account of what occurred. Marion here makes a brief distinction between *Geschichte* (the historical event as it occurs) and *Historie* (the historiographical account of it as it is documented and transmitted). Marion contends that *Geschichte,* in such complex events as the battles of Waterloo or Austerlitz, appears suddenly and from itself, namely as saturated phenomenon. For *Historie* to become possible, it must be treated under a "plurality of horizons," which "demand an endless hermeneutic in time" (BG, 229; ED, 318). This means that the historical event will require a multiplicity of historiographical narrations, none of which will do full justice to the event and none of which would be capable of turning it into an object. The richness of the event precisely defies any such objectification. He claims consequently that "the romantic fiction of Chateaubriand, Hugo, Stendahl shows as much, better no doubt, than the factual reports of the memoirists or the quantitative historical analyses" (BG, 229; ED, 319). Historians certainly recognize the complexity of the events they study and the need for a plurality of interpretations. Yet to claim that literature and imagination can provide *better* accounts of historical events than historical research constitutes a surprising dismissal of history as a discipline. What does it really mean to speak of a historical event as a "paradox"? Is utter incomprehensibility the sole alternative to a total objectification of a historical event? Are these the only two options?

It is interesting in this context that, the first time Marion employs the category of quantity and speaks of a saturated phenomenon that is immense and without measure, he uses art and painting to illustrate this instead of a historical event. Cubist painting serves as a "privileged example" because the "infinite number of facets" "continually proliferate and accumulate" (BG, 201; ED, 282). Marion gives several examples of cubist paintings that "always give more to see, and by far, than we make of them" (BG, 201, trans. mod.; ED, 282). Cubist paintings are impossible and make visible the endless quantity of the saturated phenomenon explored here. They cannot be foreseen and yet try "to let appear" what cannot actually be seen. The saturation of intuition in terms of quantity is characterized by unforeseeability and amazement. This indicates an interesting slippage between art and history that is exacerbated by Marion's almost exclusive use of literary and poetic texts for the historical events he does discuss and by his claim that they give a better account of history as event than historical research does. As the next chapter makes evident, the work of art and the artist's activity actually come to define Marion's overall project in important ways.

In Excess devotes one chapter to "the event or the happening phenomenon" (title of chapter 2). Again, Marion stresses the "self" of the phenomenon in the opening of the chapter. Somehow events show the phenomenon's self more fully than other saturated phenomena do. Givenness precedes the self-showing of the phenomenon. The unforeseeable phenomenon of the event can provide insight into manifestation of phenomena more generally (IE, 31; DS, 36). Marion also again distinguishes strongly between "objects" and "phenomena." He illustrates the event-character of all phenomena by analyzing the ways in which the lecture hall manifests itself on that particular evening of the lecture. It does so without precedent, and that particular event can never be repeated in that kind of composition. Even at the next moment, everything will have changed. Marion suggests that his description covers all phenomena, including objects. In fact, to understand an event as an object is to have "dulled" the phenomenon and "lowered" it to objectivity (IE, 34; DS, 40, 41). This suggests, however, that the degree of "richness" or "poverty" in the appearance of the phenomenon depends on our perception of it, on the way in which we perceive or receive it. To experience something as an object seems to mean to have "lowered" and "dulled" a much richer experience, hence ultimately not to have experienced it adequately.

Despite Marion's insistence that no correct historical account can ever be given, judgment does seem implied here—there are right and wrong ways of experiencing or at least of depicting phenomena. A dull account is "bad" precisely because it does not recognize the richness, fullness, and ultimate incoherence of the event. By trying to explain it, the "real," namely saturated, nature of the event is not recognized.[11] Mackinlay rightly detects here a tension "between phenomenology as *description* of the way phenomena *actually* appear to us, and phenomenology as *prescription* of the way in which we should endeavor to encounter phenomena."[12] Marion will make similar judgments for the other types of saturated phenomena and especially for phenomena of revelation. This leads to a paradox (but one rather different from what Marion calls paradox): Any attempt at explaining or making intelligible is always already a betrayal and only a recognition of the unintelligibility of the event can possibly be adequate in some way. As we have seen, in Being Given, Marion suggests that understanding historical phenomena as saturated events leads somehow to a better comprehension of them. Here he appears to say, in contrast, that any attempt at comprehension or understanding is deeply problematic and a kind of betrayal. This question of understanding will have to be explored more fully, especially as it is also central to the treatment in Certitudes négatives.

It is striking that most of the rest of the chapter focuses on the ego or the self instead of on the phenomenon of the event per se. Next to nothing is said in chapter 2 of *In Excess* about history or the historical event. The main examples, first the lecture hall on that evening, then the friendship between Montaigne and La Boétie, finally the event of my birth, have little to do with historical research. Marion speaks here at the same time of the event-like character of all phenomena and of certain phenomena that particularly qualify as such events: "We still have to take another look at the description of the event-like character of phenomenality in general, focusing for now on phenomena indisputably thematizable as events." These "indisputable" events are "collective phenomena," which he identifies as "historical" and which include "political revolution, war, natural disaster, sporting or cultural performances, and so on" (IE, 36, trans. mod.; DS, 43). It is far from clear, however, that these all qualify as "historical" phenomena in any straightforward sense or that they are all equally "saturated." Throughout the treatment in this chapter, Marion deliberately collapses any distinctions between public and private events, and between historical phenomena and any other kind of minor event, ostensibly to show that his analysis covers a wide range of phenomena. Yet this actually complicates his account because the differences between these phenomena seem ignored in favor of their saturated character. It is far from clear that saturation can be said to apply to all these events in exactly the same way, even if they are indeed all experienced as saturated in some fashion.

Marion indicates that these phenomena fulfill at least three requirements. The three features are (1) unrepeatability or irreversibility, (2) inexhaustibility or lack of explanation because of surplus of effects / causes / explanations, and (3) unforeseeability or unpredictability. Again, he insists that these characteristics apply to both public and private phenomena, as illustrated with the example of friendship, which he contends confirms and parallels his analysis of the historical event in *Being Given*. The friendship begins as a surprise without any sort of expectation, as an accident or sudden arrival. It is immediately established as a fait accompli. Marion applies all the characteristics of the given phenomenon he has outlined in part 3 of *Being Given* to the saturated phenomenon of the event of the friendship between the two men. They are employed here not to indicate the givenness of all phenomenality, but precisely to show the phenomenon of friendship as a "pure and perfect event," one that imposes itself "such that it gives itself without contest or reserve" (IE, 38; DS, 45). Yet, one may well wonder whether the surprise encounter that develops into a friendship is really the same sort of surprise one experiences in the outbreak of a war, whether the fait accompli of the friendship is the same kind of experience as that of a historical event. Mackinlay worries about this conflation of the general event-character of phenomena and the particular saturated phenomenon of the event, although I would suggest that it is not correct that Marion's "position is best interpreted by regarding all events as saturated, and even by regarding saturation to be the normal way in which most phenomena appear."[13] Instead, it seems to me that Marion has lost the "poorer" phenomena from view or, more exactly, that he is focusing so exclusively on saturated phenomena that he fails to investigate the ways in which they might serve as a paradigm for all phenomena, as he had originally suggested to be the case. He says briefly, for example, that phenomena that are "temporalized as objects" may keep "a trace of event-like character" although the Kantian transcendental ego "is absolutely not phenomenalized as an event" (IE, 39, trans. mod.; DS, 46). He continues to contrast objects with events in this treatment.

In the remaining and considerably longer part of the chapter on the event in *In Excess,* Marion focuses entirely on the ways in which the self experiences such a saturated phenomenon of the event and analyzes the phenomena of temporality, birth and death. Death, for example, only shows itself as an event and cannot become an object. The death of the other already is a "pure event" to which I do not really have access, but the anticipation of my own death appears even more fully as an event of possibility.[14] The event of my death remains inaccessible to me but gives itself as a "perfect event" in "pure givenness" and with complete excess in the possibility of impossibility (IE, 40; DS, 48). Again, Marion applies the language of arrival and fait accompli to this event. It is "unforeseeable, irreversible, unrepeatable as such, immediately past and devoid of cause or of reason" (IE, 41; DS, 48). It entirely escapes objectivity and constitution. One may ask again: Is this irreversibility and unforeseeability of my death identical to the irreversibility and unpredictability of a cultural or historical event? Does it matter, for example, that (historical) wars cause countless (personal) deaths and hence establish a relation between the communal and the personal phenomenon that experiences one as an effect of the other? It seems that Marion is primarily interested in providing the general outlines of the structural appearance of events here instead of giving phenomenological depictions of particular experiences. Doing so, however, might provide important nuance and textuality to his account.

To this analysis of death, Marion adds an account of birth, relying on and appealing to Romano's discussion of this topic. While the phenomenon of birth does not show itself to me, insofar as I am not yet present at the moment of birth, it does affect me as an event and in fact originates me. Again, birth according to Marion "does phenomenalize itself, but as a pure event, unforeseeable, unrepeatable, exceeding all cause and rendering possible the impossible . . . surpassing all expectations, all promise, and all prediction" (IE, 43; DS, 50). These privileged phenomena hence give themselves without actually even showing themselves. The phenomena of birth and death are saturated phenomena of the event; they turn me into a devoted, a self given over to and receiving itself from the event instead of controlling it as an object. Marion examines the recipient or respondent to the phenomenon here in more detail, insisting again that *l'adonné* goes beyond the dichotomy between activity and passivity: *"L'adonné* is therefore characterized by reception. Reception implies, indeed, passive receptivity, but it also demands active capacity, because capacity *(capacitas)*, in order to increase to the measure of the given and to make sure it happens, must be put to work" (IE, 48; DS, 57). This work consists not in constituting or controlling the phenomena, but rather in receiving, showing, and responding to the phenomenon.

This is an active stance, then, not merely a passive position. While it is not the strong subjectivity of the tradition (the versions of the ego in Descartes, Kant, and Husserl), it is an important role and privilege of the recipient who "phenomenalizes the given" and ultimately "reveals the given as phenomenon" (IE, 49; DS, 58). Mackinlay, who generally stresses the passivity in Marion's account of the self, does worry that "if saturated phenomena are only able to appear as saturated when we *refrain* from reducing them to objects, does our *allowing* them to appear as saturated compromise their initiative and independence in showing themselves, and perhaps even result in a form of constitution?" (original emphasis).[15] Marion is fairly clear, however, that this reception and revelation happens in a mode of resistance and response, not in terms of constitution. He consistently holds in tension the more passive and more active aspects of such receptivity in a way that we will encounter over and over again. Marion suggests that the excess and abundance of saturated phenomena are received by "bearing up" under them, by resisting their impact and thereby making them visible. The more firmly the recipient can stand under the weight of the given, the more of the given will become visible through the ways in which the effect or impact is marked on the recipient. Already in this context Marion describes this as moving from the unseen *(l'invu)* to the seen, something he explores much more fully in his discussions of art. Here he puts it entirely in terms of visibility by employing the metaphor of photography or the image of a prism: the one devoted to the phenomenon blocks the impact of the light, which hence becomes visible on the *adonné* as light does on a screen, but not when it travels through empty space, where it meets no obstacle. Yet although the incoming phenomenon has full initiative, the recipient is not merely passive: Marion compares him to a "goalkeeper blocking a shot" or "a receiver sending back a winning return" (IE, 50; DS, 59). Receiving the given requires patience, skill, and steadfastness.

One wonders why Marion never applies this analysis to the person engaged in historical research. Providing historical accounts of events in the past requires great patience and skill. The person who collects the data and organizes them into a coherent narrative precisely make the historical event visible in some fashion, and we indeed talk about this as a kind of illumination. And obviously the historian is actually constrained by the given. Unlike literary authors and poets, historians cannot let their imaginations run wild but must be faithful to the phenomena, portray them as they actually give themselves to them. Historians seek to illuminate the data as accurately as possible, to reveal them in all their complexity while making them "visible" for the first time through the coherence they attempt to give them. The data were not invisible before, but they were indeed "unseen" in precisely the sense Marion seems to give that term.[16] The good historian helps us "see" the historical event in a way that was "unseen" before. And historical research often happens precisely because someone is "struck" in some way by an event or a historical period, because it grabs the attention in some unprecedented way and inspires the research. Historians are neither completely passive before events and their data, nor do they "control" or manipulate the data but are informed by them. This is precisely what it means to "document" a historical event. It is a form of historical witness that tries to be extremely careful with the data in order to let it speak "for itself" as much as that is possible.[17] Historical research is characterized by a careful tension between activity and passivity in such a way that the phenomena can appear most fully as they give themselves.[18]

Instead of speaking of the historical event and the historian, Marion again appeals to the artist and the work of art in this context: "the painter renders visible as a phenomenon what no one had ever seen before, because he or she manages, being the first to do that every time, to resist the given enough to get it to show *itself*, and to do so in a phenomenon accessible to all. A great painter never invents anything, as if the given were missing, but rather suffers a resistance to this excess, to the point of making it render its visibility" (IE, 51; DS, 61; original emphasis). He quotes Mark Rothko, on whose work he focuses in the following chapter on the idol or work of art, as confirmation of this. The background or screen (*écran*) of the painting here becomes equated with the screen (*écran*) on which the phenomenon is projected.[19] And Marion explicitly identifies this ability to bear the impact of the given as a kind of genius: "Genius consists merely in a great resistance to the impact of the given revealing itself" (IE, 52, trans. mod.; DS, 62). In this sense indeed, all saturated phenomena appear as events and the event is anything that is revealed as saturated. Any phenomenon that "gives *itself* in what shows *itself*" has an event-like character (IE, 52; DS, 62; original emphasis). In his interview with Arbib he also affirms: "I think more and more that the event is the most determinative of all saturated phenomena, that all the other kinds of saturated phenomena are each in their own way governed by eventness" (RC, 270).

Marion suggests in the conclusion of the chapter on the event from *In Excess* that this opening of phenomenality to saturated events instead of merely metaphysical objects allows us to treat the events of (religious) revelation as phenomena that can now be properly examined within phenomenology.[20] One may well wonder whether establishing this is what finally motivates his work and is one of the reasons that historical research is treated in such incidental fashion in the context of events identified as "historical." That is not to say that the category of "event" as saturated phenomenon has no value for phenomenological investigation of historical events. But it may explain why Marion's treatment spends so little time engaging with concrete historical writing. He does stress here—as he also does in many other places—that phenomenology "covers all givens" of varying degrees: "from the poorest (formalism, mathematics), to the common (physical sciences, technical objects), to saturated phenomena (event, idol, flesh, icon) up to the point of the possibility of phenomena combining the four types of saturation (phenomena of Revelation)" (IE, 53; DS, 63).[21] Thus, although the event does indeed mark or characterize all given phenomena, especially saturated ones, in some fashion, this event is pictured as essentially artistic not primarily historical. Artistic genius can make events visible and provide an account of them. In the next chapter I return to the role of the artist, but let us turn now to the possibility of rendering an account of such phenomena.

Negative Certainty in the Event

Marion's discussion of the phenomenon of the event in *Certitudes négatives* stresses again most strongly its contrast to the object.[22] He begins by showing that only little of what is given actually appears as a phenomenon to us, much never catches our attention at all (CN, 243). Among the given that do become phenomena for us, one can make further distinctions between the different ways in which such phenomena appear to us. The first seemingly obvious distinction is between phenomena that can be constituted objectively (i.e., as objects) and those that appear more subjectively and to which no clear, certain, objective description can be given. This corresponds to the distinctions we commonly draw between the natural sciences that examine objects and the human sciences that are more subjective (CN, 244–46). In one case there is clear understanding, while the other seems considerably more imprecise. While the object appears under clear parameters, insofar as it is predictable, reproducible, the result of causality and easily depicted, none of these parameters apply to the apparently more subjective phenomena. It seems hence that investigation of such phenomena must dispense with any call for certain knowledge and instead be satisfied with approximations that remain in the realm of mere hermeneutics (CN, 247). This appears to lead to an absolute dichotomy between objects on the one hand and more subjective phenomena on the other. Marion challenges both the apparent hegemony of the object and the absolute distinction drawn between the two types of investigation or knowledge. He therefore addresses the question of how the two types of phenomenality relate to each other far more explicitly here than in his prior work.

Marion shows the ways in which object and event seem diametrically opposed to each other and how the criteria of knowledge for one do not work for the other. The rationality of the object makes other phenomena seem "uncertain, imprecise, and confused, in short, as being at the margins of knowledge and even quasi-irrational, hence subjective" (CN, 248). Yet these phenomena operate with a different kind of rationality and arise from themselves, imposing themselves without cause or preparation as "autonomous, spontaneous, accomplished" on their own (CN, 248). Such phenomena appear as events. Their intuitive excess imposes itself and constitutes any understanding as always already too late. Yet an absolute distinction between these two realms is untenable (CN, 250). Marion argues that they operate in a different light, in a different sort of temporality and according to a different rationality. The distinction between the two types has to be examined more carefully (CN, 251). Only metaphysics assumes an absolute caesura between them. Phenomenology may well show us that they belong to the "same phenomenality, where they only diverge by the variations they introduce within it" (CN, 251). In fact, he suggests that they might diverge only in degree "according to the scale of these variations" (CN, 251). The object may be a "gradation" of the non-object, namely an impoverished and restricted version of the phenomenon of the event, although they still participate in the same phenomenality (CN, 252). Although Marion had hinted at such degrees in *Being Given,* he explores this possibility that the object might appear as an instance of the phenomenon more generally much more fully here.

Marion describes the object as a kind of colonizing phenomenon that takes up space and attention, while the other phenomena hide in the background, pushed aside by the object (CN, 253). Marion defines the object along Cartesian parameters: it is what can be known clearly and distinctly, hence with certainty.[23] The object is the result of a reduction that reduces the thing to an x exposed to the objectifying gaze (CN, 256). Only mathematical parameters finally fit this sort of abstraction; even most "things" are considerably more complex in their materiality and temporal appearance. This kind of mathematical abstraction, in fact, "eliminates the least residue of the event-like character in things in order to constitute them as object and dismiss them [*les destituant*] as events" (CN, 257). Drawing on Kant, Marion argues that something becoming an object depends on its constitution by the transcendental ego, which means that it looses its "autonomy and phenomenological spontaneity." It appears no longer as an event but under the conditions that turn it into an object of perception. It hence suffers from "phenomenological diminution" and becomes "poor in phenomenality" (CN, 259).

Marion reiterates the four Kantian conditions of phenomenality—quantity, quality, relation, and modality—showing each time how phenomenality is reduced in the case of the object to something that can be measured and constituted and which is, in fact, abstracted from its materiality and spatial and temporal context. The object no longer appears as event, because it is completely formalized and idealized as "reproducible and disposable" (CN, 262). By becoming objects, things are alienated from themselves, cease to appear as events, and are constituted by the ego. "The conditions of our thought (experience)" become for Descartes and Kant "at the same time the conditions of the phenomenality of things and no longer the opposite; consequently *objects* either do not appear at all or become *subject* to our conditions of thought" (CN, 268). In light of this, Marion suggests that we must choose between phenomena appearing as events and appearing as our conditions of thought. Yet if objects are presupposed to be what appears in our realm of thought and to depend upon it, the experience of phenomenality in general, that is, that of the event, is excluded a priori (CN, 268). Existence of the object becomes "the result of a production" and therefore forbids the event (CN, 269).

Marion then goes on to question this primacy of the object by pushing the comparison between object and event further. Experience must be freed and inverted from the conception of the object. Marion employs Kandinsky's surprising encounter with his own painting as an example of this reversal (CN, 272). The painting arises in indescribable beauty, cannot be foreseen or predicted, and is incomprehensible. It is an event in every sense (CN, 273). The event comes from itself without causality or correlation or analogy to objects of experience. It is not marginal but instead shows the phenomenological diminution of objects: Events open up phenomenality, whereas objects restrict it: "One must admit that, in fact, even if we only comprehend objects, because they alone accept the conditions that we impose upon them, that through and in which we have being and life, what we breathe as our pervasive air, is only given to us through events" (CN, 276). Some phenomena appear as events instead of as objects and therefore phenomenality can be divided into manifestation as objects and as events (CN, 276). Phenomenality can henceforth be divided into diminished phenomena, that is, objects, and saturated phenomena, that is, events (CN, 280).

This distinction, however, seems to reinstitute the kinds of divisions Marion was ostensibly trying to overcome. Although this may not be an absolute distinction, as both are claimed to be kinds of phenomenality, yet "degrees" or "variations" of phenomenality seem to have disappeared from view. A phenomenon is *either* "poor" *or* "saturated," and the way in which these two possibilities are experienced are reversals of each other: while one is completely predictable, the other is utterly unpredictable; while one is subject to causality, the other defies all causality and imposes itself as effect without cause; while one is completely subjugated to my conditions and fully comprehended, the other imposes itself on me and defies all attempts at comprehension. Instead of being degrees of each other, these two hence seem utterly opposed to one another. Marion does indeed speak of the two as "opposed to each other" and shows how that is so by applying all the parameters of the object to the event in a reversed fashion (CN, 281).

Yet, why must phenomena necessarily be experienced only in one or the other extreme? Why can it not be possible to comprehend, in terms of prediction, causality, and conditionality, to some extent or degree? And why must there be competition between the two? Why is one an "impoverished" version of the other, a "loser" or "outcast" (CN, 276)? Marion clearly implies that the event is somehow "better" than the object: "On the contrary [to being a 'loser'], in freedom from causes or conditions on its execution, the event stigmatizes the phenomenological diminution of the object, its submission to the gaze that delineates it, its alienation from any manifestation of itself and by itself. The event does not limit phenomenality—it opens and protects it. The object does not accomplish phenomenality—it impoverishes, restrains, and in the end, masks it" (CN, 276). It is obviously better to experience and describe something as an event rather than as an object. I return to this implication that there are "better" phenomenological experiences or accounts for them much more forcefully in the next chapter in regard to the work of art and aesthetic judgment.

Marion again makes a distinction between collective or "historical" events and private or individual ones.[24] He employs Baudelaire's poetic description of a woman passing by as an illustration of a rich event that cannot (or should not) be reduced to an object. No causality can be assigned here, as the event would otherwise be destroyed as event. Marion uses language of obligation: "How *must* I review this event if I want to find its rationality? Precisely as that which I will never be able to repeat or reproduce" (CN, 285, emphasis added). So how does the mere fact that it cannot be repeated provide greater rationality for the phenomenon? While Marion states this quite often, he has not yet spent much time exploring how this provides a real increase in rationality or understanding, besides consistently stressing that it cannot lead to full comprehension. Marion argues that the phenomenon of the passing woman gives full, even excessive, intuition. The fact that I cannot (and should not) constitute her as an object bears witness to the excess of intuition, not its lack (CN, 287). Instead of comprehending the encounter as an object, the saturated phenomenon encompasses and attains or constitutes me. It turns me into a witness, and "I must renounce claiming to be a transcendental subject" (CN, 287).

As in *Being Given* and *In Excess,* in this example in *Certitudes négatives,* one also becomes devoted to the phenomenon and constituted by it. In this context, however, Marion continues to draw out the opposing characteristics of object and saturated phenomenon. The event reverses the determinations of the object in all respects. Marion here deals briefly with the objection that "object" and "event" might merely be two different ways of *understanding* the same phenomenon instead of two different types of phenomena. In response, he suggests that this fails to maintain the distinction between theoretical and practical reason and does not recognize that saturated phenomena are known by practical reason instead of comprehended through theoretical reason (CN, 290–91). Unfortunately, this tantalizing suggestion is meager and not elaborated in any detail, although Marion appeals to his more general and frequently reiterated claim that "loving" is a different form of knowing.[25]

Marion also responds to the objection that any event must first of all appear as an object. He rejects this as patently absurd: many events appear without it being possible to constitute them as objects at all. While the object is completely dependent upon the gaze that envisions it, the event does not "subsist in permanence" (CN, 292). He discusses birth as an example of such a "pure event" that can in no way be reduced to an object or ever appear as an object to me, again relying heavily on Romano's analysis (CN, 293). While death might be appropriated in some way metaphysically, this is impossible to do with birth (CN, 295). He relies on Henry to show that birth cannot occur to objects but only to the living (CN, 296). In fact, birth is the phenomenon of the event par excellence, because it makes the very event-character of phenomena possible. It is also a perfect gift in that it marks givenness itself as such (CN, 298). One wonders whether it is true that birth can never be treated as an object. Can it not also become a mere line in a statistic, treated only as a factual record? And what about situations in which the birth of the child is not desired, where the infant might even be immediately abandoned, like a parcel on a doorstep? Is birth still experienced as a "perfect gift" in that case? Here, as in many other places, Marion's discussion seems to assume the most benign versions of the phenomena he employs as examples.

Marion ends this chapter on the event with a reflection on interpretation. Here finally he returns to the possibility of transitions and degrees: "The pure event (if there is such a thing) and the pure object (if there is such a thing) only mark the two extreme poles between which the prism is spread of all the other phenomena of various shades and mixtures. The object and the event hence are no longer opposed like two regions separated by an insuperable wall and which would each retain a pure and exclusive character: they range from one to the other by as many transitions as possible" (CN, 299). This is indeed a promising statement, suggesting that infinite variation and degrees might be possible and that object and saturated phenomenon only mark the limit cases of phenomenality. Marion recognizes that this seems to contradict the previous opposition between the two types, and he raises the question of the phenomenological status of such transitional phenomena. He replies to the apparent contradiction by pointing to his previous distinction between poor and saturated phenomenality. There are hence not only two types, object and event, but four: poor phenomena, common-law phenomena, simply saturated phenomena, and doubly saturated phenomena. It is not entirely clear, however, how these are, in fact, variations or transitions, as Marion indicates that poor phenomena and common phenomena appear as objects, while all saturated phenomena appear as events (CN, 301). While this reply relieves the accusation of contradiction, it also eliminates the range of transitional phenomena just introduced and returns it to the basic distinction between the two extreme types that oppose each other in paradoxical fashion. It would seem, however, that these transitional phenomena—the range, plurality, and diversity of phenomena neither utterly "poor" nor absolutely "saturated"—constitute the majority of our phenomenal experience. Examining them would add important nuance to Marion's excessive focus on the outer poles of phenomenality.

In regard to the phenomenological status of the transitional types, Marion employs the idea of hermeneutic variation from Kant and legitimates it with Heidegger's tool analysis. In being used, the hammer disappears as object and appears as phenomenon that is ready-to-hand (CN, 304). The phenomenological gaze determines the mode in which phenomena appear. Marion claims, however, that the distinction between present-to-hand and ready-to-hand does not correspond to his distinction between object and event, because the event goes beyond both and is not subject to use and predictability in the same way that the hammer is subject to them (CN, 307). Yet Marion does claim that Heidegger's analysis confirms the possibility of hermeneutic variations in phenomenality. As in "The Banality of Saturation," he suggests that it "depends only on my gaze" whether a stone appears as a saturated phenomenon or whether God is reduced to an object (CN, 307). The extent to which a phenomenon appears as event is the extent to which it is saturated, saturation varies according to the event-character (CN, 307). Marion ends the chapter with this tantalizing suggestion, which he does not explore further.

These claims, of course, raise the same questions as those in "The Banality of Saturation": Does whether something appears as a poor or saturated phenomenon depend solely on the gaze? In what sense, then, can the phenomenon be said to appear "from itself" without any conditions imposed by the recipient or observer? Are there better and worse ways of "seeing," as Marion frequently suggests, and if so, how are distinctions between these ways possible? Apparently, the same phenomenon can move from appearing as "poor" to imposing itself as saturated. How does it do so, except by being subject to a different interpretation? Yet is not interpretation something imposed, at least to some extent, by the interpreter? In the earlier version of the essay, Marion had suggested that I could "allow myself to be informed by the meaning that it [the phenomenon] would impose on me."[26] In both versions, he concludes by saying that everything gives itself by itself and comes from itself (CN, 308).

In the conclusion to the whole book, he portrays hermeneutics as a first expansion of phenomenology, the discovery or creation of saturated phenomena as a second enlargement, and his new proposal of "negative certainties" as a third such expansion of the domain of phenomenality (CN, 314). Each goes further than the ones before it. Already in his discussion of the event in *In Excess,* he had briefly suggested that the event gives rise to hermeneutics in some fashion: "A hermeneutic would have to be deployed without end and in an indefinite network" (IE, 33; DS, 39). What Marion seems to be saying is that we can supply lots of interpretations, because the event is incomprehensible. This suggests, however, that all of them are equivalent and even that maybe all are ultimately meaningless, because in his view no adequate account can really ever be given, and no real distinctions can be made among the infinite number of interpretations. The reference to hermeneutics, then, appears to be purely gratuitous. Hermeneutic work here actually does not lead to any greater comprehension or intelligibility. Both are ruled out a priori, as events precisely defy comprehension and intelligibility. Yet is not hermeneutics absolutely essential, especially for accounts of historical events?

Historical Events and Interpretation

While Marion's depiction of the event as saturated phenomenon is valuable in several respects, it does raise important questions, especially if such events are said to be historical. I have already suggested several questions: First, are historical phenomena best depicted as saturated in this extreme fashion? Second, what implications does Marion's insistence on incomprehensibility have for historical research? Can any historical accounts be given that attempt to make sense of these events in some fashion? Third, what is the role of hermeneutics in historical writings? Finally, what does it mean to "witness" a historical event? Obviously, all these questions are closely connected. Each is briefly discussed in the remainder of this chapter.

First of all, Marion's account raises questions about the historical phenomena themselves. Is the outbreak of a world war with the slaughter of millions of people really on the same scale as a woman passing by or the tasting of a morsel of madeleine, even when poetically described? Do not historical events, even when it is recognized that they can never be fully described or constituted, appear with different degrees of complexity and incomprehensibility? Similarly, is the element of surprise or sudden arrival of the same kind and degree in the various phenomena Marion mentions or indeed in the many other examples that could be listed? One might suggest, for example, that the outcome of the Battle of Waterloo was more surprising than the outcome of a war in which the forces involved are less evenly matched (maybe the partitions of Poland by the far more powerful nations surrounding it), even when no clear causality or entirely linear trajectory can be assigned to either. And, as mentioned above, the element of surprise that begins a friendship seems qualitatively different from the surprise accompanying the rise of Napoleon. Although both may well be surprising, are they really surprising in exactly the same fashion? Similar questions could be raised for the other aspects of saturated phenomenality (anamorphosis, fait accompli, and so forth), which Marion applies fairly indiscriminately to all these phenomena. Even when historical phenomena are recognized as saturated, not all are saturated in the same fashion or to the same degree.

Furthermore, are overwhelming saturation and complete reduction to objectivity really the only two options for phenomena? The alternative in Marion's treatment consistently is *either* object *or* event, *either* complete control of the poor *or* total exposure to the overwhelming saturated. Why only these extreme and absolute alternatives? Ultimately, Marion does affirm that even the object appears as a phenomenon, just as an extremely impoverished one. So why not a range of phenomena that are "poor" or "rich" (to use Marion's language) *to some extent*? Why not *degrees* of givenness or saturation? Are historical events not experienced in a variety of ways, with some proving considerably more overwhelming and complex than others? Marion's description of the saturated phenomenon may well be appropriate and illuminating for some phenomena, but is it really adequate for *all* historical phenomena, as he seems to suggest?

There are indeed some historical phenomena that seem to defy any description and that are completely unprecedented. That is certainly some of the language that has been used of the Shoah, even as it is often employed as a paradigm for and measure of all kinds of other evils, in obvious contradiction to its supposedly immemorial character.[27] Yet not all historical events are of the magnitude of the Shoah or a world war and yet not therefore at the level of simple objects. Intermediary degrees of phenomenality must be possible. And even for such heavily saturated phenomena, continued research and further analysis of phenomenality must be possible, in fact, is absolutely essential, as the case of the Holocaust denier attests. And even in situations of encountering utterly unprecedented phenomena, a search for greater understanding is necessary. Such extreme phenomena may actually call more insistently for explanation and deeper comprehension. Historical events, then, require ongoing historical research that in fact attempts to make sense of facts and data. Historical research seeks to establish the most honest, coherent, and convincing account possible, always realizing that it is not possible to give a full account or to establish only one truthful account (which does not mean that some accounts are not more truthful than others).[28] And one arrives at such honest and coherent accounts not only by having the event "impact" us in some utterly overwhelming fashion, but through meticulous research that collects as much data as possible, establishes criteria for evaluating the data, and weighs and represents them as accurately as possible.

It is one thing to emphasize the complexity of historical events and to refuse reductionistic accounts, but it is an entirely different matter to present historical events as being of such overwhelming magnitude that they become utterly incoherent and that no understanding whatsoever is ever possible.[29] This makes a virtue out of incoherence and incommunicability, with serious consequences. On the one hand, it becomes next to impossible to provide accounts that would either establish or challenge national or political continuity and identity. On the other hand, it gives no recourse when historical events are denied and justice refused.[30] A complete denial of the possibility of giving an account seems to equate the Holocaust denier with the philosophers of the immemorial. Richard Kearney suggests that this is precisely what has happened in some excessive accounts: "Of course, no fictional retelling can ever presume to retrieve the depth and detail of the actual suffering of those who died. However, some testimonies can do better than others and the blanket condemnation of all literary narrative remembrances of the Holocaust is, it seems to me, purist and self-defeating."[31] He argues both for the need of poetic and literary genres in dealing with traumatic historical events and against the erasure of any distinction between the genres of literary and historical writing. Sometimes literature or poetry can be eminently helpful for conveying something of the pathos of an event that a dry historical account might not provide, yet the distinction between the two genres is important and should not be erased or minimized.[32]

Another interesting example is provided by the "poetry of witness," advocated by Carolyn Forché.[33] Although she highlights the poetic character of the historical sources she collects, she thinks of this as bearing witness to historical (not fictional) events, albeit in a manner that also testifies to their "broken" character. She explicitly speaks of these events as "extremities" and stresses that the "truth" of the poems cannot be measured in terms of "accuracy."[34] On the one hand, she depicts the impact of the poems in ways that resembles Marion's language: "These poems will not permit us diseased complacency. They come to us with claims that have yet to be filled, as attempts to mark us as they have themselves been marked." Yet, on the other hand, she draws important distinctions between the event itself and its poetic expression: "Unlike an aerial attack, a poem does not come at one unexpectedly. One has to read or listen, one has to be willing to accept the trauma. So, if a poem is an event and the trace of an event, it has, by definition, to belong to a different order of being from the trauma that marked its language in the first place."[35] While she stresses the inability of the poetry of witness to tell a full story or give full voice to the victims, she attends to the need to provide accurate historical data about the trauma witnessed in the poetry. The poems are "evidence of what occurred" while their fragmentation also recognizes the inability to do justice to the trauma of the event: "The reader is strangely aware of what has been left out, what cannot or has not been said. The French call this procedure *récit éclaté*—shattered, exploded, or splintered narrative. The story cannot travel over the chasm of time and space. Violence has rendered it unspeak-able."[36] Her work constitutes a valuable example of how a recognition of excess or saturation (in the sense of horror or trauma) can enable responsible historical accounts with nuance and integrity.

Oral histories of war veterans and trauma survivors attempt to achieve a similar balance. As Ricoeur recognizes, such "witness accounts" are not iden-tical to historical research in their "accuracy" and yet they provide an important complement in our search for "truthfulness" (rather than "scientific" accuracy).[37] While the line between literature and history is thin, it should not be entirely erased. For example, Toni Morrison's fictional account of a World War I soldier's trauma and the demise of a historically black village in *Sula* or her novel about early colonial struggles and the roles race and gender played in them in *A Mercy* give readers access to aspects of historical events in an important manner, and even make "visible" in some ways what was previously "unseen"—Marion's cate-gories make lots of sense here—but they do not purport to be historiographical writings.[38] The distinction between history and fiction matters.

Recognizing the magnitude and complexity or even the surprise and horror of an event does not amount to a complete lack of understanding or coherence. Some understanding, albeit proximate, is not only possible but necessary, even imperative. To deny this, according to Kearney, "endangers the very notion of memory itself" and "makes the past itself unnecessarily inaccessible to us."[39] In Kearney's view, "the postmodern cult of the 'immemorial' amounts to a whole-sale rejection of critical hermeneutics." Although he does not deal with Marion in this particular context, he has repeatedly charged him with a similar tendency to excess that disregards the need for hermeneutics.[40] Such a cult of ineffability is dangerous for Kearney because "historical narrative is outlawed" and the right of the victims to be remembered is denied. Instead, he suggests, we must pursue "a certain judicious mix of phronetic understanding, narrative imagination and her-meneutic judgement."[41] Throughout his work, Kearney reminds us of "the moral obligation to bear witness to history" and "to continue to remember."[42]

There is hence not only a range of historical phenomena with many vary-ing degrees of saturation. There are also degrees of approximation in historical research: There are better and worse accounts that can be given of an event. Ac-counts can be improved with more research, more acute observation or critical evaluation, better presentation (or representation), and further explanation. While insight is not purely a measure of quantity (despite what might appear in Mari-on's use of the category), that is, the lack of being able to "grasp" a historical event is not merely a matter of not having enough data or information, an increase in understanding in more than merely quantitative terms surely is possible. We can understand better when we see or investigate anew, when we change the angle of our view, and also when we uncover "more" information. All these increase our knowledge about and understanding of an event, even when such knowledge or understanding can never be total. So the "negative certainty" for historical events is not absolute: Although we may certainly know that we can never get back to the "event itself" (such as it occurred) or can never fully comprehend, never completely understand, yet depending on the event and the circumstances and the data still available, there are certainly a great many things we can indeed know and understand. Our knowledge is not completely lacking or "negative" in every way. That's simply too absolute and total.

And hermeneutics indeed plays an important role here and a far larger role than the somewhat dismissive "endless interpretations" that Marion occasionally concedes. It is not only that there is an endless variety of completely arbitrary interpretations all competing with each other in equal measure. Rather, there are certain kinds of interpretations appropriate for certain kinds of events. And while new interpretations are always possible and may well prove illuminating, not all interpretations are possible, and certainly not all interpretations are equal. Some give a better account of the historical phenomenon than others. Some, such as the Holocaust denials, are simply wrong. And they are wrong precisely because they do not match the data, because their account is not coherent or convincing, because it does not "fit" the phenomena. Good interpretation assumes a "fit" between the data and the theory provided to make sense of it. Good interpretation increases our understanding, provides meaning in a way that is convincing to us.[43] Especially for historical events, this requires a plurality of interpreters and listeners, often in collaborative ways.[44] A singular and isolated interpretation only becomes convincing (a "good" or "true" interpretation) if it actually convinces, that is, if it proves illuminating to a group of people, possibly even a very large group of people. This is of course not subject to a simple "majority" vote, but often something that happens within the discipline or even a certain narrow subfield of the discipline. But hermeneutics always assumes the audience that listens and responds to the interpretation, that affirms or rejects it.

Marion speaks of the witness to the event as the one who "yields to an infinite hermeneutic" and "is encompassed by it" (BG, 267; ED, 369). But hermeneutics needs to be exercised responsibly. One does not simply "yield" to hermeneutics, but rather engages in its circular motion on many different levels. And while new interpretations are always possible, hermeneutics is not "infinite" in this vacuous sense. It is not an ocean that "encompasses" us and in which we drown. Hermeneutics is a method, a tool for careful investigation and interpretation, not something that washes over us and leaves us stunned and stranded. An event may well affect us in such a way (though certainly not all events do), but hermeneutics also has a much more active and responsible element. Marion's account of hermeneutics feels like an abdication of responsibility instead of a call for discernment.[45] And, of course, he does not actually counsel an abdication of responsibility. His section on "Responsibility" calls for a response by the one devoted to the call. Marion claims, in fact, that he wants to expand responsibility. It no longer applies solely to the realm of ethics (or "the face of the other"), but to all realms of phenomenality. Each saturated phenomenon exercises a call and thus gives rise to a corresponding responsibility to heed this call and respond to it. In the case of the event, this means that the self becomes the witness "charged with its reconstitution and its hermeneutic" (BG, 293; ED, 405). A fuller and more nuanced account of such hermeneutic would go a long way toward explicating this responsibility.

Marion discusses the witness in somewhat more detail earlier in *Being Given* in the section on the given, after he has introduced the saturated phenomenon and its overcoming of the four Kantian categories, yet before identifying them as the phenomena of event, idol, flesh, and icon. He posits the "witness" as an initial response to the "paradox" before identifying it more fully as the one devoted or given over to the saturated phenomenon. The witness is the self as constituted by the phenomenon; it depicts the counter-experience of counter-intentionality. Marion defines it as follows: "Constituted witness, the subject is still the worker of truth, but he cannot claim to be its producer. With the name *witness,* we must understand a subjectivity stripped of the characteristics that gave it transcendental rank" (BG, 217, original emphasis; ED, 302). The witness does not impose meaning, much less constitute it, but merely responds to what is already given.

In this context, Marion initially suggests that the correct interpretation is already provided by the phenomenon itself to the witness, although he later qualifies this claim somewhat. The witness does not impose interpretation or interact with the phenomenon, but merely receives the interpretation ready-made. Marion puts this forcefully: "In space, the saturated phenomenon swallows him with its intuitive deluge; in time, it precedes him with an interpretation always already there" (BG, 217, trans. mod.; ED, 303). The witness is "stupefied and taken aback" by the phenomenon. Here interpretation actually is not possible at all: "The witness . . . does not see the given phenomenon in its totality . . . cannot read or interpret the intuitive excess" (BG, 217; ED, 303). We are judged by the phenomenon instead of judging it. This portrayal is almost entirely passive: a self-manifestation of the phenomenon that exceeds all horizons or constituting subjects. Although Marion qualifies this account later, this description gives the impression that the self becomes entirely passive, maybe even an object for the phenomenon that has been instituted as the new subject. That the tension is more dynamic only emerges in the later discussion in book 5 (and maybe even there not sufficiently—at least in some respects).

This analysis of the witness remains somewhat problematic. Research on witness and testimony shows that witness accounts are notoriously unreliable. The witness is not just "swept away" by the event but almost always imposes particular interpretations upon it. Overall, one would wish that Marion had emphasized the responsibility of the recipient's response more strongly. We have to respond to the "face" of the phenomenon, including the historical event. Yet what are the parameters for such a response? The problem is not so much that Marion does not call for a response or dismisses the self as completely passive, but rather that he does not give us any parameters for response, that any response is made in total anonymity, in utter "fear and trembling." This also means that any response is completely individual, made only under the weight of the singular call directed to me personally and to which I alone can respond.[46] No one else can invalidate or even question my response, because it arises from the weight of the call felt by me and never to be made visible (except in my individual response). I am bedazzled and blinded by the saturation of the incoming phenomenon: What guarantee is there that my response is remotely adequate? In fact, Marion specifically points out that it is not and never can be. The phenomenon is so overwhelming that no response can ever do justice to it. But how, then, can we know when justice has been approximated? The historical account for Marion becomes like the work of art: It is created by a "gifted" in response to what he or she alone has "seen" or experienced and cannot be questioned or invalidated.

Yet, it seems that it is only the account of the saturated phenomenon that cannot be questioned, because it is so utterly dependent on overwhelming and blinding intuition. Marion clearly does question when someone else does not see anything or sees only objects—that person has not seen rightly. He invalidates or at least evaluates their response. What enables him to make that evaluation, to judge one response to be better than another, namely one that identifies the incoming phenomenon as saturated instead of as a poor object? We will return to this question over and over again in regard to several of the phenomena Marion discusses, but here the distinction appears fairly arbitrary. Indeed, in *Being Given,* Marion insists heavily on the anonymity of the call that is decided and identified only in the response (BG, 296–300; ED, 408–413). This gives the apparently passive witness an incredible power. He or she alone can identify the call, is indeed "master" of the given, not just its servant (BG, 319; ED, 438).[47] And in this context, Marion does envision the possibility that there might be "false" witnessing, which really means insufficient testimony.

First of all, the witness can refuse to make the phenomenon visible at all: "The saturated phenomenon appears next in terms of quantity, as the event that happens without the gaze ever being able to foresee it, because the indefinite sum of its parts is continually increasing and never equals its final sum. Submerged by the excess of this flux, the gifted can renounce rendering visibility to the given, even the visibility of a paradox" (BG, 315; ED, 433). Yet, if the recipient indeed refuses to make this phenomenon visible, how do we know that it is a saturated phenomenon? Marion also suggests that to tell "little stories" (instead of meta-narratives?) of the phenomenon is a second way of falsifying it, because it simpli-fies the event and makes it seem arbitrary and insignificant. This is reduction (in the sense of impoverishment or trivialization, not phenomenological reduction) of the weightiness of the event into little meaningless facts. Such an activity ulti-mately "masters the event, whose unforeseeability vanishes" (BG, 316; ED, 434). Again, Marion here clearly judges this account as insufficient and false: "Such curi-osity . . . denies the event its paradoxical character in order to exempt *l'adonné* from having to lose him- or herself in this excess of intuition" (BG, 316, trans. mod.; ED, 434). Thus, judgment is implied, but the judgment refers only to whether the event is received as overwhelming (and made visible as such) or reduced to an object.

Again, this seems to make it impossible to judge or discern between more and less truthful accounts of history. On Marion's reading, it appears that any account that stresses the overwhelming nature of the historical event will do. But what of a depiction that glorifies acts of tremendous injustice and horror? Is it sufficient that the account stress the incomprehensibility of the event without also somehow at-tempting to give a voice to the victims, or at least acknowledging their suffering in some at least partial fashion? A mere acknowledgment of lack of certainty can become a kind of abdication of responsibility or even a refusal to attend to the suffering of the victims. It also can become reductive and simplistic, precisely by refusing to pay careful, meticulous, close attention to detail, including the collect-ing and sifting of data, its quantitative and qualitative analysis, its evaluation and presentation.[48] Ultimately, maybe Marion is best read as a call for richer accounts of history that are acutely aware of history's complexity, but not as a description of historical events as so absolute that no account can be given of them at all. We are, in fact, under a moral obligation to give the best and most honest accounts we possibly can, especially when injustice has been wrought. And while the lit-erary imagination can play an important role here, as Ricoeur and Kearney have shown, it cannot replace careful historical research that tries to provide as much (dry) factual information as possible, even if it cannot—and probably should not aim to—establish causality.

TWO

Art and the Artist

Marion has written fairly extensively on art, although this topic has not been discussed much in the secondary literature on his work.[1] One of his early works, *The Crossing of the Visible,* is an extended reflection on the status of the image in art and contemporary culture. In his later writings, the work of art occupies a central place as the second type of saturated phenomenon, saturated according to quality. A "mediocre" Dutch painting and the practice of anamorphosis employed in painting is an element of the discussion of the given phenomenon in general in *Being Given,* and the chapter on the idol in *In Excess* discusses the work of Mark Rothko. Not only does "event-ness" characterize all given phenomenon, but so does their bedazzling aesthetic quality.[2] An article for a collection on "idol anxiety" again reflects explicitly on the artist and the work of art. A further book on art, focusing specifically on the artist Gustave Courbet, is due to appear shortly.[3]

Overall, visibility and invisibility play an important role in Marion's work, which is characterized by heavily visual language. Even the overwhelming nature of the saturated phenomenon is usually put in visual language and imagery: it is bedazzling, blinding, too much for the "too narrow aperture."[4] Marion frequently employs paintings to illustrate a point: a mediocre Dutch painting serves as a test case for the first development of givenness early on in *Being Given,* and Caravaggio's *The Calling of Saint Matthew* provides an illustration for the call of the saturated phenomenon later in the book. He also mentions Turner's paintings at several points in his discussion, commenting especially on their treatment of light. Mark Rothko's painting *Number 7* appears on the inside front cover of the French text, and it appears on the front cover of the first printing of the English translation.

This great focus on visibility is interesting, especially in light of Lévinas's critique of the Western tradition's obsession with the visual and his own emphasis on hearing and the auditory sense. Marion appears to ignore Lévinas's emphasis on hearing or, maybe more exactly, he interprets it as limited only to the fourth saturated phenomenon of the face of the other. Although Marion mentions music once or twice in his treatments, the auditory sense is rarely considered, and it is not entirely clear that a piece of music would work for the second instance of the saturated phenomenon, the work of art, considering how heavily he emphasizes painting and visibility in his explanation of its appearance. I begin by discussing what Marion says about the work of art and then turn to his comments about the artist. This is a somewhat arbitrary distinction, as he often (though not always) discusses the two together. Yet Marion's discussion of the artist has an important dimension that calls for special focus and critique. I ultimately argue that Marion's discussion of the artist and even of the experience of the work of art assumes a quasi-Kantian notion of genius and that this dimension of his discussion causes him to undervalue the hermeneutic dimension in art and to exclude the possibility of an increase in degrees of givenness.

The Work of Art

Already in the early work *The Crossing of the Visible,* originally published in French in 1991 and based on even earlier articles, Marion describes the work of art as paradigmatic of visibility more generally and as maintaining a paradoxical relationship between the visible, the invisible, and the unseen. These two points remain central to his various writings on this topic. This brief work on art and image begins by claiming that the "exceptional visibility of the painting thus becomes a privileged case of the phenomenon, and therefore possibly one path to phenomenality in general" (CV, ix, trans. mod.; CdV, 7). I would suggest that, for Marion, it always remains such a "privileged case of the phenomenon." Painting, and a particular understanding of the artist, remains central to his conception of the saturated phenomenon and its reception throughout all of his treatments. Marion begins the first study of the book by defining the paradox as the entry of the invisible into the visible. The paradox, just as slightly later the saturated phenomenon that is of course described as a paradox, "dazzles, taking the mind by surprise and shocking the gaze [la vue] in such a way that, far from fulfilling or satiating them, its very excess of visibility injures them" (CV, 2; CdV, 12). Although this discussion precedes the formulation of the saturated phenomenon, this is precisely how Marion describes its impact in *Being Given* and *In Excess.*

In a sense, this discussion provides the transition between Marion's earlier discussion of idol and icon (in *Idol and Distance* and *God without Being*) and his later use of them (in *Being Given* and *In Excess*) as instances of the saturated phenomenon. His contrast of the conceptual paradox with visual perspective, the discussion of the way in which the gaze travels and the contrast between idol as false image in our media-obsessed culture and icon as the true envisioning of the self in prayer, all recall the earlier treatments that juxtaposed idol and icon against each other in a way that clearly preferred the icon as a more authentic way of seeing, while not denying that the idol witnesses to a real experience or vision of the divine. At the same time, the language of excess, saturation, and the move between invisible and visible previews the later discussions that see idol and icon as different but essentially equivalent instances of saturated phenomena, or at least do not draw an evaluative distinction between the two types.

In *God without Being*, Marion had distinguished between idol and icon as two ways of seeing, "two manners of being for beings," or two forms of visibility, two "variations in the mode of visibility" (GWB, 8, 9; DSL, 16, 17).[5] In the case of the idol, the gaze travels from the viewer toward the phenomenon, is absorbed and filled by it, and then returns onto itself: "The idol fascinates and captivates the gaze precisely because everything in it must expose itself to the gaze, attract, fill, and hold it" (GWB, 10; DSL, 18). Indeed, Marion suggests that the gaze creates the idol and makes it visible: "It dazzles with visibility only inasmuch as the gaze looks on it with consideration. It draws the gaze only inasmuch as the gaze has drawn it whole into the gazeable and there exposes and exhausts it. The gaze alone makes the idol, as the ultimate function of the gazeable" (GWB, 10; DSL, 19). The idol hence becomes an "invisible mirror" because it perfectly delineates the viewer's desire (or aim) and ability to bear the bedazzlement of the visible (GWB, 12; DSL, 21). Such an idol is an authentic vision of the divine, albeit one delineated by the religious artist's gaze.[6]

The icon, in contrast, allows the gaze to travel through and beyond it. Instead of sending the same gaze back onto itself, it directs another gaze toward the viewer and hence envisages him or her. Marion here makes a distinction between "seeing" and "appearing" that he continues to maintain throughout his writings. While the idol is *seen* by an intentional gaze, the icon *appears* to the viewer and produces an effect (GWB, 17; DSL, 28). The icon then, more correctly, deals with the appearing of the *in*visible rather than with the visible as such. Marion puts this as follows: "The icon summons the gaze to surpass itself by never freezing on a visible, since the visible only presents itself here in view of the invisible" (GWB, 18; DSL, 29). Marion is clear in this early treatment that idol and icon are two kinds of seeing, two types of phenomenality, although his focus here is on the theological, not the aesthetic, implications of this claim. His subsequent analyses take up these assertions about the gaze in regard to the visibility of the divine and apply them instead to the gaze vis-à-vis the work of art.[7]

In his more explicitly aesthetic analysis in *The Crossing of the Visible*, Marion discusses various periods of painting, as well as issues of space and perspective (CV, 2–4; CdV, 13–15). The interplay of visible and invisible are central to this discussion already: "The real space, empty or not, nevertheless cannot be seen without a gaze. Yet this gaze stretches the visible by the power of the invisible" (CV, 4, trans. mod.; CdV, 15). Marion brings together the relief texture of painting or sculpture, the sublimation (relief as *Aufhebung*) worked by Hegel's dialectic, and the relief as release of pressure more commonly evoked by that term: "The relief of the visible comes to it from the invisible, which relieves it by hollowing it out and crossing it, to the point of uprooting it from the humus of flatness where unidimensional perception ends up. The invisible pierces the visible with transparency only in order to relieve it, even to discharge it, rather than replacing it (as in military 'relief') or soothing it. . . . The invisible gives relief to the visible as one gives a title and a fief [territory]—in order to ennoble" (CV, 5, trans. mod.; CdV, 17). From this, Marion concludes that "the visible increases in direct proportion to the invisible. The more the visible is increased, the more the visible is deepened" (CV, 5; CdV, 17). Marion stresses this throughout his discussion of painting here, although interestingly enough in his later discussion in *In Excess* he argues that the work of art is given entirely to visibility without any remainder.[8] Marion uses several examples to illustrate the ways in which the invisible (the backside of characters portrayed or the various layers of perspective) functions in painting. Various treatments of perspective and arrangement of space in painting also form part of his discussion.[9]

Already in this early work, Marion speaks of "anamorphosis": the painting must be seen from a particular point or position. Only when seen from this position does its arrangement of color become organized into a meaningful visible. He suggests that the gaze in these particular paintings functions as "equivalent to the aim of intentionality" (CV, 12; CdV, 29). In contrast to the later discussion of anamorphosis, here the gaze is intentionally directed at the work of art and determines or constitutes it in some fashion. Marion also points in this context to the important role of interpretation that turns something merely visible into a spectacle, something actually seen or perceived (CV, 13; CdV, 30). He says: "The gaze, which exercises the phenomenological function of intentionality, namely seeing the ultimate object through these experiences and interpreting the sensible visual as an irreal but accomplished object. Intentionality sees its object through the lived experiences. Perspective crosses the visible from the invisible in order to see there even more. In both cases the gaze sees in depth" (CV, 13, trans. mod.; CdV, 30). The gaze is directed at the painting and controls it.

To this Marion contrasts other styles of painting, such as impressionism, that do not provide such a clear image. He opposes the kind of painting that allows for intentionality to these other kinds that confuse the gaze and do not provide a straightforward image. Instead of a spectacle, they create an experience. Such a painting "suspends what Husserl calls the principle of phenomenological correlation—namely, that each experience of consciousness is intentionally related to an object that, thanks to this intentionality alone, concentrates the visible in itself, precisely because it plays the role of invisible authority" (CV, 15; CdV, 33). He suggests that various contemporary and minimalist works of art similarly suspend the interaction of consciousness with the visible and the invisible. One can see here a progression in works of art that corresponds to the phenomenological progression Marion outlines: from clear images that allow the viewer to be in control, to fuzzier ones that are not as amenable to intention, to the ones that impose themselves on us in overwhelming bedazzlement and entirely determine our gaze by the effect they have on us.

This is not a purely historical development, however, because not only does Marion go on to read the history of painting as an increasing disintegration (in the next chapter), but he posits the religious icon (which chronologically precedes most of the history of Western painting he otherwise discusses) as the highest instance of this "progression." In the icon, the intentionality of the gaze is entirely reversed. Marion contrasts the icon to the painting, primarily because the invisible plays a much larger role in the icon despite the fact (or maybe because of the fact) that it does not use perspective in the way in which Western art since the Renaissance does. The icon shows a gaze instead of being exposed to our gaze. It hence envisions, or "envisages," the person at prayer who is exposed to this gaze: "The invisible moves across the visible, in such a way that the painted icon supports the pigments less by the wood of its plank than by the liturgical and oratory exchange of gazes that meet one another there" (CV, 20; CdV, 42). Marion's description of the crossing of gazes here and later in the same book is identical to his description of the erotic relationship. Marion himself points this out: "In fact, the exchange of gazes across the visible (one concerning the mode of prayer, the other concerning the mode of blessing) carries the erotic exchange to the extreme: two invisible gazes crossing each other through the visible witness of their bodies" (CV, 21, trans. mod.; CdV, 43). I return to this parallel in the chapters on love and on prayer (chapters 4 and 6).

As in *God without Being,* the relationship between visible and invisible are reversed between painting and icon: While in the work of art the invisible "serves" the visible and is subordinate to it, the visible serves the invisible in the case of the religious icon. No longer does the spectator view a spectacle, but we find ourselves envisioned by the gaze of the icon (CV, 21; CdV, 43). Here this seems like a purely religious analysis, whereby icons appear to be interpreted as clearly superior to paintings and much closer to what Marion ultimately advocates: the overwhelming experience of the given. Yet later, Marion applies almost the same description to the idol as the work of art. In his later treatments, he no longer speaks of paintings as subject to an intentional gaze, but almost exclusively as imposing themselves in the manner he describes the icon doing here.

The second chapter of *The Crossing of the Visible* goes on to discuss the role of the painter, to which I return more specifically in the next section of this chapter. Marion outlines the "glory" of the painting as it is created by the artist who gives it visibility. In contrast to such authentic art, Marion suggests that contemporary painting has lost this kind of glory and that it no longer functions as authentic art should. Instead, today we have a flood of spectacles, all subject to our gazes and control. Marion interprets the history of painting as a decline from its original authenticity (in the religious icon?) from Monet via Matisse and Masson to Pollock and Picasso, culminating in contemporary action painting or performance art where the "master" is in complete control of the production. Painting is in crisis together with a world in which the visible itself is in crisis (CV, 34; CdV, 64). Marion also suggests that "authentic paintings" are often not recognized by their viewers. We ignore them and dismiss them, until suddenly we are pierced by their gaze and respond to their call.

This discussion makes intriguing—and maybe somewhat problematic—assumptions about authenticity and inauthenticity. Authentic works of art impose themselves on us; inauthentic ones are subject to our control. How are authenticity and inauthenticity determined? In this context, as in *God without Being* for the "making" of the idol, the distinction seems to rely on a decision of the gaze, hence a kind of interpretation. Marion here introduces the notion of counter-perspective, "which is no longer organized in terms of the external gaze of the spectator," but instead proceeds from the unseen toward the spectator (CV, 39; CdV, 72). He uses forceful language, with erotic and even violent connotations, to describe the effect of the painting on the spectator: "In fact, it might be more accurate to say that it is our gaze that could vanish before the dangerously unrestrained torrents of ectypes, orgiastic and unleashed, driven wild with the desire of their appearing. The canvas yields, like the depths of the unseen from which it originates, under the assault of the ectypes. The painting offers to our terrified eyes the spectacle of an unseen barrier, which gives way under the very pressure of the desire of appearing. The flood of the visible invades it" (CV, 40, trans. mod.; CdV, 73). Unrestrained torrents, frenzy, orgasm, assault, flood: No wonder we are "terrified."

As in Marion's later discussion of the saturated phenomenon in general and the erotic phenomenon in particular, this excess bedazzles and overwhelms us, comes to us with a violence that is hard to avoid. And yet at the same time he stresses that this excess of the painting must always be welcomed by the gaze and hence depends at least to some extent on our reception of it (CV, 43; CdV, 79). The painting gives itself and demands our surrender and complete devotion. It comes absolutely. But it is only phenomenalized when and if we choose to receive it and, indeed, if we are able to bear it. This is precisely the kind of language Marion uses later of the reception of the saturated phenomenon by the *adonné*. The saturated phenomenon comes as an utterly bedazzling and overwhelming experience, yet it is only phenomenalized when the recipient gives him- or herself over to it in total devotion and agrees to bear the weight of its glory. Although Marion insists that this is "not yet a matter of revelation," he does suggest that the givenness of the painting invites veneration (CV, 44–45; CdV, 80–81).

The third and fourth chapters are no longer about painting as such but rather about the ways in which the religious icon can combat the trivialization of the image in our contemporary media culture. While the first two chapters of the book speak for the most part positively about painting, the third speaks of the image primarily negatively (the fourth focuses entirely on the icon). The idol is here used as a contrast to the icon as false or inauthentic in a much stronger sense than in *God without Being*. The image as idol is "arrogant," has no original, no reality beyond it, has become a trivial spectacle, completely controlled by the viewers' whim. The televised and mass-produced image stands for (and is the result of) the nihilism of our culture (CV, 51; CdV, 93). It is only in his later writings that Marion rehabilitates the notion of idol as standing for the work of art in general. As chapter 6 of this book focuses more specifically on this discussion of the icon in the context of prayer, which is the focus of the final chapter in *The Crossing of the Visible,* it is not further explicated here.

Again, it is noteworthy that images invite such strong condemnation. While this is certainly also inspired by the larger French intellectual discussion of images at the time (e.g., in Jacques Ellul, Jean Baudrillard, and Michel Henry), painting and images are the only context in which Marion articulates such vigorous ethical condemnation. Most of the time he seems either uninterested in ethics or even views it as a kind of restriction: Lévinas has focused phenomenology too exclusively on ethics, thereby ignoring many other important phenomena.[10] Yet a discussion of the ethical dimension of painting also accompanies the analysis of the idol (now interpreted positively) as work of art and second type of saturated phenomenon in *In Excess*. I return to this question in that context later in this chapter.

In *Being Given*, Marion repeatedly speaks of paintings. Early on he utilizes a "mediocre" painting in order to criticize Heidegger's tool analysis and to suggest that phenomena appear not simply as objects (as he contends they do in Husserl) or as beings (as in Heidegger), but as "givens" (BG, 40–53; ED, 61–78). Even such a banal painting, which only inspires pleasure not overwhelming fascination, is not experienced (1) as an object, "reducible to a subsistence" (BG, 41; ED, 62–63), or (2) as a useable object "ready-to-hand" (BG, 42–45; ED, 63–67), or even (3) as a being making "manifest the truth of beings" (BG, 45; ED, 67–68), but rather by and of itself as it gives itself and especially in the effect it produces on the viewer (BG, 48–49; ED, 72–73). The painting is not an object or a being, but it acts: "To different degrees but always, the painting (like every phenomenon) does not show any object nor is it presented as a being; rather, it accomplishes an act—it comes forward into visibility" (BG, 49; ED, 73). Marion explains what he means by the effect of the painting, in a way that parallels his later analysis of perlocutionary speech in love: "'Effect' obviously must be understood here with all its polysemy: effect as the shock that the visible provokes, effect as the emotion that invades the one gazing, effect also as the indescribable combination of the tones and the lines that irreducibly individualize the spectacle" (BG, 49; ED, 73–74). This notion of "effect" is important throughout *Being Given*, as later discussions in that book contrast cause and effect and stress the effect as prior to the cause and giving rise to it, reversing the usual metaphysical assumptions and connections.[11]

Marion here already has moved the initiative of phenomenality to the painting. The painting imposes its own meaning; meaning is not imposed upon it. This raises the hermeneutic question again: Can meaning be lodged entirely in the phenomenon, imposing itself in some absolute fashion? Or is meaning dependent upon interpretation and hence on the one who receives this phenomenality? Marion also seems to imply here that the effect can come in different strengths, instead of being an either/or experience, as he insists in later works. The painting has an effect "to different degrees" (BG, 49; ED, 73). He even comments on a more general application: "The painting (and, in and through it, any other phenomenon to always different degrees) is reduced to its ultimate phenomenality insofar as it gives its effect. It appears as given in the effect that it gives" (BG, 51–52, trans. mod.; ED, 76). Deliberately employing a "mediocre" painting also suggests that different degrees of intensity and quality must be discernible. At this stage, it seems possible to envision degrees, yet in subsequent writings the painting as such becomes the paradigm for all phenomena. He already hints at that in this context: The painting as given defines the object (as a defective given) instead of the reverse (BG, 50; ED, 74).[12] I return to this possibility of "degrees" of phenomenality at the end of the chapter.

Once Marion has introduced the notion of the saturated phenomenon, the painting appears as the second instance of such a phenomenon. It is saturated in terms of quality, unbearable because of its great magnitude and its excessive degree (BG, 203; ED, 284). It cannot be anticipated and is radically heterogeneous to anything else. This phenomenon is overwhelming: "Before this excess, not only can perception no longer anticipate what it will receive from intuition; it also can no longer bear its most elevated degrees. For intuition, supposedly 'blind' in the realm of poor or common phenomena, turns out, in a radical phenomenology, to be blinding. The gaze cannot any longer sustain a light that bedazzles and burns. The intensive magnitude of intuition, when it goes so far as to give a saturated phenomenon, cannot be borne by the gaze, just as this gaze could not foresee its extensive magnitude" (BG, 203; ED, 285). Vision is filled and bedazzled by the glory of the visible.

Marion provides a variety of examples here: the blinding sun in the allegory of the cave, Oedipus's blinding, the danger of the divine (BG, 203–206; ED, 285–89). In all cases an excessive experience blinds, although one may well wonder whether Oedipus's realization that he has killed his father and married his mother and therefore blinds himself is equivalent to the experience of blindness in the encounter with the divine. Some nuanced distinctions between different kinds of blindness and excess seem called for here. Already in the treatment in the first part of the book, Marion stresses the play of light in the painting (BG, 51; ED, 75–76). Marion here is adamant that trying to portray or paint light is central to what the painter does. Turner tries to make light appear in his paintings (BG, 205; ED, 287). Light and visibility are central to the analysis of this particular saturated phenomenon, but to some extent also for all saturated phenomena. They are all consistently described as bedazzling and blinding, which is precisely the most determining feature of this saturation of quality. The painting hence again comes to serve at least to some extent as the paradigm for saturated phenomena in general.

Marion goes on to identify this qualitatively excessive phenomenon as the "idol." The terminology here has clearly shifted from his earlier treatments in *Idol and Distance, God without Being,* and *The Crossing of the Visible,* inasmuch as the idol is no longer a false or heretical vision of the divine, but a positive instance of the saturated phenomenon. Yet his use of the term also has significant continuity with his prior treatments: the idol still is the first stopping point for the gaze and fills it completely with visibility (BG, 229; ED, 320). It does also still function as a mirror by returning the gaze to itself. Marion contends that "the privileged occurrence of the idol is obviously the painting . . . , not to speak too generically of the work of art" (BG, 229; 320). The more we seek to understand the painting and to learn more information about it, the less we are able to grasp its givenness (BG, 230; ED, 320–21). This encounter with the saturated phenomenon makes us realize our finitude (BG, 206; ED, 289). The painting always "arrives" in the form of surprise and imposes itself as an anamorphosis, namely as determining even the place the viewer must occupy to "see" it. The painting individuates me by addressing me directly and in solitary fashion, hence provoking "an ineluctable solipsism" (BG, 230; ED, 321). Marion later analyzes Caravaggio's painting *The Calling of Saint Matthew* as an instance of the invisible call that requires a response (BG, 282–85; ED, 390–93). Although he is no longer specifically examining the second type of saturated phenomenon, the painting comes to stand for the call of the witness or devoted more generally. Again, the example of painting significantly shapes the more general analysis of saturated phenomenality and serves as paradigm for it.[13]

Chapter 3 of *In Excess* is titled "The Idol or the Radiance of the Painting." Although the second type of saturated phenomenon ostensibly is the work of art more generally, here the discussion again is limited to painting and relies heavily on the "look" or "gaze" and on Marion's previous discussions of visibility and invisibility. It would be hard to imagine this as a discussion of a piece of music instead, although Marion has certainly in other contexts identified listening to a musical performance as a saturated phenomenon.[14] Marion begins the discussion by stressing the importance of the visible and of visibility for us on personal, social and cultural levels. Even blindness is defined in terms of visibility. He explicates a certain kind of blindness as a particularly acute kind of vision. He also draws a distinction between seeing (*voir*) or looking (*regarder*) that parallels his discussion of various paintings in *The Crossing of the Visible*. Looking has an intentional aim that is able to discern meaning. This kind of looking tends to turn the visible into an object and to exclude the invisible. It aims to organize and control the visible. It remains blind to the unseen (*l'invu*) and represses it from appearing in the visible (IE, 57; DS, 68–69). Throughout, it is the realm of the "invisible" or "unseen" that occupies Marion's attention the most.

To this "intentional looking" Marion contrasts an "admiration of painting" (IE, 57, trans. mod.; DS, 69). The visible given in paintings exercises a fascination upon us, it attracts our gaze to it and fixes it upon itself. It hence reverses "the center of gravity of visibility" by capturing our fascinated and admiring gaze and holding it prisoner (IE, 59–60; DS, 71). The idol is precisely what captures and holds our gaze entirely, exhausts it, and makes it unable to move on. The gaze hence functions as an invisible mirror: "Name your idol, and you will know who you are. . . . My idol defines what I can bear of phenomenality—the maximum of intuitive intensity that I can endure while keeping my gaze on a distinctly visible spectacle" (IE, 61; DS, 73). Again, interpretation that assigns meaning to the phenomenon is dismissed as an illicit assertion of control over the phenomenon, as a failure to be informed and overwhelmed by its own meaning. An attempt to provide meaning essentially turns the phenomenon into an object because it becomes determined by intentionality instead of being envisioned by counter-intentionality. Two kinds of blindness are at work here: "Looking" is blind because it misses the unseen and prevents it from becoming visible. "Admiring" is blind because it is overwhelmed and bedazzled by the phenomenon. The first kind of blindness is a shortcoming that invites censure. The second kind, like Plato's liberated prisoner who faces the sun, is the blindness of sight, knowledge, and illumination.

He describes the painting as what completely fills the gaze and "hoards all the admiration" (IE, 62; DS, 75). While objects in the world can never present all sides at once, the painting gives itself to full visibility and holds nothing back (IE, 62; DS, 75). The painting excludes what is only appresented and fully presents the visible (IE, 63; DS, 76). Here relief and perspective seem less essential, although it is still curious that Marion unequivocally claims complete visibility. On the one hand, this does not apply to works of art in other media, such as sculpture, which obviously can never be seen from all sides at the same time. On the other hand, it does not seem true even of paintings that they have no backside and that apperception plays absolutely no role in them. Texture, relief, even the frame and the backing play an important role in our experience of a painting.

Here also Marion stresses the light portrayed in several paintings, a light that overwhelms the viewer. He equates cubism with religious art, which presents several scenes at once. In painting "we see directly the vision of the painter" (IE, 65;

DS, 79). Again he insists that everything becomes visible in the painting: "All is there to see, nothing is kept in absence or sheltered by appresentation. The painting carries presence, to the point of bearing even absence (appresentation) to direct visibility. The painting *adds* presence to presence, where nature preserves space and thus absence" (IE, 66; DS, 79; original emphasis). Marion shows how Paul Klee makes the invisible visible in his paintings: the visible is saturated to its highest degree and becomes unbearable (IE, 67; DS, 80). He defines what the painting accomplishes as follows: "the non-physical space where the visible alone reigns abolishes *l'invu* (the invisible by default) and reduces the phenomenon to pure visibility" (IE, 68; DS, 81; see also IE, 72; DS, 87). Marion argues that the painting is an important case for phenomenology, because of its complete appearance into visibility without appresentation. It shows for him that phenomena can be given in pure self-givenness outside the constraints of intentionality in the Husserlian sense. The painting not only first accomplishes, but perfectly illustrates, the setting aside of "metaphysical" intentionality in favor of nonmetaphysical givenness.

We cannot see a painting in only one instance, but must always go to see it again and again. Marion here presents the museum as a kind of cathedral to the saturated phenomenon: We go to look at it just as a sanctuary is the goal of a pilgrimage (IE, 70; DS, 85). The aesthetic injunction imposes itself upon us, and it calls many of us: It cannot be reduced to the singular gaze, but requires a public that returns to admire it again and again. The painting itself "demands" such a plurality of gazes or looks (IE, 71; DS, 86). The phenomenon of the painting neither "educates" our gaze, nor do we "progress" when returning to see it multiple times, nor do the commentaries of critics ever do justice to it. Rather, "each authentic painting consists. . . . in the sum of all its potential visibles. . . . It opens an arena of space and time to all the contemplations to which it gives rise. It exposes itself as the potential sum of everything that everyone has seen, sees, and will see there" (IE, 72, trans. mod.; DS, 86). In that respect, the great work of art is like the historical phenomenon, which also in some way creates a community through the great variety of accounts given (BG, 229; ED, 319). The painting does indeed have an event-like character (IE, 72; DS, 87). Unfortunately, this communal dimension is not further explored in either of these two references. Most of the time, indeed, the experience of the saturated phenomenon seems entirely singular or even solipsistic. It is hence interesting that here community is mentioned, at least for the activity of interpretation. One would wish that Marion had explored this suggestion further.

The paintings of Paul Klee and Mark Rothko feature particularly prominently in his analysis in this chapter. Rothko is said to show especially well the ways in which painting gives everything to the visible. In Rothko's art, "the idol rises up before us, silent, irresistible, worthy of adoration" (IE, 74, trans. mod.; DS, 90).

This complete visibility of the painting comes with certain ethical obligations. It has a special obligation to tell the truth, especially in light of the fact that it aims at complete visibility while realizing that not everything can be shown in visibility. The ethical dimension becomes, in fact, an explicit topic in this discussion. This is interesting in light of the aforementioned fact that Marion almost never writes about ethics. In this chapter, however, he establishes a connection between aesthetics and "ethical responsibility," relying on Lévinas's discussion of the face. Art bears an ethical responsibility for the visible it introduces into the world (IE, 61; DS, 74). Rothko, Marion contends, has a sense of the ethical obligation of painting in his refusal to paint the face. To paint the human face would be to disfigure and mutilate it. This is a "truly ethical decision" (IE, 76; DS, 92).

Because the painting with its flat surface cancels all depth and gives everything to be seen, makes everything visible, it would be unethical to portray a human face as flat or to give it completely to visibility. The alternative is between killing the face or refusing to portray it: "Rothko, then, had perfectly foreshadowed what Levinas means: The facade forbids us to paint the face, and therefore it is necessary to choose between either killing the face in enframing it in the flatness [platitude] of the painting [as Marion claims Picasso does] and putting it to death in the idol, or 'mutilating' oneself as a painter and giving up producing the face directly in visibility" (IE, 78; DS, 95).[15] This full visibility is, then, in fact a kind of idolatry because it seeks worship and excludes the human and ultimately the divine face, neither of which can become fully visible. Marion ends, therefore, by commenting on the lack of sacramental presence in Rothko's Houston chapel. It was unable to receive the "eucharistic presence of the risen Face" because it lacks the divine Name that can only appear in an icon (IE, 81; DS, 98).[16] This discussion of paintings and of Rothko, like the earlier treatment in The Crossing of the Visible, already alluded several times to the specific role of the painter or artist for the work of art. I now turn to this role more specifically.

The Artist

Marion first examines the role of the painter in the second chapter of The Crossing of the Visible. He suggests here already that the artist puts on canvas something only he or she has seen, the particular artistic vision: "The painter sees and so gives to be seen what without him would remain forever banished from the visible" (CV, 25; CdV, 50).[17] This expresses succinctly something Marion claims repeatedly, not just for the artist but also for the theologian. Artists have special access to a realm that remains unseen by other people. They are able to discover or see phenomena there, which they can—more or less successfully—transfer to the realm of visibility and thereby make accessible to others. Sometimes Marion speaks of this as a "discovery" of phenomena that already exist in this realm of the unseen. The artist merely transfers them to the realm of visibility. At other times he speaks of it as an "invention" or as genuine creativity. The phenomena do not exist beforehand, but are invented by the artist. As this important ambivalence is significant for Marion's overall work, I refer to it repeatedly in this discussion and turn to it explicitly in the final section of this chapter.

In this particular context, Marion stresses that the artist's work produces a real increase in visibility. The painting "adds an absolutely new phenomenon to the mass of already-seen or possibly anticipated phenomena" (CV, 25, trans. mod.; CdV, 50). This new phenomenon adds to the realm of the visible, that is, it increases the number of visible phenomena:

> The painting—at least one that is authentic—imposes in front of every gaze an absolutely new phenomenon, increasing by force the quantity of the visible. The painting—the authentic one—exposes an absolutely original phenomenon, newly discovered, without precondition or genealogy, suddenly appearing with such a violence that it explodes the limits of the visible identified to that point. The painter, with each painting, adds yet another phenomenon to the indefinite flow of the visible. He completes the world, precisely because he does not imitate nature. (CV, 25; CdV, 50)

The stress Marion places here repeatedly on the "authenticity" of the painting is significant. A painting is only authentic when it provides new phenomena to the world, when it introduces new "visibles" from the unseen to the realm of the visible. Authenticity is measured by newness and by an increase in visibility. There is also again the language of violence here (which increases in his talk about love). Finally, art is interpreted to be something utterly new, radically different, and original, appearing completely without context, without precedent, without "genealogy." It is in no way an imitation—and apparently it can do entirely without any hermeneutic context for apprehending or experiencing it.

Marion here also introduces more fully the language of the "unseen"—what is *unseen* is not strictly speaking *invisible*, inasmuch as it can become visible precisely by being seen and subsequently portrayed. Artistic creation depends on this kind of creative vision, which has access to a realm of phenomenality that remains invisible to other people but can be made visible by the artist. He portrays the artist in language that approaches a kind of magic: "With the painting, the painter, like an alchemist, makes visible what without him would have remained definitely invisible" (CV, 25; CdV, 51). The painter is quasi-divine in that he or she has special access to the unseen and "grants visibility" to it. This is a special gift: "If the painter rules over the access of the unseen to the visible, his gift thus has nothing to do with his vision of the visible but with his divination of the unseen" (CV, 26; CdV, 52). The metaphors Marion employs are telling: alchemy and divination. Painting hovers between magic and divinity or at least divine service. Marion compares the realm of the unseen to the dark waters preceding the creation. The painter "works before the creation of the first light" and "goes back to the creation of the world, half witness, half archangel-laborer" (CV, 27; CdV, 53).

Here also Marion insists that "painting directly and essentially involves a matter of moral choice" (CV, 27; CdV, 53), although he does not elaborate what that might mean in this particular context. The painting snatches the unseen from the underworld, maybe from the realm of the dead, and brings it to our world. The religious language is again heavy here: "Every painting participates in a resurrection; every painting imitates Christ, by bringing the unseen to light" (CV, 27; CdV, 54). The same ambivalence about the painter's work noted in the previous section emerges also in this context. Marion had just previously suggested that the painting introduces *new* phenomena into the world and hence is creating them, while here the painter seems to *resurrect* them, merely bringing them to light and hence re-creating them. Later in this text he talks of a kind of discovery, which also seems to indicate that the phenomena already "exist" in some fashion, only waiting to be discovered by someone lucky or gifted. At times it appears as if these "unseen" phenomena are something like ideas in the divine mind that we need only discover or render visible. Indeed, the painter is always "ordained" or "consecrated" (CV, 28; CdV, 54). Marion claims again that painting is neither merely a reproduction of what is already visible, nor merely an interpretation of the visible, but rather a production or creation of *new* phenomena.[18] Yet, if such phenomena already "exist" in the "unseen" and are merely transferred to the realm of visibility, how are they truly "new"?

At this point in *The Crossing of the Visible,* Marion is much more positive about contemporary art than in chapter 3. Even "ready-made art," which portrays everyday objects, participates in the realm of the unseen, because "between the store and the museum, the bottle holder has taken a bath in the unseen, and its absolutely new visibility has no other legitimacy than the fact that it has just made it through. The ready-made makes an impression not so much because it is blatantly trivial as because it has been immunized from such triviality by being bathed in the unseen, and then, indeed especially, because it reemerges, visible among the visibles" (CV, 28–29, trans. mod.; CdV, 55).[19] It is hence precisely this connection to the realm of the unseen that turns something into a work of art. Marion again uses heavily religious language in this context: "Baptized by the unseen, but also saved from the waters of the unseen, the visible painting lives on a risen life—new, pardoned, imprescriptible" (CV, 29, trans. mod.; CdV, 55).[20] Painters create miracles.

Consequently, paintings exercise a kind of authority over us; they impose themselves on us, and no questioning is possible. The painting does not gain authority by its monetary value or the number of visitors to its spot in the museum; rather, the painting itself calls out to us and we are compelled to come to see it again and again. The painting is the "phenomenon par excellence" because "it shines with the dazzling, irrepressible brilliance of those who have been miraculously saved" and attracts "the fascination of the gaze by the irresistible attraction of its weight of glory" (CV, 31; CdV, 59). Paintings have such great impact on us because they are filled with glory and have something like a salvific function. And in that sense they provide the paradigm for all phenomenality. This glory also validates the authenticity of the painting. Because it arises from the realm of the unseen, "the authentic painting defies us, provokes us, sometimes with the mischievous arrogance of some upstart who has reached visibility, more rarely with the royal and sacerdotal holiness of a master of appearance. To think about it properly, it would be necessary to be purified before entering its presence. For glory threatens, even when it saves" (CV, 31; CdV, 59). The painting hence belongs to the realm of the religious: It has redemptive qualities, it requires special preparation, it is holy and threatening.

Thus the painter never seeks to master or control the painting and is not the authority on what the painting "means." This is precisely what happens in the mass production of images and in the case of kitsch: All these become mere objects over which we have mastery, which we can simply produce. They require no creation, no gifted access to the realm of the unseen. Again, Marion distinguishes between authentic and inauthentic art. Authentic art and authentic painters introduce phenomena from the unseen and do not seek control them. They become the venue for revelation without exerting mastery over it. Inauthentic "art," in contrast, merely produces objects over which it has complete control and which it can use for profit or manipulation (as in advertising). Although Marion does not mention the moral dimension of art in painting in this context, a moral judgment is certainly implied about such mass-produced art. Only the "authentic" painting can serve as the paradigm for Marion's phenomenological project: "The authentic painting fulfills the expectation of the painter and the visitor precisely to the extent to which it surprises, disorients, and overwhelms this expectation. It fills not the expected expectation but a different—unexpected—expectation" (CV, 32, trans. mod.; CdV, 61). The painting surprises us and gives rise to new possibilities, new desires, new expectations. Marion sees this culminating in the icon, because (at least at this point) the idol does not fully accomplish the inversion of the gaze and the absolutely new expectation. Yet, it seems that the "authentic painting" therefore functions as an icon and not as an idol: "The authentic painting would not give itself to be seen in such glory if it had not taken and surprised our scope of expectation" (CV, 33; CdV, 62). In his later treatments in *Being Given* and *In Excess,* Marion accords full authenticity and saturated phenomenality to the idol as the work of art and employs the icon instead for other purposes.

Marion's depiction of the painter hovers ambiguously between activity and passivity. On the one hand, the artist is completely passive and does not impose any will or control on the work of art: "The truly creative painter, then, is characterized not by a plastic inventiveness imposing his will, but rather by a passive receptivity; which, from among a million equally possible lines, knows to choose this one that imposes itself from its own necessity" (CV, 36; CdV, 66–67).[21] Thus, although the artist has special access to the realm of the dead and gods, he or she is also quite passive before the authority of the unseen. At times, Marion goes so far as to treat the artist as a mere recording device: "The painter traces nothing. He only pinpoints, like one divining water, which can (and therefore must) well up from below. . . . The painter records, he does not invent" (CV, 36; CdV, 67). The painter sketches the traces of the unseen, hence works under special, quasi-divine, inspiration. The unseen functions as stigmata, imposing itself upon the painter: "The painting bears the stigmata of the unseen: like scars, half-healed wounds of fractures imposed upon the neutral, still virgin screen of the visible" (CV, 37, trans. mod.; CdV, 68). Marion compares this activity to the seismograph that detects volcanic tremors and records the breaking of the earth: "Like the surface of the earth, which is fractured and folded under the pressure of the invisible telluric forces, from the magma of the unseen well up the folds that take shape from the inside in the frame of the painting, rising to its surface like the fossils deposited by a torrent of lava. The painter, with his sensitive and quasi-vulcanologist hand, follows with a flowing brush—the most trembling, that is to say, the most sensitive kind possible—the radically unforeseen trait that imposes itself on him" (CV, 37, trans. mod.; CdV, 68). All these images and metaphors—divination of water sources, stigmata and scars, seismographic inscription—seem to indicate complete passivity before the imposition of the work of art. Yet, elsewhere in his work, as we have already seen, Marion claims that the painter does invent and actually creates new "visibles." This tension between passivity and activity, between total response and a certain measure of initiative, marks his treatment throughout his writings on art.

This more active language becomes somewhat stronger in the chapter on art in *In Excess,* where Marion again argues that the work of art adds to the visibility of the world by introducing new "visibles" into it. At first he still phrases it in more passive terms, identifying it explicitly as a kind of genius: "The painter renders visible as a phenomenon what no one had ever seen before, because he or she manages, being the first to do that every time, to resist the given enough to get it to show itself—and then in a phenomenon accessible to everyone. A great painter never invents anything, as if the given were missing; he or she suffers on the contrary a resistance to this excess, to the point of making it render its visibility. . . . Genius only consists in a great resistance to the impact of the given revealing itself" (IE, 51, 52; DS, 61, 62). He spells this out more fully in his article on art, which is discussed momentarily.

The painter gives visibility to something not seen in nature or anywhere else before (IE, 60; DS, 71). Then, the language becomes decidedly more active: Such a painter "hunts" for what is unseen and makes it available to be seen. There is also again language of violence here, but in this case one of strong activity, not of passivity. The painter not only goes hunting in the realm of the unseen, but then "tears from" it the unseen and introduces it visibly into the realm of the seen. Here newness, invention, and active creativity are stressed: "With each painting, a new visible comes to dwell among us, definitive resident of our phenomenality" (IE, 69; DS, 83). Indeed, the painter is a "king" and is ignored only at society's peril (IE, 70; DS, 84). The same ambivalence discovered earlier emerges again: The painter creates something new, yet at the same time only finds or discovers it in some other realm. The newness, then, appears to concern only the production in the visible world; it concerns not the phenomenon itself but only its phenomenality, assuming that the two could be artificially separated in this manner.[22]

Marion's "What We See and What Appears," his most extended article on art, carries this discussion the furthest.[23] He begins by raising the question of aesthetic visibility. Not everything that is seen visibly actually "appears" to the gaze. There is a meaningful and indeed ethical distinction between what he calls "common visibility" and aesthetic visibility. To approach this distinction, Marion first examines cases in which something appears without actually becoming visible, employing Flaubert's description of Frederic's "vision" of Madame Arnoux getting into a boat on the Seine in his *Sentimental Education*. This event "appears" only to Frederic because his gaze settles on her, because he is struck by her. Although visible to everyone else, it does not actually appear to anyone else, in the sense that it is not noticed. Reiterating a distinction already made in *God without Being*, Marion claims that only metaphysical objects are *seen*, while phenomena *appear*. Such "objects" are the fulfillment of an aim that envisions and controls them. The aim actualizes and realizes the object. The object is foreseen, and one can have full knowledge of it. Because objects are the result of an aim and dependent upon it, they are reproducible and in fact need not even appear in order to be seen. Marion relates this to the "common phenomenon" of *Being Given;* it is the standard Kantian and Husserlian phenomenon for which intuition merely validates prior concepts. Relying on various examples of technical objects and Heidegger's tool analysis, Marion claims that objects only "appear" when something is wrong with them. Usually they are only seen, but they need not or do not appear. Most of the time, their visibility or intuitive fulfillment is unnecessary because the concept determines them fully.

The painting, in contrast, appears even without being seen. Marion reiterates his analysis from *Being Given* that paintings appear by the effect they have, not because they are useful or have monetary value. The painting cannot be foreseen, it must appear from itself. He employs the notion of anamorphosis here even more fully than in the earlier treatment. Anamorphosis in painting assumes that the painting will truly appear to the gaze only from a particular standpoint or perspec-

tive. The painting imposes the location of the gaze; it appears from itself. Anamorphosis annuls perspective, because it imposes itself on the gaze instead of allowing the gaze to control it. Frederic has a vision of Madame Arnoux because she
appears to him in an absolutely unique way. Marion suggests that this helps us define or identify a great work of art:

> They are those visibles that cannot be foreseen, they are after-seen.
> One can say of them that nobody has ever seen them. I insist on this
> point: What is a "work of art"? (I'm using this expression so dated and
> narrow that it is meaningful.) What do the people, the middle-class,
> call a "work of art"? Or the expert? A work of art is that to which one
> returns (*ce que l'on revoit*). The work of art is not something that one
> sees (*voit*), but it is to what one returns (*revoit*), what one goes to see
> again (*va revoir*). The object is what one does not see as such, it is what
> one foresees and what one tries to see as little as possible as long as it
> works or functions. The work of art, in contrast, is that of which one
> can never say: I have seen it. If someone says: "I have seen a painting
> and hence I have no need to see it again," either it is not a painting or
> the speaker is a fool. The definition of the painting, of the work of
> art, is that it is always necessary to go see it again.[24]

Even "knowing" a painting requires going to see it over and over again. One goes
to see it again not to study a particular aspect of the painting or to gain more factual information about it, but rather to feel its effect again. It is a saturated phenomenon that floods us with intuition and cannot be grasped or contained. Marion
says: "The painting and I share a life; that is to say, the painting will change to the
extent that I will have seen it. The more I see it, the more it will give me to see,
and the more my concepts will lag behind."[25] The painting forbids intentionality.

This, Marion contends, is particularly true of the artist. Even the artist cannot intend the painting or foresee it in any fashion. The painting takes the initiative and imposes itself upon the painter and the devotee. Again, the artist is the
one who has seen what is unseen and introduces what was formerly invisible into
visibility, hence producing new phenomena in the realm of the visible. The artist
makes a real contribution to phenomenality by creating new phenomena that are
not found in the world and did not exist before. As this passage encapsulates much
of what is essential in Marion's discussion, I quote it in full:

> The painter (and the photographer, etc.), the artist has this Pro-
> methean privilege never to reproduce the world. He or she adds some-
> thing visible, something so far unseen to the total of visible things in
> the world. Aristotle said that art either imitates nature or fulfills it,
> implying that it adds to nature. The painter increases the quantity, I
> might say the density, of the visible, that is to say of the world's phe-

nomenality. And that is something we sense physically when we travel to countries without museums or without painting, for there are such places: there is a weakened density of visibility. I almost would dare say that in this sense museums are sanctuaries of intensity of appearance that enhance the visibility of the world in some way. Museums do not contain a different visible, but the same visible, quantitatively and qualitatively stronger, so much so that we see the common visible that is outside the painting in some way on the model of the visible of the painting, because the visible of the painting is more visible than the common visible. This is so much so that the landscape I see in Aix (I live in the region of Ornans, home to Gustave Courbet), I see according to his paintings. Paintings are not reproductions of landscape, but exactly the reverse. In fact, I believe I see the visibility of the landscape and what I see is what Courbet has produced (I do not say: "has put there"), has added to it. We see inside of paintings. Paintings are the paradigm of shared visibility.[26]

Paintings add phenomenality to the world and change the ways in which we see. The painter is able to create phenomena and reorient our vision, although the phenomena created by great art may themselves have been a prior phenomenological experience, an artist's vision of the previously unseen.

The work of art shocks because of this intensity of intuition that transforms our vision of the world. It conveys "the absolute truth of experience."[27] And in this context Marion carries this discussion one step further by claiming even more emphatically that the artist has a special talent for vision, a kind of inspiration of seeing. The artist is the one uniquely able to bear the weight of the saturated phenomenon. While ordinary mortals usually fall short, are so bedazzled and blinded by saturated phenomena that they cannot see them, or, conversely, so blasé and indifferent that they are entirely blind to them in the first place, the artist has a special ability to see and appreciate. This does not give the painter control over the work of art. Rather, "contrary to what the discourse of the painter as king, as creator, as prince has long allowed us to assume, in painting, the one who sees it is precisely not the one who produced it. That is to say, the experience of seeing the aesthetic visible is an experience in which the one who sees is not the master of his or her vision, is stripped of vision, in contrast to ordinary vision." According to Marion, this makes possible "a theory of genius" "in the sense of the romantics."[28] The genius is the one who "sets the limits of that for which we can become witnesses."[29] The artist, then, is "gifted" in a very particular way, gifted with a special visionary talent and a privileged access to the realm of the unseen.

Marion suggests several times in the course of this article that this is not merely a description of one specific saturated phenomenon, but that aesthetics has implications for phenomenology more generally: "In this way the aesthetic phenomenon, aesthetic visibility, should be conceived as a privileged and particular case of visibility, in opposition to the visibility of the object for instance, but also as one of the places from which the whole question of phenomenality is raised. This means that aesthetic questions are too serious to be left to people who specialize in questions of aesthetics. It is fundamental for philosophers, because it is here, that the possibilities, not at the extreme but standard for phenomenality, are in part defined." The aesthetic phenomenon, in fact, is "absolutely normative for poor phenomena."[30] He concludes this discussion of aesthetic visibility by stating that "what is decisive, and without doubt why phenomenology pays such almost obsessive attention to questions of painting and of aesthetics in general, is that what is at stake there is an exceptional realm of visibility. Phenomenology in particular realizes that, far from being marginal, it is one of the access roads to the original situation of the manifestation of phenomena."[31] Aesthetic visibility, then, in some way becomes the very paradigm of phenomenality and the genius of the painter becomes the paradigm for the one gifted with a special talent for bearing up under the saturated phenomenon and making it visible.

Genius and Visibility

This discussion of the artist is interesting for several reasons. First, it is unique in Marion's work to date in regard to the reception or presentation of saturated phenomena. Although the artist presumably is only active in regard to the second type of saturated phenomenon, namely the work of art, no similar talented individual is assigned to the other types. There is really no equivalent to the artist in regard to the other saturated phenomena, with the possible exception of the phenomenon of revelation, where the theologian seems to play a similar function to the artist, as we see at the end of this chapter. The artist produces the work of art as saturated phenomenon or at least as an expression or representation of the saturated phenomenon as it has affected him or her. While the immediacy of the flesh probably does not require such production, it is interesting that the historian is never accorded similar privilege, except in the occasional use of great literature to illustrate historical events. Thus, maybe Stendahl or Baudelaire are on a par with the artist—and, of course, they are literary artists—but nothing of the sort is suggested of more strictly historical writers. And although the lover plays an important role in responding to the face of the other in Marion's fourth type of saturated phenomenon, this role is quite different from that of artistic genius.[32] There is really nothing like an author who introduces the unseen into the visible for other saturated phenomena (again, except the theologian who discovers phenomena of revelation and introduces them into visibility). This confirms the privileged place of art in Marion's work that we have seen emerge throughout this chapter.

Even more interesting, and perhaps more troubling, however, is the close affinity this account of the artist has with Kant's theory of the creative genius, which it seems to reproduce on a phenomenological level. Kant defines the artistic genius as the one who can make the judgment of taste.[33] The genius has special talent for perceiving and identifying the beautiful. Similarly, only a genius can create great works of art, again because of a special talent or endowment. As we have seen, Marion briefly acknowledges this identification. In Kant this has strong connotations of order, teleology, and control, but although Marion would reject some of this teleological orientation, there is actually a sense in which the two accounts are parallel, even on this particular issue. For Kant, the relationship between nature and artistic creation is reversed. The genius does not follow certain rules, but rather imposes rules upon nature. The work of art arises from this originality and freedom (from rules) and itself becomes then the measure for beauty and order. While art assumes certain rules for Kant, merely following rules or techniques will never produce a great work of art. Such a work is not an imitation of nature or of the work of other artists, but each time a new and original creation, which henceforth in some sense comes to serve as a paradigm for art. Similarly, for Marion the work of art does not follow rules but makes its own rules. It does not imitate but always creates anew via the special vision the artist has of the realm of the unseen and the unique ability for making it visible. The great work of art imposes absolute truth, its own truth.

Furthermore, as for Kant, genius also seems required on some level for seeing something as a great or authentic work of art. Truly seeing or appreciating a great work of art requires special talents. Not only the "producer" but also the observer of great art must be a genius, someone especially capable of "bearing" the "weight" of the "glory" of the work of art.[34] Marion says that works of art make us their devotees: we must "go to see" them over and over again (IE, 70; DS, 84). One "viewing" or "seeing" is not sufficient. The "seeing again" is infinite: we have never "got" everything in the work of art, we cannot control or master it. Even the genius with great capacity of appreciation remains ultimately inadequate before the great work of art, but is certainly far ahead of ordinary mortals in terms of creation and appreciation of art. It is in this context that Marion's strong emphasis on "authenticity" in the work of art can be understood. The artistic genius is the one able to create a truly authentic work of art, because of the special access he or she has to the realm of the unseen. The artist has an unusual talent for bearing the weight of the unseen and transferring it most authentically and most faithfully to the realm of the visible. And the especially talented "viewer" of the work of art can distinguish its special creative brilliance, is able to bear the weight of its glory most authentically and can hence distinguish between more and less authentic renderings of the unseen. "Authenticity" here really refers to the faithfulness a painting as a phenomenon exhibits to its "original" in the realm of the unseen. Only genius can recognize this.

This turns the experience of the saturated phenomenon, at the very least of that of the work of art, into a rather elitist experience, if only those with special talent or endowment are able to have access to them. It also seems to sever the experience from any historical or cultural context. As Gadamer argues, this constitutes a subjectivization of aesthetics.[35] Beauty receives a kind of a priori principle in which the freedom of feeling is the highest value. For Gadamer, Kant's preoccupation with nature and its teleology still keeps this subjectivization in check, but it runs rampant in Kant's successors where "the concept of *Erlebnis*," that is, of the personal experience of aesthetic pleasure, becomes "the very stuff of consciousness."[36] Art becomes an experience (*Erlebnis*) of the individual as an expression of the whole life, a transformation that "is based on the experience of an inspired genius who, with the assuredness of a somnambulist, creates the work of art, which then becomes an experience for the person exposed to it."[37] Art "freed itself from all dogmatic bounds" and became "defined as the unconscious production of genius."[38] Gadamer rejects this view and suggests that, for most of human history, art was an intricate part of religious and secular life, instead of a peculiar "aesthetic pleasure."[39]

Although Marion certainly does not speak of the subject in the same way as do the romantic appropriators of Kant's theory of genius, his account of the genius seems similarly isolated and dependent on individual feeling and endowment, although now explicated phenomenologically. The encounter with the great work of art, as he describes it, also appears as a fairly isolated experience, a bedazzlement that overwhelms the individual before it. Although Marion once briefly mentions that works of art give rise to a community of devotees (IE, 71–72; ED, 85–86), it does not seem that any sort of more "communal" appreciation would really be possible here, as it relies on individual special endowment. In fact, as already cited, at one point he says that "the idol provokes an ineluctable solipsism" and individuates me "radically" (BG, 230; ED, 320). The work of art is so rich and saturated that no adequate account of it can ever be given. Shared description hence could never become possible.

More troubling still, it does not seem that anyone could invalidate or judge anyone else's creating or seeing—unless also a genius with special access to the unseen.[40] The artist and the person viewing the art are alone in their respective creating and appreciating. In fact, what Marion says about authenticity actually serves to strengthen this emphasis on the exclusivity of the artist's vision and its reception instead of allowing for some sort of judgment. The work of art is authentic and true precisely when it imposes itself absolutely and renders impossible any sort of critique or reduction into an object. Authenticity is employed in order to exclude and defy aesthetic judgment, which is seen as belittling and objectifying. No discussion is possible about the work of art, we stand alone before its overwhelming imposition—and we stand only in the particular space indicated to us via its anamorphosis. The vision the artist has had of the unseen is true and unassailable, although it is always possible that the artist is unable to bear the full weight of the unseen and that rendering it into the visible could thus be insufficient in some way. Presumably that is what distinguishes greater from lesser works of art, although it is hard to conceive how one might know that the artist fell short of bearing up under the vision of the unseen.

This connotation of genius or giftedness does not remain limited to Marion's analysis of art, but in fact will be extended to any reception of saturated phenomena. Although there is no special person of genius assigned to the other types of saturated phenomena, there is a sense in which the artist's special "giftedness" does in some fashion become the paradigm for the one who receives and becomes devoted to the saturated phenomenon. Jeff Kosky translates *adonné* as the "gifted" in *Being Given*—presumably with Marion's approval. This is not what the word actually means. *Adonné* means to be devoted or given over to something, even addicted or attached to it. The translation of "gifted" of course tries to preserve the parallels between the section titles: givenness, the gift, the given, the gifted. *Adonné* is clearly related to the French term for giving (*donner*), and most English ways of preserving this parallel terminology would be awkward indeed. Kosky indirectly justifies his choice of "gifted" in his "Philosophy of Religion and Return to Phenomenology in Jean-Luc Marion":

> In other words, what gives itself shows itself in or, perhaps more precisely, as the response it receives from the gifted who receives himself from it. In its passive work of phenomenalizing givenness in and through its witness thereto, the "gifted" here takes on another sense: echoing Kant's theory of genius, the gifted is the one endowed or inspired with a talent or aptitude for making more of the given visible than heretofore has been seen. Receiving himself in the passivity of giving himself over to the given, the gifted registers or witnesses the appearance of the given to varying degrees depending on how gifted he or she might have been. Some gifteds are more gifted than others and so let more givenness show itself. The degree of giftedness is seen in the extent to which the gifted gives himself over to the call.[41]

In his translation of *In the Self's Place*, Kosky explains his choice as follows: The gifted "should be taken in the sense of having a talent for . . . (for converting the given into the seen) but also as a substantive made from the passive form of the verb *to gift*. This latter sense is meant to convey that the self, too, happens originally in and through a givenness in which I receive myself at the same time as and along with the given" (SP, xx). He is certainly right that Marion's account of the one devoted to or receiving the phenomenon has a connotation of special endowment: the "gifted" somehow has a particular gift of seeing or receiving the phenomenon (however, I think this is neither particularly clear in *Being Given*, nor does it serve as the primary connotation of the devoted there).

This connotation becomes much stronger in Marion's subsequent work. In "The Banality of Saturation," Marion addresses the contention that most people "see nothing" where he sees a saturated phenomenon. He responds that it takes a special capacity to see, that one might even need to be trained to see. Some people see more than others. Some see nothing at all, they are literally blind, not only blinded (VR, 124; VeR, 151–53). His book of reflections on faith is called *Le croire pour le voir*, which indicates that one might need to believe in order to be able to see. Instead of "seeing is believing," as we commonly say, this title claims that "believing is seeing" (or that we believe "in order to see"—no form of the verb "to be" appears in the French title). All this indicates that the saturated phenomenon requires a particular predisposition, even a kind of genius or talent, a gift for seeing. This means, however, that the phenomenon does not merely come out of nowhere and overwhelm us. We are not all passive equals before the phenomenon. Rather, some are considerably more active than others; they are prepared with special talents that enable them to receive the phenomenon in ways that other people cannot. And while Marion does not speak of interpretation in his discussion of the idol in *In Excess,* he does admit in the previously discussed essay on aesthetic visibility that in some way interpretation is indeed required: "The better I know a painting, the more research I must undertake. That is why I want to undertake a hermeneutics that would have no reason to stop short."[42] Once the phenomenon has imposed itself, even the gifted recipient must interpret it endlessly because no interpretation will ever do justice to the experience.

Yet the idea that certain people have been prepared to "see," namely through a certain kind of belief or talent or even increased research, would suggest that hermeneutics does not merely come after the event, but provides an important prior context. Someone who has seen many paintings or has listened to many operas will appreciate the saturated aesthetic event much more fully. The prior experience provides the context within which this new experience can precisely be experienced as saturated. It is not merely an arbitrary endless number of interpretations after the fact, but a continuous cycle between more exposure to the painting and increased appreciation. And except for the one brief reference to hermeneutics just cited, most of the time Marion does not allow for or at least does not mention any sort of role for interpretation in the encounter with the work of art; instead, he stresses that we experience it as something before which we are completely speechless and overwhelmed. That is why we must go to see it over and over again (which is also the result of the "endless interpretations" in "What We See").

In fact, Marion is occasionally fairly dismissive of art critics, both in regard to paintings and music. They totally miss the experience because they turn it into an object. Yet, a certain hermeneutic context does seem required in order to acquire the talent to see "aright" (or at least to see better). Having some training on how to view art, maybe some knowledge of the artist, his or her time period, the particular techniques of painting, the subject portrayed, and so forth, can enable a greater appreciation of the work of art and hence a better way of "seeing." Some such preparation may even be necessary for the phenomenon to appear as a work of art at all. Furthermore, this analysis of art also seems to call for a greater variety of degrees of saturation, for a more nuanced account of the many ways in which works of art appear to us. Are paintings really only either "poor objects" or excessively saturated masterpieces that overwhelm us utterly? Even Marion's own use of the "mediocre" painting, which nevertheless still has an effect, discussed in the first part of Being Given, suggests otherwise. There must be a way of depicting phenomenologically a whole range of aesthetic works and experiences that are saturated in different ways and in an endless variety of degrees with many types of mediocrity and mastery, without these degrees depending only on a failure to see adequately. There should be a way of depicting phenomenologically how a painting impacts the average mortal and not just the artistic genius and how different kinds of painting affect us differently.

The parallel between Marion's claims about art and about religion is also significant in this context, especially considering how heavily religious language characterizes Marion's treatment of aesthetics throughout. The artist has access to certain "unseen" phenomena that are introduced through the work of art into the realm of phenomenality and thus enrich it by adding phenomena to it. Similarly, Christianity has discovered, and the Christian philosopher has introduced, certain phenomena into our experience that would otherwise have remained unknown (VR, 74; VeR, 110). And it is precisely in this context that Marion is most dismissive of hermeneutic activity as "mere" interpretation, completely arbitrary and relative, not concerned with truth. If "'Christian philosophy' can be reduced to a hermeneutic, then it remains secondary, derivative, even elective in comparison with one instance, philosophy, the only original and inventive one" (VR, 69; VeR, 104). Furthermore, "reducing 'Christian philosophy' to a hermeneutic leads to branding it as arbitrary" (VR, 70; VeR, 104) and ultimately denies the newness of Christian revelation. Christian philosophy, instead, should pursue a "heuristic" function by discovering new phenomena: "'Christian philosophy' is not practiced as a simple, possibly ideological, hermeneutic of a natural 'given' already accessible to rationality without Revelation, in short as an interpretive supplement under strange command. It offers entirely new natural phenomena to reason, which reason discovers because Revelation invents them for it and shows them to it" (VR, 72; VeR, 108). The language of privileged access to another realm and of an "invention" of "new" phenomena exactly parallels his analysis of aesthetics.

Marion examines several examples of such phenomena that have been discovered by Christian revelation. He speaks of the Christian philosopher in a fashion exactly parallel to how he describes the artist: "As a consequence, 'Christian philosophy' would remain acceptable only as long as it invents—in the sense of both discovering and constructing—heretofore unseen phenomena. In short, 'Christian philosophy' dies if it repeats, defends, and preserves something acquired which is already known, and remains alive only if it discovers what would remain hidden in philosophy without it" (VR, 74; VeR, 110). In a much more recent article about "the service of rationality in the church," he defines a genuine intellectual as someone who "invents and produces information, concepts, images, and so forth, which would have remained unknown without him and through him become available to others" (CpV, 108). And Marion consistently interprets his own project in that way: He is providing new phenomena to the realm of phenomenality (or at least formulating them rigorously so they can become visible), namely saturated ones. This is ultimately what Marion really wants to do: He seeks to discover and introduce new phenomena, to make visible what has heretofore remained unseen.[43] Maybe this is one of the key reasons that he focuses so strongly on the most excessive and extreme phenomena. Mundane phenomena do not require special talents for seeing them or showing them to others.

Yet the same ambivalence between "invention," "discovery," and "interpretation" characterizes the task of the Christian philosopher as that of the artistic genius. On the one hand, the phenomena introduced from revelation into the realm of philosophy are said to be absolutely new, unexpected, unforeseeable, impossible to access without the theologian's vision of them. On the other hand, they are discovered and first seen in another realm (that of Revelation) where they seem to exist already. In that sense, they are only "transferred" from one realm to the other, not created in any novel fashion. The only thing new about them is that they have now become visible when they were heretofore unknown. Finally, although that suggestion is explicitly rejected in the article on Christian philosophy, these phenomena do seem to rely at least on some level on interpretation. Only someone who has access to the "realm of charity" can really "see" them. They hence apparently rely on the *interpretation* of the phenomenon as saturated instead of a mere object, an interpretation that depends on the particular "giftedness" of the interpreter but does not seem verifiable in any other sense. This ambiguity is central to Marion's project and reappears over and over again. Are phenomena somehow *in themselves,* per se, saturated and not experiencing them as such is hence an identifiable failure? Or, if they are truly *phenomena* and hence given to experience in consciousness, are they only *experienced* as saturated or poor and hence the level of saturation is not somehow in the phenomenon itself? The *same* phenomenon can hence appear as saturated to one person but as poor to another, saturated at some time and in some contexts but not at others.[44] And how saturated it appears seems to depend in important ways on the person's (hermeneutic?) preparation for the experience, on the particular (hermeneutic?) context, and on the person's (hermeneutic?) ability to "see."

Marion's project has, in fact, made us more aware of excessive phenomena, which we certainly encounter in a variety of ways. In some sense, he captures well the manner in which a great work of art can affect us at certain times, the way in which a musical performance can transport us. His account might even shed light on the need we have to take recourse to artistic creation after experiences of great trauma. It is not incidental that one of the most significant responses to dealing with the tragedy of 9/11 in its immediate aftermath consisted of the creation of poetry and artistic memorials, as well as an abundance of concerts on the following weekend or already scheduled concerts explicitly dedicated to the victims.[45] Art—music at least as much as imagery or poetry—can indeed be experienced as a saturated phenomenon in Marion's sense: utterly overwhelming, bedazzling, sweeping us off our feet, having an effect utterly inexplicable in state, rational terms. But to describe *all* of art, *every* aesthetic experience in this way lacks nuance. Not to have an overwhelming experience before the *Mona Lisa* or Monet's water lilies is not always necessarily a personal failure, a lack of the kind of genius that would be able to bear their glory. A phenomenological description of aesthetic experience must cover a wide range and variety of phenomena and employ careful hermeneutic tools for analyzing and interpreting them in a way that does not reduce them to mere objects. Acknowledging a hermeneutic context, such as artistic training or aesthetic education, for experiencing works of art and examining the various ways in which they appear and impact us in various degrees, enriches an account of aesthetic experience instead of impoverishing it.

THREE

Nature and Flesh

Instead of examining a phenomenon that Marion already depicts as saturated, this chapter focuses on one he does not discuss. I will suggest that nature and various nonhuman beings can appear to us as saturated phenomena, both on Marion's own terms and in the sense in which I have argued in respect to the first two types of phenomena examined: as displaying degrees and requiring hermeneutic context. Hence this chapter is not specifically about Marion's discussion of the third saturated phenomenon, that of the human flesh. Yet, as we see later in this chapter, there might be some connections between "nature" and "flesh." I use "nature" here loosely to refer to what are generally understood to be "natural phenomena": the land, the weather, the habitat of species, and so forth, including nonhuman animal and plant life and perhaps even our own "animality." Nature is distinguished, however, from what Marion calls "technical objects." As emerges near the end of the chapter, technology often subverts and covers over nature, making us forget our intrinsic connection with it and dependence upon it, often even destroying it. While a discussion of nature need not necessarily have "environmental" or "ecological" concerns, such concerns are not excluded in this discussion.[1]

Could elements of "nature" appear to us as what Marion calls "saturated phenomena"? While at first glance this suggestion might seem an obvious one, to date Marion has not employed natural phenomena as examples for his notion of the saturated phenomenon and has rarely engaged environmental concerns in his writings.[2] He focuses almost exclusively on humans (the self and its encounter with the other) and on the divine. Yet, he does obviously contend that some other phenomena can appear as saturated to us: historical or cultural events, paintings and other works of art, gifts or sacrificial items, and our own human flesh.[3] And, in fact, in *In Excess* he fleetingly identifies a natural disaster as an "event" together with "political revolution" and "sporting or cultural performances, and so on" (DS, 43; IE, 36). Why not animals or trees or ecosystems or planets?[4] Katharina Bauer similarly wonders whether saturated phenomena could include "*also* the natural phenomenon, *also* the beautiful or sublime in nature, *also* the flesh [*Leib*] or gaze of an animal" (original emphasis).[5] In this chapter I examine the possibility that natural phenomena may indeed be interpreted as "saturated" in Marion's sense despite his own neglect of them. I use the word "interpret" here advisedly, as I suggest that the hermeneutic element plays an important role in this, one much larger than generally acknowledged by Marion in his phenomenological account. The first section of this chapter discusses in what sense natural phenomena might appear as saturated in Marion's sense. The second section argues that hermeneutics has to play an important role in identifying such phenomena as saturated. A third section considers the usefulness of speaking of nature as saturated, at least to some extent, especially for ecological concerns. Finally, a possible connection between nature and the immediacy of the human flesh, which Marion does identify as a saturated phenomenon, is suggested.

Might Natural Phenomena Be Given as Saturated?

As we have seen in the introduction and more fully in the previous chapters, saturated phenomena according to Marion are phenomena of great complexity and richness. They take the initiative by imposing themselves upon our consciousness, and it is impossible to constitute them as objects (or at least any such attempt is both inadequate and does injustice to the phenomenon by minimizing or trivializing it). Saturated phenomena are rich in intuition and noematic content, that is, they are given or give themselves in abundance and our intentionality is overwhelmed by them. The gaze cannot grasp them or comprehend them, but is bedazzled or even swept away entirely. They exercise a counter-intentionality: the phenomenon comes to constitute or affect the recipient instead of a transcendental ego controlling or determining the phenomenon. The saturated phenomenon gives too much, far more than the recipient can bear or receive. It is an excessive and radical phenomenon and the appropriate response to it is awe, wonder, maybe even worship. The historical event cannot be quantified or adequately described, the great work of art must be contemplated over and over again, the lover must give him- or herself in complete devotion to the beloved (see next chapter). Can we have this sort of encounter with "natural" phenomena? Might a nonhuman phenomenon—or at least one not created or heavily influenced by humans in the way in which that is the case for the work of art or the historical event—give itself in such a saturated fashion?[6] Can nature overwhelm us and maybe even constitute or reshape us in significant fashion?

Marion himself does not make this application. There is almost no reference to (nonhuman) animals anywhere in his work and a tree is mentioned only once and in that case is listed together with a triangle as a "technical object" and thus a "poor" phenomenon (BG, 126; ED, 179). To be more exact, there are actually two brief mentions of trees in that particular context. In the first, Marion speaks of the "intentional objects" of "tree" or "triangle," which are objects in the flux of lived experiences like the objects of mathematics and indicates that a distinction between natural, temporal, or purely theoretical objects "is not pertinent here" (BG, 126; ED, 179). Shortly after that, he briefly suggests the notion of "habitual phenomena" (an idea to which he so far has never returned) and mentions a tree in the desert—which most interestingly "opens a world," left entirely unexplored—together with a taxi as two phenomena that "impose" themselves on me as I am in need of them.

It is difficult to ascertain exactly what status these examples and many others, primarily of "technical objects," have here, as they are used to develop the "anamorphosis" of the given phenomenon, which later becomes applied to saturated phenomena. As I explained in the first chapter on the historical event, anamorphosis, arrival, surprise, fait accompli, and even an event-like character are said by Marion to apply to all given phenomena, but are then later focused more narrowly specifically on saturated phenomena. In the conclusion to the section, Marion indicates that instead of a firm "either/or" distinction between poor and saturated phenomena, phenomenality might be envisioned to increase in "degrees of givenness" and he suggests that these objects mentioned earlier might hence be a first, shallow, degree of givenness. He never returns to explore this notion further, except for the brief reiteration of this claim at the end of Certitudes négatives, which is examined in chapter 1.

Although Marion almost completely ignores natural phenomena, there is little reason why nature may not appear or give itself (or be given) as saturated at least in certain contexts. The primary characteristic of a saturated phenomenon, as we have seen, is its overwhelming nature, which floods us with intuition. Saturated phenomena give too much: They cannot be constituted and defy any reduction to an object. They affect us in radical ways, turn their recipient into someone given over to, devoted to, even addicted to them. They come from themselves instead of being caused or produced by us. They arise in surprising ways and present us with a fait accompli. And they impose themselves as anamorphoses, determining the place at which we must "stand" in order to "see" them. They are given and received, not produced or otherwise determined by us.

One need not point to Kant's notion of the sublime or the most recent natural disaster to realize that nature can indeed present itself in overwhelming and even threatening ways. Both the breathtaking beauty and the raw power of certain natural phenomena affect us in overwhelming, threatening, and bedazzling ways. Many, if not most, natural phenomena cannot be fully understood or constituted by humans, as much as research in biology, botany, geology, and natural history may try to do so. Clearly a biotic system such as a wetland, a tidal pool, a region of rain forest, even an anthill, are complex phenomena that cannot be completely grasped by human consciousness. Although we can certainly try to impose concepts upon them or turn them into an object (as obviously happens and maybe must happen in much scientific study), these always remain inadequate.[7] Natural phenomena—whether singular, such as a specific animal or individual tree, or more complex, such as an entire ecosystem—are *not* technical objects in Marion's sense of easily manipulable, mass-produced, and highly determined objects. Since they cannot be fully constituted by human consciousness, they must appear as "saturated" at least in some respect. And many, although obviously not all, people who encounter nature as saturated become devoted and addicted to it, just as some people are struck by a particular painting while others do not feel the same effect.

This possible "saturation" of natural phenomena becomes particularly evident in the depictions of encounters with nature in much nature writing that certainly qualifies as phenomenological, even when it is not explicitly identified as such. Whether it is Annie Dillard's moving meditations at Tinker Creek, Bernd Heinrich's careful observations about the Maine woods,[8] Edward Abbey's gripping accounts in *Desert Solitaire,*[9] John Muir's inspiring experiences in the Sierra Nevada,[10] Aldo Leopold's meticulous descriptions that precede and ground the more theoretical final chapter in "A Land Ethic,"[11] or any of the many similar writings about "nature experiences," natural phenomena are consistently described as saturated phenomena in these texts. Here is just one example from Dillard's *Pilgrim at Tinker Creek:*

> The secret of seeing is, then, the pearl of great prize. . . . The secret of seeing is to sail on solar wind. Hone and spread your spirit till you yourself are a sail, whetted, translucent, broadside to the merest puff. When her doctor took her bandages off and led her into the garden, the girl who was no longer blind saw "the tree with the lights in it." It was for this tree I searched through the peach orchards of summer, in the forests of fall and down winter and spring for years. Then one day I was walking along Tinker Creek thinking of nothing at all and I saw the tree with the lights in it. I saw the backyard cedar where the mourning doves roost charged and transfigured, each cell buzzing with flame. I stood on the grass with the lights in it, grass that was wholly fire, utterly focused and utterly dreamed. It was less like seeing than like being for the first time seen, knocked breathless by a powerful glance. The flood of fire abated, but I'm still spending the power. Gradually the lights went out in the cedar, the colors died, the cells unflamed and disappeared. I was still ringing. I had been my whole life a bell, and never knew it until at that moment I was lifted and struck. I have since only rarely seen the tree with the lights in it. The vision comes and goes, mostly goes, but I live for it, for the moment when the mountains open and a new light roars in spate through the crack, and the mountains slam.[12]

Dillard's encounter with the tree bedazzles and overwhelms her; she finds herself envisioned by it instead of imposing her vision on it; it impacts her when she did not expect it or prepare for it—it has all the connotations of saturation and counter-experience Marion outlines.

Examples of this sort could be multiplied endlessly from the texts of the authors mentioned above. In general, these books contain bedazzling, overwhelming, unsettling, at times breathtakingly beautiful and deeply moving accounts, calling us to cease our objectifying of nature and to experience it differently, precisely as saturated with meaning and as valuable on its own terms.[13] The very power of their impact on us is precisely this dimension of excess or saturation that either overwhelms us and makes us feel small or maybe even makes us permanently devoted and even "addicted" to natural phenomena. Many environmentalists are committed to ecological actions and policies precisely because of their own profound experiences of nature as saturated or because they were moved by reading such accounts. To receive something as a saturated phenomenon is to assign a value to it that cannot be measured or objectified.

Yet the idea of the saturated phenomenon might apply not only to such more "positive" encounters with natural phenomena, which have at times been criticized—maybe somewhat unfairly—as a "romanticized" version of nature.[14] In light of Marion's account of the event, we might well speak of instances of environmental destruction, such as a terrifying storm or especially global climate change, as saturated phenomena. Certainly the 2011 earthquake and subsequent tsunami in Japan (and the one that caused such destruction in Indonesia, Sri Lanka, and other countries on the day after Christmas 2004), the 2005 flooding of New Orleans and its surrounding areas by Hurricane Katrina, the 2011 tornado that devastated Joplin, Missouri, or Hurricane Sandy's impact on New York City and the Jersey shore in the fall of 2012 were beyond all description, overwhelming in magnitude or even in "quality," though certainly not in the positive sense usually described by Marion.[15] The exorbitant release of carbon into the atmosphere has unleashed forces that seem overwhelming and indeed often blinding in their complexity. Not only do we still know very little about the real consequences that climate change will have on the planet, but we realize increasingly that it is such a complicated phenomenon that we may never fully understand it. Climate change is so complex that we cannot possibly make entirely certain predictions about how it will affect our planet, because even the weather as a chaos system cannot be foretold with complete confidence.[16] We have no way of being sure about such things as the runaway impact of feedback loops or of the capacity of the ocean to continue to absorb carbon. In many of these cases, it is not merely a matter of not having sufficient information but of the very complexity of the event and its countless interactions with other phenomena.

These events cannot be understood as "effects," not because they do not have a "cause," but because there is an abundance of possible causes, not because there is too little information, but because there is too much of it (BG, 167; ED, 235).[17] Marion's depiction of the event seems to fit the complexity and incommensurability of climate change well: "In effect, what qualifies it as event stems from the fact that these causes themselves all result from an arising with which they are incommensurable" (BG, 168; ED, 237). The same is true of climate change: Although the human release of carbon dioxide is identified as one cause—precisely by looking back from the effect—no single perpetrator can be neatly identified or made responsible. Rather, many causes over a long period of time have accumulated in a way that makes the effect of climate change incommensurable with any one of them or even with their combination. This may suggest that not only "positive" phenomena such as works of art or gifts might be experienced as saturated, but that terrifying, violent, or appalling phenomena are similarly saturated and impose themselves from themselves. Marion does not explore this possibility, but it does not appear excluded by his account. (The closest he comes is in his frequent references to war, which I examine more fully in the next chapter.)

Here the notion of "negative certainties" might also prove quite helpful. Marion claims that we will never have complete understanding or full comprehension of saturated phenomena, precisely because they are the kinds of phenomena that escape definitions of knowledge in terms of certainty. We know "certainly" that we will never have complete understanding, but that such understanding is not only impossible but would destroy the very nature of the saturated phenomenon by turning it into an object. Natural scientists are increasingly realizing that this is true in studying many natural phenomena, especially when they are living beings. The work of several feminist philosophers of science is particularly noteworthy in this regard, as they argue precisely for a more caring and involved scientific approach to the phenomena.[18] Animals especially cannot be treated as mere objects, but one can learn from them only by encountering them, maybe even living with them. They affect us far more deeply than our study of them affects them (unless it is destructive in some fashion, as of course much scientific study has been in the past and occasionally still continues to be, for example, in experimentation on animals). That does not mean, of course, that no knowledge is possible at all. Knowledge can increase over time, even if it can never be total or complete. This is a point to which I return later in the chapter.

So far I have discussed nature primarily as a saturated phenomenon to suggest that Marion's account of saturation can provide important insight for these phenomena, which he himself does not explore. Yet as I have argued for art and history, nature also might push us to less absolute terminology. The extreme terminology fails to deal with the possibility that there might be phenomena that are neither as absolutely saturated as the ones Marion examines nor merely technical objects or even "common" phenomena, but in any number of variations in between. Phenomena might be saturated to some extent, yet not be utterly overwhelming and completely pure. Phenomena of nature, I would suggest, may well extend along a whole spectrum of phenomenality from fairly limited to very rich, including a whole range of experience along that spectrum without abrupt flip into paradox from poverty to riches. Are there not degrees of givenness in our experience of nature, degrees that cannot be reduced to only two or three instances (poor, common, rich)? Not always is it given to us as supremely saturated, but it does not thereby become an object. There are many levels and degrees between these two extremes. A small backyard garden may be less saturated than a beautifully manicured public park, while neither is entirely "poor" or "saturated" in Marion's sense. A flourishing coral reef may well qualify as a "saturated phenomenon" while one that has been bleached entirely maybe is a mere object or at least a "poor" phenomenon, yet there is clear progression from one to the other state during which the coral reef presumably appears in various levels of saturation; it does not suddenly "flip" from one state to the other. A tornado or blizzard may be experienced as a saturated phenomenon, while a gentle rain or flurry of snowflakes is not experienced in such a saturated fashion but is therefore not merely an object.

Furthermore, a particular natural phenomenon may present itself as saturated to some degree or in some respect, but not in others. A tidal pool may give itself as more "saturated"—somewhat ironically—when the tide has subsided rather than when it is filled with ocean water. A certain mountain or stream may have served as a sacred locus of overwhelming saturation for a people, is encountered as saturated to some lesser extent by a group of avid hikers, is experienced with even a lesser degree of saturation by someone who contemplates it from the foot of the mountain or beside the stream, maybe even from the person's house, where mountain or stream have become more habitual phenomena and only occasionally catch real attention, and is experienced even differently by an artist trying to capture something of the aura of the place on canvas. Certain aspects of a wetland might be well understood and have become quasi-objects, while species within it or their interaction with each other remain saturated to a much higher degree.

And these various examples reproduce the ambiguity of saturation in Marion's own account: Does the same phenomenon move, depending on time, context, and reception, from poverty to saturation, or is it merely the interpretation that changes in certain circumstances? Does the level of comprehension determine the level of saturation, and does a phenomenon that is better understood hence becomes less saturated? Does frequency of experience make the phenomenon appear less saturated? (That clearly is not the case in the work of art, at least on Marion's account.) To some extent, all of these may be the case and indicate the need not only to distinguish between various levels and degrees of saturation, but also to pay attention to the context and purpose of encounter with the phenomena when making such distinctions. This raises the hermeneutic question that I now turn to in more detail.

The Hermeneutic Context for Natural Phenomena

In the case of natural phenomena, as maybe also in that of works of art, it is particularly obvious that not all people experience them in the same saturated fashion. Nature certainly does not seem to have the same impact or effect on everyone. Apparently in the eighteenth century, some travelers covered their eyes when they crossed the Alps since the mountains' lack of geometry was perceived as ugly. Many tourists who go to national parks spend a few minutes there and don't see much more than the visitor center.[19] Some of today's children have little sense that food comes from anywhere but the supermarket. And our increasingly technological culture removes us further and further from experiences of nature. So much of our lives is conducted in a virtual or highly manipulated reality that lacks any meaningful connection with earth and sky, weather and seasons, whether because "real life" is conducted on screen or because even when we are not on cell phones, Facebook, or the internet, we still live in highly climatized environments designed to insulate us from the effects of nature as much as possible.

Apparently a way of "seeing"—as Dillard stresses in her account—and hence a hermeneutic dimension, is necessary in order for someone to become sensitive to nature as saturated. The accusation of "romanticism" about nature in regard to these accounts seems very similar to the accusation made by some critics that, where Marion experiences saturation, they see nothing. Marion responds that this does not mean there is nothing there: "The fact or the pretense of not seeing does not prove that there is nothing to see. It can simply suggest that there is indeed something to see, but that in order to see it, it is necessary to learn to see otherwise because it could be a question of a phenomenality different from the one that manifests objects" (VR, 124; VeR, 151). One requires "eyes" to see, a kind of attunement to the phenomena. Some see more than others. This, however, clearly seems to imply a hermeneutic dimension to such phenomenal "seeing." We only see if we have been prepared in some way by our context, by instruction, by previous exposure, by a certain predisposition, maybe even by various versions of "belief," religious or otherwise.

And some sort of choice also seems implied: Seeing nature as valuable, maybe even as creation or as intrinsically alive in some fashion, makes us more open to encountering it as saturated. If we regard it merely as a resource to be exploited for our pleasure or convenience, it will be much more difficult for us to experience it as saturated. And yet there are certain excessive moments, such as violent natural disasters, when it is almost impossible not to be overwhelmed and swept away by the phenomenon. This points precisely to the kind of problematic ambivalence Marion consistently maintains: The saturated phenomenon is given as saturated—we do not merely interpret it to be so in some arbitrary fashion. And therefore to miss its saturation, to refuse to see it or be unable to see it, is a deficiency or lack of some sort. At the same time, some instances of saturation require a special kind of preparation or even genius: only the great artist has access to the unseen and the talent and devotion to portray it in the visible. To some extent, then, whether a phenomenon is experienced as saturated depends on the capacity and interpretation of the consciousness experiencing it. This kind of seeing is not the hermeneutics Marion disdains, the "mere" interpretation that renders the phenomenon utterly relative, dependent solely upon the recipient's (by implication capricious) "interpretation." Rather, it is a—to some extent prior—hermeneutic context that makes seeing possible.

Marion makes an intriguing suggestion at the end of *Certitudes négatives,* which heightens the tension of the ambivalence just discussed. He mentions as an example that it might be possible to treat a stone as saturated and God as an object (CN, 307). The second is clearly problematic and might indicate that the first one is, as well: stones should not be experienced as saturated, just as God should not be turned into an object. Yet, at least in this context, Marion does not censure this saturated encounter with the stone, although interestingly enough it occurs again in a built environment—in the courtyard of an old hotel instead of some more "natural" environment. Regardless of whether such interpretation is acceptable or false, it does raise the hermeneutic question forcefully: If stones can be interpreted as saturated, does all experience of saturation depend on interpretation?[20] Similarly, in the interview with Dan Arbib, he says that "everything can therefore become a saturated phenomenon as long as the way in which it gives itself does not become shut down, as occurs in the way in which the everydayness of the technical world imposes itself in a univocal objectivity" (RC, 151). Is it only our interpretation that assigns poverty or saturation to a phenomenon? Is a rock inherently a poor phenomenon and God a saturated one—as most of *Certitudes négatives* would suggest—or do they both become "poor" or "saturated" only when they are experienced as such? And if phenomenality is indeed about our experience of something as a phenomenon instead of about the "thing in itself" or its existence in the real world, questions that are set aside by the *epoché,* does this distinction between inherent and interpreted even make sense? If, however, such a completely different experience of the phenomenon is a genuine possibility, then might we teach people to perceive certain phenomena as saturated instead of treating them as poor? Can one be guided into having a saturated experience of natural phenomena? Might a description of a natural phenomenon as excessive—

as happens in the nature writers mentioned earlier in this chapter—open others' eyes to see differently? Besides the phenomenological concerns and possibilities it raises, this is obviously a question with tremendous implications for our dealing with the ecological crisis.

This qualification of the hermeneutic task in regard to saturated phenomena also points to the importance not only of a possible prior preparation for experiencing something as saturated but also of the need for discernment in such interpretive exercise. Not to admit that our burning of fossil fuels is connected to climate change is a willful misinterpretation of the phenomena. Evidently, not all interpretations of climate change are correct. Although we may not have complete knowledge and may be faced with an overwhelming phenomenon that can never be fully understood, some distinction between interpretations is possible and necessary. To some extent, Marion is quite right to worry about the completely arbitrary interpretation of phenomena. The climate change deniers certainly constitute one example of such arbitrary interpretation that has been severed from all responsibility to the phenomena as they actually appear. Yet, most contemporary hermeneutics stresses the importance of being able to distinguish between better and worse interpretations.[21] Interpretation does not mean that "anything goes" or that all interpretations are equally correct—and hence equally false.

One such way is via engaging in the hermeneutic circle, where a constant back-and-forth between the phenomenon and its various facets can both confirm and invalidate various interpretations, while remaining open-ended and allowing for further hermeneutic activity in the future. And Marion's discussion of the "seeing" necessary for experiencing a phenomenon as saturated can actually prove helpful here. For example, the simplistic solutions occasionally proposed to "solve" the ecological crisis may well qualify as a minimization of the saturation of the phenomenon: turning a complex and ongoing event into a mere object—and technology, especially in its guise as supposed savior of all our problems, plays an important role here.[22] Similarly, the destruction of rich ecological environments or elimination of whole species could be interpreted as turning saturated phenomena into poor ones. We return to this suggestion at the end of the next section.

Implications of Interpreting Natural Phenomena as Saturated

Considering that Marion himself does not identify natural phenomena as examples of saturated phenomena, it might be worthwhile to ask how identifying them in this way is helpful and does productive work. What difference would it make if natural phenomena were regarded as saturated? Such implications can be twofold: On the one hand, this proposal may well have implications for Marion's own project, opening it to a greater consideration of phenomena not produced by humans (such as the work of art or the historical event) and possibly clarifying the need for hermeneutic context and degrees of phenomenality. To some extent I have already addressed this issue and return to it in a discussion of Marion's account of the flesh in the final section of this chapter. On the other hand, such a proposal may have significant implications for environmental thinking, especially eco-phenomenology and environmental hermeneutics. Let me briefly explore the latter suggestion here. What can the proposal of saturated phenomena add to the environmental discussion?

First, it might make us more reluctant to think that we can give quick answers to environmental problems or solve them with advances in technology. In fact, for Marion, the opposite of the saturated phenomenon is precisely the "technical" object. Although at times he contrasts what he calls "common-law" phenomena (as poor) to saturated (rich) phenomena, often he employs the language of "technical object" and comments precisely on this link with technology.[23] Indeed, besides mathematical concepts, many of his examples are products of technology. At times he even censures our fascination with technology: "It could even be said that the world is covered with an invasive and highly visible layer of poor phenomena (namely, the technical objects produced and reproduced without end), which ends up eclipsing what it covers over" (VR, 125; VeR, 154). Earlier in the same paragraph he points out that "if these phenomena with no or poor intuition assume the status of technically produced objects (which is most frequently the case), their mode of production demands no other intuition than that which gives us their material (a material that itself becomes at once perfectly appropriate to each 'concept' and available in an in principle limitless quantity)" (VR, 125; VeR, 154). Technology provides us with objects, not with saturated phenomena. Its very goal is mastery of the material and complete control over it.

On other occasions, he links this ability to constitute technical objects easily into concepts to the inherent disposability of the technical object. He contends that technology first imposes a concept and that whatever it "manufactures" as object is a mere result of this concept.[24] It should thus not even be called the "production" of an object. Real production or creation happens only in the case of saturated phenomena. At one point he comments on "the monstrous commercial city, almost unlimited and without form, oozing its own vulgarity, awash in items for sale" (BG, 129; ED, 183). Although his critique of technology is not as trenchant as that of Michel Henry, on whom he largely seems to rely here,[25] or that of other French thinkers such as Jacques Ellul or Jean Baudrillard, he certainly agrees that technology reduces humans to objects and is quite critical of its pernicious effects especially in his more recent work *Certitudes négatives*. In that book he refers repeatedly in derisory fashion to "technoscience" and describes the way in which medical and economic adoption of technique reduces humans to mere objects (CN, 49–66). Similarly, in a Lenten address on the topic of "Faith and Reason" at Notre Dame de Paris, he condemns "the dehumanization of humans to improve humanity, the systematic sapping of nature to develop the economy, injustice to render society more efficient, the absolute empire of information-distraction to escape the constraints of the true" (VR, 151; CpV, 24). In all these contexts Marion seems to condemn the perilous effects of technology on contemporary culture, including effects on the environment. The reduction wrought by technology, destroying saturated phenomena and turning them into mere objects, is a useful insight for environmental thinking. This tentative critique of technology could profitably be explored further.

Furthermore, if a phenomenon such as global climate change were to be recognized as a saturated phenomenon, it would also be admitted that it is overwhelming in its complexity and requires deep and thorough engagement and maybe even a kind of humility before its enormity. The proposal of the saturated phenomenon insists that there is something rich about the phenomenon even when it is not recognized. Although there is no phenomenon without a recipient or witness, some ways of receiving or witnessing are better than others, more appropriate for the phenomenon. We have already seen that the way in which we reply to the saturated phenomenon has a certain ethical dimension. To encounter a great work of art as saturated is more appropriate than treating it as an object for sale. One might hence insist that experiencing nature as saturated is a *better* reception than reducing it to an object. Marion explores this possibility of "misapprehending" the saturated phenomenon:

> This danger [of solipsism], while no doubt undeniable, results less from the saturated phenomenon itself than from the misapprehension of it. When this type of phenomenon arises, it is most often treated like a common-law phenomenon, indeed a poor phenomenon, one that is therefore forced to be included in a phenomenological situation that by definition it refuses, and it is finally misapprehended. If, by contrast, its specificity is recognized, the bedazzlement it provokes would become phenomenologically acceptable, indeed desirable, and the passage from one horizon to another would become a rational task for the hermeneutic. The saturated phenomenon safeguards its absoluteness and at the same time dissolves its danger when it is recognized as such, without confusing it with other phenomena. (BG, 211; ED, 295–96)

Here recognition and misapprehension play an important role. Although a phenomenon may impose itself as saturated and absolute, it must be recognized and received as such and may be misapprehended as poor and relative.

How is it properly received? Presumably by being interpreted as saturated instead of as poor. Being overwhelmed by the beauty of a mountain, encountering it as a saturated phenomenon, is better than treating it as an object for strip mining. Encountering the ocean and its creatures in all their excessive beauty and diversity is better than overfishing its varied species or using it as a garbage dump. Recognizing the limitless diversity of a flourishing ecosystem as a fluid habitat for many creatures, which we will never fully understand, is better than seeing it as merely a space for a housing development, mall, or parking lot. This is especially the case for the rich environment of the rain forest, which is so "saturated" with species that researchers continue to be stunned by its immense diversity and to deplore its destruction. Experiencing all these and countless other phenomena as saturated not only changes our attitude toward them, but such an altered attitude is also increasingly realized as a more appropriate response to natural phenomena than treating them as mere exploitable resources. This also calls, even on Marion's own account, for hermeneutic endeavors that would give a variety of analyses of the event, recognizing that one version alone will never do full justice to its complexity. We hence need much richer and more complex accounts of nature as saturated phenomenon, accounts that are able to convey some of the "non-constitutable" excess of natural phenomena. Providing such narratives makes us more aware of our environment and integrates the natural and the social more fully; as a result, we may be able to forge a path to experience both realms as saturated and hence not reducible to an object. Here the "world" opened by the tree, to which Marion refers fleetingly in *Being Given,* may well become a rich world depicted and envisioned by a diversity of narratives.

This implies, then, that speaking of individual natural phenomena as saturated, especially as such phenomena are frequently depicted by nature writers, might give us greater sensitivity to the animal and plant "other" and might even make it possible to contemplate what it might mean to respond to this "other" in more ethical ways, as has begun to be envisioned by several thinkers for our encounter with the animal.[26] This could be clearly pushed beyond encounters with other animals to encounters with trees or mountains. No tree or animal is merely an object for human consumption, no natural place merely a possible site for human use. To treat trees, rivers, springs, and even gas deposits in the Marcellus Shale merely as resources is to reduce their saturation to that of an object and to believe that we know them completely and with certainty when we treat them as such. It is to ignore the complexity and excess of the saturated phenomenon: instead of being blinded by it, we turn a blind eye to it. Much environmental destruction is precisely a result of having reduced complex ecosystems to mere objects of exploitation without recognizing the excess of life present in them (as just mentioned, this is particularly true of the rain forest, which contains more species than we can presently imagine, most of which remain undocumented and unexamined). Scientists involved in botanical, zoological, ethological, ecological, and geological research frequently witness to this sense of abundance or excess and acknowledge the limitations of their research.

This, of course, indicates a need *for* further research, not for ceasing it. Saturation here precisely does not function as a way to stop our examination of the phenomenon. Just as I have argued that the historical event requires continued investigation that can lead to an increase in knowledge without violating the recognition that there can be no full comprehension of such an event, natural phenomena call for careful and sensitive research that can indeed increase our knowledge and appreciation of them without thereby turning them into mere objects or pretending to comprehend them fully. One might suggest here also an affinity with Marion's account of the artist. As the artist has a special genius for depicting the "unseen" on canvas, so the scientist may have special talents for investigating the complexity of natural phenomena, as long as such investigation does not reduce the phenomena to objects but instead opens up our encounter with them to a richer experience. And yet the scientist does not merely have talent, but has undergone training, has increased in his or her ability to investigate such phenomena. That ability is hence not merely "genius," but requires hermeneutic preparation. Maybe this also is a kind of "giftedness" that comes with a heavy responsibility.

One might suggest, then, that the ambivalence whether saturation is "in" the phenomenon or whether it depends on the recipient's response to it, is not merely arbitrary, as I have tended to present it in the first two chapters. Even "censure" of "inappropriate" reception, namely a reception that disregards a phenomenon's richness, may not always be entirely problematic. If proper training, preparation, and context are provided, a phenomenon may be experienced as saturated when it would not be experienced as such without such preparation or context. Distinguishing between "better" and "worse" interpretations of a phenomenon imply the possibility of discernment in regard to phenomena and their reception, as well as judgment of the conclusions reached about them and the ways in which they are portrayed. The ambivalence is not vicious if it refers to a circular and ongoing movement of exposure to the phenomenon, confirmation of the experience, renewed encounter, correction of the initial phenomenological description, and so forth, including communication with others and testing out "hypotheses."

This entire process, however, is deeply hermeneutic, both in terms of the recognition of context or horizon and training or preparation for the experience and in terms of a hermeneutic circle of confirmation and discernment that cycles through various interpretations in order to find the most faithful ones for this particular occasion and context. This does not mean that the phenomenon has been reduced to an object, that it is fully understood, or that we can arrive at some "final" and definitive interpretation. It does mean, however, that a phenomenon can only truly give itself in its fullness and richness, or be received as saturated, if it allows for a phenomenological horizon or context that enables the recipient to prepare for it, to "see" it, to bear its impact fully, and to discern it as "rich" rather than "poor" or "common."

Such discernment also has ethical connotations. As we have seen in the previous chapter, the work of art does have an ethical dimension for Marion. The artist bears responsibility for what is portrayed in the painting. Marion attributes this ethical dimension only to the portrayal of the human face, which raises similar issues as various environmental discussions of Lévinas, which ask whether animals have a "face" or access to speech, in Lévinas's sense of the term.[27] Would it be possible to speak of the "otherness" of nature in a way that requires it to be depicted as more than an object? Does it impose itself as the "other" does in Lévinas? Does it require that I not "kill" it? As I can become utterly desensitized to the mute appeal of the other's face asking me not to hurt or kill it, certainly we can (and have) become desensitized to the mute appeal of nature to leave it alone—an appeal clearly still heard by many native peoples, which we often dismiss as "romantic" or "primitive." The problem is not that nature does not speak or feel anything, the problem is that we have come to think in such materialistic and technological terms that the very idea seems ridiculous to us, so that stories and poetry from cultures that speak of nature in more personal terms are dismissed as anthropomorphic or rejected as pantheistic.[28]

This of course returns us to one of the fundamental problems of phenomenology, namely how one can speak of anything outside oneself or of the experience of another beyond the experience of one's own consciousness. In order to speak of nature adequately, we must be able to give a phenomenological account of its impact on or manifestation to consciousness as one different from simple "objects." Do I respond to the mouse or cockroach running through my kitchen differently than I do to the countertop or floor? Do we experience a rose differently than the pot in which it grows? Marion would suggest that we do: "For that matter, the rose, when it opens, arises like an event, just as the event blossoms—when it is ripe" (BG, 170; ED, 240). Is such difference of experience merely a matter of my "view" or my particular interpretation? Can I give an account of nature's impact on my consciousness that would parallel the neighbor's obligation imposed on me as something I can avoid or ignore only at mine and the other's peril? How can recognizing natural phenomena as saturated influence our response to them and ultimately change us? Marion's criticism of Lévinas's focus on ethics in favor of a greater emphasis on love might actually prove useful in this context. Maybe "love" for nature and natural phenomena can motivate us to care about them and consider them worthy of protection instead of exploitation. Recognizing them as "saturated" could make us "devoted" to them, addicted to them, or even given over to them in a way that forbids treating them as objects or resources there merely for our use and abuse. Possibly, love could even "individuate" natural phenomena in the way in which the lover individuates the beloved according to Marion. I return to the topic of love more fully in the next chapter, but explore one more implication of Marion's treatment for environmental concerns here.

Identifying some natural phenomena as saturated might change not only our attitude toward them, but it might also help us rethink more deeply what it means to be human. Marion consistently stresses that his analysis of the saturated phenomenon has profound implications for the notion of the self, which is no longer a Cartesian self-sufficient subject.[29] Instead, the one who responds to the saturated phenomenon is the witness, the one devoted, given over, even addicted to the phenomenon. The recipient of the "self" of the phenomenon only becomes a self of his or her own in this encounter with and response to the "self" of the phenomenon:

> Therefore, the *self* of what shows *itself* and gives *itself* can never be verified through inference or constitution, which would collapse it equally into the in-itself of the object (or the thing without phenomenality). But it could be through the impression, or rather through the pressure that it exerts over the gaze (and, of course, over the other modes of perception). This pressure bears down in such a manner that it makes us feel not only its weight, but also the fact that we cannot in any way master it, that it imposes itself without our having it available to us—we do not trigger it any more than we suspend it. The *self* of the phenomenon is marked in its determination as event. (BG, 159; ED, 225–26; original emphasis)

Thus, if natural phenomena can be recognized as saturated in this fashion, this may well help us address some of the anthropocentric dilemmas that continue to haunt environmental thinking. The aporia of how to move away from anthropocentric thinking that values the human as superior to all other species and focuses exclusively (or primarily) on human concerns toward a more biocentric or ecocentric position that values other forms of life for their own sake always is complicated by the fact that it is the *human* who continues to speak and to articulate even the biocentric or ecocentric position. How would a human really know what an animal felt or what the world might look like from the point of view of a plant?

This aporia seems addressed at least to some extent in the paradox Marion continually articulates in the notion of the counter-experience of the witness. While all phenomenology is about human consciousness of phenomena and thus recognizes that it is contextual and that we cannot literally climb into the consciousness of an other (whether it is the other person, the divine, or indeed animals or plants), Marion, following Lévinas, articulates a phenomenology that is primarily a response to the other. Here the self becomes possible only as it responds to and receives the incoming of the other who has the initiative. And, unlike Lévinas, Marion does not insist on the other as human, but envisions the possibility that any phenomenon could have such an initiating "self." If an encounter with a painting or the experience of a historical event can individuate me, why not an encounter with a nonhuman animal or the experience of natural rather than historical phenomena? Peter Steeves describes such an encounter:

> And then one night while doing dishes in the back washroom a black lizard the size of my thumb crawled in through the barred window above the sink and sat on the wet cement near the faucet. He moved impossibly fast; his toes were spread impossibly wide in a graceful fan at the end of each foot; he stuck impossibly to the dripping wall of the sink, cranked one eye in my direction and turned to face me. Self-conscious, I froze. The moment was pregnant with possibility. . . . But the lizard. . . . His motions, his thoughts were unscripted. The relationship was open on both ends. We could become anything together.[30]

Here it is the encounter with a specific animal that gives me to myself in some fashion and provides an opening for new possibilities. The phenomenon of the lizard is indeed encountered as saturated in some fashion. It comes from itself and by itself, in a surprising way, as a fait accompli. It freezes me in a particular position, from which I must see it. If I move, the lizard surely will be gone. And henceforth my becoming is no longer isolated but is connected in some way to that of the lizard: we become together.

Approaching nature as saturated phenomenon then opens the possibility of understanding ourselves differently and experiencing ourselves envisioned (transformed and constituted) by the non-human other. And this might also open up Marion's account to an important dimension lacking in his phenomenological analysis. As Derrida suggests in *The Animal That Therefore I Am* (mostly in response to Lévinas and Lacan), a phenomenological account that ignores our animal nature and does not recognize nonhuman others is no longer viable today. We cannot extract ourselves—even philosophically—from the ecosystems that sustain our life or ignore the destructive impact we have on them. This connects to what Marion, following Henry, describes as the most intimate experience of myself as my own flesh. While the phenomenon of nature is not identical to that of the flesh, especially as Marion depicts it, it may well have some important connections to it.

The Saturated Phenomenon of the Flesh

Marion's third type of saturated phenomenon, that of the experience of the flesh, at first glance has nothing to do with nature at all. I am certainly not suggesting that the two are equivalent. The most important characteristics of the saturated phenomenon of the flesh, as Marion presents it, is its utter immediacy that makes any relation impossible. I am not related to or distinct from my flesh, precisely because I *am* my flesh. The experience of the flesh is indistinguishable from

the experience of the self. Clearly, we do not encounter animals or plants or ecosystems as that immediate or intimate. We certainly experience them as outside of
us and often even as strangely "other." Yet the experience of our flesh and that of
nature or natural phenomena might not be as disparate as they seem at first glance.

The phenomenon of the flesh is the one least prominent in Marion's account.
Although he always mentions it as one of the four types of saturated phenomena,
he devotes only one brief chapter to it (chapter 4 of *In Excess*) and rarely returns
to it as a separate phenomenon aside from the lists in which it features as one of
the four.[31] And although Marion does interact with Romano on the saturated phenomenon of the event, with various painters and their writings in regard to the
phenomenon of the idol, and with Lévinas in regard to the phenomenon of the
icon, his reliance on Michel Henry's phenomenology for the phenomenon of the
flesh is much more extensive. Marion basically adopts Henry's account of the self-
affection of the flesh and merely illustrates how it can be understood as a saturated phenomenon of relation, inasmuch as it is absolute and completely without
analogy (BG, 209–212; ED, 289–92).[32] It is self-affection, because "affection refers
to no object, according to no ecstasy, but only to itself; for it itself is sufficient to
accomplish itself as affected. . . . The flesh auto-affects itself in agony, suffering,
and grief, as well as in desire, feeling, or orgasm" (BG, 231; ED, 322). Joy and pain,
anxiety, fear and trembling, "all arise from the flesh and its own immanence" (BG,
231; ED, 322). This phenomenon can never be seen and makes intentionality impossible because it is so utterly immediate that no distance can intervene. It most
profoundly accomplishes individuation and even "demands solipsism" (BG, 232;
ED, 323).

Chapter 4 of *In Excess* explores further this "givenness of the self" that the
flesh accomplishes. Marion discusses self-givenness and the flesh via an analysis
of Descartes's analysis of feeling and the senses and Husserl's distinction between
flesh and body. He criticizes Descartes's assimilation of the "bodies of the world
(sky, earth, and so on)" and "my body gifted with sense," arguing that they are "absolutely not identified" (IE, 84; DS, 101). Although he questions Descartes's dismissal of the sentient body in favor of the mind, he will not wonder about Descartes's much stronger rejection of the "bodies of the world" that supposedly feel
nothing (which at least in the case of many animals is patently untrue). Marion
insists that "as feeler, my body is radically distinguished from the bodies of the
world, only felt, but never sentient as feeling" (IE, 84; DS, 101–102). He rehabilitates Descartes against the charge of dualism by arguing that Descartes did have
a sense of this feeling body, but leaves the dualism between my self-affection and
the non-sentient rest of the world in place.[33]

In *Sur la pensée passive de Descartes*, Marion returns to this aspect of Descartes's
work by arguing for Descartes's thought as "passive." He explores the final two

sections of the *Meditations,* supplemented by some of Descartes's letters and his work *The Passions of the Soul* in order to reread the strong account of the Cartesian cogito and show that Descartes actually thinks of the human being as receptive and passive. He argues that Descartes proceeds in three stages in his work, the first two corresponding to the two versions of metaphysics that Marion has outlined in his earlier work—one version with the ego cogito as grounding principle and one with the divine as guarantor of all being—while the third is one at which Descartes arrives only in his latest texts and which speaks of the self in terms of affectivity and passivity. Marion examines Descartes's analysis of the flesh in terms of its sensations, especially that of pain (PPD, 86–87). The affectivity of the ego's flesh hence becomes the foundation for the existence of material things and the relation between soul and body. Descartes emerges as a phenomenologist in disguise (PPD, 92). Marion's analysis culminates in a reading of *The Passions of the Soul* that stresses the passivity of the Cartesian self affected by the passions, which was briefly examined in the introduction. The connection between the flesh and its passivity via affection, grounded to a large extent in Henry's analysis of the flesh, also characterizes Marion's more explicitly phenomenological account of the flesh.

In chapter 4 of *In Excess,* Marion employs Husserl in order to argue that the flesh "spiritualizes," that is, "renders visible the bodies of the world that would remain, without it, in the night of the unseen" (IE, 89; DS, 107). The world cannot be phenomenalized except through my flesh. (Marion provides an illustration of this in his account of how the saturated phenomenon is experienced through the five senses in "The Banality of Saturation." I return to this momentarily.) In this context, Marion explores the phenomena of suffering, pleasure, and aging as examples of the phenomenon of the flesh. He contends that I cannot appear to myself or even become a self without experiencing myself in this fashion. I cannot withdraw or distance myself from my flesh (IE, 92; DS, 111). In the case of suffering, "I do not suffer from the fire and from the iron—but, because immediately they hurt *me,* they only hurt me. I suffer *myself* by them. . . . Suffering rivets me to myself as one rivets something to the ground—by earthing [*par la prise de terre*]" (IE, 92; DS, 111; original emphasis).[34] The self-affectivity of the flesh is accomplished in a similar way through pleasure. Both pain and pleasure render me completely passive, overcome me, and manifest themselves in me by manifesting me to myself. The phenomenon of aging also confirms "the inseparability of the flesh" by manifesting how the passage of time is marked in my flesh (IE, 94; DS, 114). Our face becomes an archive of time, which cannot itself be perceived, but "appears in the accumulation of its marks, which leave their traces to ruin the physical body . . . but especially living flesh and, more than any other flesh, the flesh of my face" (IE, 95; DS, 115). Marion takes all three of these experiences to confirm the phenomenalization of the ego in its incarnation in the flesh. Flesh individuates me in my facticity and it does so in a way that reason or understanding never could (IE, 97; DS, 117). The flesh of the other always "remains absolutely inaccessible to me" (IE, 98; DS, 118). I receive myself from my flesh. Marion concludes that "birth, original taking flesh, does not therefore have a biological status but rather a phenomenological one" (IE, 98; DS, 119).

Yet, must biological and phenomenological origin of the flesh be so completely disconnected and exclusive of each other?[35] Indeed, is this account of the flesh really possible without some attention to nature and the earth? In "The Banality of Saturation," Marion explicates our experience of saturated phenomena in terms of the five senses. For all five senses, his examples are primarily of human performances or products: the colors of the traffic light versus the colors in Rothko's painting *Number 212,* the human voice over the loudspeaker in the train station versus the diva singing in an opera, the odor of gas in a house versus the smell of perfume, the taste of poison versus that of fine wine or a sumptuous meal, the stumbling in a dark room versus an erotic encounter with another's flesh (VR, 127–33; VeR, 157–65). Why does Marion instead not depict the colors in a rainbow, the sound of gently trickling rain, the fragrance of a rose, the taste of fresh fruit, the feel of the wind in my hair or caressing my skin? After all, on the most basic level, our sensory experiences are rooted first of all in nature. All our fleshly experiences require the earthy substrate of nature in obvious or more hidden ways. Even the perfume and the wine require the materials of nature of which they subsist, as do the canvas and paint in a less obvious fashion. The voice of the diva and the flesh of the beloved are obviously directly physical, although the particular context here makes that difficult to recognize. Our most basic needs of respiration, nutrition, and reproduction are "earthy" and physical. They are indeed impossible without connection to the air, the ground, and the elements that constitute the human body and only enable it to become a sensing "flesh." Unless we are surrounded only by technology and eat only highly processed food, most of our experiences are immediately based in natural elements, particularly obvious for nutrition but also true of most other experiences.

The pleasure and pain, joy and suffering, experienced immediately in our very flesh are central to this analysis. Yet, can a phenomenologically "thick" description of pleasure or pain be given without a recourse to nature: the joy over the beauties of nature or the pleasure of fresh food grown in healthy soil, the suffering or pain caused when our bodies break down, affected by the natural system of aging and response to disease? An adequate phenomenology of the flesh cannot be developed without being grounded at least to some extent in the "earthiness" of nature, from which we come, with which we are intimately connected in manifold ways, which sustains our very life, and to which we ultimately return. Hunger and thirst, fatigue and elation, are intimately linked to the conditions of our animal bodies, even if we experience them consciously in our immanent flesh. "Body" and "flesh" should not be separated so firmly and absolutely, one as a mere object and the other a saturated phenomenon. Pleasure or pain cannot be experienced without the proper functioning of our bodies, without the concrete physicality of our limbs, skin cells, neurotransmitters, and so forth. An awareness of these conditions of experience does not automatically lead to a reduction of the body to a mere object, as Marion at times seems to suggest (e.g., in his discussion of a hospital experience [CN, 51–54] and the dismissal of a biological account above [IE, 98; DS, 119]). While that is certainly true in some contexts, where bodies become objectified as mere objects for research, it is not necessarily the case. The real physicality of our experiencing flesh cannot be completely excluded from an account of our immediate consciousness within it.

Marion consistently prefers to lead a discussion of the flesh in more theological directions. In the final line of his fullest treatment just discussed, he suggests that an account of the flesh might enable us to think philosophically about the theological notion of incarnation (IE, 103; DS, 124). Yet, even theologically speaking, the incarnation is an affirmation of the material and fleshly.[36] In his brief treatment in the first chapter of *Certitudes négatives,* where he focuses primarily on a reduction of the human face but mentions the flesh occasionally, he claims that a more adequate understanding of the human face would need to see it as an image of God and connect the indefinability of the human to the incomprehensibility of the divine (CN, 69). Ultimately, the human must be understood as a "God" (CN, 74). The final two sections of this chapter explore how the "secret of the human" is linked to the divine and explicitly try to decouple the human from any definition as an animal, which are interpreted to be reductive (e.g., CN 83). Yet can such a complete separation between humans and animals be sustained? Do they not ignore something important about our experience of ourselves?

Emmanuel Falque, drawing his inspiration from both Marion and Henry, explores this animal dimension of our experience more fully in his *Les noces de l'agneau.*[37] He insists that we must pay much closer attention to our animality, to our concrete organic existence in an analysis of our fleshly experience. Falque continues to draw a strict distinction between our own animal nature, which he calls animality, and that of other animals, which he refers to as bestiality. This distinction seems arbitrary, however.[38] Exploring our own animality more fully may well open the path to our becoming more attentive to the animality of other creatures and possibly even to more general organic and inorganic life. That certainly is the implication of much ecophenomenological writing on this topic. Marion suggests at the end of his discussion of the flesh in *In Excess* that this discussion of the flesh despite its apparent solipsism might open a new path toward speaking of encounter with the human other in what used to be called "intersubjectivity" (IE, 103;

DS, 124). If that is a genuine possibility, it should similarly enable us to begin to explore an account of nonhuman flesh and its affective experience, maybe make it possible to speak of "inter-animality" in a more coherent and convincing fashion.

Furthermore, our experience of pleasure and pain is dependent not only on the proper functioning of the animality and physicality of our own flesh.[39] It also relies on many other "natural" factors. Our mood, whether we experience pleasure or pain in something, is influenced by the weather and even by the temperature. Heat and high humidity can make us sluggish and lethargic, can erode our enjoyment of a summer day. Extreme cold can make us intensely miserable or even incapable of functioning. Polluted air and poisoned waters can sicken us and hence cause actual pain. Besides physical pain, they can also cause emotional pain, as when such pollution causes greater incidences of miscarriages, leukemia, and various cancers, where we may lose someone beloved or lovingly anticipated. The phenomena of the flesh, which Marion depicts in his treatment, such as birth, death, and aging, are not unaffected by the natural contexts in which they occur. Henry identifies our experience of such phenomena as an encounter with the call of "Life." Might they also constitute an encounter with the call of "nature"? Is it possible for us to hear such a call phenomenologically? All these remain mere questions and tentative explorations at this point and all deserve fuller explication. Yet, at the very least, they suggest that bringing Marion's phenomenology of givenness together with phenomenological accounts of nature and animality may prove mutually enriching. Not only can the notion of the saturated phenomenon play an important role in environmental thinking, but an increased attention to the earthiness and materiality of our experience may bring nuance and greater complexity to Marion's account of the flesh and of givenness more generally.

FOUR

Love and Violence

The lover "declares his love as one declares war" (EP, 79; PE, 129). So insists Marion repeatedly in his investigation into the nature of the erotic phenomenon. War, of course, is here "only" a metaphor illustrating the absolute commitment of the lover. Yet the fact that this analogy is used several times throughout *The Erotic Phenomenon* seems to indicate that it is not insignificant. Rather, it points to a problematic aspect of Marion's treatment of eros, namely the extreme—if not almost militant—character of this love. And the careful reader finds the connotations of absoluteness exacerbated by another subtheme, stated even less obviously: the parallel between this phenomenological analysis of eros and Marion's earlier theological analysis of charity. Combined, they lead to a troubling conclusion. The lover, on Marion's account, will turn out to be like a God declaring war. In this chapter I (ab)use four of Marion's comparisons of love to war in order to highlight the absolute character of his treatment and show how in each case the divine emerges surreptitiously. I maintain, instead, that the phenomena of the other in general and that of love in particular require, on the one hand, distinctions between types of love and between degrees of love, and, on the other hand, an account of the hermeneutic context that makes any relationship with the other, especially a loving relationship, possible. Before analyzing these comparisons more carefully, however, let me briefly provide some context for Marion's exploration of love.

In some form or other, Marion has been occupied with the topic of love throughout most of his work. His most extensive discussion in *The Erotic Phenomenon* (2007, originally published in 2003) merely crowns an older concern that was previewed in *Idol and Distance* (2001, originally published in 1977) and prepared in *Prolegomena to Charity* (2002, originally published in 1986, although several of the essays collected in it are considerably older), especially in its chapter 4, "The Intentionality of Love" (originally 1983). In that chapter, Marion argues against Lévinas that only love can truly individuate the other and confer particularity (or *haecceitas*) on the beloved. Love enables a counter-intentionality where I experience myself envisioned by the gaze of the other (PC, 82–83; PaC, 102–103). It displaces the strong subjectivity of the Cartesian subject in favor of a self addressed by the injunction of the other and allows the other to emerge as an invisible but non-substitutable and irreplaceable other (PC, 98–101; PaC, 118–20). One hence gets the sense already in that early chapter that the phenomenon of the other for Marion is closely linked if not identical to the phenomenon of love. In this early exploration, he describes love as a "crossing of gazes"[1] where the lover's gaze crosses with and weighs upon that of the beloved other who envisions the lover in a mutual, although not reciprocal, fashion: "To render oneself to the unsubstitutable other, as to a summons to my own unsubstitutability—no other than me will be able to play the other that the other requires, no other gaze than my own must respond to the ecstasy of *this particular* other exposed in his gaze" (PC, 101; PaC, 120; original emphasis). Love will remain the privileged way to approach the other throughout Marion's work, including his treatment in *In Excess,* in *In the Self's Place,* and of course especially in *The Erotic Phenomenon.*

Although the fairly short chapter on the icon in *In Excess* focuses on the face, it follows the analysis of a crossing of gazes laid out in *Prolegomena to Charity.* Marion here carries further the suggestion that while I cannot know or have access to the other's flesh, I must presuppose it like the gaze of the other that I cannot see proceeding from the empty pupils of the eyes (IE, 114–15; DS, 138; also BG, 232–33; ED, 323–24). Marion draws on Lévinas's account of the face, but then goes beyond it by criticizing its exclusive emphasis on ethics and claiming that the order to love is an even more important injunction of the face (IE, 118; DS, 142). I am envisaged by the other's invisible gaze and called to respond to its truth and signification. The face gives rise to an infinite hermeneutics because no final signification can be given to it, and hence an endless number of stories have to be told about the other's life. Therefore, this hermeneutic truly begins only after the other's death (IE, 123; DS, 148). And such hermeneutic is most faithful when one has lived with and deeply loved another: "Only someone who has lived with the life and death of the other knows to what extent he or she does *not* know that other. Only such a person can hence recognize the other as the saturated phenomenon par excellence, and consequently also knows that it would take an eternity to envisage this saturated phenomenon as such—not constituting it as an object, but interpreting it in loving it" (IE, 126–27, trans. mod.; DS, 152; original emphasis). Already in *Being Given,* Marion similarly claims that the icon "gathers together the particular characteristics of the three preceding types of saturated phenomena" and hence carries them to their highest degree (BG, 233; ED, 324). He also suggests in the final lines of that book that love might be a better way to speak of the face of the other than Lévinas's supposedly exclusive emphasis on ethics and that "the phenomenology of givenness" might be able to restore to love "the dignity of a concept" (BG, 324; ED, 443).

In his more fully developed treatment in *The Erotic Phenomenon,* Marion outlines what he calls an "erotic reduction" in six meditations. Such an erotic reduction sets metaphysical constrictions aside and reconfigures the notions of time and space. It is also able to overcome the metaphysical dichotomies of subject and object, on the one hand by articulating a self after the subject that is not autonomous and self-sufficient, and on the other hand by approaching a truly individuated other. Marion begins with the claim that we are today no longer concerned with Cartesian certainty but that questions of meaning and affirmation touch us more profoundly. We particularly desire the assurance that somebody loves us. He shows that we are unable to provide such assurance ourselves by outlining the failure of self-love that ultimately leads to hatred of both self and others. He therefore suggests that love must start not with my own desire to assure myself that I am loved by someone else, but rather with my decision to love another. Love is articulated first of all as a meeting of the flesh (instead of bodies) where I phenomenalize the flesh of the other while the other phenomenalizes my flesh: we both give each other the experience of our own flesh. Marion speaks of this again as a mutual, yet not reciprocal, relationship. He then goes on to show how this love incarnate in the flesh must always come to a halt (e.g., after the rapture of orgasm) and therefore seeks to express itself in a "third" that would bear witness to the fidelity and reality of that love. The child can do so only temporarily and unsuccessfully. Marion therefore concludes by articulating a language of love that would express the whole range of its experience, even as it always admits its inability to express this impossible event. Outlining and describing these moves, Marion also provides analyses of seduction, betrayal, hatred, jealousy, fidelity, friendship, and various other aspects of love, many of them beautiful and moving depictions, rooted in intensely personal experience and description.[2]

War or violence is not an explicit aspect of this treatment. Marion does not extensively compare love and war; there is no separate section on the relationship between or similarity of love and war. Yet he uses war as an analogy for love several times and in different contexts, albeit only in passing. It is this apparently innocent metaphor and especially its repeated occurrence that makes us aware of something disquieting emerging in Marion's treatment of love. In this chapter I consider four of these comparisons, each emphasizing a different aspect of Marion's account of love: the lover who declares love; the beloved to whom love is declared; the language of this declaration of love; finally, the quality of this love and especially its univocal character. In the last two sections of the chapter I draw out the implications of this analysis and argue for a less "absolute" treatment of love.

The One Who Declares

The first comparison is the one mentioned at the opening of this chapter and appears when Marion begins to insist on the lack of reciprocity in the loving relationship, which must escape all danger of metaphysical reason and economy.

Marion compares love and war as both beyond reason in their escape from calculation and commerce: "Just as, in the end, a war breaks out without reason, in a deflagration and a transgression of every good reason, the lover makes love break out. He declares his love as one declares war—without any reason. Which is to say that he does so sometimes without even taking the time or the care to make the declaration" (EP, 79; PE, 129). We engage in both love and war with passion and abandon, without cool consideration, without hesitation, without rational boundaries. What Marion emphasizes in this context (as is, of course, also very evident in the comparison itself) is the importance of the lover's initiative. Marion had originally begun his treatment with the desire of the subject to find meaning in life. In order to escape the attack of "vanity" or meaninglessness, I wish to be assured that I am loveable and that somebody does actually love me. It is in consequence of my failure to love myself sufficiently or to find another who will love me satisfactorily, that Marion suggests we must abandon all search for self-fulfillment, assurance of being loved, and even reciprocity (EP, 67–70; PE, 111–16). Instead of requiring to be loved by the other, I must take the initiative in loving; I must first become lover before I can find myself beloved. Marion insists that this separates love from "being" and overcomes metaphysical constrictions.[3] He compares the love that I give freely, even if it is not returned, to the gift that escapes any commerce or need for reciprocity. In loving with abandon, even if that love is rejected by the other, I find meaning and assure my identity and dignity as lover (EP, 76; PE, 122).

To some extent, this emphasis on making the first step in love seems to connote selflessness, vulnerability, and generosity, which are obviously all aspects that Marion wishes to stress. Yet even these apparently so positive connotations seem problematic if they indicate an exclusive emphasis on the lover. And the insistence on the primacy of the lover becomes even stronger in a following section, where Marion argues that the mere decision to love is already sufficient to mark me as lover.[4] Marion highlights the significance of this decision to love first: Even if I do not love well or perfectly and cannot measure the quality of my love, I must make a decision to love as first lover. This decision is fully accomplished even if my love never elicits any response (EP, 91; PE, 146). Since I could never accomplish love perfectly anyway, I need not wait for a complete performance of love. The decision alone suffices. My phenomenality decides itself only in my decision for the other. I can and must at least decide to love, "love to love" (*aimer aimer [amare amare]*) (EP, 92; PE, 148). Although I can never love fully, it suffices to love "love" in order for me to appear as lover. I must act *as if* I love. The initiative of love lies fully with the lover who seems to act in complete independence. I fall in love only on my own account, not by chance or by accident or by the other's initiative.

Throughout these passages Marion emphasizes repeatedly the lover's sole initiative on which everything depends here (EP, 89–97; PE, 146–52).[5] Yet a lover who can become lover solely by his or her decision, by a solitary choice, and needs no interaction with another in love seems extremely problematic. Surely loving *love* is decidedly not equivalent to (nor the first step toward) loving *another.* Marion would likely respond that we are still in the beginning of the treatment, that we have not yet spoken of the intimacy of the flesh or even of the necessary appearance of the third in the figure of the child. Yet the fact that love must necessarily begin with my initiative and that I can become lover solely by my own choice and without interaction with the other still is somewhat alarming. Indeed, Robyn Horner suggests that Marion is here presenting a critique, not an analysis that he advocates.[6] Claude Romano, in turn, sees Marion's insistence on the primacy of initiative of the lover as the most central claim of his analysis: "What are these requirements [of love]? In truth, they boil down to a single requirement from which all the others flow: to love first, to arrive ahead of the other in love."[7] It seems to me that the passage is best read as a stage in Marion's depiction of the erotic phenomenon. Although the isolation of the lover is later mitigated by the mutual crossing of gazes, the requirement that the lover act entirely without expectation of return or reciprocity is indeed an essential first step for Marion, as he reiterates in the interview with Arbib (RC, 193). And Marion is right to refuse a requirement of reciprocity in the loving relationship and to describe love primarily as a freely offered gift, yet neither of these aspects ought to lead to an elimination of the role of the other in this relationship to the point where the sole focus is on the choice of the lover.

Marion insists on the absolute importance of this initiative of the lover because, so he suggests, it individuates the self for the first time fully:

> I do not become myself when I simply think, doubt, or imagine, because others can think my thoughts, which in any case often do not concern me but, instead, the objects of my intentionalities; nor do I become myself when I will, desire, or hope, for I never know if I do so in the first person or only as the mask which hides—(and is propped up by) drives, passions, and needs that play within me, yet without me. But I become myself definitively each time and for as long as I, as lover, can love first. (EP, 76; PE, 125)

I become individuated in my acts as a lover and in my choice to love, because neither depends on other objects or on a reciprocal relationship. I gain assurance not of another's love, but of my own ability or decision to love. This assurance allows me to overcome my self-hatred and counters the "attack of vanity." By thus assuming what is "most proper to me," I am able to become truly myself and am no longer dependent on anything else to affirm my existence or my worthiness.[8] Basing himself on Marion's previous analyses of *capax/capacitas* in Descartes for his interpretation of the lover's capacity, Stephen Lewis explains that "the lover makes an act of the will in deciding to advance without pre-payment or guarantee; thus the advancing lover's decision is a free action, but it is not aimed at exercising a sovereign power over a field of objects. Instead, the decision to advance in love discloses an infinite human will that is both passive and active, one that seeks to participate in the other through reception of the other's gift of participation, rather than seeking to dominate the other through the exercise of a power or capability."[9] True love is generous abandonment and gift of self.[10]

This first love that has to be prior to any response, that is freely given as a gift (and that apparently speaks more of me than of the other), already seems to carry religious overtones. And, in fact, biblical imagery pervades the treatment. It is a love thoroughly kenotic in character, patterned on the infinite divine love for finite humanity.[11] Marion explicates what he calls "remarkable postures of love" by taking up the Pauline definitions of love from 1 Corinthians 13: The lover supports all and prepares everything for the beloved (EP, 85; PE, 138). The lover believes all and endures all with a kind of "sovereign power" that requires no response (EP, 86; PE, 139). The lover loves without sight and thus hopes all (EP, 87; PE, 140). Marion articulates this even more forcefully in his book on Augustine, *In the Self's Place,* where he is particularly interested in the discovery of the self. Love, he concludes, "makes me myself more than I make me myself, love is established as the ultimate condition for the possibility of the self" (SP, 271; LS, 365). Here also the decision to love comes first and is required for becoming a self: "Love weighs on myself like the sky at the horizon, not that it oppresses me with a lid of anxiety but because it discloses to me an opening that will never be closed again: the opening onto the unshirkable, absolute, inalienable, but still always undetermined, possibility of deciding to love, of having to love whatever comes, whatever I might want, and whether I want it or not" (SP, 271; LS, 366). As Stephen Lewis warns regarding *The Erotic Phenomenon:* "We run the risk of rushing past the fact that the ego when it decides to love loving discovers the truth of its nature."[12] Love is the condition of possibility for the self, the only way to "know" the self, the very creation of the self.

This love is not only self-emptying but also overpowering in its intensity. It abandons itself in complete commitment and profound vulnerability. Yet it is consistently the lover who makes the first move, who decides to love, and who prepares all conditions for intimacy to become possible. Marion insists on this precisely in order to avoid the need for reciprocity in love, but one wonders if any beloved would still be able to resist such powerful advances. Maybe this is an appropriate description of the incarnation, but is it also a good paradigm for all human love? Marion goes on to argue that my initiative as lover does not merely serve to individuate me but also the beloved. Yet even the distinction itself between "lover" and "beloved" appears to suggest the superiority of one and the dependence of the other.[13] It is always the "lover" who phenomenalizes the "beloved" and allows him or her to appear.[14] The next comparison highlights this even more clearly.

To Whom One Declares

This second (briefer) instance appears only a few pages after the first in the context of Marion's analysis of Don Juan as an example of the advance of the lover (EP, 80–82, 84–85; PE, 131–32, 133–35). Marion claims that "those to whom he declares his love, like those against whom he declares war (often the same people), appear in their increasingly extreme singularity" (EP, 82; PE, 134). The seducer especially exemplifies love in his or her abandonment and total commitment to the cause that is akin to that of the soldier. Both are passionately devoted to the "object" of their pursuit, which is thus highlighted in its singularity and specificity. Again the initiative of the lover (as the one who makes the declaration of love or war) and his or her complete dedication to the movement of eros are emphasized. Yet what Marion also highlights in this case is that the lover actually allows the phenomenon of the other to appear for the first time in the way in which a declaration of war singularizes the enemy.

Not only does my initiative as lover allow me to find myself, but it also becomes the condition for the individuation of the other. In the erotic reduction, the beloved appears for the first time as an individuated person and not merely as an object of my consciousness. This carries further the argument Marion makes in "The Intentionality of Love" (chapter 4 in *Prolegomena to Charity*).[15] Love individuates the other in a way that Lévinas's ethics cannot, because *any* other can appear as face and all faces equally require my response. The ethics of the face does not impose singularity or uniqueness in Marion's view (PC, 83–86; PaC, 103–106; EP, 101; PE, 161).[16] Love does. Marion argues that the lover allows the other to emerge and makes him or her visible through the erotic reduction: "The other is phenomenalized in the exact measure according to which the lover loves him or her and, as an Orpheus of phenomenality, tears him or her from indistinction and makes him or her emerge from the depths of the unseen" (EP, 80; PE, 130). Making something "emerge from the depths of the unseen," as I discuss in chapter 2, is an expression Marion generally uses in order to depict the work of an artist (especially in painting). Creativity means to make visible as a phenomenon what was before unseen.[17] Yet although the work of art is not an object (as Marion obviously wants to insist also about the beloved) but a saturated phenomenon—a bedazzling and incomprehensible experience—it still seems extremely problematic to imply that the lover "creates" the phenomenon of the beloved in a manner similar to the painter's creation of a work. Here the ambivalence of describing the new self as a "gifted" or quasi-genius, already examined in previous chapters, acquires another dimension.

And Marion continues to emphasize this parallel. Only the lover sees truly and allows the other to emerge: "The lover alone sees something else, a thing that no one other than he sees—that is, what is precisely no longer a thing, but, for the first time, just such an other, unique, individualized, henceforth torn from economy, detached from objectness, unveiled by the initiative of loving, arisen like a phenomenon to that point unseen" (EP, 80; PE, 131). The lover is the condition of possibility for the phenomenon of the beloved who appears on the horizon of the lover's consciousness. This seems to go beyond vulnerability and generosity to give the lover both power and control over the beloved, despite all Marion's affirmations of the contrary. Even if the beloved saturates or even explodes the screen of consciousness, the lover must first provide the screen and horizon that is being transgressed. If the lover allows the beloved to emerge, allows the beloved to become visible, and is like the painter who permits the invisible phenomenon to emerge, then this primacy includes at least a measure of mastery.

In *Prolegomena to Charity,* Marion describes this even more strongly: "Only charity (or however one would like to call it, if one is afraid to acknowledge its name) opens the space where the gaze of the other can shine forth. The other appears only if I gratuitously give him the space in which to appear . . . I must take from myself, in order to open the space where the other may appear" (PC, 166; not included in PaC). The lover seems to provide the entire context for love to become possible and for the beloved to emerge and become individuated. The beloved, and indeed the phenomenon of love, hence seem to depend on this prior choice of the lover (namely to engage in the act of love, to give him- or herself without expectation of reciprocity) and on the lover's preparation (the enacting of the advance). Although the lover has no expectation of love being returned, love is fully accomplished by the lover. Stressing this aspect of Marion's treatment, John Milbank posits that Marion has returned us entirely to a Cartesian subjectivity or even to a Hegelian account of complete closure. He contends that "this phenomenon [of the other] is only present for me by fiat of my will" and becomes a "voluntarist decisionism" that "exits phenomenology altogether."[18] Unfortunately, many of Milbank's claims are highly rhetorical and not worked out fully so that his criticism does not convince entirely.[19] It is clear, however, that Marion's account of the role of the lover implies fairly strong activity and not solely passivity.

And, in fact, quite a bit of this insistence on the initiative of the lover even likens him or her to God.[20] In *Prolegomena to Charity,* Marion compares the lover's initiative more explicitly to a divine one while also using the imagery of creativity: "It is up to me to set the stage for the other, not as an object that I hold under contract and whose play I thus direct, but as the uncontrollable, the unforeseeable, and the foreign stranger who will affect me, provoke me, and—possibly—love me. *Love of the other repeats creation through the same withdrawal wherein God opens,* to what is not, the right to be, and even the right to refuse Him" (PC, 167, emphasis added). The lover like God prepares all the conditions for love and loves indeed with the same sort of overwhelming power, albeit a kenotic kind of power. The imagery of painting therefore becomes loaded with a weightier creation, the divine one. Although Marion does not make the same connection explicit in *The Erotic Phenomenon,* he affirms later that God is the first and primary lover, and is therefore the one who precedes us and by whom we are always loved prior to our own loving another (EP, 222; PE, 341). We return to this later in the chapter.

Marion's employment of the figure of Don Juan in this context seems particularly unfortunate. Although he censures Don Juan's obsession with seduction, he praises him for his advance. He explains that the problem in this context is not that Juan advances in his desire to seduce, but rather that he breaks off too quickly and thus continually and obsessively repeats the movement with a new person. In true love, the lover would need to maintain the initiative more faithfully and more persistently toward the same person: "Don Juan does not love too much—on the contrary, he loves too little, too short of the mark, without impetus; he loses his advance. Don Juan loves too little, not because he desires too much, but because he does not desire enough, or desire long enough, or desire persistently enough" (EP, 85; PE, 137). Yet is there not something deeply problematic about seduction, apart from its lack of fidelity and its need for repetition? Is it only an issue of "too much" or "too little" in love, or does the *kind* of love matter, as well? Surely "advance" can here quickly become demanding and violent. The space to resist or reject this advance of the seducer seems to recede from view, especially as Marion calls for an even more persistent pursuit, ideally one that lasts to eternity.[21] Is persistence or eternity identical with the *quality* of the love? And not only does Marion take recourse to biblical imagery and theological language here, he also calls for such language in the discourse of the lovers, as we see in the context of a further comparison of love to war.

How One Declares

In this third passage, Marion points to the repetition of the imagery himself: "Once again, lovers declare love like one declares war: to say that one loves is equivalent to provoking it" (EP, 147; PE, 230). As in the previous occurrences, Marion wishes to stress the absolute and total commitment implied in one's declaration of love that is like one's total involvement in a war, yet he is particularly concerned with the *language* of love in this context. Like the *declaration* of war, the *declaration* of love is performative, not descriptive. In declaring my love (as in declaring war), I do not describe a state of affairs or investigate an object, but I engage in an activity to which I commit myself completely. Erotic language is performative or pragmatic in two ways. On the one hand, it does not really "say" anything, because it makes no statements of fact or description and often does not even make sense. It is therefore neither descriptive nor logical speech. On the other hand, it makes possible the actual "performing" of the activity: it excites the flesh and enables its reception, it invites the coming of the other, it commits the lover by an oath of fidelity. Like the declaration of war, it announces an incoming event and makes this activity possible, instead of describing something that has already happened.

Again, what Marion says about the language of love parallels what he has said in his earlier, more theological work about the language of prayer and praise. He has repeatedly employed the threefold Dionysian distinction of an affirmative (or kataphatic), a negative (or apophatic), and a third way, a hyperbolic way of praise, which is not prescriptive or descriptive but purely performative.[22] In the liturgical acts of prayer and praise, the person praying approaches God and allows himor herself to be envisaged by the divine, to become open to the crossing of gazes that happens within this act of prayer. The performative language of prayer therefore accomplishes a relationship similar to that between lover and beloved. It individuates the self in a parallel fashion to what we saw in the previous section. Marion speaks of the activity of prayer the most fully in *The Crossing of the Visible*. His analyses of art or painting in general, of the contemporary status of the image in our media-centered world, and finally of the significance of the religious icon center around a rethinking of the subject as a kenotic self that is radically envisaged by another (namely God) and receives true identity as a person only from the one who holds it in this divine gaze.[23] The icon initiates a liturgical exchange in which "the gaze looks at the one who, in prayer [*orant*], raises his gaze toward the icon" (CV 20; CdV, 42). Distance must always be preserved here, for the "crossing of gazes" is a kind of participation in a dance, not a simple amalgamation or direct identification.

This is a paradox of self-giving where I abandon myself to the gaze who envisions me. The emphasis on abandonment and self-sacrifice is here connected with a recovery of personhood and self-identity. In contrast to contemporary culture, where I lose all identity because I am constituted only by the gazes that evaluate me as an image on a screen, where I become an idol, fully seen and fully determined by the tyranny of the other's gaze, and where all invisibility is eliminated, the icon makes possible a recovery of self through vulnerability and devotion to God. The icon thus invites veneration, welcomes the crossing of gazes instead of aiming at control or possession. The self is dispossessed, dislocated, and unsettled in prayer as it is in the erotic experience. Kenosis means not to lose one's face before the other but to expose oneself to the other's gaze in a fashion parallel to the vulnerable exposure of my flesh in the intimacy of love. Only such prayerful exposure ultimately makes a communion of love that preserves distance possible.

Hence, even in this analysis of prayer, Marion identifies the encounter as a move-ment of love or charity. Prayer or praise is the performative language that accom-plishes the loving relationship. I return to this parallel with prayer in chapter 6.

Prayer, then, neither describes nor denies description, but it performs an ac-tivity. Like the performative language of love, praise and prayer are not logical, at times not even coherent. And like love, prayer opens me to the coming of another, commits me to a certain kind of life. This similarity would not be troubling if it was a mere parallel: prayer is one example of performative language, and the dec-laration of love is another. Yet Marion actually insists in his analysis of eros that the language of mystical theology is absolutely essential for an appropriate expres-sion of erotic love and as the culmination of such talk. The erotic word "must *in-evitably* borrow words from mystical theology" (EP, 149; PE, 233; emphasis added). "Come," the word of the eschatological future of erotic reduction, he points out, is also the final word of Revelation. The erotic word *must* employ "the language of spiritual union of man with God" (EP, 149; PE, 233). The excess that is repre-sented by the excitement of the flesh overflows in a discourse that for Marion is al-ways that of mystical theology. The language of love *must* express itself in a mysti-cal and quasi-divine discourse. Marion even explicitly likens the three vocabularies for love he has outlined (obscene, infantile, mystical) to the three ways of Diony-sian theology (EP, 149; PE, 233). Erotic language must not only employ the vo-cabulary of mystical theology, but any terminology it does employ finds its place in a relationship of discourse patterned on theological affirmations about God. Of course erotic imagery and language have indeed been employed in mysticism and theological language has been used to describe sexuality. Yet to insist that erotic language must *of necessity* be theological and that chastity is "the erotic virtue par excellence" (EP, 183; PE, 283) seems too extreme.[24]

Within *The Erotic Phenomenon,* Marion mentions this "necessary" connection of erotic language to mystical theology only briefly. He explores the parallel be-tween the two in greater detail in chapter 6 of *The Visible and the Revealed,* "What Cannot Be Said: Apophasis and the Discourse of Love," where he analyzes the nature of erotic statements in greater detail. He contends that "I love you!" does not "say something about something" (a locutionary act that is signifying or pred-icative) or even "performs what it says" (an illocutionary or performative act), but that it "does what it says to someone."[25] He identifies this as a "perlocution-ary" act, namely, one that intends to have an effect on the interlocutor, although it need not necessarily accomplish this intent. Such effects might include provoca-tion, intrigue, compulsion, or seduction and are concerned more with the person to whom one speaks than with either the utterance or the speaker.

After identifying erotic language as such a perlocutionary act, Marion goes on to analyze what he sees as its "three paths," which correspond again to the three paths of mystical theology (VR, 101–104, 112–16; VeR, 119–23, 135–39). He spells out an affirmative, apophatic, and hyperbolic path in erotic dialogue, employing the example of Clélia's declaration of love to Fabrice in Stendahl's *The Charterhouse of Parma*. Although "I love you!" cannot be verified (it is neither locutionary nor illocutionary), it does affirm the effect that it intends to produce, namely to individualize the other and to open the space for a response. This affirmation leads to negation in that the speaker must listen to the effect the speech act has produced, knowing that no clear response is possible at this moment. There is always a temporal delay in an answer, and it is always fraught with ambiguity. The affirmation of love hence must ceaselessly be repeated in a final *hyperbolic* movement: "I keep saying and repeating 'I love you!' precisely because, on the one hand, I cannot guarantee it, and, on the other hand, I cannot give up trying. Short of answering the question, 'Do you love me?' I repeat the perlocutionary act that instigates it, 'I love you!' It is neither a question of kataphasis, nor of apophasis, but rather of a temporalizing language strategy, a repetition that affirms nothing, negates nothing, but that keeps alive a dialogic situation" (VR, 115; VeR, 139). One may wonder whether there is a parallel here with the need to see a great painting again and again.

Marion concludes the chapter on apophasis by linking this erotic discourse explicitly to mystical theology and by insisting on their univocality (VR, 116–18; VeR, 140–42). He denies the suggestion that the two discourses are merely parallel but wants to establish a deeper connection between them. Both types of language "mobilize three types of names" for the beloved (or God) and do so in a parallel fashion. He employs the story of Christ's threefold question to Peter whether he loves him to show that its three stages exemplify the path of mystical theology and of erotic discourse. Consequently, "between God and man everything remains ambiguous except, precisely, love" (VR, 118; VeR, 142). Already the theological nature of this phenomenological exercise has become apparent. This is made even more explicit in a final comparison of love to war in *The Erotic Phenomenon*.[26]

Why One Declares

This final instance occurs when Marion is speaking of the need for a third to witness to love, while simultaneously pointing out the insufficiency of the child to do so. The fact that the child will grow and no longer witness to the couple's love he sees as further consolidating the impossibility of reciprocity between lovers. He emphasizes this: "The lover enters in advance, like one enters into war or into religious life—by burning his ships behind him, and without hope (or the least desire) to return to the balance of exchange" (EP, 204; PE, 315). This comparison is again intended to stress the complete and total character of love and the abandon with which one engages in it, one that allows no reflection or reversal. Yet, in this case, religion is included in the comparison, making explicit what has become clear in the preceding: the univocity between divine and human love.

Indeed, Marion insists repeatedly on the need for a univocal description of love. He outlines how important it is that anything having to do with love, including the moves of seduction and betrayal, can be described with the same paradigm. Purely carnal desire, friendship, affection between parents and children, erotic intimacy, religious or mystical union with God—all must display a similar pattern. After comparing the most extreme cases (of desire for money or drugs with love for a human being or God), Marion concludes that there can be no equivocity in love: either erotic reduction is practiced fully and in the same fashion, or there is no love involved in the desire at all (EP, 217; PE, 335).[27] For Marion, all types of love function in the same manner, even erotic love and friendship. Friendship does not "formally" differ from erotic love except in "the tonality of its figures" (EP, 218; PE, 336). One may well wonder why all these instances of love should be the same. Are they really mere modulations of the same phenomenon? It appears inadequate, for example, to describe the affection of a young girl for her grandmother as a mere immature stage of a later development of deeper erotic sentiments and sexual urges. Nor does it seem appropriate to describe friendship, as Marion implies, as erotic love minus orgasm.[28] The fact that there is no "object" involved or that neither is concerned with possession or economy is surely not enough to indicate the phenomenological identity of the various figures.

Yet, to show the univocal character of love is one of Marion's explicit goals from the very beginning of the treatment. Even in his introduction, he claims that to distinguish between different kinds or modes of love is to compromise its unique character: "A serious concept of love distinguishes itself by its unity, or rather by its power to keep together significations that noneerotic thought cuts apart, stretches, and tears according to the measure of its prejudices. The entire effort consists in maintaining for as long a time as possible the indivisibility of the single garment of love. . . . Univocal, love is only told in *one way*" (EP, 5; PE, 14–15). One ought not to oppose eros and charity or even eros and agape to each other. A true concept of love, for Marion, must of necessity be a univocal one. The apparently so strict distinction between his earlier theological reflections on charity and his present phenomenological treatment of eros, then, is far from clear. The insistence on love's univocal character and the rejection of any distinctions between eros and charity / agape make evident that Marion does seek to appropriate his theological insights for his phenomenological treatment, or at the very least that he wants to guide the phenomenological consideration back to theological reflection. Indeed, he says that "theology knows what love is all about" but is unable to "render justice" to the phenomenality of passion (EP, 1; PE, 10).

This connection becomes even more explicit in the final paragraphs of *The Erotic Phenomenon*, where Marion examines the traditional distinction between human eros and divine agape and rejects it, as true human love does not possess the other (and thus is like agape) and as God's desire is as strong as any human eros (and thus qualifies as erotic). He concludes that God loves in the same way that we do and performs the erotic reduction in a parallel fashion to us: "God practices the logic of the erotic reduction as we do, with us, according to the same rite and following the same rhythm as us, to the point where we can even ask ourselves if we do not learn it from him, and no one else. God loves in the same way we do" (EP, 222; PE, 341). All love then ultimately functions in an identical fashion for Marion. The various aspects of eros that he has outlined, apply to all human beings and to God in the same way. Erotic intimacy is an indication of divine agape. And God's love provides the blueprint for any truly loving human relationship.

This is of course also something Marion has argued in his earlier theological work. In an article on the ascension, Marion depicts the relationship between the disciples and Christ as the paradigm for a self that is related in total abandonment and love to God.[29] The disciples take on the role and persona of Christ. Christ was the first to measure the divine distance successfully and to do so as a human being. To assume the role of Christ is to be able to engage in the play of distance with right measure and to recognize that it is a game of charity that is played only with the measure of love. The disciples (then and now) must live out this new vision of charity by playing the role of Christ in mutual love, as if it were a performance in a theater that they must continually reinvent (like a *commedia dell'arte*): "Distance allows the disciples to become not servants but friends, not spectators but actors of the redemptive and revelatory action of Christ. They themselves occupy the place, the role, and the charge of Christ" (PC, 145; PaC, 171). To instantiate love truly is to become like Christ, maybe even to become divine.[30]

Marion has pursued this argument in greater detail in *In the Self's Place,* his interpretation of Augustine's *Confessions,* in which love is a central topic, and he also argues again explicitly for its univocity. Marion portrays Augustine as delineating many of the same moves he has explicated in more general terms in *The Erotic Phenomenon.* He argues that "there is nothing optional or facultative about love; it predestines us absolutely (*schlechthin*), with an irrecusable, inexcusable, and irremediable possibility. All that's left is to decide how and what to love" (SP, 272; LS, 367). Marion explicitly connects self-love, love of the (human) other, and love of God, arguing that these display an essential univocity and only differ in respect to modes: "Such a transcendental determination of love implies that, formally at least, it is put into practice in the same way and according to the same logic, however different its object and occasions appear. Whatever I love, I always love for the same reasons and in the same fashion, which vary no more than love itself ever ceases to love—*dilectio vacare non potest*" (SP, 272; LS, 367). Marion is certain that Augustine's conception of love is entirely univocal and rejects Nygren's interpretation in the strongest terms, which he calls "a groundless and insignificant polemic." Instead, "love remains univocal in the role of transcendental horizon all the while being perfectly capable of being distinguished in different modes" (SP, 275; LS, 371).[31] Marion does not explain in this context how he conceives of the difference between a "transcendental horizon" and "modes," but primarily shows how Augustine's apparent distinction and even opposition between different loves is to be read as affirming a univocal claim about all love. Just as Augustine's two cities do not differ in their nature (given by God and hence good) but only in their respective wills, so love is essentially the same but can become perverted.

Love of neighbor and love of God are intimately linked because one is found in and made possible by the other: "Therefore, it's not a question of two parallel or opposed loves but of two modes of the same love: creatures, myself or my brother, can therefore be loved, and even loved *with enjoyment,* provided that they come to be loved *in* the enjoyment of God: the *propter Deum* (which should be understood more as *in view of God* rather than as *with God as the motivation*) becomes *in Deo,* a place and the place for all enjoyment, the enjoyment of God and therefore in it of every other thing" (SP, 277; LS, 273; original emphasis). It is not the nature of love that is different, but only its mode of expression. Marion explicates this in terms of three paradoxa correlating to what are often thought to be three types of love: love of self, of the neighbor, and of God. None of them contradict each other, but one always loves oneself and others *within* one's love for God. Love for the neighbor is an instance of love for God. The plurality of loving expressions all "articulate the singular playing field of love" (SP, 281; LS, 379). Charity comes to me and gives me my place by excluding the world. I "am" only where I love (SP, 282; LS, 380).

Thus, finally, not only do all loves proceed in a parallel manner, but for Marion, all erotic love ultimately appears to drown in divine agape. One loves authentically only when one loves like God in an abundant, self-giving kenosis. Human love and divine love are exactly parallel. The experience of love is always univocal and the same discourse must be used to describe them. As we have already seen, the initiative of the lover seems to parallel the divine initiative. The arising of the other parallels a kind of creation. The language to describe this encounter is that of mystical theology. And so Marion concludes his entire treatment of the erotic phenomenon by making explicit what has been implicit all along—that divine love is the origin and culmination of all human loves:

> When God loves (and indeed he never ceases to love), he simply loves infinitely better than we do. He loves to perfection, without a fault, without an error, from beginning to end. He loves first and last. He loves like no one else. In the end, I not only discover that another was loving me before I loved, and thus that this other already played the lover before me (§ 41), but above all I discover that this first lover, from the very beginning, is named God. . . . God precedes and tran-

scends us, but first and above all in the fact that he loves us infinitely better than we love, and than we love him. God surpasses us as the best lover. (EP, 222; PE, 341–42)

God is the only true lover. All human love is authentic only as it approaches the character and direction of this divine love. All humans must consider themselves loved by God before they are truly capable of love. Ultimately, their love becomes a mere repetition of the divine one. God enables, sustains, and perfects all human love.[32] While this might be a convincing *theological* account of love, it seems rather problematic as a *philosophical* analysis of eros.[33] Despite all of Marion's ground-breaking work on the erotic phenomenon and at times beautiful descriptions of its various aspects, this love seems too overwhelming. A love initiated by an absolutely committed lover who prepares all conditions for the beloved and declares this love in a divine fiat—such love really does seem to strike the bedazzled beloved like a "declaration of war."

Degrees of Love

Even without the strong parallels to divine love, the emphasis on violence and the absolute nature of love seems problematic. Should it not be possible to distinguish between kinds of love: the love between parent and child, between friends, between romantic lovers (maybe even between homosexual and heterosexual love),[34] between humans and other animals, the love of certain pursuits or activities, and so forth? It is not clear that these are really only different "modes" of what is fundamentally the same. Rather, they appear as different *kinds* of loves with some areas of overlap, with certain similarities, but also with important distinctions and differences. Love also does not manifest itself as equally absolute in all of these instances. Phenomenology ought to be able to explore these different experiences in a way that enables meaningful description, which includes and requires distinctions and comparisons, if it is to be specific to the particular experience examined. Even if love always requires some sort of strong commitment—this seems the most essential feature of love for Marion—one might still wonder whether the *kind* or *nature* of commitment or attachment in all these phenomena is identical. Is not the love of a child for the parent different in its nature from that of two friends who enjoy the same hobby?

Furthermore, it seems evident that love can, in fact, increase and decrease. Surely it does not qualify as love only when it is total and absolute. This is no longer a question about types or kinds of love, but about degrees within the same sort of love. Can one not learn to love, starting with a fairly minimal degree and growing to higher intensity of attachment? Part of the problem in the lack of stability of relationships in contemporary Western society seems to be precisely the ways in which love is regarded in extreme and absolute terms, which see "falling in love" as the kind of experience that sweeps one completely off one's feet in an instant and trumps all other commitments. It might be more profitable to identify stages in love and to acknowledge that the phenomenon of love is experienced in many different degrees of saturation. If the phenomenon of love really appeared only when it is a complete and total commitment, utterly selfless and without any expectation of reciprocity whatsoever, it would cease to be a phenomenon actually experienced. Love in this "perfect" sense does not occur or occurs only rarely. Maybe Marion merely wants to paint such love as a limit-experience, as the ideal toward which we strive. Yet if that were the case it would need to be stated much more clearly, otherwise the *phenomenon* of love disappears entirely. This is not to argue, as Milbank does, that love always requires reciprocity.[35] It is merely to wonder whether the excessive and utterly kenotic phenomenon that Marion depicts can actually ever become a phenomenon in the sense of a lived experience.

One may also wonder whether this absolute and excessive account of love really leaves room for a refusal. Marion affirms repeatedly that it does. The kenotic nature of this love is heightened precisely because it does not expect a response yet always knows that it can be rejected. Marion's consistent refusal of reciprocity in his account of love is in accordance with this. Reciprocity would rely on an expectation of response and on an economic exchange where my gifts must be returned in kind and where my loving devotion will naturally produce a response. It is consistent with Marion's account to reject such reciprocity. Yet, while love surely should not be reduced to some sort of reciprocal exchange, one wonders to what extent the declaration of love in Marion's treatment really leaves the response completely free. If the declaration of love is like a declaration of war, can I still maintain a neutral stance? Marion repeatedly emphasizes that my love is meant to have an effect on the other. Can I then remain unaffected? If the lover truly provides all conditions for the beloved's response and if the lover loves with God's boundlessly self-giving love, must not the beloved be so stunned, so overwhelmed, so deeply affected, that the freedom of the response is already fundamentally compromised? And is it still the kind of self-sacrificing love it desires to be, if it has curtailed the other's freedom? Has the other not already been shaped to some extent in my image of him or her, my vision of the beloved?

In fact, Marion's account of love has been criticized in several of these respects. In his own development of a phenomenology of marriage, rooted in the recognition of the "organicity" of our flesh, Emmanuel Falque disagrees with Marion's emphasis on the univocity of love and seeks to draw distinctions between different types of love.[36] Romano, as already mentioned, also feels uncomfortable with the univocal approach. He suggests that Marion achieves his coherent account only at the expense of defining love very narrowly and simply refusing to call anything love that does not fit that definition; Marion's argument hence becomes somewhat circular.[37] He also wonders about the coherence of an erotic *reduction* in Marion's sense, which does not seem to correspond to what Husserl understands by reduction, because it is too particular and it is unclear what is actually being reduced. The internal logos or rationality of love that Marion wants to show, following Pascal, therefore focuses almost exclusively on a refusal of reciprocity in love, which is also the central presupposition.[38] Finally, he objects to Marion's exclusion of being or metaphysics from the phenomenon of love and insists that the existence (or "being") of the other, at least in memory or anticipation, *does* matter to our ability to love the other.[39] Similarly, Robyn Horner does not think that Marion has overcome metaphysical accounts of intersubjectivity as successfully as he claims. She also feels uncomfortable with his references to God as supreme lover at the end of *The Erotic Phenomenon*.

Many of these concerns and objections could be allayed with a more nuanced and more hermeneutic account of love. And to argue for degrees and distinctions in phenomenological descriptions or analyses of love is not to say that love does not appear, at least some of the time, as a saturated phenomenon, or that it is not, at least on occasion, experienced as overwhelming and excessive. Nor does it imply that it is completely false to demand that love be selfless and generous and not count on a response. Not at all. Rather, what is problematic in Marion's treatment is the fact that this becomes the *sole* way of depicting love and that he requires that *all* love appear and be depicted in this fashion. It is the complete alignment of love with violence and absoluteness that is unsettling, not the fact that love can on occasion appear violent or absolute. Yet surely when it appears as violent, that should serve as occasion not for praise but for critique or correction or safety measures. Marion's univocal definition of love makes a hermeneutic judgment: it defines love in one particular fashion, namely as utterly kenotic and concerned solely with the other. It simply refuses the name "love" for any other, more totalizing or at least problematic versions of "love," such as desire or seduction, where the line between love and violence is much less clear. Surely the relationship of love to violence and even hatred is considerably more complicated than this.

Indeed, the phenomenon of love usually appears in a much more "mixed" version where desire and need and self-sacrifice and attraction all play a role to a larger or lesser extent and cannot be neatly divided from each other. Motives are notoriously difficult to identify and distinguish, and this is particularly true in the phenomenon of love, which rarely if ever appears in the purified and utterly selfless fashion Marion employs as the paradigm. While a completely selfless and selfgiving love may well be the ideal for some instances of love, it is not helpful to posit this as the *only* true love. If we are to investigate love phenomenologically, there must also be a place for a description of first attraction, of a child's maybe immature but still genuine expressions of love, of an elderly couple's devotion to each other that may be colored and burdened but also deepened by illness and impending death. What exactly do all these versions of love have in common that qualifies them as the same type of love? Is it merely the kenotic excess that Marion claims characterizes all of them? That seems to imply that the considerably more "selfish" love of a young child is not love at all. And if indeed it is possible to speak of "degrees" of love, it also does not seem correct to depict these degrees as organized in a simple linear fashion where one expression is at the bottom of the scale of love and the other (erotic intimacy? divine love?) at the top. Yet for Marion, it appears as if the only true and authentic love is a divine love that completely empties itself and ultimately dies for the other. No other love matters except inasmuch as it approaches and arises from this divine paradigm in some fashion.

And all this is surprising in light of Marion's fundamental claim, especially in his work on Descartes, but also in *Idol and Distance* and various other more theologically oriented pieces, that *any* univocal language of God is inappropriate and ultimately blasphemous.[40] He condemns first Galileo, Kepler, Mersenne, and Bérulle, and later Descartes, for employing the same kind of language for both divine and human.[41] In the case of Kepler, Galileo, and Mersenne, this is epistemological univocity, which claims that God knows in the same way we do with the same mathematical parameters. In the case of Bérulle and some others, this is ontological univocity, which applies the language of being to God in the same way as to humans.[42] In the case of Descartes, this is causal univocity by defining God as *causa sui* and making the divine subject to human notions of causality. Marion condemns all of these moves that establish parallels or connections between divine and human as deeply problematic because they do not uphold the distance and difference between divine and human. The same concern motivates *Idol and Distance,* where any talk about God that eliminates distance is judged idolatrous. No univocal talk about divine and human is ever acceptable. Why should the language of *love* escape this rejection of univocal language? What makes it different from these other discourses?

The difference for Marion lies in the nature of love: Unlike being and knowledge, love is self-emptying, gives itself as pure gift, does not impose any limits or seek to control. Most importantly, it cannot be measured or defined, hence the univocity here actually provides no concrete content. Already in *God without Being,* Marion had claimed that love does not make the same totalizing moves as being (GWB, 102, 196–97; DSL, 148, 275–77).[43] It is a more appropriate name for God, because it does not define the divine or limit it to a concept, but rather designates self-emptying and overflowing abundance: "In distance, only *agape* can place into givenness every thing on earth, in hell and in heaven, because only *agape* is, by definition, not known, is not—but gives (itself)" (GWB, 106, trans. mod.; DSL, 153). Love is a gift and therefore by definition is unlimited and overflowing. In that respect, it is utterly unlike other kinds of language or other types of knowledge. Love, then, occupies a privileged place in Marion's work as the only move that can escape from the idolatrous and blasphemous metaphysical approaches he consistently condemns. Love is the answer to all the phenomenological aporiae Marion uncovers in Husserl and Heidegger or in the phenomenological tradition more generally. It provides us with the sole appropriate name for the divine, with the only nonmetaphysical approach to the self, the only possibility for genuine individuation of the other, and the best parameter of knowing as an alternative to Cartesian certainty.

Marion has spoken of love as an alternative way of knowing throughout his work. Already in his early texts he proposes it as Christian philosophy's most important contribution to the "rationality" of the world (PC, 160–69; VR, 74–79, 151–54; VeR, 111–17; CpV, 25–29).[44] Repeatedly, he hints that love is a kind of practical knowing (in Kant's sense) that pursues its own form of reason (appealing especially to Pascal) more appropriate to the phenomena (CN, 290–91). In his book on Augustine, he puts this explicitly in the language of the saturated phenomenon: "Hence the problematic of bedazzlement, which can in fact be borne only by the courage, endurance, and suffering of love, arises each time that the phenomena to see pass beyond the common use of the faculties. Love must then open (and keep open) the mind to truth, simply because in the case of divine things, it is an issue par excellence of the truth of the saturated phenomenon—'invisable,' unbearable, irregardable, and absolute. But the same love (or the same hatred) should intervene for every other type of saturated phenomenon." (SP, 135; LS, 192). Already earlier in the book he had explicated a strong link between knowing and loving, in this case in respect to knowledge of the self: "More intimate to me than any equality of the self to itself thus turns out to be the distance of the lover to what he loves. Whoever travels this distance knows himself because he knows the other *self* who resembles him more than himself—a self more him than he himself" (SP, 96; LS, 142; original emphasis). The Augustinian self emerges as both lover and beloved, receiving itself as lover via the love first given to it by God. For Augustine, love and wisdom are united; the truth is reached through loving. Augustine performs an "erotic reduction, in which truth can be known inasmuch as it is loved" (SP, 143; LS, 202). Indeed, for Augustine on Marion's reading, love is higher than the will and determines it: "The will therefore follows what I love, and what I love precedes my will. . . . The radicalization of the will into love reverses the advance—the intentional advance of the *I* toward the object of its willing reverts into the delay of the *I* with regard to the place of that which the self loves. . . . As much as I will be an intentional advance, so much I love in the delay of desire" (SP, 184; LS, 254; original emphasis). Marion reiterates this displacement of the will by the passions that speak of the self's passivity and receptivity in his analysis of Descartes's late text, *The Passions of the Soul*. Consistently, this commitment to love emerges as a form of knowing phenomena that cannot be "grasped" via certainty because that kind of comprehension would miss or even destroy them.

Not only is this posited as a special type of knowledge it also is the stance that most fundamentally characterizes the receptivity of the one who responds to the saturated phenomenon. The *adonné* really is the one who loves the saturated phenomenon, who is utterly devoted to it, who becomes addicted to it. This includes all the connotations of desire, devotion, erotic attachment, and kenotic self-emptying Marion has outlined in *The Erotic Phenomenon* and his analysis of Augustine. Joeri Schrijvers rightly points that "one single theological model governs both the thinking of distance and the later notion of phenomenological givenness: revelation as God's full, definitive, unique and universal abandonment to the world through love."[45] For Schrijvers this applies especially to Marion's account of the self: "Love is then the answer to the question of just how we should abandon or give—*s'abandonner* or *s'adonner*—ourselves (over) to that which has always and already been given to us and has advanced towards us. The only appropriate response for the human being to God's gift is indeed to abandon ourselves to God with the very same love that Christ did."[46] This is also why this is neither a solely passive nor a solely active stance, why even that distinction misses a significant part of what is at stake here. Loving receptivity, total devotion, and complete openness are in some sense utterly passive, completely given over to the other, and yet they are also eminently active, wholly directed toward the phenomenon, deeply engaged with it. Stephen Lewis is right to point to the important role of "capacity" in this context and to see it linked to the will.[47] Both are indeed always at work in Marion's explications of the *adonné*, as his discussions of Augustine and Descartes highlight even more forcefully.

Does this imply, however, that love has given up on other kinds of rationality? Marion often portrays this alternative kind of knowing as incommensurable with philosophical (or "metaphysical") kinds of knowing as "certainty." Charity belongs to a higher order that cannot be seen or experienced from the order of certainty (VR, 77; VeR, 114; MP, 306–345; PM, 325–69; RC, 172, 186). The two are completely incompatible. At other times, Marion affirms more continuity between "secular" or even "scientific" knowledge and the rationality of Christian faith or theology. Both include elements of belief and elements of reason (VR, 145; CpV, 17). If the "rationality" of love or charity really were completely incommensurable with all other kinds of knowing, it is hard to see how such love can still be said to constitute a form of reason or knowing. Some continuity or overlap must be permissible, and hence conversation between the kinds of knowing must be possible. Any such conversation, especially when there is a fear about the confusion of languages and forms of knowing, requires hermeneutic tools. Marion's account of love, then, requires hermeneutic discernment on several levels: to articulate the various modes of love, to distinguish love from violence and to recognize "genuine" love, and to relate the rationality of love to other kinds of knowing or comprehending.

Love and Hermeneutics

Love requires interpretation in order to appear as love. I have to interpret the other's claim to love me and judge by the actions and possibly the gifts that accompany it. Is this a manipulative relationship where the other is trying to gain some benefit or take advantage of me? Is this person insecure, in need of affirmation, maybe hoping that I will care for him or her and provide solace for previous disappointing experiences? Is the other genuinely interested in me, but seeking a relationship of intellectual exchange or mutual entertainment or sharing in a pleasant activity together? Or is the other romantically attracted to me and this attraction one of desire or the kind of selfless giving Marion advocates? It is not necessarily easy to recognize the lover's advance as such or even possible to discover the various motives involved. Interpretation is hence always required. And when speaking of such a complex phenomenon as love, it seems that hermeneutic discernment is particularly necessary. Due to the intense level of emotion often involved in love, it is especially prone to abuse and manipulation. So many instances of violence—from spousal battering to child abuse to marital rape and various kinds of emotional manipulation—are at least on some level connected to various facets of love, devotion, and desire, in ways that cannot always be easily separated from each other. Why does a battered spouse stay with a violent partner? Why does an abused child still cling to the abusive parent? Although these are extreme cases, they show the complicated ways in which love and violence are often intimately connected and defy easy description. This may suggest that Marion's link between love and war is telling in ways he does not intend. While he employs the imagery of war to show love's pure and total commitment, the violence that often accompanies love shows its impurity and contamination by other motives and nonloving practices. Love is rarely the purified total kenosis Marion depicts. Interpretation is always required to recognize and identify love.[48]

Beyond the hermeneutic discernment that seeks to interpret the phenomenon of love as it occurs or has been experienced, some preparatory hermeneutic context might in fact also be necessary to experience love. Love is learned by imitation, by seeing other people treat each other in loving ways and through being loved oneself. I am not entirely sure that one must really always love first without expecting any love in return, as Marion insists, or that this is even possible. Research with children who suffer from reactive attachment disorder because of neglect or abuse has shown that lack of love can have dire consequences and indeed can make certain people incapable of love.[49] If children are not loved and their needs not met on a consistent or reliable basis, they grow to distrust the world and the people around them and become incapable of reaching out to others or even accepting help from others. Children who have never been loved and have never learned to attach to a person are incapable of love without significant interventive help—and often not even then. Maybe we do actually need to be loved before we can love in return and can offer the kind of selfless love Marion depicts.

Furthermore, how we understand and practice love is prepared to a large extent through our environment and context. We neither experience nor offer love in a vacuum. Even Marion's own description of love is clearly determined hermeneutically by a Christian context of self-emptying love of incarnate kenosis. We find his account convincing if we have been habituated to recognize such selfless love as the highest instance of love, to see agape as superior to eros. This we have learned from the Christian tradition, from the Johannine epistles, from Augustine, Bernard of Clairvaux, and many others. The parallels to Marion's theological assumptions in his account of love are telling. They show precisely that his vision of love is informed by a particular theological context that thinks of God's incarnate and kenotic love as the pattern for true love. To affirm that our love is like that of God who loves with complete abandon and without any requirement of return, who gives selflessly to the point of death and never demands that such love be requited, is to employ the hermeneutic context of Christian charity as the paradigm for love. This may be a useful and enlightening paradigm, but it is grounded in a particular hermeneutic context that interprets love in a specific fashion.

Finally, if love truly is a kind of knowing, a predisposition for approaching and understanding saturated phenomena, as Marion frequently suggests, it is itself a hermeneutic approach. As Horner affirms, "love in some manner functions as a hermeneutic principle, and we cannot underestimate the importance of this point in the context of Marion's theology. . . . Love is not only a way of seeing, but a will to see in a particular way."[50] Love is the interpretive lens that enables us to recognize a phenomenon as saturated and to bear its impact. Love is the hermeneutic preparation and the training for such phenomena, the language that allows us to depict them adequately. Marion's frequent judgments about appropriate and inappropriate reception of saturated phenomena, of being able to "see" their bedazzling splendor rather than remaining blind to them, rely on the insight that loving devotion enables us to see in a new way and to know more authentically. This loving knowing is precisely the hermeneutic dimension that enables such seeing or knowing. Preparation or "training" for receiving saturated phenomena engage in a hermeneutic circle of increasing openness to the given—but always against the horizon of previous exposure to such phenomena or comparison with other phenomena. If love is really a way of "knowing" the phenomenon, it cannot come completely out of nowhere, falling upon us without any preparation whatsoever. Yes, "falling in love" may begin with a singular glance, a sudden and utterly surprising encounter. Yet even on Marin's own terms, "genuine" love requires fidelity and commitment, sustaining the advance, engaging with one another, possibly even "without end" and unto infinity (IE, 127; DS, 153).[51] This lifetime of growth in love provides the hermeneutic context for offering, recognizing, and responding to it. Love, then, requires both hermeneutic context and hermeneutic discernment. Hermeneutics is involved at all kinds and levels of love. Love is not recognized as love until it is prepared via loving context and interpreted as loving gesture. Both are necessary for love to make an appearance and to be "known." In that case, while love may still be experienced as overwhelming and rich in manifold ways, it no longer need have the kind of violence that strikes me as a declaration of war and where I no longer have any possible response but utter submission.

FIVE

Gift and Sacrifice

Marion is maybe most well-known as a philosopher of the gift. Already in a widely read article, titled "Sketch of a Phenomenological Concept of the Gift," he attempted to illuminate the topic of the gift.[1] His major phenomenological work, *Being Given*, explores phenomenology as fundamentally about "givenness" and includes an entire section titled "The Gift" (part 2). He engaged in extensive debates with Jacques Derrida on the gift and economy, especially in the highly publicized debate of the 1997 conference "Religion and Postmodernism I: God, the Gift, and Postmodernism."[2] In the English-speaking world, this debate (somewhat unfortunately) dominated the early secondary literature on Marion.[3] Only slowly have other aspects of his work also been recognized. Yet in his 2010 books *Certitudes négatives* and *Le croire pour le voir*, Marion returns to the topic of the gift, indicating that this question continues to be important for his thought.[4] The gift is central to *Certitudes négatives*, occupying two of the five chapters. In these chapters, as in *Being Given*, the gift figures as a significant phenomenological figure within the exposition of larger phenomenological claims. The theme of the gift also appears repeatedly in the more theological work, *Le croire pour le voir*, including one essay entirely devoted to the gift, with the title "La reconnaissance du Don" ("The Recognition of the Gift"). Finally, a 2011 English collection, edited and translated by Stephen Lewis, brings together four pieces on the gift under the title *The Reason of the Gift*.[5] Three of the pieces in that book, which exists only in English, are now part of Marion's 2012 *Figures de Phénoménologie*, while the final piece is an earlier version of one of the chapters in *Certitudes négatives*.

This debate over the gift originates in Marcel Mauss's important sociological study of gift giving in various societies, in which he describes how the gift ultimately functions as an economic exchange, deeply marked by obligation and reciprocity.[6] Its second impetus was Derrida's philosophical commentary on Mauss's insights in his *Given Time*, where he argues that a purely gratuitous gift is impossible.[7] Gratuity—that is, a free giving not marked by obligation or economic exchange—is central to the gift. Yet, as Mauss had shown and as Derrida articulates philosophically, all our gifts immediately enter this horizon of exchange, where they are marked by expectation, reciprocity, and obligation. In *The Gift of Death*, Derrida continues this discussion by analyzing Patočka's discussion of sacrifice and Kierkegaard's portrayal of the sacrifice of Isaac and the connotations of "mystery" and "secrecy" always involved in these religious discussions of sacrifice.[8] He also remarks extensively on the "heavenly economy" established in the Matthean version of the Sermon on the Mount, where Christ counsels "secret giving" while promising reward for it in heaven. Marion's earliest discussions of the gift respond to Derrida's early text on the impossibility of the gift and try to show that a phenomenological concept of the gift is possible. His more recent treatments develop the phenomenality of the gift further and also speak of sacrifice in light of Derrida's treatment in the later text.

One may then ask why Marion returns to the earlier debate in these more recent texts. Is his thought marked by a significant development on this subject? In this chapter I explore Marion's discussions of sacrifice and forgiveness, setting them in the context of his earlier work on the gift and examine to what extent these constitute a development or adjustment of that earlier work. I also raise questions in regard to these expositions and by extension of Marion's phenomenology of the saturated phenomenon more generally. As in previous chapters, I argue for the need to articulate degrees of givenness in regard to the gift in order to provide a fuller account of its phenomenological character and also highlight an important hermeneutic dimension for speaking of and identifying the gift.

The Gift in the "Sketch" and *Being Given*

The "Sketch of a Phenomenological Concept of the Gift" is the earliest phenomenological statement of Marion's thought about the gift, although he had already frequently referred to God and God's love as gift in his more theological writings, such as *God without Being*. This essay provides a preliminary outline of the sort of arguments Marion develops more fully in *Being Given*, although this early text begins by identifying the gift as a phenomenon of revelation, while *Being Given* examines it more fully as a strictly philosophical phenomenon. In "Sketch," Marion identifies gift and givenness with each other and explicitly connects both to revelation. He suggests: "Givenness, therefore, is not limited to the very restricted case of the phenomena of revelation but defines all phenomenality in a universal fashion. Therefore, rather than reflection abandoning revelation when it considers the gift, on the contrary, it may be that revelation traces the only possible path toward it: givenness as the first level of all phenomenality, the gift as the final trait of every phenomenon revealing itself" (VR, 80–81). He goes on to develop a "concept of the gift" in the rest of the article.

He first considers a "metaphysical" concept of the gift, which would describe it primarily in terms of causality. Although drawing on Derrida's analysis, Marion especially emphasizes the way in which most accounts of the gift make it subject to Aristotle's four causes, relying on reciprocity, and ultimately subjecting givenness to the principle of sufficient reason.[9] A phenomenological concept of the gift must free itself from this notion of causality and from the reciprocal economy of exchange, just as a phenomenology of givenness does not accord with any principle of sufficient reason, but must exceed all metaphysical rationality. We see here again how overcoming metaphysical paradigms is one of Marion's primary motivations in his phenomenological analyses. As in the preceding discussions, metaphysics is defined in terms of reciprocity, causality, and a project of grounding and justifying fully in purely rational terms.

Marion asserts that giver, recipient, givenness, and the gift must all be suspended in some fashion in order to escape a metaphysical economy of the gift. He outlines the aporia he perceives in the gift as follows: "Either the gift presents itself in presence and it disappears from givenness in order to embed itself in the economic system of exchange, or the gift does not present itself and no longer appears, thus closing all phenomenality of givenness" (VR, 84). Marion renounces the "horizon of economy" in order to reveal a different "truth" of the gift under the "horizon of givenness." The gift would then no longer be impossible: "Describing this givenness is a question of thinking through the gift under the rubric of givenness itself, without referring it to economy, because the impossibility just noted does not concern the gift as such but rather its economic interpretation" (VR, 88). Exchange, reciprocity, causality, and objectivity must be excluded from a phenomenological reading of the gift. When the "conditions of the impossibility of the gift" are reversed, they become the conditions of its possibility.

Marion seeks to accomplish this by "suspending" or "bracketing" each of these metaphysical conditions phenomenologically. He describes situations in which the gift would not be an object or where the object itself only serves as symbol for the gift (e.g., a ring for the gift of love, the transfer of a crown for giving power to another). The gift comes to determine and even give rise to the giver through a kind of obligation it imposes upon the giver by acting completely from itself: "The gift gives *itself* by giving its giving" (VR, 92). The giver is obligated not only by the gift, but also in some way by the recipient, who must accept the gift in order to accomplish it fully, yet can refuse it through ingratitude, indifference, or malice. Yet, reception obligates the recipient: "To decide to receive the gift amounts to deciding to become obligated by the gift" (VR, 94). This again shows the phenomenological priority of the gift: "The gift decides about its own acceptance by deciding about its recipient. . . . The gift gives *itself* by giving its reception" (VR, 94, original emphasis). Marion draws two conclusions from this analysis: "The first is that the gift, as that which decides *itself* by itself, supposes nothing other than the moment of givenness and thus does not belong to the economy of exchange but is accomplished even and mainly in a regimen of reduction. The second conclusion is that this gift, reduced to what decides *itself,* takes its character of the given from givenness alone, that is to say, from itself, without depending on any extrinsic relation—neither upon exchange nor upon the giver nor upon the recipient. The gift gives 'itself' intrinsically in its *self*-giving" (VR, 94–95). Consequently, the gift "appears in the horizon of givenness, where it properly (by itself) gives (as all phenomena give) as what (par excellence) gives *itself*" (VR, 95). We can see here already how the gift functions as a paradigm or preparation for a phenomenology of givenness as such.[10]

Marion goes on to work a similar suspension of metaphysical categories by bracketing or setting aside the giver and the recipient in turn. Both "bracketings" belong integrally to the gift as phenomenon, as it determines them from itself; recipient and giver both depend on the gift. Marion gives the examples of an enemy who does not recompense the gift. Even when the gift is refused, it is still fully given, because given in abandon.[11] Marion says: "the ungrateful person reveals negatively the gift reduced to givenness in all of its purity" (VR, 97). The invisibility of the recipient enables the gift to emerge phenomenologically, because it is no longer dependent on the recipient's acceptance, but appears entirely from itself. Similarly, the giver can be bracketed, as in the situation of an inheritance (where the giver is deceased) or a charitable donation (where the giver is unknown). In all these cases, the gift still appears fully and from itself, precisely because the absent giver is no longer in control of it. Such a gift cannot actually be returned, reinstituting the reciprocal economic exchange, because the giver has permanently disappeared from the circle of exchange.

Thus, "far from marking the impossibility of the gift, the absence of the giver manifests the reduction of the gift to givenness" (VR, 99). At the same time, it infinitely obligates the recipient, who cannot return the gift and relieve himself of the debt. It thus removes the recipient from metaphysical autarchic subjectivity. The self is received as a given instead of being seen as an originating principle of exchange, in control of the exchange. Marion summarizes his account as follows: "I have reduced the gift to givenness in order to expose the fact that beyond all objective support and any economy of exchange, *the gift intrinsically gives itself from its self-giving.* I also bracketed, first, the recipient in the figure of the *enemy* (of the ungrateful and the anonymous one) and then the giver, in the figure of the unsolvable *debt*" (original emphasis). He concludes: "This yields the following paradox: *the gift, reduced to givenness, decides to give* itself *as an unsolvable debt given to an enemy.* Thus, one may suppose to have reduced gift, recipient, and giver also to givenness. This triple reduction obviously does not aim to abolish the gift, the recipient, and the giver. On the contrary, it makes them play freely according to

the mode of pure givenness" (VR, 100; original emphasis). Marion ends the essay
by suggesting that this sketch of the gift parallels the abundant (and abandoned)
givenness of revelation.

While the "horizon of givenness" and the parallels between gift and given
are only hinted at in the early "Sketch," in *Being Given,* Marion develops the gift
as an important example of his notion of givenness. He had anticipated this very
briefly in the conclusion of *Reduction and Givenness,* where he proposed a third reduction to the call or to givenness, which "gives the gift itself: the gift of rendering
oneself to or of eluding the claim of the call" (RG, 204; RD, 305). In *Being Given,*
he now speaks more fully of givenness as the central characteristic of the phenomenon. Phenomena do not simply appear; they "give" themselves.[12] They can
only be experienced truly, if they are allowed to give themselves in their full givenness without imposing conditions on them. All preconceived notions and conditions must be set aside (or "reduced") so that the phenomenon can appear fully
as it is given,[13] leading him to posit as the fundamental phenomenological principle "as much reduction, so much givenness" or that what appears, shows itself
inasmuch as it gives itself.[14] Marion then proceeds to an analysis of the gift, again
using Derrida's reflections on the gift as guideline, but attempting to refute them
at the same time. He adopts Derrida's claim that a gift that is subject to economic
exchange immediately annuls itself. A true gift has to be gratuitous, freely given,
and not involve any connotation of debt or return. Yet, any gift however concealed
or however liberally given, will by definition elicit at the very least gratitude or the
consciousness of having given, and thus a kind of obligation. It will be no longer
a purely gratuitous gift but will always contain connotations of debt or economy.

In *Being Given,* Marion tries to tackle this aporia of the gift (i.e., its automatic
reduction to economic reciprocity or causality) by considering every pole of the
gift exchange: that of the notion of giving, of the giver, of the recipient (translated
somewhat awkwardly as the "givee"), and the gift-item or object itself.[15] While the
earlier sketch focused primarily on the gift itself and spent considerably less time
on the giver or recipient, these poles receive much more attention in *Being Given,*
although Marion reuses most of his earlier examples. As in the "Sketch," he illustrates with these examples that each of the poles of giving can be conceived to be
set aside or bracketed in particular circumstances. For example, in the case of an
inheritance or a charitable donation, the giver either is no longer present or does
not know the recipient; in the case of ingratitude or rejection of the gift, there is
no real recipient although the gift may have been truly given; in the case of a ring
or the promise of fidelity, there is no real gift-object or the object itself is not the
gift but only represents it. In *Being Given,* Marion argues even more strongly that
we can indeed speak of a phenomenon of the gift and thus overcome its aporia if
we regard it as reduced in this fashion. It escapes economic exchange (reciprocity)

and metaphysical causality (the principle of sufficient reason) and shows itself in pure givenness and immanence (BG, 113–17; ED, 161–67).

In the later part of the book he articulates the notion of the saturated phenomenon, which is an excessive givenness where the phenomenon presents too much to consciousness and thus cannot be held or contained (BG, 199–221; ED, 280–309). Although he does not extensively apply this analysis to his earlier treatment of the gift,[16] it does seem that the gift appears as such a saturated phenomenon. This also becomes clear when one compares his analysis here with his article, "The Gift of a Presence," first published in *Communio* (1983) and then included as the final chapter of *Prolégomènes à la charité* (penultimate chapter of the English translation). Although this is a heavily theological article and Marion does not yet employ the terminology of "saturated phenomenon," his depiction of Christ's absence in the resurrection and ascension narratives (the topic of the article) displays many of the paradoxical characteristics of the excess in the "gift of absence" and bedazzling blindness he later associates with the saturated phenomenon.[17] The article is explored in more detail in the next chapter. In fact, as emerges both in this and the remaining chapters, there is significant overlap between Marion's treatments of the gift, of prayer, and of the Eucharist. Although the gift is ostensibly a purely philosophical phenomenon, it will emerge as a particular apt theological phenomenon, as well. And Marion will finally characterize the gift of the Eucharist as the very paradigm not only for the gift as such but for all of phenomenality.[18]

In these early treatments, Marion's analysis of the gift seems driven by two main concerns. First, the gift helps establish and confirm his more general focus on givenness as the central characteristic of phenomenology. It serves as a "test case" and confirms the analysis of givenness provided in the other parts of the book: "Givenness determines the gift as much as and in the same sense as the phenomenon because the phenomenon shows *itself* as such and on its own basis only insofar as it gives *itself*" (BG, 118; ED, 168; original emphasis). The gift is a privileged phenomenon that uniquely overcomes metaphysical parameters and "attests the fold of givenness" where all phenomena show themselves as they give themselves from themselves (BG, 118; ED, 168). It is interesting in this regard, that *In Excess* does not say a word about the gift.[19] At that stage, the gift appears to have done its work and need no longer appear in the discussion.

Second, much of Marion's analysis of the gift in this early account speaks of our obligation to the gift and makes a kind of indebtedness to the gift central to the analysis. This is not the debt of economy and exchange, but instead it functions primarily to establish that the gift is given from itself and therefore can turn the one to whom it is given into a recipient (or "givee" or "gifted"). The strong Cartesian subject is dislocated by the phenomenology of the gift, becomes addressed by the gift, indebted by it, and devoted or even addicted to the given. Indebtedness to the gift confirms the priority of the gift and the response of the recipient, which are Marion's most central concerns in these earlier treatments. These two results, the centrality of givenness for any self-showing of the phenomenon and the overcoming of the subject, are explicitly listed as the two accomplishments of *Being Given* in the conclusion to the book (BG, 320–24; ED, 439–43). The gift in this context functions primarily to develop and confirm them.[20]

Gift and Sacrifice in *Certitudes négatives*

In *Certitudes négatives,* Marion returns to the phenomenon of the gift. Two chapters focus in detail on this topic, although the notion of givenness pervades the whole book and to some extent provides the presupposition for the exploration of "negative certainties." These apply precisely to phenomena that give themselves in a "counter-experience" and cannot be constituted by consciousness.[21] As in *Being Given,* the notion of the gift seems to make this particularly clear. In the first of these two chapters, "The Unconditioned and the Force of the Gift" (chapter 3), Marion takes up many of his earlier treatments, referring extensively to *Being Given* and even the early "Sketch" but revising them significantly.[22] In the second of these, "The Unconditioned and the Variations of the Gift" (chapter 4), he explores the phenomena of sacrifice and pardon (for-"give"-ness)[23] as illustrations of the gift.[24] They are ultimately what make the gift appear in all its richness. *Le croire pour le voir* also contains a discussion of the gift, which similarly draws on the earlier treatments but ends on a theological note by culminating in a discussion of the Eucharist as the very paradigm of the gift. It is explored in more detail in the context of that discussion.

Marion begins his analysis in this work by reviewing the aporiae of the gift already outlined in *Being Given* and with a brief summary of his earlier treatment, especially in regard to the suspension of one of the poles of the gift relation in order to allow it to appear in its pure givenness. Yet, in this context he goes further. He recognizes that his earlier account is predominantly negative in method: It responds to the economic reduction of the gift to exchange by freeing it from its causal and reciprocal connections, but it does not allow the gift to appear from itself in a more "positive" or "authentic" fashion (CN, 161–62). As an example of a gift that appears from itself, immediately within the horizon of givenness instead of being torn from the horizon of exchange, Marion examines the notion of paternity. According to him, the gift of life given by the father who is not directly involved with the child and who must always leave the child (both after conception and later on to provide for it) is a freely given gift where no economy or reciprocity is at stake (CN, 163–168). The child can also never return this gift to the father. He concludes that "paternity hence deploys, in fact and by right, the entire phenomenality of a gift reduced to pure givenness" (CN, 168).[25] There is no reciprocity present in this phenomenon of the paternal gift.[26] It also challenges the metaphysical principles of self-identity and equality, thus showing the excess and possibilities present here. Marion affirms that this abandon of the gift outside exchange and reciprocity applies not merely to the idea of paternity but to all instances of freely given gifts (CN, 173). The gift hence is truly a saturated phenomenon in the way outlined in *Being Given* and *In Excess*. Again, the central elements of the discussion here are on the one hand the freedom of the self-givenness of the phenomenon, giving itself without any conditions, and on the other hand the impossibility of return or reciprocity. Both serve to show a self given to itself by the phenomenon instead of a strong metaphysical subject.[27]

Marion then outlines two apparent requirements of a gift: one must decide to accept a gift and one must see what it is one accepts. Yet both of these requirements emerge to be regulated by the gift itself and hence serve even further to imbalance the notions of final reason and self-sufficiency that had determined the metaphysical concepts of the gift: The gift itself must accomplish its own acceptance (CN, 178). This notion of the acceptability of the gift is a phenomenological necessity, not a moral one or a kind of seduction. The gift is phenomenalized when it shows itself as it gives itself, thus confirming the fundamental principle of phenomenology, as Marion has laid it out. This fully reduced gift fulfills the definition of the phenomenon par excellence: it shows itself from itself and gives rise to giver, recipient, and gift object. As in the "Sketch" but even more forcefully, the gift becomes "the paradigm of all [or any] phenomenality" (CN, 181). Instead of conforming to the rationality of economic exchange, the gift has its own reasons: "Always coming in excess, it demands nothing, removes nothing, and takes nothing from anybody. The gift is never wrong, because it never does wrong. Never being wrong, it is always right (literally, has reason). Therefore, it delivers its reason at the same time as itself—reason that it gives in giving itself and without asking any other authority than its own advent. The gift coincides with its reason, because its mere givenness suffices as reason for it. Reason sufficing for itself, the gift gives itself reason in giving itself" (CN, 184).[28]

Marion concludes this chapter by arguing that his analysis provides a way of combating contemporary nihilism and the absolute rationality of economic exchange. The gift gives itself in complete freedom, without any conditions whatsoever, and thus has its own reasons outside of the logic or rationality of contemporary society.[29] The privileged example of the gift shows that instead of conforming to established horizons, saturated phenomena give rise to their own horizons and introduce new events and visibility into the realm of phenomenality (CN, 185).[30] In a sense, Marion here simply reiterates his earlier account: The gift operates completely from itself and gives itself freely and gratuitously. Yet he also goes much

further by articulating this as a kind of rationality of the gift (parallel to the rationality of love explicated in the previous chapter) that is thereby able to function as
a response to contemporary nihilism. This concern with nihilism emerges much
more fully in Marion's later work, especially in *Certitudes négatives* and *Le croire pour
le voir.* I return to this below.

In chapter 4, Marion explores the notion of sacrifice and pardon.[31] They play
a special role as "variations" of the gift and in allowing the gift to appear. How do
they do so? Marion begins by rejecting the sacrifice as destruction or annihilation
in the case of the terrorist, which serves as a negative example to illustrate that sacrifice cannot be defined in these negative terms. Even a definition of renunciation
(sacrificing for an "other") is not sufficient, as it immediately returns to a kind of
economic reciprocity which the analysis of the gift has already rejected. Sacrifice
is "abandon without return" or without conditions and hence faces similar aporiae as the gift (CN, 195).

> The sacrifice supposes henceforth a gift already given, which it is not
> a matter of destroying or of rejecting, nor even of transferring to an-
> other owner, but of sending back to the givenness from which it came
> forth and of which it must always carry the mark. The sacrifice re-
> turns the gift to the givenness from which it comes forth, by sending
> it back to the return itself which constitutes it originally. The sacri-
> fice does not leave the gift, but lives in it totally: it maintains the gift
> in its status as given, in reproducing it in an abandonment. (CN, 203)

This is not a counter-gift or a reciprocal return, but a recognition of the gift, a way
of allowing its givenness to appear: "Sacrifice does not give the given to the giver
by taking it from the recipient, for that would simply annul the first gift. Sacrifice
makes givenness visible by re-giving the gift as such, that is to say as an abandoned
gift [*un don abandonné*]. The origin of this abandon can no longer be concealed by
any attempt to take possession, nor can its status of given be undone. Sacrifice effects the redounding of the gift in abandon [*la redondance du don dans l'abandon*]"
(CN, 204).[32] The sacrifice makes the gift "safe" and allows it to appear as a gift.

Marion illustrates this notion of sacrifice with the biblical story of Abraham's
(almost) sacrifice of Isaac. He argues that Isaac had been given to Abraham as a
completely gratuitous gift, not only because according to Jewish tradition all firstborn children belong to God,[33] but because Isaac's birth was even more specifically a gracious gift from God: both Abraham and Sarah were too old to conceive
children, and the birth of the child was announced by the visit of angels, making
clear its miraculous character. Yet Abraham and Sarah had begun to treat Isaac as
a possession, as *theirs* and no longer a gift from God. In asking Abraham to sacri-

fice Isaac and hence to give him up completely, Abraham is reminded of the gift-character of Isaac: "Abraham hears himself asked not so much to kill his son, to lose him and return possession of him to God (according to the common concept of the gift), as, first and foremost, to return him to his status as gift given by reducing him (leading him back) to givenness. In the strict sense, [this means to ask him] to abandon him [to God] in order to assure the redounding of the first gift" (RoG, 87; CN, 208).[34] The sacrifice makes visible the gift, allows it to appear, reminds Abraham of its nature. He receives Isaac back as a gift, a gift now duplicated by the sacrifice. The abandon of the sacrifice reveals the gift and provides access to the giver and the process of givenness (from the point of view of the recipient). Marion concludes here that God alone truly gives the gift by providing for the sacrifice. God is manifested as the true giver who appears as the origin of the gift.

The second illustration of the gift in this chapter on the "variations" of the gift concerns the notion of pardon or forgiveness where the gift that has been reduced to exchange by the recipient is restored by the pardon granted (again) by the giver of the original gift.[35] At first sight, sacrifice and forgiveness seem opposed to each other: While the former assumes an equal exchange with a kind of justice, the latter assumes precisely an injustice, something that has not been accepted and in which no equality is at work. For justice to be reestablished, equality and exchange have to be restored. Marion argues, however, that sacrifice and pardon are actually counter-images of each other: In the case of sacrifice, the gift has been given and reduced to exchange *in* its reception by the recipient turning it into a possession; in the case of pardon, the original gift was *not* received precisely because it was reduced to exchange. While sacrifice makes the gift and the giver of the gift visible from the point of view of the recipient, forgiveness makes visible the gift from the point of view of the giver, who grants forgiveness precisely to confirm the original gift that had been refused or not recognized, thus making it visible.

Marion relies here on Hegel's account of recognition in the master-slave dialectic of *The Phenomenology of Spirit,* which he applies to the recognition of a fully abandoned gift. The inequality of exchange is reproduced by the impossibility of mutual recognition of consciousness (CN, 215). Both master and slave are dependent on each other and one cannot do without the other. Yet, their "exchange" is unequal and nonreciprocal, characterized by injustice. In the same way, giver and recipient of the gift cannot engage in any mutual recognition of consciousness, but such exchange would similarly do injustice to the gift. There is no apparent solution here: any attempt at retributive justice to reestablish reciprocity wreaks new violence. And yet, this is how pardon is usually defined: it reestablishes justice after the injustice of non-recognition. According to the logic of exchange, but of an exchange already recognized as unequal, "pardon sanctions the abandonment of the ruined gift irrevocably" (CN, 218).[36] The gift hence seems to presuppose injustice. This forgiveness becomes a kind of negotiation with all sorts of conditions attached to it. It is no longer a freely offered gift.

Marion acknowledges that it seems that great injustice cannot be pardoned without trivializing it or committing further injustice, but, like Derrida, he insists that, structurally, pardon always concerns the impossible and thus is beyond the exchange implied by the notion of justice. This is particularly obvious in such extreme cases of injustice as the Shoah, where it seems that forgiveness is no longer possible. A pardon that is demanded or negotiated in order to remit a debt is not really forgiveness, but remains unjust and ultimately imprescriptible (CN, 220). There cannot be any prescribed conditions for forgiveness. Pardon only becomes possible when it is impossible, as Derrida had already suggested in his discussion of Jankélévitch (CN, 221).[37] Consequently, pardon cannot be defined as payment of a debt or any other way that would envision it as an exchange implying the possibility of reciprocity. Forgiveness has nothing to do with exchange or even with justice, but only with a purely gratuitous gift freed completely from conditions of any sort. The discussion of forgiveness in the case of such great evils as the Shoah serves here merely as a confirmation that forgiveness seems impossible and does not rely on conditions of exchange. Marion is not really adding to the discussion surrounding Jankélévitch's treatment, but merely employing it to confirm the claim that true forgiveness cannot be reduced to retributive justice.

Marion uses Shakespeare's play *King Lear* as an illustration of such excessive forgiveness. Lear initially believes that love can be exchanged for power and thus does not recognize the gift of love offered by his daughter Cordelia. The forgiveness asked of (and granted by) Cordelia to her father, which is given freely and is gratuitous though undeserved, first makes the gift of her love for the father appear, a love that was not apparent to him before and that he originally scorned. And in fact, her father does not forgive (his other two daughters), but rather *receives* Cordelia's forgiveness. While his relationship with the two older daughters relies entirely on economic exchange, his encounter with Cordelia becomes marked by the gift, which is able to reappear on account of her forgiveness. Forgiveness is only possible when there has been a prior gift. It cannot be based on exchange. The gift is the "condition of possibility" for forgiveness: "Forgiveness does not correct a deficiency of justice in regard to the exchange, but a deficiency of visibility in regard to the first gift. Forgiveness hence works the phenomenality of the gift" (CN, 226). Forgiveness frees the gift from being inscribed into the economy of exchange to which it submits so quickly and easily. Only when the giver completely "abandons" the gift by giving without any conditions whatsoever and by disappearing him- or herself, can the gift appear as such (CN, 227).

The unforgivable concerns what is not preceded by a gift; forgiveness always relies on a prior gift and on the giver's willingness completely to abandon the gift or even to view everything as gift.

Marion ends this chapter in *Certitudes négatives* with a reflection on divine forgiveness as what accomplishes the impossible.[38] Here God is the absolute paradigm of forgiveness: God can forgive all because God has created all and thus gives perfectly. In fact, "God alone can forgive absolutely with a forgiveness that is impossible for us" (CN, 228). God alone can forgive sins, because he alone is the origin of all gifts. All faults are hence ultimately faults against God. The impossibility of such goodness and forgiveness in humans is precisely an instance of negative certainty in Marion's view (CN, 231). Marion employs the parable of the prodigal son to show what he calls "the hermeneutic process of forgiveness," which includes a kind of conversion and recognition of the forgiveness already given. Forgiveness converts the interpreter and corrects the false interpretation, which thinks of the gift in terms of exchange. Here Marion speaks explicitly of hermeneutics: "The hermeneutics of the gift as such makes forgiveness thinkable, but under the condition that it is permitted by a conversion to the gift; and, inasmuch as this conversion to the gift remains first of all and most of the time problematic, the failure of this conversion requires forgiveness. One must hence describe a circle, itself hermeneutical, which leads from the gift to forgiveness by passing from hermeneutics to conversion and returns from the failed conversion to forgiveness—always sought but always also already presupposed" (CN, 232). I return to the "hermeneutics" proposed here in the final section of this chapter.

Marion's analysis of the parable of the prodigal son makes the same point as his interpretation of *King Lear* does: The son disregards the gift of the father's paternal love by requesting an economic exchange of the father's life in the form of an inheritance. This attempt at possession leads to a disregard of the gift and its loss and, in fact, to the disappearance of both "father" and "son," who no longer act as fathers and sons should. In his forgiveness, the father gives the gift of his love again to the son so that he becomes anew a son of the father: "Via forgiveness, the re-giving gift, the father does not give him what the exchange had lost (possession), but reestablishes him in the movement of the given gift, hence appears to him hereby for the first time as giving father and shows him for the first time as receiving son. Forgiveness makes the entire phenomenon of the gift visible for the first time" (CN, 237).[39] The reaction of the older son confirms this in Marion's view, because he also did not see the gift of the father's paternity but took it as a kind of possession. He also does not love his father but regards himself merely as a badly compensated servant. Not having experienced the same loss as his younger brother, he remains ignorant of the gift. We all stand before God as these two sons and have to make our own choice about accepting forgiveness and the corresponding gift (CN, 240). We can only recognize either the gift or its process; never are both visible at the same time (CN, 241).

The parallel of this use of the biblical story here not only to Marion's interpretation of Shakespeare's play but also to his employment of the sacrifice of Isaac earlier in the chapter is striking. There also, he had claimed that only God gives truly and is the giver of all gifts: "God hence gives himself to see inasmuch as he gives in an originary fashion, inasmuch as he shows that all gifts come from him" (CN, 209). Like love, the gift hence emerges as rooted in and originated by the divine. We can love and give gifts only because God loves us first and creates us in pure gratuity. All gifts and all love proceed from the divine. This becomes even more obvious in my chapter 7, where we see that Marion ultimately posits the Eucharist as the supreme gift of love that determines the phenomenality of all other gifts and possibly of givenness as such. There is continual slippage between the gift as paradigm for *any* phenomenon and the specifically religious connotations of sacrifice, forgiveness, and Eucharist. And this "slippage" or parallelism is much more explicit in *Certitudes négatives* than in the treatment in *Being Given,* where Marion presented his analysis as strictly phenomenological and kept religious or biblical references to a minimum.

At the same time, this more recent treatment develops Marion's earlier one in important ways. No longer is the focus as strongly on establishing the proposal of givenness as such or of the displaced self, results that are now taken as accomplished. This enables Marion to focus more explicitly on the phenomena of gift, forgiveness, and sacrifice themselves instead of examining them primarily as validations of the larger project. He has also removed basically all references to indebtedness in the phenomenon of the gift. Although it still operates from itself and by itself, this is no longer expressed in terms of an obligation of debt for the recipient. Both the phenomenon of sacrifice and that of forgiveness allow Marion to describe encounters between the parties involved with the gift much more fully, without either reestablishing an economy of exchange or rendering the recipient entirely passive. Neither Abraham nor King Lear can be said to be entirely passive in the face of the gift, but they actually play an important role in making the gift appear through sacrifice (Abraham) and forgiveness (Lear). This suggests again that Marion does not think of the phenomenological recipient as entirely passive, but rather marked by a tension that involves elements of both activity and passivity, namely a capacity to receive and to respond. He stresses this also in his interview with Arbib: "The term passivity is insufficient, because I can precisely not remain passive before the event: I become available or avoid it, I take the risk or flee it, in short, I still decide and respond, even in refusing to respond. In order to be passive in such an encounter, a certain kind of activity is necessary, one must expose oneself to things with a certain amount of courage. It is hence not just a

matter of passivity" (RC, 141). Bauer similarly recognizes that this is no mere passivity, but requires a certain attitude vis-à-vis the phenomenon in order to receive
it properly and allow it to give itself.[40]

In *Certitudes négatives,* Marion also seems far less confident that the gift can
appear as such and indeed seems to see its very inability to appear (at least "on its
own") as axiomatic. That we cannot provide an adequate account of the gift precisely illustrates its excessive character. It would not be a gift, could it be described
in terms of objectivity and causality. Gift-character is by definition excessive and
uncontainable. The earlier account in *Being Given* obviously also does not read
the gift in terms of objectivity or causality, but it actually explicitly seeks to avoid
these metaphysical constructions of the gift. Yet in that context, Marion does still
seem to claim that the gift can appear as a phenomenon if one of the "poles of
exchange" is suspended. His account in *Certitudes négatives* goes much further by
having the gift only appear "negatively" via the phenomena of sacrifice and forgiveness, where the gift has always already disappeared and only "appears" via this
very disappearance. Overall, the notion of the gift is much more central than it is
in the earlier work, where it seemed to serve primarily as a test case and validation
of the more general account of givenness.[41]

Yet what continues to be problematic about this account, indeed what has
emerged as a larger worry with Marion's phenomenology overall, is its absolute
and excessive character. A gift is a gift only if it is completely and utterly gratuitous. Love is love only when it is completely and utterly kenotic. Sacrifice counts
only when it goes to the point of complete and utter self-abandonment and ultimately may only be given to God in response to God's gifts. Forgiveness must be a
total divestment of self, given completely without regard of circumstance or condition and ultimately can only be granted by God. *Any* definition or determination
of the human or the divine or the gift (or indeed any rich phenomenon) is entirely
reductive and nihilistic and must be radically excluded. While there is certainly a
sense in which all these statements may be true and indeed an accurate depiction
of *some* phenomena of gift, sacrifice, and forgiveness, to what extent can they constitute a phenomenological account of *all* gifts, *all* instances of sacrifice, *all* expressions of love, *all* gestures of forgiveness? Is this a phenomenology that can actually
be said to describe the phenomena experienced by the average mortal? Can one
ever give a gift when the requirement of the gift is such excessive abandon? Can
one ever love, if it is only possible in this completely kenotic mode? These are the
questions I examine in the final two sections of this chapter.

The Excess of the Gift

The gift has become the very paradigm of the impossible in phenomenology.
The excessive depiction of the gift is certainly not particular to Marion. Jacques
Derrida, John D. Caputo, Edith Wyschogrod, and any number of other interpret-

ers speak of the gift in such superlative and excessive terms. Pure gratuity belongs
to the very definition of the gift. Yet pure gratuity is never possible in our concrete
human situations. Thus, the gift, as such a pure giving, becomes impossible. In
Derrida's account of forgiveness and sacrifice, by which Marion is influenced here
and to which he responds even when he does not cite Derrida explicitly, this purity
and contamination continually cross each other. Derrida does not give up on the
purity of the gift, and it is surely as excessive as Marion's account, even if Derrida
does not identify it as a saturated phenomenon or even as a phenomenon at all.
For Derrida, the gift and forgiveness are "the impossible." Forgiveness is only truly
forgiveness when it forgives the unforgivable. The gift is only truly given when it
is so pure that it disappears as a gift entirely.

     And yet Derrida recognizes that this purity, although it is essential and under-
girds any idea of gift giving or forgiveness, is never actually enacted in real life.
Our gifts are always contaminated by exchange, our forgiveness always marred by
debt. This is necessarily so and cannot be otherwise. Although this contamination
and debt must be continually criticized, this does not mean that they will ever go
away or that we might actually be able to accomplish an instance of purity. Derrida
claims that a purely gratuitous gift is "impossible," that no real gift can ultimately
be given. This is so in a necessary and structural way: the very notion of the gift
implies its pure gratuity, its free nature that is not tied to any notion of exchange
or reciprocity and not contaminated by any expectation of response or even gratitude. Yet, as Derrida points out repeatedly and as we know from intimate experience, no such completely pure, gratuitous gift ever occurs. Our gifts are always im-
pure and fall short of absolute gratuity. For Derrida, the gift functions as an ideal,
as a structural limit case that gets us continually to reexamine our assumptions and
transactions, to discover and even highlight their impurity, and always to explore
opportunities in which we would be more deliberate, more aware, and more just
in our transactions, while keeping the structural impossibility of the ideal as a continual criticism and impetus for the concrete, less ideal and more contaminated
instantiations. This is not merely a resigned acknowledgment that we will never
reach some impossible ideal, but the impossible itself—whether gift, forgiveness,
messianism, the democracy to come or hospitality—are structurally involved in
all the less ideal instantiations. The very notion of "gift" requires the "impossible"
and unreachable ideal of purity and gratuity, the very notion of forgiveness relies
upon the impossible of the unforgiveable that alone could truly be forgiven, any
practice of hospitality is dependent upon and even parasitic on a notion of complete openness exposed to hostility and abuse even when it practices hospitality
in only partial fashion by protecting oneself and being open only to some guests,
choosing whom to host. Even mundane and contaminated gifts—which are indeed Derrida's concern—always rely on the impossible as such (the pure gift, ab-

solute forgiveness of the unforgiveable, unconditional hospitality). The idea of selfless and free giving, although it ultimately always breaks down, does inform giving as such and indeed is absolutely essential for it. The gift, or the impossible, functions as a structural limit case and at the same time as the core notion, which alone makes possible the mundane, actual, flawed exercises of generosity, forgiveness, and hospitality, while also always challenging and correcting them, making us realize their flawed and incomplete nature.

Derrida's project obviously is significantly different from that of Marion. Derrida has no desire to establish a pure phenomenality or a phenomenology of givenness. One might actually suggest that his very project is the opposite: to tear down any attempt at pure or complete phenomenality and to show the impossibility of any first or last phenomenological project such as Marion's. Marion, in turn, argues that Derrida's notion of the gift remains metaphysical, because he defines it in terms of what is impossible for *us* and so the human is the measure for the phenomenon of the impossible. This is also why he speaks more often of the "unconditioned" rather than the "pure" gift. Marion contends that the gift crosses metaphysical limits and must be understood from the given itself not from our metaphysical parameters. This claim highlights again what is central to Marion's phenomenology but at the same time causes the most difficulties for it: In order to "escape" metaphysics one must receive and describe the given as it gives itself, without any presuppositions and entirely outside our "normal" parameters. Yet if we are to receive or indeed describe the given, must we not receive it *as* human, understand it against the horizon of our previous experience—even if it crosses, unsettles, or even explodes that horizon—and use our human language to describe and interpret it? And if this absolute given does indeed provide the paradigm for all givens and radically reorients phenomenology, so that even the most lowly conceptual object must be analyzed in terms of it, how can a relation be established between the saturated and the poor? What are the implications of the excessive gift for the less excessive, for the more mundane and lowly phenomena Derrida examines?

These, then, are the questions that Marion's account seem to raise: How might the "banality" of saturated phenomena help us for recognizing degrees of givenness that allow for stages of development and might even make it possible to distinguish between kinds of gifts or types of givenness? Is there any value in depicting phenomena of sacrifice, forgiveness, and giving of gifts that might not show themselves in such a radical fashion? And if there is not, if only the completely excessive gift matters, only the absolutely abandoned self-sacrifice counts, how does this still constitute a description of phenomena, as they are actually experienced by human beings in the world? Are the unconditioned gift, the complete sacrifice, the absolute act of forgiveness really phenomena, or are they rather imaginative ideals that can be thought but not actually experienced? Can they really be said to convey "the truth of the gift" (or even "the reason of the gift," as Marion's titles and subtitles indicate), if they have so little connection to how gifts are actually experienced by most people?[42]

One might ask then whether there is a way in which Derrida's recognition of the contamination of the real world can be appropriated phenomenologically in a way not incompatible with Marion's project. Is it possible to give a phenomenological account of less abundant gifts and partial forgiveness or do only extreme cases give us phenomenological insight? A phenomenological description of actual gifts, even when they are contaminated by some notions of exchange or reciprocity, teaches us important things about the phenomenality of our world, our actions within this world, and the ways in which they appear to our consciousness. Even if it is recognized that the "unconditioned gift" might be a saturated phenomenon in the extreme way in which Marion outlines it, degrees of givenness and giftedness are required to take account of the phenomena as they actually give themselves to us. While the unconditioned gift may be a limit case of phenomenality, the most excessively saturated phenomenon of the gift, lesser versions of saturation or excess must be possible and might even be necessary for the gift. Must any gift be completely abandoned in order to qualify as a gift *even to some degree?* It should be possible to give an account of phenomena that are found somewhere *along the spectrum* between economic exchange and pure gift. It is really too extreme to posit these two as the only options. Not all gifts congregate at the outer limits of poverty or saturation. If gifts are always completely saturated phenomena, then really only God gives truly, as Marion indeed suggests. Yet what would it mean for such an excessive account to become the *paradigm* for all other phenomena? And, indeed, if it functions as a paradigm, then the depiction of the gift as impossible must give us concrete help for recognizing less excessive phenomena. But so far it does not really tell us much except to insist that the gift is excessive to an intense degree. What else do we learn about the gift from Marion's account besides the fact that it is overabundant (and completely "abandoned") and cannot be grasped?

Let me use the example of gift giving at Christmas to illustrate what I mean. Many people mourn the commercialization of the Christmas holidays.[43] Gift giving has become required—it is expected to give gifts on this feast. Stores gear up for the holiday shopping season months ahead of time and in the U.S. economic crises are measured by the lack of pulling a profit on the day after Thanksgiving (the so-called "Black Friday"). The entire culture (at least in Europe and the Americas) moves into this commercialized holiday mood, often for several months. Gift giving becomes obligatory even in many business settings. Clearly, these are in no sense absolute or radical gifts; they are heavily conditioned by economic considerations on many different personal, social, and cultural levels. And yet does not this very implication in social or cultural conditions tell us important things about our culture and our personal conduct within it?[44] Do not precisely these conditioned gifts speak most fully about who we are, how we conduct ourselves, and the values we hold and the meanings we create? The event, especially as it comes at the end of the year, encapsulates our contemporary world, in its mix of past traditions, appropriated by a contemporary heavily commercialized and mediated age, our desires and relationships, and the ways all these are characterized and defined in particular ways by our own unique versions of gift giving.

"Gifts" and their perception dominate the displays in stores and various forms of advertising, particularly in areas where more traditional Christian symbols associated with the holidays have been banned or at least become questionable. Ironically, many people go heavily into debt each Christmas season in order to give "gifts." And while most—maybe all—of these gifts are deeply characterized by economic and commercial structures of expectation, reciprocity, and comparison with others, the assumption of a "purer" or more abundant giving, one that is unconditioned and beneficent with no expectation of return, still underlies this culture of giving—and ironically occasionally drives people more deeply into debt in their attempt to make larger and more "generous" gifts. The idea of an absolute gift, of a gift that would shatter obligation, that would be given completely gratuitously and out of "genuine" generosity, does on some level inform our giving, as we strive to exemplify it. Many of these gifts are not primarily given in order to receive a recompense, despite the fact that obligation (to give or to give "back") is always at work on some level.

And even in this array of less absolute gifts, there are many gradations of giving, from the business gift, calculated only to keep the customer or commercial partner engaged in continued economic exchange, to the gift swap of many social gatherings that relies entirely on reciprocity but is certainly not characterized by exactly the same economic connotations, to a gift given primarily to gain recognition or praise or outdo another and hence assert a form of control while probably also wishing to bestow enjoyment of the gift. All these clearly fall prey to the conditions of economy, reciprocity, and contamination. None of them is an unconditioned or saturated gift. Yet they are "conditioned" in very different ways and probably to different degrees—none of them is entirely "poor" and can be reduced solely to concepts. And other gifts are given more freely: a special gift selected to please a friend, where much consideration may have gone into what that friend might most enjoy, or the simple gift of a child, maybe even homemade but involving great energy and dedication, given out of love for the parent. Both of these cases are probably still characterized by an eagerness to please and a desire at least for a certain amount of gratitude or recognition of the gift, but they are far less tied to the relations of economic exchange than the previous list of gifts, and they are given more genuinely from themselves. They are also not identical to each other. And while they are certainly not "unconditioned" gifts and not saturated in the way Marion describes, they approach a "genuine" gift far more than those that are more obviously characterized by obligation and reciprocal exchange. They are certainly not "poor" phenomena.

In fact, it seems odd that so much of the discussion surrounding the gift is so negative.[45] Often it appears that for these philosophers the ungrateful refusal of a gift says more about the phenomenon of the gift than something the average person would recognize as a gift. If phenomenological analysis really carries us back to "the things themselves," should it not find a way of allowing these more mundane and average gifts to appear and show themselves as phenomena? These less excessive gifts also require phenomenological analysis, and their very lack of absolute abundance renders them more fully lived phenomena. While it might make a great deal of sense to regard the "pure" or "unconditioned" gift as a limit case of phenomenality or even as a paradigm for the gift and maybe to begin there in some fashion, the precise ways in which such a limit case serves as paradigm for all other phenomena should be explored much more fully. Might it be possible to describe the ways in which gifts and giving shape social bonds and establish communal and political identities without being merely about economic exchange?[46] How might we speak of a large variety of gifts that are neither entirely "poor" nor wholly "saturated" and maybe not at all connected to the horizons of economy and exchange? To a large extent that is precisely what Marion seeks to do in his work on the gift, yet it seems that a fuller hermeneutic depiction of a range of such phenomena would be helpful in this context. Phenomena are not only varied in their degree of givenness, but hermeneutics can help us see how that is the case.

The Hermeneutics of the Gift

As already mentioned earlier in this chapter in the analysis of the parable of the prodigal son, Marion explicitly, albeit only fleetingly, speaks of a hermeneutic process and even a hermeneutic circle in the case of forgiveness. The gift had been misinterpreted in the first instance as an item of exchange. In Marion's example, the prodigal son confuses the father's gift of love with the father's property. In the son's acceptance of the father's forgiveness, this false interpretation is corrected. The gift of the father's love is no longer understood as an item of exchange but is seen from itself. Here (as already cited in that context), Marion speaks explicitly of hermeneutics: "The hermeneutics of the gift as such makes forgiveness thinkable, but under the condition that it is permitted by a conversion to the gift; and, inasmuch as this conversion to the gift remains first of all and most of the time problematic, the failure of this conversion requires forgiveness. One must hence describe a circle, itself hermeneutical, which leads from the gift to forgiveness by passing from hermeneutics to conversion and returns from the failed conversion to forgiveness—always sought but always also already presupposed" (CN, 232). Marion hence distinguishes between a false and a correct interpretation. The hermeneutic circle is enacted to move us from the false interpretation to the correct one, although the move itself is motivated by the phenomenological experience. The experience of forgiveness makes it possible to interpret the gift "correctly," because we have been "converted."

That is striking language. It is not interpretation that "judges" correct perception of the phenomenon, but phenomenal experience "judges" the process of interpretation. Marion has reversed the relationship between hermeneutics and phenomenology. Hermeneutics does not serve to prepare for, articulate, interpret, and discern the phenomena. Rather, the phenomena give rise to and judge the interpretation. As in the other places where Marion speaks of hermeneutics in a positive sense (especially in *God without Being*), it is said to be imposed *by* the phenomenon instead of *upon* it. Through its overwhelming self-givenness the phenomenon provides the correct interpretation. No other interpretation seems possible. And yet Marion has stressed in other contexts that false interpretation certainly is possible. We can turn God into an object, not see the beauty of the painting, or trivialize the historical event by assigning it a simple cause. And this certainly applies to the gift: We can misunderstand the gift as a tool of manipulation or a bribe. And we can certainly refuse the gift in these and other cases. In these cases the "poverty" of the phenomenon depends only on the false interpretation instead of being intrinsic to the phenomenon in some sense, that is, it is *really* a saturated phenomenon, but the recipient experiences it as a poor one due to weakness or misinterpretation. How would one distinguish these cases of poverty from the other cases, where one really is confronted with a poor phenomenon?[47] No recourse to hermeneutics can be taken here, if hermeneutics is actually part of the problem of misapprehension.

And yet it is the very task of hermeneutics, at least as articulated by Heidegger, Gadamer, Ricoeur, and other thinkers, that enables us to address some of these questions. First of all, hermeneutics provides an important context for experiencing the phenomenon that would help negotiate some of this tension. If I am in a loving relationship, I am hermeneutically predisposed to appreciate the gratuity of the gift given to me (even if it is never completely unconditioned). If I am in a highly manipulative relationship, I am warned by prior experiences to interpret the "gift" carefully, as it probably comes with all kinds of strings attached to it—certainly far more so than in the previous case. The context in which one receives a gift matters not only to its reception, but to the very way in which it appears as a gift. And this context certainly also helps in the interpretation of the gift.

The hermeneutic circle both precedes the phenomenological experience and follows it: it occurs within its context. The continual back-and-forth between lived event and interpretation enables the event to become meaningful against the horizon of prior lived experiences and in turn to influence the horizon within which future experiences are encountered and interpreted.

Furthermore, it is hermeneutics that enables discernment between various kinds of experiences and between better and worse interpretations of these events. This is not to say that hermeneutics provides "the" truth of the event or some sort of absolute answer or foolproof guide of measurement. In fact, events are continually interpreted and even judged as we encounter them. The very identification even of a saturated phenomenon—as an event or work of art or gift or encounter with the divine—is hermeneutic in character inasmuch as such identification is an interpretation of the recipient. The decision to devote oneself, to become addicted to or give oneself over to the phenomenon, to give oneself to the gift, is a hermeneutic decision that relies upon a process of interpretive discernment. Even to judge a gift as completely unconditioned and gratuitous, utterly excessive and overwhelming, still implies judgment of some sort, even if that judgment does not imply any (ability of) control over the phenomenon. And this is particularly true if gradations or degrees of givenness are admitted. To discern degrees of saturation and particular contexts of economy and reciprocity, to distinguish between commercial and gratuitous aspects of "mixed" gifts, to ascertain the particular degree and character of the gift, to become aware of the extent to which it imposes itself upon us and escapes our attempts at manipulation—all these are important hermeneutic exercises.

Such hermeneutic discernment does not necessarily imply that control is asserted over the phenomenon or that it is pushed into a particular mold and hence regarded as an object. Rather, it means that it is examined carefully, namely that an attempt is made to ascertain its meaning in constant sensitivity to its particular appearance within specific contexts, but also to become aware of the ways in which the horizon of the gift or phenomenon intersects and interacts with my concrete horizons of experience and the larger cultural and communal horizons. All these are significant hermeneutic dimensions that allow us to experience the phenomenon more fully because they make us more sensitive to all its ways of manifestation. Hermeneutics is not a way of shutting down the gift or imposing arbitrary interpretations upon it, but a variety of processes that allow for a sensitive exploration of saturated phenomena in ways that actually permit their levels of saturation to emerge more fully and to be appreciated more deeply. As Thomas Carlson points out in the context of an analysis of Marion's notions of blindness and bedazzlement: "Humiliation, then, which dispossesses me of my arrogance or self-reliance, is itself a necessary gift of the given, the gift required in order for me not only to see the given but also to see what my arrogance prevents me from seeing: that I see the given always inadequately, that my response always falls short."[48] Hermeneutics does not erase the excess and saturation of the gift or cover over my inadequacy or inability to "bear" its weight, but it allows us to experience a whole range of abundant and less excessive gifts in more meaningful fashion. Hermeneutic discernment is not a question of "imposing" conditions upon the phenomenon, but a means for allowing it to emerge more fully *from* itself but also *to* us.[49]

Acknowledging the role hermeneutics can, does, and should play at all stages of phenomenality, not merely after a phenomenon has already occurred and been received by consciousness, therefore does not destroy or eliminate the self-givenness of the gift and its transgression of metaphysical limits and boundaries. Rather, its cyclical process prepares us for the incoming of the phenomenon and helps us discern more accurately the kind and degree of the particular phenomenon encountered. Interpretation is not arbitrary because it is not merely imposed on the experience but continually corrected by it. It is not a limit placed on the given phenomenon, but an openness to it, a willingness to hear and encounter it on its own terms, but also against the horizon of previous experience and understanding. This horizon is not a limitation, because it is not fixed but continually moves with and is expanded by the phenomena we encounter. Indeed, no exceeding of the horizon in Marion's sense could be possible, if there were not first a horizon to be thus exceeded. This does not mean that the recipient now "controls" the phenomenon or imposes previous conceptions or parameters upon it arbitrarily. Instead, this is a way of depicting the receptive capacity of the *adonné*: complete devotion to the phenomenon as a result of its impact is not at all excluded. The manner in which a particularly "saturated" phenomenon crosses and unsettles the horizon may still bedazzle and stun precisely because previous experience has taught the recipient that this phenomenon is extraordinary and does not fit into the usual categories. At the same time, a hermeneutic circling back and forth between the phenomenon as it gives itself and the ways in which it impacts the recipient's consciousness and shifts the horizons of understanding, enables to discern the level of saturation of the phenomenon and hence makes possible phenomenological depiction of a plurality and great diversity of experiences, distinguishing between their many types and degrees of saturation. Let me confirm these claims by examining the most saturated experiences Marion describes, namely experiences of revelation, such as they are encountered in prayer and the sacrament of the Eucharist.

SIX

Prayer and Sainthood

Prayer is a fairly prominent topic in Marion's writings, although it is not a concern addressed much by the secondary literature on his work.[1] Already the early distinction between idol and icon in *God without Being* is to a large extent about prayer or worship, about the human approach to the divine that can be expressed in idolatrous adoration or authentic prayer before an icon. The former is idolatrous for Marion because it becomes an invisible mirror that returns entirely upon the self, while the other is authentic because it is emptied of self and exposed to the divine gaze. This account is deepened and focused more fully on prayer in *The Crossing of the Visible*, where the final chapter examines explicitly what it means to pray before an icon. Somewhat surprisingly, the final chapter of *In Excess*, which really should examine the possibility of a phenomenon of revelation if it consistently followed the outline of the five kinds of saturated phenomena (event, idol, flesh, icon, revelation) as presented in *Being Given* and the first chapter of *In Excess*, instead examines the kind of language appropriate for the divine. This language turns out to be prayer or praise. In some sense, then, this simply continues the earlier distinction between an idolatrous and an iconic way to approach the divine. Yet, formulated as a response to Derrida on negative theology, it is a much more conscious articulation of the linguistic element in prayer.[2]

All this is not disconnected, of course, from the possibility of a phenomenon of revelation. In a sense, prayer encapsulates how we are to encounter, receive, and respond to the phenomenon of the divine as it gives itself to us. It hence also brings to a head the tensions uncovered so far between the utter self-givenness of the phenomenon and the need for its "appropriate" reception, including the difficulty of how to determine "appropriateness." These tensions and difficulties emerge in even more poignant fashion in a brief discussion of what it would mean to speak of—much less identify—someone as a "saint." Marion does indeed speak of the "phenomenon of the saint" or the "phenomenality of sainthood," and yet this is an "invisible" phenomenon, because the saint can never appear or be identified. It is striking that Marion's accounts of prayer and sanctity ultimately appear to have a greater concern with God in the interaction of prayer than they do with the person at prayer or the communal dimension of worship. Marion does not seem to speak of the more corporate dimensions of prayer primarily because of his desire to protect God in his accounts of the language of prayer. His analysis of prayer is ultimately primarily about how the individual person at prayer can speak rightly about God, rather than how such prayer might be informed by or contribute to the community of faith. This may be partly due to the fact that prayer, as the other experiences we have examined, is presented in its most excessive and absolute sense and that his treatment does not consider less radical forms.

Despite Marion's occasionally strong ecclesial concerns in his more theological writings, it seems that his accounts of prayer remain limited in this fashion because they so strongly depend upon his phenomenology: His talk about prayer parallels his explication of the undeniable and surprising nature of the appeal and his phenomenological account of love. As the claim that comes to the phenomenological recipient must be invisible, silent, and undetermined, God's name must remain radically undetermined in prayer. As love is described phenomenologically as the crossing of two invisible gazes, prayer becomes collapsed into erotic vision by being defined in almost identical fashion. The strong focus on the recipient or dative self in Marion's phenomenology is thus carried over into his theological depiction of prayer, making it more individualistic and personal than corporate and ecclesial. Such is the case because Marion is more concerned with the *form* of prayer than any particular content or ethical dimension of prayer, paralleling his emphasis on the structure of a phenomenology of the given as such as opposed to more particular phenomenological concerns or ethical implications.[3] Marion's more general phenomenology therefore strongly influences—or maybe even jeopardizes—his phenomenologies of prayer. This is visible also in a reflection on sainthood that similarly relies heavily on his phenomenological proposals and parallels his description of prayer. In this chapter I examine Marion's various accounts of prayer and highlight the questions they raise. I then show that an account of degrees and of hermeneutic discernment is particularly necessary when speaking of prayer, worship, and sanctity.

Prayer as a Crossing of Gazes

Marion's first full account of prayer in *The Crossing of the Visible* is set in the context of an exploration of aesthetics, in particular an analysis of painting, examined already in my chapter 2. Marion considers a phenomenology of the image, broadly conceived. He analyzes the status of the image in contemporary society and its impact on how persons perceive themselves. Ultimately, so he concludes, we become defined and imprisoned by the image that we must convey to our visually obsessed media culture (CV, 46–65; CdV, 85–98). He thus proposes to liberate us from the tyranny of the image by an analysis of the religious icon. In this context, his explication of the icon is far more clearly linked to Byzantine theology and iconography than in his earlier treatment in *God without Being,* to the point of quoting from Patristic treatises defending the use of icons and using phrases from the Byzantine liturgy (CV, 68–75; CdV, 122–33). The icon no longer functions here primarily as a defense of a certain speech about God or a protection of God from such speech, although it is still to some extent opposed to the idol as the "image" projected by a heavily mediated culture. The icon is read as a "kenosis of the image" and an alternative to its detrimental effect upon people (CV, 62; CdV, 111).[4]

Marion examines the use of the icon for prayer in light of the "crossing of gazes" within it. The icon, Marion contends, is a particular doctrine of visibility of the image and of the use of this visibility (CV, 59; CdV, 106). Before the icon, I both see and am seen. Yet, unlike the image, which is completely exposed to visibility, the icon does not ultimately give itself to be seen but must be venerated. An icon is painted (or "written") as a window to another reality and must hence be traversed in response to the gaze, which transits across it and imposes itself upon the person praying.[5] The two gazes cross and expose themselves to each other. The icon is kenotic because God humbles God-self to appearing in an image or a figure, thus showing not only the face of Christ but a trace of God. The icon therefore provides a transition from the invisible to the visible and makes the invisible visible in a way similar to what Marion later claims for painting more generally (CV, 60, 62, 72; CdV, 108, 110, 131).[6]

Here this transition is only possible in prayer and cannot be accomplished by any other attitude. Marion describes this movement of prayer: "The icon can only be contemplated honorably by the gaze that venerates it as a stigmata of the invisible. Prayer alone can thus go back from the visible to the invisible (according to the type), even as the spectator can only compare the visible to the invisible (according to mimesis). The holy things for the holy: prayer alone traverses the icon because it alone knows the function of the type" (CV, 75, trans. mod.; CdV, 133).[7] The inverse perspective of the icon attempts to draw our gaze into it toward the invisible. The icon imitates inner-Trinitarian life: the transferal of glory that takes place between the Father and the Son. It performs the same movement of holiness and glory, directing it to an other than itself. The icon is a sign, a figure of the distance of the invisible. In the icon, I always see an invisible gaze that envisages me (CV, 76, 77, 83; CdV, 134, 135, 138, 147).[8] To pray is to open oneself to a gaze coming from elsewhere but located in the medium of the icon, which refers to the other to whom one prays. The icon hence becomes an instrument of communion between the one praying and God, and it allows for an encounter between them (CV, 85–86; CdV, 151–52). Marion concludes: The icon "defines itself as the other gaze of a prototype, which demands the veneration of my own gaze climbing, across this type, toward it. The icon has as its only interest the crossing of gazes— thus, strictly speaking, love" (CV, 87; CdV, 153). The crossing of gazes in prayer and the crossing of gazes in love are here explicitly identified with each other.

Prayer is therefore the balanced tension between two invisible gazes that cross each other and weigh upon each other. Prayer allows God to become incarnate and simultaneously allows humans to ascend toward the divine: "In the icon, the visible and the invisible are set ablaze by a fire that no longer destroys, but lights up the divine face of humans" (CV, 87, trans. mod.; CdV, 154). At least to some extent, this represents a development in regard to the analysis of the icon in *God without Being*, where the human gaze was solely "envisaged" by the divine. In *The Crossing of the Visible*, Marion takes much greater pains to speak of God's vulnerability and self-giving in love to the believer or the one praying.[9] A mutual response of gazes ensues: Not only does the person before the icon find him- or herself envisaged by the divine gaze that proceeds through it, but a movement of the human gaze ascending to the divine is also envisioned. Yet these two gazes seem enveloped in a fairly narrow relation that concerns only them. The depiction of two gazes that cross each other, hold each other in balance as they weigh upon each other, does not only closely correspond to Marion's description of the erotic relationship, but it cannot possibly be accomplished by more than the two gazes involved. Such prayer always borders on the solipsistic: The praying person is alone with God and invisible to the world. It seems that this kind of prayer cannot happen within community, and in effect it shuts out the fellowship of others as it exists in splendid isolation, a soul intoxicated with its individual mystical experience of divine love.

Marion uses terminology and description for this account of the relation between God and the person at prayer that is exactly parallel, if not identical, to this definition of love. Both love and prayer are analyzed phenomenologically as a "crossing of gazes." Both expose two gazes to each other in vulnerability and ecstasy. Both are invisible and incommunicable to all others. And as we have seen in the chapter on love, Marion explicitly affirms these parallels. Erotic language and the language of mystical theology influence each other, are used in similar contexts, maybe are even identical to each other on some level, as the language of mystical theology is said to be essential for erotic discourse and prayer is marked by the erotic gaze. All our love is a response to divine love. As the erotic phenomenon is ultimately a response to the divine, so the prayerful crossing of the two gazes across the icon is ultimately an erotic one. It is hence invisible (and presumably irrelevant) to all others. Prayer is an intensely personal experience of love, not one that could be communicated.

While entirely consistent with his larger phenomenological work, Marion's depiction of prayer here also seems significantly influenced by his personal experience. In an interview with Dan Arbib, he remarks repeatedly on the importance the practice of the adoration of the blessed sacrament has had on him from early on (RC, 41, 42, 52, 187). He describes the "dialogic character" of the spiritual life as experienced in "eucharistic adoration" in the terms *God without Being* and other texts consistently use for talk about the divine: "With eucharistic adoration a fundamental psychological change takes place, because it is a matter of putting words in the mouth of a reality, if I can put it like that, or of causing the words spoken to be actually those of One who is here now, facing me, infinitely more than me" (RC, 53). He stresses that this means that God is not found as utterly transcendent "in some other world" but that "the spiritual life becomes the space where all else takes place and is not a part, a margin, or a limit of experience of the world." And he concludes that "the consequence for intellectual life is not slight: speculative theology or neutral rationality are no longer on one side and the spiritual life on the other, but the same place envelops both" (RC, 53). Personal mystical experience becomes the ground for theological speech. Later in the interview he stresses eucharistic adoration again as "a very vivid and determinative experience in my life" (RC, 187) and speaks of prayer as divine address (RC, 245). These accounts go a long way toward explaining why individual contemplation plays such a strong role in Marion's writing about prayer, although they do not necessarily justify it as the sole or most adequate account of prayer more generally.

Prayer as Protection of God

Similar to his concern in *Théologie blanche, Idol and Distance,* and *God without Being,* Marion's intent in the final chapter of *In Excess,* titled "In the Name: How to Avoid Speaking of It," is to protect the name of God and to preserve it from blasphemy and idolatry. This concern takes up his earlier analysis of idolatrous and iconic language for the divine even more clearly than the account of prayer in *The Crossing of the Visible.* His title picks up on two of Derrida's discussions of negative theology: *Sauf le nom* (translated in *On the Name* together with two other essays) and the earlier "How to Avoid Speaking: Denials."[10] Marion responds in this chapter to what he contends is Derrida's claim, namely that negative theology is still descriptive and onto-theological, merely re-inscribing the description and ultimate affirmation of the divine on a higher level via apophatic discourse. Marion takes issue with Derrida's writing on "negative theology," which he prefers to call "mystical theology," and argues instead that mystical theology escapes any kind of determination and is not metaphysical.[11] He engages in an analysis of Dionysius's treatises *Mystical Theology* and *On the Divine Names* and finds in them three movements: one of predication or affirmation, one of denial or negation, and a superior or third way, which he describes as a way of "eminence" or "un-naming" (IE, 134–42; DS, 162–71).[12] Derrida, so Marion argues, only recognizes the first two ways and therefore remains stuck in predicative language about God (or at least accuses negative theology of such).

Marion wishes to explicate this third way that Derrida misses in his view. He speaks of it as a way of prayer or praise, which moves beyond both affirmation and negation in a movement of praise that no longer seeks to say anything determinative about God.[13] It is a way that plays outside of the duality of affirmation/negation, synthesis/separation, true/false, and thus transgresses the values of truth that are exercised by logic and metaphysics. In so doing, it shows the insufficiency of the first two ways (IE, 138; DS, 166). Marion sees the three ways inscribed in a hierarchy: negation is superior to affirmation (and more appropriate than it), eminence and praise is superior to both (and more appropriate than either). All names for God are denied and disqualified. The point is neither "naming" nor "not naming" (both remain ultimately idolatrous), but "un-naming" (which is iconic), and the very pertinence of all predication is thus eliminated. Similarly to his "radical" phenomenology that explicates the purity of the "claim as such" and not any particular determinate claims, Marion seeks to move beyond concrete manifestations or specifications of God to a "pure" naming that is no longer predicative. I pursue this parallel in more detail later in this chapter.

Prayer, then, transgresses the metaphysical function of language (IE, 143–44; DS, 173). The point of praise is no longer to say but to listen: to be said, recognized, and "loved by goodness" (IE, 148; DS, 178).[14] Marion concludes that we must ultimately be silent about God in order to protect God from our idolatrous namings.[15] The theologian must practice deconstruction (IE, 153; DS, 185). This silence itself, however, has to be both deserved and qualified. It is not an ignoring of God or a "silencing" of theology, but an appropriate silence, one of awe in which the focus moves from me talking about God to God addressing me. It is not so much that Marion is interested in the effect of this speech or silence on human beings, but his reversal of emphasis designates the important impossibility of speaking about God. God cannot be named; there cannot be any conceptual possession of God; God's name and essence must be protected (IE, 150–58; DS, 181–90). Again, this move may be said to parallel his more general phenomenological reversal, in which I no longer control the phenomenon, but the phenomenon comes to me. Prayer thus becomes dissolved in pure (and mute) praise.

Furthermore, instead of speaking adequately of God, in this kind of prayer the movement is inverted and the one who is praising becomes named by the one whom he or she seeks to praise, in a move that parallels to some extent the crossing of gazes in *The Crossing of the Visible*. The person praying no longer speaks but gives him- or herself to the one whom the prayer "unsays." According to Marion, this constitutes a pragmatic function of language not a predicative one (IE, 140; DS, 168). He links the movement of prayer with that of naming and ultimately of baptism (IE, 142–58; DS, 171–90).[16] Prayer, then, does not consist in making the one invoked come down but in raising us toward God "by sustained attention" (IE, 144; DS, 174). Marion concludes that "the Name no longer functions by inscribing God within the theoretical horizon of our predication but rather by inscribing us, according to a radically new praxis, in the very horizon of God. This is exactly what baptism accomplishes when, far from our attributing to God a name that is intelligible to us, we enter *into* God's unpronounceable Name, with the additional result that we receive our own" (IE, 157; DS, 189; original emphasis). Mystical theology hence does not find a name for God but helps us receive our name from such prayer. Prayer becomes an openness to the divine naming that envisages me and reduces me to awe and bedazzlement.[17] Relation is here ultimately impossible, because the distance is so great.[18]

Reflection on the phenomenon of prayer in this article therefore returns to a consideration of the possibility of revelation (IE, 158–62; DS, 190–95). Prayer, for Marion, although it begins with the praying subject, really is a way of getting at a sense of God's activity. Prayer is not about what we do or say or who we become, but first about what we should not say and secondly about what God does for us. Unlike the earlier account in *The Crossing of the Visible,* where two gazes cross mutually and weigh on each other, here the person at prayer appears rather passive and merely marks the response to the divine other who is the primary or even sole actor, similar to the description of being envisaged by the gaze proceeding from the icon in *God without Being.* This phenomenology of prayer, then, becomes a way of acknowledging our impotence to speak of God and the highest articulation of what happens in the overwhelming phenomenological encounter. Indeed, that is the actual point of the article. It is primarily an explication of the impossibility of speaking about God or saying anything adequate about the divine. Prayer simply serves as a name for the awe inspired by the unnameable and as a way of claiming that such awe is no longer predicative.[19] Despite this fairly brief treatment, however, it does remain a representative indication of Marion's views on prayer as he describes the "right" human attitude before God consistently as an experience of excessive bedazzlement to which awe and silence can be the only appropriate responses. This kind of prayer, then, is not primarily meant to be practiced in community or to transform an individual or a group of people, but rather provides a safeguard to protect the divine name. Prayer is the apparently passive response to the excessively saturated phenomenon of revelation.[20]

The person at prayer then closely parallels the recipient of the saturated phenomenon, the one who is completely devoted and "given over" to the phenomenon. Prayer serves as the screen on which the "incoming" of the phenomenon of revelation marks its impact. This impact is made visible in praise and in the kind of language employed about the phenomenon. Instead of creating a work of art or bearing witness to the historical event, the person at prayer praises the God who has been encountered. Yet, the description of prayer seems to make the recipient considerably more passive than the account of the saturated phenomenon more generally. There is no sense here in which the person at prayer could serve as the "master" of the given. Rather, the prayerful person becomes envisioned, named, and baptized by the divine call. No response can possibly be adequate to this experience. Indeed, Marion stresses this negativity and incapacity throughout, not only with the language of "un-saying" and the parallel between "non" (no) and "nom" (name), but also by insisting that silence and even stupor are requirements for approaching the divine phenomenon because "God is never given intuitively" (IE, 161; DS, 193). Rather, the intuitive excess is so large that it "is accomplished in the form of stupor, or even of the terror that the incomprehensibility resulting from excess imposes on us" (IE, 161; DS, 194). At the same time, it gives rise to an obsession with invoking the name we can never truly name. We must continually un-say it and learn to "dwell" in it. Marion does not elaborate on what "dwelling" "in the Name" could mean beyond stressing that it transfers all initiative to the divine whom we allow to "say, name, and call us" (IE, 162; DS, 195).[21] Revelation renders us considerably more passive than the other saturated phenomena, which are, after all, still dependent on the recipient's willingness and ability to bear their respective impacts. In the case of revelation, even far more so than for the experience of history, art, or the flesh, it is abundantly clear that we could never sustain its impact. The divine is much too excessive.

Prayer as a Corporate and Corporeal Phenomenon

Marion's accounts of prayer, then, focus almost exclusively on the divine name and exposure to the divine gaze. Although he identifies prayer as a language of praise, there is little discussion in these accounts of worship in a more communal sense, that is, in the setting in which praise usually occurs. Yet despite this apparently exclusive focus on solitary prayer, Marion certainly has ecclesial concerns. This is most evident in an essay in which he explores the notions of presence and absence in light of the accounts of the ascension.[22] He finds an important link between presence and blessing. Only in the disciples' blessing of God can God become present and be recognized. The gift of God's presence is given when it is received as gift and blessed in that reception. In recognizing the gift and blessing it within the temple, the disciples are transformed into Christ and become themselves a paschal gift of presence. They imitate Christ's gift, repeat his sacrifice, and become "actors of presence" (PC, 130–31; PaC, 156–57).

Marion links the body of Christ that has ascended into heaven to the body of the Eucharist and to the disciples constituting Christ's body as the church. This gift of presence can be assimilated when it is recognized as such in prayer and blessing. Blessing, Marion insists, also relates to mission. The disciples have to perform the mission of Christ and thus become actors of Christ as they act in love or charity. He argues that the community is newly constituted by the resurrection and supposed to perform the body by its becoming or "playing" Christ as in a *commedia dell'arte*. Marion even points to the eschatological nature of this liturgical action: "Presence: not to find oneself in the presence of Christ, but to become present to

him (to declare oneself present, available) in order to receive from him the present (the gift) of the Spirit who makes us, here and now (in the present), bless him
like he blesses the Father—until and in order that he return. The highest presence
of Christ lies in the Spirit's action of making us, with him and in him, bless the Father" (PC, 145; PaC, 171). The focus, however, is still almost exclusively on praise
of God. It appears that this "instantiating" of the role of Christ and even making
Christ present today is more occupied with safeguarding the divine than with any
transformation of the community or the community's activity within the world.

Despite Marion's recognition of the significance of Eucharist and mission in
this text, his depiction remains a fairly individualistic one. It is the individual believer who is inscribed into the divine life of the Triune God and is patterned on
Christ. Marion claims that in liturgy all our senses are brought together and directed to God, but he describes this sensual experience as a "spectacle," something
which the believer observes the celebrant perform. It is the celebrant who acts in
the person of Christ and takes on his role. Christ is touched, seen, eaten, heard,
breathed in Scripture and eucharistic body, but in Marion these actions affect not
the body but only the gaze. The attitude of my gaze before the liturgy parallels my
attitude before the crossing of the visible by the invisible in prayer (CV, 64; CdV,
114). Liturgy, for Marion, guides us to the "decision" of "accepting to pray," which
"signifies allowing the other to observe my gaze" (CV, 65; CdV, 115). The "participant" in the liturgy is merely passive, an adoring observer of what the priest performs in the place of Christ. Only the priest acts *in persona Christi* and performs
the work of Christ.[23] The congregation seems like an "audience" without active
participation in the liturgy. Any appropriation of this sacrifice happens only in an
individual attitude of prayer before what is performed by another for me and in
my place—or possibly through individual adoration of the sacrament. A coming together of this assembled people into one body active for justice and peace,
transforming this present world into the one promised, is not considered in this
context. Believers may bless God and may take pains not to speak God's name
inadequately or idolatrously, but there is little discussion of how they are transformed by their prayer.[24]

This is qualified somewhat by the claim that our gaze is affected by the divine
in prayer. In both his discussions of prayer, Marion does insist that our gaze is exposed to the divine in prayer and by implication the divine has some sort of impact on us. In the discussion of the divine name in *In Excess,* he puts this in terms
of our naming: we receive a name from God in baptism (IE, 157; DS, 189). And, as
we have seen, we are invited to "dwell" in this Name. Marion certainly does not
exclude that prayer could have a transformative effect on us and indeed seems to
expect it. In the discussion of the icon in *The Crossing of the Visible,* our gaze becomes inflamed in love for the divine. Our gaze clearly does not remain unaffected
in prayer. Yet the most immediate result is that the person at prayer becomes more

careful about how to name the divine and is prevented from reducing God to an object. Thus, God seems to "profit" most directly from these effects on the prayerful gaze. What appears to be missing in this account is the kind of transformation that would make a difference in the world, one that might compel us to work for greater justice and peace. Such an account would in no way be incompatible with what Marion has outlined so far. He just has not ever gone on to elaborate any of these possible implications.[25]

Parallels to this early account of the effects of the ascension on the believer who becomes like Christ in *Prolegomena to Charity* and the effects of the divine gaze on the person at prayer in *The Crossing of the Visible* can be found in a much more recent reflection on the saint and sainthood in *Le croire pour le voir* (CpV, 207–16).[26] In this piece, Marion contends that holiness is by definition invisible, as no one can ever attribute holiness or judge the saintliness of another person, much less of oneself, because it would require judging the virtue of another and the purity of the other's heart to which I have no access. Holiness relies on the paradox of invisibility itself (CpV, 209). Marion compares the witness of holiness to the witness of extermination in the death camps. No one who was exterminated can testify to it, yet a survivor has not really experienced the extermination all the way to the end. Holiness is presented as a similar limit-experience. As death or the sun cannot be faced, holiness is too blinding to be viewed directly. Marion's analysis culminates in Christ: the only true witness about death because he truly experienced it and yet was raised from it. Christ is hence the only true saint (CpV, 212). Drawing on various Hebrew accounts of God's overwhelming glory and sanctity, Marion concludes from this that "God's holiness is manifested as such and as a result is manifested as invisible. Holiness marks the realm of God's very phenomenality as unreachable, unconceivable [*unvisable*] invisibility" (CpV, 213).[27] Christ alone epitomizes this divine holiness in his earthly life, yet it remains ultimately invisible, inasmuch as it cannot be turned into an object for inspection. In Christ, it culminates in the most kenotic disfiguration of an ignoble death, what seems furthest removed from the divine holiness and glory. Finally, Marion suggests that saints are visible only in the third order of charity or holiness; they remain invisible to the world or to philosophical thinking because they belong to a different realm of phenomenality that cannot be grasped by these other attitudes (CpV, 216).[28] Holiness can be seen only by the holy and remains invisible to anyone else. It is hence completely parallel to other saturated phenomena that remain invisible to anyone who "does not have the eyes to see" them, albeit put in even more excessive terms.

This account of saintliness has parallels both to the treatment of prayer and eucharistic presence just outlined as well as to Marion's more general discussions of the third order of charity as escaping the metaphysical order of certainty. It also makes Marion's apparent disinterest in ethical or communal dimensions glaringly obvious. Surely a discussion of sainthood would prove an eminently suitable con-

text for speaking of the ways in which the encounter with God transforms believers and directs them to service to the poor, outcast, and vulnerable. Yet Marion's account focuses exclusively on the "excess" and invisibility of the saint and
ultimately denies sanctity to anyone but Christ. While people acknowledged as
saints by their communities have certainly often rejected such ascription, and obviously sainthood cannot be claimed for oneself, it seems that some account can and
should be given for how it is manifested within the world. And, historically, such
manifestation has often been seen to be through acts of charity, kindness, compassionate care, or even explicit social and political action on behalf of the poor and
marginalized of society. Marion stresses only the purity of the heart but says little
of outward actions. Again, these may be in no way incompatible, but the more
corporate, corporeal, and concrete dimensions remain unexplored.

Furthermore, this essay on sanctity makes use of the argument already hinted
at in *Being Given*, first set out explicitly in "Banality of Saturation" and explored
much more fully in *Le croire pour le voir*, that certain phenomena (especially saturated ones and in particular phenomena of revelation) might be seen only if one
believes in them or has eyes to see them or is prepared for them in a certain fashion. That, as I suggest in previous chapters, is an important hermeneutic dimension Marion does not acknowledge sufficiently. Such a dimension is particularly
important for practices of prayer, which arise within specific ecclesial traditions,
just as sainthood is defined in particular ways by the concrete context in which it
is acquired through certain fairly clearly circumscribed ascetic practices. Prayer,
for much of Christian history (and in fact also for many other religious traditions), has been regulated by both oral and written traditions, which outline specific stages through which one progresses in various concrete practices of prayer
intending to lead the person to greater sanctity. Prayer and holiness are indeed
closely linked throughout the Christian tradition. There is no sanctity without intense practices of prayer, and prayer makes possible and sustains the connection
and similarity to the divine in which sanctity consists. Marion is certainly right to
point out that Christian notions of holiness are patterned on Christ and rooted in
the call to be holy as God is holy. Yet this need not be a purely individualistic enter-
prise, nor does it mean that holiness must always appear in the exclusively excessive manner Marion suggests. Rather, it is often practiced in seemingly mundane
fashion via the "cup of cold water" offered to the thirsty and care for the needy
and downtrodden in ways that are less dazzling and spectacular.[29] Let me take up
each of these claims in turn.

Prayer and Hermeneutics

An account of prayer actually requires many important hermeneutic dimensions. First of all, prayer is made possible and prepared by a hermeneutic context

that informs how prayer is understood and practiced. We learn to pray through the various traditions of prayer to which we are exposed when we are young or when we first come to prayer. These could consist in scripted morning and evening prayers in some traditions, mealtime prayers, or more extemporaneous prayers for various occasions or times in other traditions. When prayers are read from a prayer book or said in unison in a liturgical space, the hermeneutic context is obvious. We participate in what has gone before us, was formulated long before we came on the scene, and we identify it as prayer because it follows the formulae or is printed in the book. Yet even more "freely" formulated (extemporaneous) prayers are significantly shaped by precedent and expectations that provide a context for what counts as prayer. These merely oral prayers are often just as heavily scripted as the ones that are written down.[30] Regardless of the style of the prayer, these various traditions of prayer provide a hermeneutic context for how prayer is identified and what practices "count" as prayer. Believers will identify a phenomenon as prayer or can give a response of praise to the divine gaze because their prior expectations shaped by their experiences within particular ecclesial traditions have hermeneutically prepared them to do so. As Hart points out in the context of commenting on Marion's account of revelation: "If we think of revelation also coming through the reading of Scripture and preaching about it we must also admit that there is an appeal to the senses. Yet this appeal is not without a horizon, for we have an intentional rapport with Scripture when reading it, and with a homily when hearing it unfold."[31] Prayer, like the hearing of the word, occurs within an ecclesial context and is prepared and informed by its horizon.

Furthermore, such prayer also always requires interpretation after it has taken place, in particular to the extent that it expects a response from the divine interlocutor. What does it mean to recognize the divine gaze in prayer, to "feel" the divine calling me or bearing upon me, to sense God speaking to me? All these require significant amounts of interpretation in order to hear this voice or see this gaze correctly, even to hear it *as* a voice or identify it *as* a gaze. Marion emphasizes the effect the divine vision has on the person who is praying. Identifying this effect as an effect of the divine gaze, however, is a hermeneutic exercise. Obviously, such identification does not happen in a vacuum but is always deeply informed by a whole (and varied) tradition of how God is understood to call or affect people. And yet the fact that this tradition is so varied itself points to the great role interpretation plays in this process.

For example, many thousands of Mormon believers agree with Joseph Smith that his encounter with the angel in upstate New York was an authentic experience of the divine. God spoke to him and gave him the instructions that became the Book of Mormon. An even far larger number of believers in a great diversity of Christian traditions do not agree with this interpretation, but consider Smith either to have heard nothing at all or to have misidentified whatever he did hear. Many Roman Catholic Christians believe that the pope, in particular when speaking *ex cathedra* (in virtue of his office), has a particularly good or even infallible sense of God's will and voice. Many other Christians strongly disagree that any person can be said to understand God correctly by virtue of office, even if only in very specific, precisely circumscribed circumstances. Christian history (not to speak of the history of other religious traditions or even Christianity's encounter with them) is littered with the casualties of various disagreements over correct and incorrect interpretations of the divine voice or gaze. Many people have claimed to hear God's voice and employed it as license for great violence or manipulation of other people. Such "false" interpretations of the divine revelation in prayer can only be rejected via hermeneutic discernment. This discernment becomes possible only through engaging in a hermeneutic circle, as the experience is evaluated by the larger community in the context of previous tradition.

Marion seems to say that if we expose ourselves fully to the divine gaze before the icon we will be marked by the divine and will respond in veneration. He does admit that one could venerate idols instead of icons, visions of the divine that are really just mirror images of my own expectations instead of a full exposure to the divine gaze. Yet is not a hermeneutic again required in order to distinguish between the vision of an idol and the exposure to an icon? What tells us whether we are admiring an idol or venerating the divine in iconic fashion? Cannot icons turn into idols? For Marion, the distinction is between whether one's gaze is held entirely by the idol and returned as a mirrored gaze, or whether one finds oneself envisioned by the gaze of the other in the case of the icon. Yet how can one distinguish phenomenologically between these two encounters? How does one know when one's gaze is held by that of another? Does it result in some special feeling? Does it transform the praying person in some way, so that one's prayerful faith could be judged by its "works"? The primary "result" for Marion appears to be more adequate, that is to say more apophatic, talk about God, at least in the distinction between idol and icon. The account in *In Excess* portrays prayer as a third stage that goes beyond even apophatic language, although its result still seems to be a more adequate, in this case "performative" or ultimately silent, talk about God.

If, however, the only meaningful difference between admiration of an idol and prayer before an icon is the language one uses of the divine as a result or the manner in which the distance between the divine and the person at prayer is crossed, this seems to require hermeneutics par excellence. How else would one discern between such types of language? How except through interpretation would one know that one language is "affirmative," another "negative," one "performative," another "effective"? When Marion speaks of hermeneutics in this context, it is always a hermeneutics exercised by the divine on us, instead of one that we employ, as we see more fully in the next chapter on the Eucharist. Yet when the stakes are listening to the divine voice or exposure to the divine gaze, must not a hermeneutic intervene that at least *attempts* to distinguish between different types of voices or different kinds of gazes? For exposure to the divine, this hermeneutic discernment is shaped in significant fashion by the hermeneutic context that precedes it: the accounts of the divine voice and gaze in the Scriptures and in the larger ecclesial tradition over the past two thousand years or so (much longer if the Jewish tradition is acknowledged as a precedent).

Marion himself actually constantly draws on this tradition in order to support and articulate his account.[32] In *The Crossing of the Visible* he has recourse to the logic of the defenders of icons against iconoclasm in order to distinguish between type and prototype and in order to define the icon over against the mere image or the false idol. In *Idol and Distance* and *In Excess,* he employs the texts of Pseudo-Dionysius in order to articulate the proper distance we should maintain in regard to divine transcendence. His discussion of baptism and the divine naming in *In Excess* depends on Gregory of Nyssa and other Patristic writings. Tamsin Jones has convincingly argued that Marion draws heavily from Nyssa's theological work, although he often does not acknowledge doing so and instead refers to Dionysius as the primary source. She shows how Marion conflates some Patristic writings and hence covers over the diversity in their accounts, presenting a fairly monolithic picture of the Fathers as speaking in a singular voice. She suggests that distinguishing more carefully between various Patristic arguments might actually have strengthened Marion's account and provided nuance to his explication of prayer.[33]

And Marion not only employs Patristic sources, but biblical references are also abundant in his work. Even in *Being Given,* a supposedly strictly phenomenological text, he draws extensively on various biblical stories in order to articulate the saturated phenomenon of revelation, such as the account of Christ's transfiguration, the calling of St. Matthew, and the calling of the prophet Samuel. As we saw in the previous chapter, he makes extensive use of Abraham's sacrifice of Isaac and the story of the prodigal son for his analysis of the gift, of sacrifice, and of forgiveness in *Certitudes négatives.* All these interpretations of the gift and its various figures are informed by the hermeneutic context of the Christian tradition, scriptural and otherwise, including religiously inspired paintings. It is striking, in fact, that almost all of these treatments—with the exception of the analysis of paintings—rely on interpretations of *texts.* Marion rarely describes contemporary experiences of the divine, but usually employs historical accounts of such encounters as they are reported in various texts. The biblical texts are probably the most significant source for him in that respect, but Patristic texts also play an important role. That may well be perfectly understandable in a written, scholarly text and there is no reason why Marion should not draw on these sources, yet employing them surely does constitute a hermeneutic exercise. Identifying them as saturated phenomena or as encounters with the divine is a particular interpretation and it is one standing in a history of interpretations that understands the texts in particular ways.

To give just one example: Marion's interpretation of the sacrifice of Isaac as Abraham's recognition of the divine gift responds to a long history of commentary on this text; Paul, Kierkegaard, and Derrida are among the most obvious characters in this diverse tradition. Marion is interpreting the story to be indeed about God calling Abraham, unlike interpreters who think that no God would ever ask anyone to sacrifice his or her own child and that Abraham would have been wrong to kill Isaac in response to such a demonic voice. Marion also interprets the sacrifice as fully accomplished by Abraham's response, in contrast to interpreters who think that it is cut short by God and not in fact completed. Some interpreters think of the story as an illustration of the transition from human sacrifice to animal sacrifice.[34] Others interpret it as being primarily about absolute faith that cannot be identified in "works" but is a passive response to saving grace. Marion's interpretation of the story is precisely that: an interpretation. It may well be a good interpretation, and it certainly "fits" his larger project, which provides the hermeneutic context for the particular interpretation. But it remains an *interpretation,* as any reading of the story must always be. It becomes meaningful to us precisely through this process of interpretation.

Similarly, the response to prayer relies upon an interpretation of what has been heard or seen in prayer. Whether it is veneration and praise or a radical transformation of one's life or a particular concrete action—possibly the sacrifice of one's only child—such response always constitutes an interpretation of what has occurred during prayer. One would surely want to maintain that there are better and worse interpretations of what has been heard or seen during prayer: going out to kill someone or starting a religious crusade we would surely now judge worse interpretations than actions of love or charity, although not all people at all times and places would have agreed. Yet, distinguishing between better and worse interpretations—love instead of violence—depends on a prior hermeneutic context and a contemporary community of interpreters, in which one can communicate about and in a sense "test" one's interpretation against that of others. An important role is then played by the corporate context for interpretation. The response to prayer is most dangerous when it happens in an apparent vacuum where the individual is no longer responsible (i.e., response-able) to other people, when there is no feedback from others about one's interpretation.[35] Feeling a divine gaze weighing on me calling me to outrageous acts of heroism that are without continuity with the kinds of things God is affirmed to be asking of people by a larger tradition may be more an indication of hallucination or mental derangement than of any authentic encounter with the divine.

There is also a sense, of course, in which prayer is not merely the utterance of a single person at a particular moment in time, but more generally defines what happens when religious communities gather together. A church service may contain "prayers" but is itself a kind of communal prayer where the people together come before God. Marion describes the person at prayer before an icon. While icons can certainly be found in people's houses (or "secret chambers"), they are more commonly found in Eastern Orthodox churches, and that is the practice that John of Damascus and Theodore the Studite defend in the treatises Marion draws on for his argument in *The Crossing of the Visible.* Yet his discussion gives the impression that he is speaking of purely solitary prayer, not of the icons found in (or forcibly removed from) the ecclesial space of these writers.[36] Even in ecclesial traditions that do not employ icons in their liturgical space, prayer is to a large extent a communal exercise. Again, distinctions can certainly be drawn between more "ordered" liturgical arrangements, usually following a particular text established by a tradition of practices, and "freer" or more spontaneous arrangements, which still follow fairly uniform practices and patterns over time, even when these are not written down or put in a code of some sort.

Prayer is understood differently by these different groups. The Eastern Orthodox tradition, for example, has an elaborate liturgy, following complicated patterns (often requiring a multitude of liturgical books for a particular occasion), rich in sensory impressions but fairly narrowly scripted. Liturgical prayer is understood to be an entry into the kingdom, a real participation of the eschatological reality of being in the presence of God.[37] A service in an evangelical Protestant church may follow no books at all, project music electronically on a bare wall, maybe illuminated with a cross, and see its primary purpose in providing a space for individual experience of the divine in a conversion of the heart, but witnessed by the community and to some extent made possible by the emotive space created through the music and the sermon. Both interpretations of communal prayer will shape how the act of prayer is exercised, how the "voice" of God is heard or how the gaze of the divine is experienced. In both cases, the ecclesial space is expected to prepare for prayer and encounter with the divine, praise is expected to occur within its context, and the gathering of the community generally is thought to be at least a minimal condition for a genuine encounter with the divine. All these are important dimensions of prayer that matter to its experience as a phenomenon and the interpretation of its phenomenal content or meaning.

These spaces and practices, then, serve as preparation or context for prayer or for hearing the divine voice. This dimension of preparation is almost entirely missing from Marion's account, which focuses instead on the surprise or unpredictability of the divine advent. Jones rightly criticizes Marion's "lack of attention to the role of preparatory practices in developing a capacity to receive phenomena

as pure givens." She suggests that "one might imagine many practices that cultivate expectancy or receptivity: bodily and contemplative practices as well as social and individual practices." As examples she lists "silent prayer; the contemplation of icons; the practice of solitude, of living in a community, of training one's
temporal experience around the liturgical seasons; restrictions on sexual practices
and diet; rules about clothing, obedience, poverty, and so on." She concludes that
"a debate could occur about which of these practices are more or less conducive to
the 'clearing away of obstacles' in order that saturated phenomena might appear as
they give themselves freely and without constraint. However, Marion never raises
the question."[38] And she links her criticism about the lack of considering preparatory practices to the absence of a discussion of discernment: "Marion never discusses how one might begin to establish a mode of judging such phenomena and
their intent."[39] Both of these concerns are hermeneutic dimensions: Prayer arises
in a context, is taught by a tradition, and interpreted within community.

Excess and Purity in Prayer

Yet even with these important hermeneutic preparations and guidelines,
prayer is hardly ever the kind of excessive experience Marion depicts. Even believers who regularly use icons for prayer do not continually or even usually experience the divine gaze weighing on them in the extreme fashion Marion describes.
Many instructions for prayer, both ancient and more contemporary, warn precisely of these kinds of expectations of excess.[40] Marion recognizes, of course,
that we do not always experience the entire extent of the saturated phenomenon.
He speaks of bedazzlement and blindness as our more usual reactions, because we
are unable to do justice to the intuitive excess and cannot bear its weight. We fail
in our exposure to the saturated phenomenon, we are not able to "bear up" under
the divine gaze. Yet, the implication always is that God's gaze is fully given, that
God is always manifested even when we do not recognize the divine. The failure
to experience the divine is always ours. Yet is this an accurate phenomenological
description of how prayer is usually experienced? Is it always an utterly abundant
experience that stops short only by my being so overwhelmed that I need to inter-
rupt it before I break down? Is this a helpful way of describing prayer as such and
useful to employ as a *paradigm* for its experience more generally?

One certainly would not want to deny that occasionally prayer can appear in
such excessive ways. The history of mysticism provides many accounts of such
rich encounters with the divine that were indeed experienced in utterly overwhelming ways. And Marion's account may indeed be very appropriate for these
instances. Surely, to speak of a saturated phenomenon is an illuminating way to interpret dramatic cases of conversion in response to the divine gaze. For example,
Joan of Arc's voices highly motivated her to courageous action although clearly

not everyone agreed with her interpretation. Teresa of Avila's extraordinary experiences of prayer enabled her to reform her order in radical ways and also made her suspicious to the Inquisition. Francis of Assisi's vision caused him to leave all his wealth behind and care for the poor and outcast of his society, much to the chagrin of his rich father whom he must have embarrassed considerably.[41] Yet are all experiences of prayer this excessive, and is it a good idea to make such extreme instances the paradigm for prayer as such? Must prayer always be this overwhelming, and is any "lesser" experience of prayer an indication of its failure? It seems impossible to identify a paradoxical "flip," in which prayer goes from the one extreme of idolatrous vision where I only contemplate myself to the other extreme of utterly kenotic exposure to the divine. Instead, it seems more accurate to portray "progress" in prayer as moving slowly along a path of prayer where motives may always remain mixed and attention often wanders at least to some extent and where God is encountered on occasion but not consistently or predictably and not always in utterly overwhelming fashion.[42] There must be degrees in one's experience of the divine. The liturgical year, for example, which alternates between feasts and fasts and more "ordinary" times, shows that we cannot always operate at the same intense level. And such need for times of lower intensity seems not *merely* a mark of our sinfulness or blindness.

The aforementioned mystics themselves, in fact, often warn against excesses in prayer practices and try to minimize the radical nature of their own superlative experiences. Teresa of Avila, for example, repeatedly tells her nuns that "God walks among the pots and pans" and admonishes them that levitations and similar extraordinary experiences in prayer are not the norm and should not be the goal of prayer practices.[43] She also is concerned with differences in persons and counsels compassion for anyone whose experience is unlike one's own: "For at times it happens that some trifle will cause as much suffering to one as great trial will to another; little things can bring much distress upon persons who have sensitive natures. . . . If you are not like them, do not fail to be compassionate."[44] She continually acknowledges that people experience and practice prayer in different ways, often drawing on her own mundane (rather than excessive) experience: "I spent fourteen years never being able to practice meditation without reading. There will be many persons of this sort, and others who will be unable to meditate even with the reading but able only to pray vocally, and in this vocal prayer they will spend most of their time. There are minds so active they cannot dwell on one thing but are always restless, and to such an extreme that if they want to pause to think of God, a thousand absurdities, scruples, and doubts come to mind."[45] She goes on to describe an elderly person who had lived a good life but seemed incapable of mental prayer (one of the supposedly "higher" stages of prayer). She concludes about this person and others like her: "There are a number of persons of this kind.

If humility is present, I don't believe they are any the worse off in the end but will be very much the equals of those who receive many delights; and in a way they will be more secure, for we do not know if the delights are from God or from the devil."[46] She continually stresses that the more active life has its own value and is not to be denigrated in favor of "pure" contemplation.

Similarly, many stories of the desert ascetics—surely a good example of excess albeit in its most minimalist version—emphasize the more mundane faith of a doctor or simple craftsperson said to be as close or even closer to God than the ascetic who has spent the past forty years of his or her life in prayer and fasting.[47] In one example it is revealed to Abba Antony that "there is somebody in the city like you, a physician by profession, who provides those in need with his superfluous income and is singing the *trisagion* with the angels of God all day long."[48] In another instance, a humble greengrocer is said to be far above an elder in holiness.[49] Many stories stress the importance of humility and warn of relying on excessive experiences.[50] In one instance, a visitor comes to discuss lofty topics of prayer ("spiritual and heavenly matters") with one of the elders who remains entirely silent. When questioned by a disciple, Abba Poemen says of the visitor: "He is from on high and speaks of heavenly things, whereas I am from below and speak earthly things. If he had spoken to me about passions of the soul, I would have answered him; if of spiritual matters—I don't know those things."[51] On another occasion, an abba counsels a disciple who feels overwhelmed by the amount of work, to do only a little each day.[52] Several particularly entertaining accounts concern young novices who try to be "like the angels" and no longer see any need for work but attempt to pray continuously. They are quickly brought "back to earth" by their respective communities. For example, when one such novice returns for food, the community members refuse to give him anything, saying, "John has become an angel and is no longer among humans." Only when the aspiring ascetic realizes his own need do they let him in, saying, "See, you are human, so you will have to get back to work again in order to feed yourself."[53] Several teachers point out that "disproportion is destructive everywhere."[54] One novice is actually forbidden to say prayers, gets in trouble when he tries to pray anyway, and is taught to move more slowly. The story concludes that *"little by little,* he became an excellent monk" (emphasis added).[55]

Besides these qualifications of the accounts of mystical prayer themselves, it seems deeply problematic to make such mystical experiences the very paradigm for prayer more generally. While prayer can appear on very rare occasions in such extreme form, much more commonly it is a considerably more mundane and ordinary practice, not characterized by any particular excessive or abundant phenomenality. Many "manuals" of prayer stress the need for faithfulness and persistent practice and discourage expectations of strong emotion or similar excessive effects.

And of course the "dark night of the soul," an experience of the absence of God where prayer seems completely ineffective, is characteristic of many accounts of prayer, including those of the great mystics themselves. How helpful is it to create in others—especially in children—an expectation of overwhelming experiences in prayer? Will they not abandon such practices much more quickly when the desired effects fail to occur? Often a loss of faith may be the result of overblown expectations of how God is to act in our lives. If encounter with God is always depicted as a thunderstorm or whirlwind experience, we will miss the "still, small voice" of the divine or be tempted to give up when we are confronted with only silence and absence.[56] Christ himself, at least as portrayed by several of the Gospels, experienced God's abandonment on the cross, and even his earthly life did not seem to be characterized by constantly saturated experiences in prayer. And surely he would have been supremely able to "bear up" under the divine bedazzlement. This alone should indicate that a lack of excess or saturation in the experience of prayer cannot be solely the result of sinfulness or inadequacy.

Another aspect that seems missing in Marion's account is the corporeal dimension of prayer. Not merely a mental exercise, prayer involves one's body. This is particularly obvious when prayer is done in a deliberate posture, such as standing before icons or kneeling. One might fold one's hands or raise them in the traditional orans position. Sometimes prayer is accompanied (and enabled) through other arrangements of the space: one puts oneself in a particular location, maybe one lights a candle or oil lamp, one ensures there is quiet and no distractions. Occasionally one prepares one's body in other ways through fasting or various ascetic practices. Physical fatigue at the end of a long day can significantly impact one's attentiveness during prayer. Bickering children or other interruptions may make focus or even prayer itself impossible. Sometimes a sigh or scream may be the most authentic prayer we can muster in certain circumstances. Prayer in a liturgical context is experienced differently from individual prayer. The phenomenological experience of prayer takes place in space and time and these are important to how prayer is experienced. Prayers differ not just in their degree of intensity, but also in manifold other ways, depending on how the experience is shaped by the context in which it occurs or is exercised. A phenomenology of prayer should be able to take account of and depict these various dimensions.

Finally, the tradition actually explicitly affirms degrees and stages of prayer. Prayer is not an all-or-nothing experience but is learned as a practice in which one can and should grow in one's experience. And usually this is a long and arduous process, marked by many disappointments and dry periods. One of the most famous examples of such an account of growth in prayer is Teresa of Avila's description that likens the four stages of prayer to the watering and nurturing of a garden, depicted both in *The Book of Her Life* and somewhat differently in *The Interior*

Castle, which itself is a larger image for the path that prayer takes through many rooms into the very interior of one's life.[57] Teresa describes this process: "Beginners must realize that in order to give delight to the Lord they are starting to cultivate a garden on very barren soil, full of abominable weeds. His Majesty pulls up the weeds and plants good seed. . . . And with the help of God we must strive like good gardeners to get these plants to grow and take pains to water them so that they don't wither but come to bud and flower and give forth a most pleasant fragrance to provide refreshment for this Lord of ours." She goes on to describe four basic types of watering, each representing a particular stage in prayer: drawing water from a well, getting water by means of a water wheel and constructed channels, having water flow naturally from a river or stream, and finally "a great deal of rain." The work of prayer hence becomes successively less laborious and more "natural."[58] While the culmination of this process may well be a kind of saturated phenomenon, the path to it and the stages through which one proceeds and learns its various practices are saturated to a much lesser extent and often characterized by loss, boredom, and various distractions.[59]

Another famous image is that of John Climacus (John of the Ladder), where prayer is described as the process of climbing a ladder on which there are many steps and many possible missteps.[60] One spends all of one's life climbing this ladder toward the divine and it is by no means a linear progression. Climacus describes the stages of prayer and sanctity in graphic detail, including many admonitions about pitfalls and slow progress. He stresses repeatedly that this path is "hard, truly hard."[61] Throughout, he counsels discernment:

> We must be very shrewd in the matter of knowing when to stand up against sin, when and to what extent to fight against whatever nourishes the passions, and when to withdraw from the struggle. Because of our weakness there are times when we must choose flight if we are to avoid death. We must watch and see (for perhaps there are times when we can neutralize gall with bitterness) which of the demons uplifts us, which depress us, which make us hard, which bring us consolation, which darken us, which pretend to enlighten us, which make us lazy, which shifty, which make us sad and which cheerful.[62]

He illustrates all thirty of the rungs or steps of the ladder with vivid stories about various monks or ascetics and their diverse practices. Many of his stories are superlative and yet they are simultaneously accounts of slow and laborious progression. He also affirms diversity. In the context of step 28 (on prayer), he says "The attitude of prayer is the same for all, but there are many kinds of prayer and many different prayers," and goes on to describe some of these differences.[63]

As these final examples have indicated again, prayer and a pursuit of sanctity are closely connected. Indeed, for much of the Christian tradition, prayer and sainthood have been linked in some fashion. Although consistent practices of prayer are not a guarantee for sainthood, sanctity is rarely attained without them. Marion focuses on the invisibility of the saint who cannot appear as a phenomenon. Yet, sanctity only becomes possible through practice and through interaction with other people. Often holiness emerges precisely through mundane and ordinary care for others in manifold small ways that accumulate over time (like the doctor shown to Abba Antony). Similarly, Kearney's discussion of Dorothy Day, Jean Vanier, and Gandhi highlights the ways in which their "sanctity" was expressed through their concrete and humble service to people on the margins of society.[64] Sanctity is seen to be produced by prayerful and loving practices over long periods of time and often under much adversity and danger.

And several Christian traditions believe a growth in prayer to be best patterned on a threefold path of growth: purification, illumination, and contemplation.[65] Sanctity is assumed to be the theoretical goal of such growth, even when it is always understood that its attainment could not be assumed from the start and can never be *claimed* for oneself but only aspired. In fact, most of the greatest saints—at least great in other people's estimation—themselves declaimed any sanctity and described themselves as the chiefs of sinners. There are countless stories in which the amazed disciple hears the saintly abba on his deathbed pray to have more time for repentance.[66] There are also many stories in which a particular elder or a community try to exclude someone who sinned and are subsequently shown to be wrong to do so. For example: "A brother who sinned was put out of the church by the priest. Abba Bessarion got up and went out with him, saying, 'I too am a sinner.'"[67] Sainthood then both increases by "degrees" and also requires hermeneutic interpretation. While in some traditions sainthood requires official recognition by an ecclesial hierarchy, it often emerges through popular devotion and commemoration. Regardless of the process, sanctity is in both formal and informal processes confirmed and recognized by other people and finally validated by the community. It becomes visible in the community's affirmation and recognition of the person's holiness. Surely not all holiness is visible, but certainly some is, although it may always require interpretation by other people.

This raises one further question that should be at least briefly explored here (although I return to it more fully at the end of the next chapter): Can one speak of phenomena such as "prayer" or "revelation" within phenomenology at all or has such a discussion moved us always already into the domain of theology? Matthew Burch criticizes Marion's account of revelation as not sufficiently phenomenological, because "Marion addresses a marginal possibility that might in fact never occur and to which very few people would claim to have first-person access." A phenomenologist would "address only those possibilities that are in principle accessible to anyone from the first-person perspective."[68] Burch thinks that "revelation does not seem to be a category of experience; rather, it seems to be a marginal, if not scarcely imaginable, metaphysical possibility." It is utterly *"unlike all other phenomenological experiences"* because "revelation is not a possibility that we have all always already experienced. The categories of experience can be seen by anyone because they are what each one of us always already *is,* and revelation is clearly not a possibility in this sense" (original emphasis).[69] The extreme language employed in Marion's account of religious experience does at times create the impression that such phenomena can be experienced only by very few people on rare occasions and even they will not be able to bear the divine excess adequately. To some extent this is precisely the worry he tries to address in his essay, "The Banality of Saturation," where he contends that saturated phenomena are "banal," frequent, and accessible to anyone. He does not engage the question of revelatory phenomena in that context.

Yet it seems wrong to claim that religious phenomena in general are only a "marginal" or "scarcely imaginable" possibility. Although surely not everyone actually *has* religious experiences, it is a possibility for everyone, at least in principle. And certainly religious faith is practiced in a variety of ways that are clearly experiential. Prayer is one example of such an experiential practice; the Eucharist— to which we turn momentarily—is another, but there are many other ascetic and spiritual practices that are experiences that can be examined phenomenologically, although this obviously does not constitute a claim about whether any particular experience originates from the divine. Steinbock's examination of mysticism is a good example of this, partly because he does focus on excessive experience and uses language of givenness in a way very similar to Marion. Yet he stresses even more fully than Marion the phenomenological character of these "possibilities of experience, essential possibilities as actualized," which evoke experience in such a way that we can see or experience it for ourselves.[70] With Marion he stresses that experience is "given as a gift" and yet much more strongly he insists that "there is not one kind of vertical experience pertaining to the religious sphere, but many modes of vertical experience that fall under the rubric of 'the religious.'"[71] The integrity of the variety of experiences is maintained by him both in his examples drawn from different traditions (Christianity, Judaism, Islam) and also stressed in his philosophical analysis: "Indeed, the encounter with 'another' way forces us to examine ourselves critically, not to reduce others to our way."[72] He also places more emphasis than Marion on the ways in which holiness is expressed in "works" and "authenticated" (though not proven) by the way in which they transform the believer.[73] His analysis bears out the possibility of a genuinely phenomenological account of religious experience.

It seems, then, that a phenomenological account of prayer is a valid philosophical endeavor. Yet, while prayer may well culminate—at least for some people on some occasions—in a supremely saturated experience or even in saintliness, that is not always the case. There are also many kinds of prayer that are not at all excessive and overwhelming, yet their lack of "saturation" is not due to some human fault or sin. Furthermore, one grows in prayer, and it is possible and even necessary to proceed through many stages and degrees of prayer. Prayer is also not always a solitary experience, where my individual gaze crosses with the divine gaze in a sort of meditative solipsism *à deux*. While prayer may on some rare occasions be such an individual experience of rapture, many other times prayer is practiced in concrete communal and corporeal ways. Finally, prayer emerges and is identified only through prior hermeneutic contexts and subsequent processes of interpretation, which also have plural dimensions over space and time. The phenomenon of prayer is "verified" by the theological context in which it is interpreted and by the witnesses to its effects on a person or community. All these are important hermeneutic dimensions of the phenomenon of prayer.

SEVEN

Eucharist and Sacrament

Marion has explored sacraments and especially the Eucharist throughout his work, beginning with his rather controversial treatment in *God without Being* and culminating with two accounts in *Le croire pour le voir*. Why is the Eucharist so important for Marion? On the one hand, it is obviously a central liturgical rite that particularly defines Christian identity. It is therefore especially significant for a phenomenology that seeks to explore religious experience. One might say that the Eucharist is Christian religious experience par excellence. On the other hand, the Eucharist is believed to be a central place of *God's* self-revelation. The Eucharist is said to be the "body of Christ" who is given to the ones who participate in the rite. Eucharist is hence not merely something religious people *do,* but it is something they receive: the eucharistic elements are *given* to us. It is hence above all a gift and, in fact, *eucharistia* means "thanksgiving."

The Eucharist consequently brings together many aspects of Marion's more phenomenological and of his more theological work: It shows us in our position as recipients of the divine and is centrally concerned with givenness and the gift. As a liturgical rite, it is also about prayer, indeed, is a form of prayer; thus it encapsulates various aspects of religious experience as Marion has treated them. I begin by examining Marion's writings on the Eucharist in some detail, showing the development from his earlier more controversial treatments to his more recent and considerably less well-known expositions. I then highlight what I perceive as some fundamental problems in Marion's account of the Eucharist as a convincing analysis of religious experience, focusing again on the elements discussed in previous chapters: the possibility or necessity to speak of degrees of givenness and the importance of the hermeneutic context for this experience.

Eucharist as Gift of Charity

Let us first consider what may be identified as Marion's "early" position on the Eucharist. This position is primarily articulated in two chapters of *God without Being,* which are probably Marion's most well-known treatments of the topic and are still often cited as authoritative, but can be supplemented by a piece that concluded *Prolégomènes à la charité,* the French edition of *Prolegomena to Charity,* and is the penultimate chapter of the English translation. I briefly summarize what Marion says about the Eucharist in these pieces and then draw out the phenomenological implications, before considering his more recent and far more clearly phenomenological statements about the Eucharist. Although these early texts are not always explicitly posited as theological, they are certainly not as fully phenomenological as the later explorations.[1] Yet Marion's phenomenological goals can already be discerned in them to some extent.

The final chapter of *God without Being* "proper" is titled "Of the Eucharistic Site of Theology," while the first of the two chapters placed "outside the text" (*hors-texte*) also concerns the Eucharist under the title "The Present and the Gift." The first of these chapters on the Eucharist claims that theology must proceed from God in order to be truly speech about God, while the second focuses on transubstantiation. As the title of the first piece indicates, Marion posits that theology arises out of the Eucharist, inasmuch as Christ himself speaks in the Eucharist as the Word and offers himself in the flesh. Ultimately, only Christ can interpret the sacred text. The account of the disciples on the way to Emmaus who recognize Christ when he breaks the bread and through this realize the import of his interpretation of the Scriptures on the road, is taken as confirmation of this (GWB, 148; DSL, 209). Marion maintains that *"the theologian must go beyond the text to the Word, interpreting it from the point of view of the Word"* (GWB, 149; DSL, 210; original emphasis). He insists that this does not mean that the theologian speaks from some sort of privileged, quasi-divine position but instead that the hermeneutic itself is located in the event of the Eucharist: "The Word intervenes in person in the Eucharist . . . to accomplish in this way the hermeneutic. The Eucharist alone completes the hermeneutic, the hermeneutic culminates in the Eucharist; the one assures the other its condition of possibility: the intervention in person of the referent of the text as center of its meaning, of the Word, outside of the words, to reappropriate them to himself" (GWB, 150; DSL, 211–12). Here the hermeneutic is regarded as originating from the event itself instead of its human interpreter. Christ appears within the Eucharist as an overwhelming presence that interprets itself and merely calls for reception and acceptance. In the Eucharist, the hermeneutic is "accomplished" and indeed "completed." All that remains to do is to welcome its fullness.

At this point, Marion has not yet developed his analysis of the saturated phenomenon, but roughly speaking this is what he takes the Eucharist to be: a mystical appearance of Christ overwhelming the recipient. It affects us instead of our controlling it: "In fact, the Word, at the eucharistic moment, does not disappear so much as the disciples, who eating his body and drinking his blood, discover themselves assimilated to the one whom they assimilate and recognize inwardly" (GWB, 151; DSL, 213). Marion speaks of this as an "absolute" hermeneutic because it proceeds directly from Christ as the divine Word: "This place—in Christ in the Word—is opened for an absolute hermeneutic, a *theology*" (GWB, 151; DSL, 213; original emphasis). When we celebrate the Eucharist we reproduce and perform Christ's hermeneutic presence: "The Christian assembly that celebrates the Eucharist unceasingly reproduces this hermeneutic site of theology" (GWB, 152; DSL, 213). This culminates in what has surely become the most contentious statement in all of Marion's work, namely his claim that "only the bishop merits, in the full sense, the title of theologian" and the further somewhat less problematic implication that theologians should not separate themselves from the ecclesial hierarchy.[2] He also concludes from his analysis that theology is not really a science but an exercise in holiness that requires the saintliness of the bishop-theologian,[3] and that no progress in theology is ever possible.[4] Marion later qualified some of these claims in an interview with Richard Kearney, where he explained that all he meant to imply with these statements was that theology cannot be separated from the life of the church, as can be seen by the fact that the early theologians were all bishops or at least held important ecclesial posts.[5] This connection between ecclesial event and interpretation of that event is actually an important point that Marion does not usually stress and that would have been useful to elaborate more fully.

This early emphasis on hermeneutics is remarkable. Most of the people who have criticized Marion for not emphasizing the role of hermeneutics sufficiently do not comment on this text. It is far earlier than Marion's discussion of the saturated phenomenon or indeed most of his explicit work on phenomenology. And this text conveys a particular "interpretation" of hermeneutics. Hermeneutics means here that multiple interpretations are possible of an event, but that only one is authoritative. The "correct" interpretation is the one provided by the event itself, if it is experienced in its fullness. Complete exposure to the event enables one to experience the event as it actually is. Only Christ can provide full interpretation here, because only Christ can truly "bear" the fullness of the event. Interpretation hence always falls short, but it falls short because we are too weak and maybe also too sinful to stand in the place of the Word who provides the truth. By becoming like Christ and standing in his place, we can approach this hermeneutic location, where we open ourselves to the Truth and which seems to function like an anamorphosis. If we were able to accomplish this fully, if we could become completely like Christ, we would indeed comprehend. No longer would our experience of the event be *one* interpretation, but it would become *the* interpretation. It is only our finitude and sin that prevent this, and hence the holier a person is, the closer does he or she approach the truth. In God, truth and interpretation merge entirely. God sees fully and hence need not interpret. Hermeneutics therefore is a provisional method of ascertaining the meaning of an event after it has occurred and it is necessary only because we are not divine and therefore do not know what the meaning is. If we had that kind of perspective, interpretation would turn to sight and no longer be necessary. This brings to a head what previous chapters have already suggested in regard to how Marion understands hermeneutics to function and what he considers its role. And indeed it is consistent with his definition of hermeneutics in the Marquette lecture:

> Hermeneutics practices a *givenness* of meaning on the given, a meaning suited to the given, in such a way that the latter, instead of returning to its anonymity and remaining in hiding, is deliberately released and freed in its manifestation. Hermeneutics does not give a meaning to the given, by securing and deciding it, but each time, it gives *its own* meaning, that is to say, the meaning that shows that given as itself, as a phenomenon which is shown in itself and by itself. The *self* of the phenomenon settles in the final instance all the givenness of meaning: it is not a matter of giving a meaning to this very object, constituted by the I as object, but of letting its own meaning come to the object, acknowledged [*reconnu*] more than known [*connu*]. The meaning given by hermeneutics does not come so much from the decision of the interpreter, as from the one who attends to the phenomenon itself and of which the interpreter remains a mere discoverer and therefore the servant. The phenomenon shows itself to the extent to which the interpreter admits to the given the meaning of *that* given itself. Hermeneutics interprets not only the given in a phenomenon, but, to do so, the interpreter must allow himself to be interpreted by the given which has to be phenomenalized. (GH, 40–43, trans. mod.; original emphasis)

Here also hermeneutics is read positively as long as it does not compromise the self-givenness of the phenomenon and its ability to phenomenalize itself. The phenomenon imposes its own interpretation. I return to this more fully in the final section of this chapter.

The second essay on the Eucharist in *God without Being* seeks to "explain the Eucharist" and essentially defends and rethinks the doctrine of transubstantiation against some contemporary criticisms.[6] He contends that absorbing the mystery of the Eucharist into a "rational, conceptual system" would be a failure even when it succeeds, although he insists that this is not what happens in the doctrine (GWB, 162; DSL, 226). Most fundamentally, he suggests, the Eucharist is a *gift* that simply must be accepted. He criticizes the displacement of "real presence" from the species of the Eucharist to the reception by the community or the individual. Both are false conceptions of presence. Locating God's presence only in the "consciousness of a collective self" devalues the Eucharist and ultimately makes it a useless performance that relegates God's presence to the past (GWB, 167; DSL, 235). Marion rejects this as just as idolatrous as the interpretation that "idolizes" the bread as a reified object of "eucharistic presence" (GWB, 168; DSL, 237), because here the individual consciousness substitutes itself for Christ. The Eucharist is to be seen as a gift of Christ, who gives himself within the species.[7] Marion argues that "eucharistic presence must be understood starting most certainly from the present, but the present must be understood first as a gift that is given" (GWB, 171; DSL, 241–42). Presence, Marion insists, "must be received as the present, namely, as the gift that is governed by the memorial and *epektasis*" (GWB, 175; DSL, 247). Past and future are hence temporalized in the eucharistic gift, which therefore makes possible a "Christian temporality": "The eucharistic present thus organizes in it, as the condition of its reception, the properly Christian temporality, and this because the eucharistic gift constitutes the ultimate paradigm of every present" (GWB, 176; DSL, 249). This is the gift of charity by which I am challenged to transformation. This requires that the presence be located outside of me, and thus transubstantiation proves a more useful account.

Again, Marion describes the Eucharist as a phenomenon that comes to me in kenotic abandon, gives itself to me as a gift of charity, and renders the phenomenological gaze unable to contain it.[8] We do not contribute anything to this gift of abundant love—we only receive it or reject it: "Love accomplishes the gift entirely, even if we scorn this gift: the fault returns to us, as the symptom of our impotence to read love, in other words, to love" (GWB, 178; DSL, 252).[9] The gift of the Eucharist confronts us, challenges us, changes us, apparently without much participation on our part. Marion rejects the idea that we could assimilate the divine to us in this phenomenon and instead insists on a kind of reversed experience where we become assimilated to Christ and ultimately to the Father.[10] He concludes in what sounds again like a preview of the later analysis of the phenomenon of revelation: "Summoned to distance by the eucharistic present, the one who prays undertakes to let his gaze be converted in it—thus, in addition, to modify his thought in it" (GWB, 182; DSL, 257). A real explanation of the Eucharist can proceed only from prayer, in which the person at prayer is completely exposed to the divine gaze and is being given the full meaning and signification by its overwhelmingly saturated intuition. While Marion does not yet use his later phenomenological language in these two pieces, they are accounts of a counter-experience of a supremely saturated phenomenon, a fully given gift of charity, that completely overwhelms the recipient through its kenotic abandon.[11] The recipient must bear up as best he or she can. The more exposed the believer is and the more assimilated he or she becomes to Christ, the more of God's presence is experienced and the more correctly can one speak of the divine. Both chapters, then, portray the eucharistic event as a fully given gift proceeding from the divine who gives in loving abandon. This gift must be received via the humble exposure to its effects.

Prolegomena to Charity also includes a reflection on the Eucharist that is strikingly similar to the second piece in *God without Being*.[12] "The Gift of a Presence," already briefly examined in the previous chapter, is a phenomenological consideration of presence in light of the resurrection and ascension accounts, where "presence" is a function of Christ's absence. Christ's presence is now a gift; the blessing at the ascension anticipates the eucharistic blessing. Marion also appeals again to the Emmaus account where Christ disappears at the very moment his presence is acknowledged through the blessing of the bread: "Christ blesses fundamentally on the basis of his Eucharist to the Father, and in view of fulfilling it" (PC, 132; PaC, 158). He suggests that the institution narrative and eucharistic rite invoke the presence of the Spirit who makes the bread into the gift of God and shows its identification with Christ. Christ makes himself recognized precisely through his kenotic abandon in the eucharistic "gift of presence."[13] Marion suggests that Christ's distance, indeed even absence, is essential, because it would otherwise annihilate our sinful world, which is not sufficiently pure to receive him:

> Let us note an evidence: the absolute accomplishment of the blessing signifies the absolute accomplishment, in the economy of the world, of the trinitarian communion; so long as this world remains subject to sin, a blessing between the Son and the Father passes beyond it, explodes it, in short annihilates it; therefore this blessing must be produced at a distance from our cosmic sin, for as long as the hour of Judgment does not arrive. And therefore Christ must remove from the gaze of the world (and even from his disciples) his communion of blessing with the Father for as long as the face of the world is not purified. (PC, 135; PaC, 161)

Here the full gift of God's presence cannot be given, because it cannot be received. And it cannot be received not because of our finitude, but because of impurity and sin.

Hermeneutic distance hence again emerges as a way of compensating for sin and lack of reception. The physical presence of bread and wine becomes the substitute for Christ's real presence, which we cannot bear because it is simply too overwhelming.[14] Yet, if we come to recognize him in our hearts, we ourselves can become imitations of him here on earth and thus reveal his presence to others.[15] This recognition again is not really an interpretation, but it is a more or less complete openness to what is fully given by Christ. The Eucharist is the gift of Christ giving himself who is invisibly present in the gifts: "Thus Christ is neither present in visible flesh, nor absent yet present in spirit or memory only, since his Eucharistic body is given to us daily" (PC, 146; PaC, 172). We receive it correctly when we ourselves come to imitate this kenotic love in our lives. He concludes "our flesh becomes word in order to bless the trinitarian gift of the presence of the Word, and to accomplish our incorporation in Him" (PC, 152; PaC, 178). Besides its similarity to the piece in *God without Being*, this essay also has important parallels to Marion's various accounts of the gift, as discussed in chapter five. Like the gift, the Eucharist is given completely and from itself. As in the gift, the giver and recipient must ultimately disappear, are never on the scene together. Neither the gift nor the Eucharist can be described as an economic exchange; such a depiction would invalidate the very essence of their meaning. God is given completely gratuitously in the gift of the Eucharist, without conditions and with complete abandon.

And as in the case of sacrifice and forgiveness, love is central also to the event of the Eucharist. As we will see shortly, the Eucharist becomes, in fact, the supreme instance of the gift and the paradigm for all truly given gifts. Just as God's love is the paradigm for all human love, the eucharistic gift is the supreme instance of all human gifts. In fact, it seems that already in these early texts the Eucharist is presented as an overwhelmingly saturated phenomenon, which proceeds from God alone and whose sole content is Christ as God's supreme gift. Not only do we encounter God directly within the Eucharist, but the focus is almost exclusively on God's self-revelation instead of on our experience. On the one hand, the theologian can (indeed should) speak from God's position. On the other hand, not to receive Christ's love offered in the gift is a human failure. Everything is fully given; it is merely a matter of accepting and of bearing up under the weight of the given. The phenomenological aspects of this treatment of the Eucharist emerge more fully in the more recent discussions, although Marion's overall position will remain very similar. These newer accounts include one explicit discussion of the sacrament as a "phenomenon of abandon" and several statements in other articles which have bearing on the earlier discussions of gift, presence, and hermeneutics.

Eucharist as Phenomenon of Abandon

Several pieces on the Eucharist and on other aspects of Christian faith are included in Marion's *Le croire pour le voir*. The essays collected in this work span the space of about ten years, but are nonetheless fifteen to twenty years removed from *God without Being* and *Prolegomena to Charity*. One essay focuses again specifically on the story of the Emmaus disciples, but this time uses phenomenological categories much more consciously.[16] Marion suggests that the disciples on the road to Emmaus were lacking concepts that would help them recognize Christ and that he provides these concepts in his explanation of the Scriptures. The disciples are confronted with an overwhelming intuition, but they are blinded and so they cannot deal with what they are given, cannot comprehend that this is the resurrected Christ with them. The appropriate interpretation of the phenomenon is provided by Christ's hermeneutic act of breaking the bread. Immediately, he disappears:

again absence itself becomes the "gift of presence" as in the earlier chapters in *God without Being* and *Prolegomena to Charity.*

In the context of this analysis, Marion dismisses various "bankrupt theologies," which he suggests are absurd precisely because they merely "rehash facts" and do not open themselves to the phenomenon of revelation before them. These theologies are blinded because they do not appreciate the overwhelming givenness of Christ:

> Before Christ, whether glorified, in agony, or resurrected, it is always words (and hence concepts) that are lacking in order for us to say what we see, in short to see the intuition that floods our eyes. When he comes among us—if he comes, or rather precisely *because* he comes— we, who are his own people, cannot "grasp him or understand him" (John 1:11). God does not measure his intuitive manifestation out stingily, as if he wanted to mask himself at the moment of showing himself. But we do not offer concepts capable of handling a gift without measure and, overwhelmed, dazzled, and submerged by his glory, we no longer see anything. The light plunges us into blackness—with a luminous darkness. What is more, the miscomprehension even appears inevitable—so much does the inadequacy of our concepts to the factual intuition of Christ result directly from the incommensurability of the gift of God to the expectation of men. (148, trans. mod.; CpV, 199; original emphasis)

This is precisely the way in which Marion describes the saturated phenomenon: It comes to us as overwhelming and bedazzling intuition; it renders us blind because none of our concepts could possibly be adequate. And indeed the end of the essay identifies Christ as a "saturating" phenomenon "par excellence" (CpV, 205). Contemporary lack of faith, he suggests, is not God's fault for being so hidden, but our fault for not seeing and receiving rightly. God is fully there and gives God's self in abandon, but we are unable or unwilling to accept and receive this gift. Our concepts and interpretations are inadequate because we cannot bear the excess of the divine gift. We are blinded and reduced to bumbling interpretations, because we are not strong enough for the truth.

Thus again, the Eucharist is read as a hermeneutic provided by Christ. In the Eucharist, Christ shows the disciples "*his* meaning, *his* concept, *his* interpretation" (150; CpV, 202; original emphasis). There is only one right interpretation given directly by Christ to the one who can hear and bear it. Marion concludes: "What we lack in order to believe is quite simply one with what we lack in order to see. Faith does not compensate, either here or anywhere else, for a defect of visibility: on the contrary, it allows reception of the intelligence of the phenomenon and the strength to bear the glare of its brilliance" (150; CpV, 203). Once the disciples accept Christ's interpretation, they are able to "constitute" a full phenomenon, to come to a meaning corresponding to the overwhelming intuition given to them, because the right meaning or signification is given to them by Christ himself.[17] Hence, not only is the Eucharist here read as the very paradigm for a saturated phenomenon, but it is also fairly clear that only one interpretation of this saturation can be valid, which is in some sense not an interpretation, but the Truth, fully and completely given by God directly to the person. For Marion, only one interpretation is ultimately adequate: that given by Christ himself via the Eucharist. Through the Eucharist we have direct access to the divine and God is fully given within its event, remaking the recipient in the divine image. Furthermore, we can see that the confluence we noticed earlier between Marion's theological and phenomenological accounts[18] has implications in both directions: while the Eucharist is read through the lens of the gift and saturated phenomenality, it also becomes the supreme paradigm for all other excessive phenomena, maybe even for all phenomena.

This is stated even more forcefully in a discussion of the gift within the same book. Marion reiterates many of his previous phenomenological statements: The gift proceeds from love and gives itself in full abandon. It can never fully appear, since it would turn immediately into an item of exchange or commerce, a metaphysical object, and Marion provides the usual phenomenological examples to confirm this. Yet he goes on to suggest that "the case of the invisibility of the gift" can only be fully comprehended by Christian theology because it has access to revelation (CpV, 182). Theologically, the gift can be identified as proceeding from God: "The gift of God consists in what God gives and that is nothing less than giving himself in the person of Christ" (CpV, 183). Again, the difficulty is not that God's gift is not fully given, but rather that the world refuses to see or accept it. Yet even the recognition of this gift is a kind of gift itself. Marion compares this gift of recognition to a sort of phenomenological epoché, in which the "natural" way of seeing is set aside in favor of a different attitude that is open to what is given.[19]

The penultimate section of the essay speaks explicitly of the eucharistic bread and wine as gifts. The kenotic gift "par excellence culminates in the Eucharist" (CpV, 189). Only this gift is completely abandoned, fully given.[20] All other gifts fall short in comparison. He concludes that "the Eucharist hence offers the paradigm of the gap between what experience gives to see and the gift that must be recognized" (CpV, 190). The usual difficulties in the phenomenological appearance of the gift hence seem to be ascribed again to human inadequacy. The divine, instead, gives perfectly. In the Eucharist, pure gifts can indeed become possible. The Eucharist is the perfect and supreme gift, in fact, the very paradigm of the ideal gift. This is the case because its materiality disappears completely and because it empties itself entirely (CpV, 190). Through this self-annihilation it manifests Christ as true phenomenon. The Eucharist is a perfect gift because it is given from above by God and because its hermeneutic is provided by God directly (CpV, 192–93).[21] Again, the fact that the eucharistic gift proceeds from God is taken as support for its perfect and full phenomenality.

This essay has already employed phenomenological language more heavily and more explicitly than the earlier more consciously theological treatments. Marion's most fully philosophical consideration of the Eucharist is posited as a consideration of the "phenomenality" of the sacrament and defines it as a "phenomenon of abandon."[22] This essay, significantly, begins by acknowledging that the sacrament is first of all a theological concern, but then insists that it employs phenomenological language and can be analyzed in phenomenological terms: "We can therefore ask: must the sacrament be received as a phenomenon, and, consequently, which particular phenomenality does it concern?" (90; CpV, 150). Marion examines the traditional definition of the sacrament as "the visible sign of an invisible grace" and then considers several interpretations of this definition.[23] He cites three traditional eucharistic models: first, a "metaphysics of substance" that describes the relationship between visibility and invisibility in terms of that between substance and accidents, second, a further metaphysical model that describes this relationship in terms of cause and effect, and third, a semiotic model that perceives the sacrament as a "sacred sign." In each case, he concludes that phenomenologically speaking this means that the sacrament "truly gives itself to see as invisible, in short, it *gives itself without withdrawal* to the point of abandon" (93, 94, 95; CpV, 154, 155, 156; original emphasis). Therefore, this must constitute the true phenomenality of the sacrament: the invisible gives itself entirely in the visible and abandons itself to it.

He examines this conclusion both phenomenologically and theologically. Phenomenologically speaking, he argues for a notion of phenomena as saturated, reiterating his critique of earlier phenomenology (from Kant onward) as concerned exclusively with objects and his own proposal for givenness as such. He suggests that Heidegger's analysis permits attributing a "self" to the phenomenon appearing "from itself" and that "phenomenality accomplishes itself in the full phenomenon insofar as the appearing gives the appearance and the appearance gives itself in its engagement in the appearing" (97; CpV, 160). Phenomenality is accomplished in complete immanence, although it does so from its own initiative.[24]

Interestingly enough, the phenomenological section says nothing about the sacrament at all, but focuses only on the relationship between appearing and what appears. In the final section, identified as theological, Marion applies these phenomenological parameters to the phenomenality of the sacrament, suggesting that "the sacrament accomplishes and reduces the intrinsic manifestation of the

Son, the transition in it from the Father's invisibility to Christ's visibility spread by
the Spirit in its Church" (99; CpV, 162). He claims that phenomena of revelation
show themselves more than other phenomena and that they do so more fully from
themselves. Hence these phenomena are not constituted, but they are simply received as they give and show themselves, making it impossible to impose any concepts upon them.[25] Intentionality proceeds only and directly from God (100; CpV,
163). Here Marion explicitly appeals to his phenomenology of saturated givenness:
"Thus, it is advisable to situate the sacrament in the horizon of God's Revelation
in his icon, Christ, and to apprehend it, by analogy with the phenomenality of the
world, as a phenomenon that shows *itself* par excellence and in excess" (100; CpV,
164; original emphasis). The theological phenomenon of the Eucharist is hence
placed fully within the horizon of the phenomenological analysis.

Marion reminds us that most things show themselves as more complex than
simply objects. Materiality itself is already rich with meaning. Yet, in the materiality of the sacrament, this saturation is raised to another level: "And these moral
and spiritual tonalities already appear at the outset, intrinsically, with the materiality of the sacrament, which *thus implements a determination of the phenomena in
general in a simply more radical mode*" (101; CpV, 165; emphasis added). Here the relationship between theology and phenomenology becomes reversed: The phenomenality of the sacrament becomes the paradigm for all other phenomena. It
is a more absolute, more excessive, more radical phenomenon, which can inform
all phenomena. As in his more general phenomenological account, the extent to
which the phenomenon can appear depends "on the width of our reception and
the meaning it carries with it" (101; CpV, 165). The sacrament is thought as the
supreme phenomenon of revelation, which gives itself in full and total abandon
and overwhelms consciousness entirely.[26] This, then, is a phenomenological appropriation of total kenosis, absolute self-givenness, complete abandon. Marion
concludes:

> The phenomenality of what gives itself extends to the givenness of
> the invisible; in short, it qualifies the sacrament as a phenomenon by
> full right, although by analogy, because what gives itself gives itself to
> the point of death and of the death on the Cross, because what gives
> it gives itself absolutely. Christ gives himself enough so that even the
> invisible face of the Father can show itself among us. *That is enough
> to qualify the sacrament as a perfect and whole phenomenality.* (102; CpV,
> 166; emphasis added)

The implication that the Eucharist is essentially about Christ's showing of the Father's invisible face is consistent with Marion's previous analyses, where the Eucharist is interpreted as God's self-revelation via the incarnate Word. Yet here this
is clearly also a phenomenological claim and not solely a theological one.

Admittedly, in "The Phenomenality of the Sacrament," Marion phrases things more carefully. He does not claim anywhere that we might move over to God's point of view, although he obviously still wants to maintain that Christ gives himself fully and with complete abandonment in the eucharistic gift. Nothing is said about hermeneutics in this treatment at all and, in fact, Marion's consideration of several explanations of the Eucharist seem to imply that a variety of approaches might be possible (although he does think they convey a common message). Marion also distinguishes more carefully between a theological and a philosophical treatment here, mostly employing his distinction that theology has access to the actuality and historicity of events of which phenomenology can only explore the possibility.[27] Yet despite his greater care, the confluence of his two projects is still plainly evident: His phenomenological project is fully applied here to the Eucharist as a saturated phenomenon par excellence given in complete self-abandon. At the same time, this phenomenon of "total kenosis" is posited again as the supreme phenomenon that can serve as a paradigm for all other phenomena. The sacrament has a "perfect and whole phenomenality" "in a simply more radical mode" (102, 101; CpV, 166, 165).

One may wonder, on the one hand, whether this does justice to the eucharistic event as a religious experience and, on the other hand, whether such a specific religious experience can justifiably be said to serve as a paradigm for all other phenomena. I have doubts on both counts, as becomes clear in the final two sections of this chapter. Following the line of argument pursued in previous chapters, I first raise questions about the absolute and excessive nature of Marion's depiction of the phenomenon of the Eucharist, suggesting that even in this supreme Christian experience degrees of givenness play a role. To some extent this is in response to the first question of whether the phenomenological account can do justice to the "theological" experience. In the subsequent section I explore more fully the hermeneutic context I think is required to speak of the Eucharist as a phenomenon. This attempts to approach the second concern, namely whether such a distinctly religious phenomenon can be said to serve as interpretive lens for all other phenomena, that is, whether a "theological" or religious phenomenon, such as a sacred rite, can serve as the paradigm for all other phenomena.

Degrees of Eucharistic Experience

Marion presents the phenomenon of the Eucharist as the most saturated of all phenomena. It is a direct encounter with the divine in all its fullness and overwhelming presence, a gift of full presence and also of the highest apophatic absence. It completely overwhelms intentionality, disabling it and shaping it in a counter-experience where all intentionality flows from the divine toward the recipient. Yet, one might wonder whether "saturation" and "excess" are really the best ways to speak of the phenomenon of reception of the Eucharist. Does "excess"

best capture what is at stake in this experience? Is the most appropriate response
to participation in the eucharistic meal a sense of being utterly overwhelmed and
blinded? Obviously, it is also participation in a mystery: for the ancient church, the
Eucharist was "the mystery" par excellence, and the sacraments are still referred
to as "the mysteries" in the Eastern Christian tradition. Yet, even at the time when
the Eucharist was surrounded with the most mystery and secrecy, Cyril of Jerusalem stresses the corporeal dimensions of the event in his mystagogical lectures:
"Sanctify yourself by partaking of Christ's blood. While your lips are still moist,
touch them lightly with your hands and bless your eyes, your forehead and your
other senses."[28] Here the Eucharist is understood as a blessing of the body and the
senses, not an experience that overwhelms and sweeps them away entirely. I return
to this corporeal dimension of the sacrament shortly.

Our "mundane" experiences of the Eucharist do not bear out this depiction
of the sacrament as an overwhelmingly saturated experience. Although "the faithful" may well partake of this meal in hope of an experience of God and of the reality of the body of Christ, they do not usually have this experience in the excessive ways described by Marion. As in prayer, people are often distracted during the
eucharistic liturgy or tired or just bored. Rarely are they overwhelmed and bedazzled every single time they participate in the rite, in the kind of absolute fashion depicted by Marion. Having a less-than-saturated experience does not necessarily imply that one is sinful or not properly prepared, as Marion seems to suggest. In fact,
theologically, the Eucharist is actually linked directly to our experiences of failure
and inadequacy. The liturgical texts in several traditions speak of it as a healing of
our "unworthiness" and an absolution or cleansing of sins: hardly a description
of mystical rapture.[29] Of course, Marion does not downplay our unworthiness;
God's gift is all the more kenotic and loving because of it. Yet Marion seems to depict sin primarily as a failure to receive the saturated phenomenon properly instead
of seeing it as intricately connected to the very experience of the phenomenon.
It is not that our sin prevents us from experiencing the Eucharist in overwhelming fashion, as Marion suggests, but rather it is at least to some extent our sin and
need that bring us to the sacrament.

Beyond this recognition that inadequacy may be part and parcel of the phenomenality of eucharistic experience, other distinctions between degrees of givenness in this phenomenon seem required. Can distinctions be made, for example,
about the ways in which the experience might differ in different ecclesial or liturgical contexts? Does a Protestant experience the Eucharist differently from a Roman Catholic or an Eastern Orthodox believer? Can a careful description of their
different experiences say something about the phenomenality of this sacrament
in these traditions? Does the phenomenality of the sacrament differ for various liturgical occasions even within the same tradition? For example, is the experience
of the Eucharist different at Pascha/Easter than it might be on an "ordinary" Sun-

day? Does the heightened intensity on a major feast day suggest something about the ways in which the particular context matters to the experience of the phenomenon? Is it possible to take greater account of all the concrete ways in which people actually experience participation in the Eucharist?[30] Several elements would be required in such a description and all of them require more variable degrees of givenness. For all these questions, the notion of the saturated phenomenon seems to overdetermine the actual experience of the Eucharist in a way that covers over the diversity of experiences in this event.

For example, it is possible that many of the historical and current controversies over what the Eucharist means refer to different phenomenological experiences of this phenomenon. While the language of transubstantiation relies on particular philosophical categories appropriated from Aristotle, these categories were employed, albeit in transformed fashion, precisely because they seemed an adequate description of the phenomenon as experienced. Zwingli's definition of communion as a "memorial" meal and the ways in which it is celebrated in many of the more radical Protestant traditions convey very different phenomenological experiences. Let us take two extreme examples: In many evangelical Protestant parishes the meal is celebrated only rarely, attached monthly or even quarterly to the end of the "regular" service. In various denominations, grape juice is used instead of wine and it is served in tiny, individual plastic cups, sometimes with the waver enclosed on top of the thimble-sized cup, protected with an additional plastic cover. After the institution narrative is read, often directly from the biblical text (usually 1 Corinthians 11:23–26 is employed in some form), the entire congregation consumes the waver and juice simultaneously. This is at times followed by silence for personal reflection and prayer. In the Eastern Orthodox tradition, the eucharistic meal is the central liturgical rite around which everything revolves. Ideally, it is celebrated by the entire community gathered around the bishop or other celebrant (i.e., there cannot be more than one eucharistic celebration per day, per priest, and per altar—multiple priests present concelebrate instead of serving successive services). After an elaborate ritual, which involves a rite before the liturgy even begins (the Proskomedia or Preparation of the Gifts), various entrances in which the gifts are presented and carried to the altar, and multiple prayers both raising the congregation "mystically" to participation in the heavenly celebration and invoking the Spirit's blessing and descent upon the gifts, all participants commune from the same cup in which bread and wine are mixed together and served on the same spoon to all communicants, including infants. These gifts are regarded as the "food of immortality," which purifies and sanctifies the participants.[31]

Although both of these celebrations are rooted in the same biblical tradition and ostensibly go back to the same historical origin, clearly they depict quite different experiences. The phenomena themselves are, in fact, not identical and they carry a different meaning. The Protestant experience depicted is a more introspective and personal experience, although simultaneous partaking clearly also affirms it as a communal rite. It is meant to affirm one's faith and one's commitment to Christ, to bind one more closely to Christ through remembering his act of salvation on the individual's behalf. The Orthodox phenomenon is meant as the community's participation in the heavenly celebration, as entry into the kingdom, which becomes present within the liturgy.[32] The bread and wine, affirmed to be the real body and blood of Christ, effect transformation of the community, bring healing and growth in sanctity. What the phenomenon means, then, does not impose itself entirely from itself but emerges through the ways in which it is practiced and enacted. These phenomena are saturated in different ways and to different degrees, and that may not mean that one is "more" saturated than the other, but that they are differently saturated or that different aspects of the experience are saturated. Both can appear as more or less overwhelming and bedazzling, but such bedazzlement and the various ways in which it might be borne are located in a different aspect of the experience and are received quite differently. This is not to say that the experience of the Eucharist in different traditions has nothing in common. But to pretend that it is only one monolithic phenomenon that always gives itself in the same way (except for inadequacy of reception) not only misrepresents how the phenomenon is actually experienced but also misses the important ways in which its meaning differs for different communities, which says something significant about the identity and self-understanding of these communities.

Closely connected to this point is another issue: The Eucharist requires a fuller account of corporeality and materiality. There is almost no consideration in Marion's treatment of the eucharistic elements and of our tasting and consuming them. And as we saw in chapter 3, Marion has certainly talked about the experience of the flesh in other places and in "The Banality of Saturation" even explicitly explored the ways in which a saturated phenomenon appears to all five senses. So far he has not applied this analysis to the Eucharist, but it would be interesting to pursue this further and may well raise questions about the more "absolute" account of eucharistic experience generally given. What might it look like to explore the ways in which the eucharistic elements are seen and tasted, the words and music heard, the incense smelled, the exchange of peace felt in one's hands and bones? All of these aspects, and indeed their presence or absence in particular ecclesial traditions, inform the concrete experience of the Eucharist.

For example, the experience of the Eucharist is different if one is sitting, standing, or kneeling, if it is preceded by a gesture of reconciliation, such as the exchange of peace in the Roman Catholic and Anglican rites, or by a gesture of communal confession and absolution, as is the case in many eucharistic rituals. One of the important historical controversies concerned whether to use leavened or unleavened bread (still practiced differently in East and West) and, on a much smaller scale, whether to use fermented or unfermented liquid (i.e., wine or grape juice) and whether to mix it with water or not. Both preparation of bread and obtaining wine presented particular difficulties when Christianity moved into areas that did not traditionally grow grapes or raise wheat. Many Protestant congregations are now experimenting with using one big loaf of bread that is then symbolically broken and shared among the entire community or even celebrating entire "agape meals" instead of only a symbolic ritual that does not involve much food per person. In all these cases, a different phenomenological experience is at work and what we see, hear, taste, smell, and touch significantly influences how we experience the phenomenon and what and how it means for us. Such a more fully embodied description that pays attention to our sensory impressions may well suggest that the account of saturation for this phenomenon requires nuance. Just as not every experience of the diva or of a painting leads to an overwhelming experience, the sights and smells and sounds and tastes of the eucharistic experience may not always be experienced at their height, and yet they are essential to the experience itself. If we do not actually taste and touch, we can no longer speak of a phenomenon of the Eucharist. The ways in which our senses participate are an essential part of the experience. It also matters theologically that the elements are taken from the earth and that they really are consumed. The phenomenological analysis should not disregard this "earthiness" of the phenomenon.

There is also little consideration in Marion's account of the fact that the species become part of our body, that they mingle with our flesh.[33] How might the analysis of the saturated phenomenon of the flesh inform this account of the Eucharist? The Eucharist is understood by the tradition to be sanctified *matter* and thus to imply a sanctification and sacralization of material reality and of all of creation. The very treatises that Marion employs in his analysis of the icon (especially in the final chapter of *The Crossing of the Visible*) make that point clearly. John of Damascus affirms that matter is holy and sanctified through the incarnation and the presence of the Spirit within it and that to deny the sacrality of matter is to be Manichean.[34] This neglect of the matter of the eucharistic elements parallels Marion's more general neglect of materiality and nature, which I examined in chapter three. Yet the very visceral reality of "eating" and "drinking" in the eucharistic experience is fundamental to the experience itself. Here matter is "saturated" in precisely the sense that Marion seeks to stress throughout his work. A truly "embodied" account of the Eucharist may well help explore the important phenomenological dimensions of the material and corporeal in a way that does not dismiss them as impoverished.[35]

The liturgical setting also plays an important role for the event of the Eucharist. Even more clearly than the phenomenon of prayer, the Eucharist occurs within a liturgical context. The symbolic movements—carrying the gifts to the altar, breaking the bread, pouring the wine, distributing the elements to the community, carefully cleaning the implements used—are all an important part of the

experience. It matters that we commune only after extensive liturgical preparation and that we do so in a particular setting, which involves bodily movement
and a community of people. Yet, Marion's single-minded focus on the self-givenness of the phenomenon portrays it instead almost exclusively as the experience
of a solitary individual.[36] Despite the fact that he occasionally invokes the church
and draws on some traditional ecclesial texts and formulations, the eucharistic experience for him seems to be primarily a solitary encounter between the self and
God, patterned on his earlier analysis of prayer before an icon (which, as we have
seen, similarly disregards that icons are generally found in churches). His account
throughout seems to assume that Christ shows himself to the *individual* believer
as he or she partakes of or contemplates the sacrament instead of depicting or
analyzing a more general communal experience. Yet, even more than for prayer,
the communal setting is absolutely essential for the eucharistic experience and
hence also for an adequate phenomenological account of the Eucharist. It matter to one's personal experience of the phenomenon that one shares in it together
with others. And an individual experience of the Eucharist (e.g., in a hospital bed)
differs in important ways from the experience that takes place in the context of
a major liturgical feast where a large crowd of people is present and participates.
The ecclesial space in which the Eucharist is received is a significant part of the
phenomenon. If the Eucharist is said to be in some way the "body of Christ" that
signifies our belonging to the *ecclesial* "body of Christ," then participation in the
eucharistic body of Christ cannot be a purely individual experience concerning only
the singular believer before God. Even our individual experience of eucharistic reception is shaped by our doing so within the context of a community and a tradition.[37] An analysis of the plural dimensions of the event is absolutely necessary in
a phenomenology of the Eucharist.

At the same time, it must be acknowledged that even when the phenomenon
of the Eucharist is experienced within the same setting, participating in the same
community and the same bread, it neither has the same meaning for every participant nor does it affect everyone in the same fashion. The hermeneutic dimension
is central to the phenomenon as the vigorous, and at times bloody, historic controversies surrounding its meaning attest. All of the elements just mentioned—
the ecclesial space, the corporeal dimension, the diversity of traditions, the liturgical context, the words and their meaning—call for interpretation and themselves
provide the interpretive space in which such interpretation is conducted and becomes meaningful. Hermeneutics is absolutely essential to the experience of the
Eucharist on a variety of levels.

Eucharistic Hermeneutics

As we have seen, Marion's earliest analyses of the Eucharist actually explicitly
speak of it as a hermeneutics. The Eucharist provides the hermeneutic of faith or,

more correctly, Christ provides the hermeneutic that enables believers to receive him within the Eucharist. The theological interpreter should ultimately move over to "God's point of view" and see the event from the divine perspective. The more recent accounts no longer counsel moving "over to God's point of view" in any explicit fashion, but even there the initiative within the Eucharist still lies entirely and exclusively with the divine. All seem to assume on some level that one could proceed from the divine as a starting point. This parallels, of course, Marion's more general phenomenological argument that grants the initiative to the saturated phenomenon, which is fully given to the recipient who must merely receive it. In the case of the Eucharist, the initiative proceeds from the divine or more specifically from Christ, who is given fully in the sacrament. Yet is the initiative of the human flesh or of a masterful painting or even of the face of someone I cherish really completely parallel to the initiative of the divine? Even in the case of the saturated phenomenon, Marion does not actually claim that I would move over to its position, only that it gives itself fully from itself. Claims of the sort that the "face of Christ" is visible in the sacrament or that God appears invisibly in the Eucharist via Christ's sacrifice seem impossible to substantiate phenomenologically, although they may well be valid theological assumptions.

In general, Marion's treatments seem heavily concerned with verifying God's sole initiative in the event. Yet if these are truly *phenomena,* then they are first of all *our* experiences. Even if they are "counter-experiences," where the initiative lies with the phenomenon, the experience can only be recognized as an experience of the *recipient.* It is still the impact on the recipient that gives us access to the phenomenon at all.[38] What would it mean to "move over to God's point of view"? How could we ever know how something manifests itself from God's perspective? Bruce Benson also raises this question in a review of Marion's *God without Being:* "Put in a theological context, does the revealed Logos break through as a 'pure phenomenon' without any horizon? Or does that Logos depend upon the context of, say, Old testament prophecies for its very identity (at least for us)? Or, alternatively, when the Logos becomes present to us in the breaking of the bread, how much does its meaning (again, at least for us) depend upon the very ordinary biological reality that bread sustains life and the very particular historical occurrences of the Passover and the Lord's Supper?"[39] Instead of claiming an absolute "arrival" of the phenomenon without any context whatsoever in an utterly surprising mode, it might make sense to analyze more carefully and show more fully what *does* manifest itself in our experience: the space and time of the gathering, the signs and movements, the sounds and smells and tastes, the memories and anticipations.

As we have seen in previous chapters, in other aspects of his work Marion places more emphasis on the modes of reception of phenomena. Some of these analyses might prove useful also for speaking of eucharistic experience.[40] For example, in *Being Given* and in several articles, Marion insists on the anonymity of the phenomenon, which is identified only in the response of the recipient who identifies the phenomenon as coming from God, from the call of being, or maybe the intimate experience of my own flesh. Here a closer analysis and description of how a particular experience marks its recipient might be desirable. Is it merely a matter of it being excessive? Or can it be identified more fully? What guides this identification? Does the context in which the phenomenon is experienced matter for its identification and for what constitutes an appropriate response? How exactly is the recipient shaped by the phenomenon? Does participating in the Eucharist, for instance, somehow make the participant more humble, more aware of other people's suffering, more careful with the material things of the earth, more loving and selfless? How can the "effect" of the phenomenon be identified? And does this effect, the particular sort of counter-experience it is, identify the phenomenon in a certain fashion? Can other (saturated?) phenomena have similar effects on us? All these are important hermeneutic questions, and how they are answered provides important insight into the phenomenality of the Eucharist and its meaning.

In this context, one must also wonder again whether a hermeneutic *preparation* is not required in order to experience this effect. Is it really true that the phenomenon is given in complete abandon and that we contribute nothing at all to it? Do we not come with conceptions and expectations of meaning, which prepare us for the experience and also help us ascertain its meaning and signification? Marion may well be right that in many ways phenomena of revelation are overwhelming and that we cannot possibly grasp everything that is given to us. Yet, they do appear against a hermeneutic horizon of previous ecclesial experience, of expectations about our feelings, of theological explanations and historical controversies, of the liturgical context of the eucharistic act, and so forth. Their meaning emerges only in interaction with these horizons not somehow separate from it. Indeed, the phenomenon may well be experienced as overwhelming only and precisely because of being *anticipated* against a hermeneutic context that identifies it as a sacrament or mystery, as a religious experience and as being something more than the consumption of ordinary bread and wine. And the difference in experience between different traditions and on different occasions may well be intricately connected to the particular hermeneutic horizon of expectations formed by these traditions or occasions. This does not mean that the recipient controls or determines the phenomenon, or even that it cannot come in surprising and overwhelming ways, rather it means that we must be "attuned" to the phenomenon, open to it in order to receive it.[41] It might then still challenge us, question us, or even profoundly unsettle and dislocate us, but if we are not even aware of its possibility as a phenomenon, it is hard to see how any reception could occur at all. As with the previous phenomena discussed, the particular hermeneutic context in which the phenomenon is experienced is essential for identifying and even for experiencing it as saturated.

Marion's ambivalence about hermeneutics actually emerges most markedly in theological settings. As we have seen, Marion repeatedly rejects "mere interpretation" in favor of getting to the phenomenality of the event, and this almost always happens when he is speaking of religious phenomena or considering the role of theology. For example, in *In Excess*, he wonders why the theologians are always privileging hermeneutics instead of focusing on phenomenology (IE, 29; DS, 34). Similarly, in the article on the possibility of "Christian philosophy," he suggests that we should reject a "merely" hermeneutic account in favor of a "heuristic" function for Christian philosophy, because "to reduce 'Christian philosophy' to a hermeneutic amounts to denying it the level of philosophy" (VR, 69; VeR, 104). With this dismissal of hermeneutics, just as with the very early affirmation of it as being worked by Christ in the sacrament, he appears to want to affirm that the phenomenon of revelation is real and actual and not merely something that depends on our interpretation or our assumptions about it. God really gives God's self in the phenomenon of revelation; it is not merely my overly spiritualized psyche that thinks this is what is happening. And yet, as we have seen, in response to various criticisms Marion has admitted that to some extent whether a phenomenon is experienced as "poor" or as "saturated" may depend on our reception of it and that it might even be possible to move from experiencing the *same* phenomenon as "poor" to encountering it as "saturated." Hence we should be able to conclude that one person might experience the Eucharist as an overwhelming manifestation of God's gift of Christ's very flesh and blood, while another might taste only ordinary bread and wine and see nothing beyond them. Whether the Eucharist functions as a saturated phenomenon, then, would depend on my reception of it, my response to it, my interpretation of it.

This might indicate, however, that phenomena in themselves are neither poor nor saturated, but that this is an interpretation imposed on them by the consciousness that experiences them as such. This, of course, is precisely the conclusion Marion seeks to avoid: As his treatment of the Emmaus disciples, for example, confirms, Christ's appearance for Marion is ("in and of itself") a saturated phenomenon. When the disciples do not recognize him, they fail to see or experience this saturation, but it is there nonetheless. Saturation does not *depend* on their interpretation, although it can only *appear* as saturation when they do acknowledge Christ's presence (precisely when he disappears). Hence, for Marion, saturation is a characteristic of the phenomenon, but the *correct* interpretation of its phenomenality depends on the consciousness of the recipient. Yet, what are the parameters for establishing "correct" or "incorrect" modes of reception? What are the rules that enable us to make such a judgment?

This dilemma, I think, can only be resolved with a different conception and employment of hermeneutics. "Correct" interpretation of a phenomenon can only be established (or at least approached) through precisely the measures that Marion dismisses, namely the hermeneutic and communal dimensions of the event: the texts that speak of its meaning, the community members who participate in it corporately and corporeally and thus can share and to some extent confirm each other's experiences. Marion regularly seems to imply that hermeneutics functions only as a way of relieving our failure or sin. Christ must provide the hermeneutic for the disciples because their finitude and sin prevent them from seeing. Christ must ascend and cannot remain with the disciples, because their sin makes them unable to bear his continued presence. But hermeneutics is not only necessary when sin is involved. It is not just a way of compensating for our failure, but something always necessary in order to identify our experience, to depict the effect of the sacrament on us, to distinguish between different experiences of the phenomenon in different settings and at different times. A hermeneutic circling is required between open exposure to the phenomenon as it gives itself and the hermeneutic horizon within which it is received and which is always corrected by more open and more honest exposure to the phenomenon in repeated encounter or more careful examination. Only this can enable authentic reception of the phenomenon as it gives itself from itself and a verification of it as a saturated phenomenon.

The larger question, of course, is whether "verifying" God's presence in the sacrament or the "correct" interpretation of it as an event of revelation, are or should be the goals of phenomenological analysis. Instead, it might make more sense to examine the phenomenality of the sacramental event as it appears in the experience of human beings instead of first and foremost as a manifestation of the invisible—without implying that this may not also be the case or that the two are not intimately connected to each other. That is to say, phenomenology can validly examine the experiences of religious believers as they practice religious rites and experience religious events and thereby reach some conclusions about the meaning of these rites and events without thereby degenerating either into mere "psychologizing" interpretations or making theological claims about God's activity in the event. It seems, in fact, that Marion's distinction between philosophical possibility and theological actuality is unnecessary in regard to concrete religious practices such as the Eucharist.[42] These are real, actual, physical practices, so there is no need to speculate about their "having taken place"—they are taking place continually and can be observed or examined again and again. One would only need to distinguish between possibility and actuality in these events if one were concerned—and of course Marion is concerned—to identify what happens as revelation of the divine, or, even more specifically, as an encounter with the Christian God as the true and only God.[43]

Yet meaningful phenomenological analysis of religious practices, such as participation in the sacraments, can be performed without needing to prove something as true in a factual sense. This seems no longer to understand truth as a revelation or manifestation, but much more like verification or correspondence. The concern with actuality is about verifying that what happens *corresponds* to a manifestation of God. But, as Marion himself continually points out, phenomenology is about a process of manifestation, about revealing how phenomena give themselves to us, concerned with having an effect on us instead of validating propositions. In light of this, it seems to make much more sense to examine religious experiences for the insight they give us into how they are meaningful to communities of believers. They can help us see why people engage in these practices and what they are meant to do, how they shape religious life.[44] And this is important work not only for understanding religious practices but also for comparing them with other kinds of experiences and for ascertaining the meaning within them.

Such an analysis may well provide insight even for nonreligious phenomena, without needing to serve as a "paradigm" for them. And it does require recognizing even phenomenological analysis as a hermeneutic exercise at least in some respects. The more "saturated" a phenomenon (to employ Marion's language), the *more* is interpretation required (not less, as Marion often seems to suggest). If a phenomenon is more overwhelming, it does not thereby prohibit interpretation because it imposes itself absolutely, but it actually calls for greater caution and vigilance, more careful analysis and more manifold interpretation. The hermeneutic exercise is not a dangerous descent into utter relativism, as Marion at times seems to fear, but, as Ricoeur stressed over and over again, it is a way to ascertain the manifold meanings of our lives in the continual struggle between concordance and discordance which includes, as Richard Kearney has convincingly argued, diacritical judgment that is able to distinguish between better and worse interpretations although it always does so in provisional ways, always in "fear and trembling."

The Eucharist in particular is the kind of event that lends itself to phenomenological exploration precisely because it is such a central practice that occurs over and over again and is experienced by many people on a regular basis. A phenomenology of the Eucharist can and should allow for a phenomenological analysis of concrete religious practices and of the ways in which such practices are meaningful and indeed life-giving to the many people who participate in them regularly. The Eucharist grapples with the concrete fleshly reality of our lives in all their fragility and brokenness, while—to employ Ricoeur's language—inviting us into a world of hope where we are challenged to imagine ourselves differently.[45] The Eucharist both embraces our vulnerable finitude, recognizing that we need healing over and over again, *and* it invites us to enter into its experience of the kingdom where all things are transformed and made whole. Eucharist is a communal and corporeal experience with cosmic and not merely individual dimensions.

It is also closely tied to the core meanings of Christian faith and might be said to express in some sense the essence of that faith. "This is my body, broken for you" is Christ's explanation of his incarnate self-giving and encapsulates the Christian message of redemption. Phenomenological analysis of this event as it is experienced in a variety of traditions and settings and by many different people may well give us a better sense also of the meaning of this central Christian rite in a way that explains both why this sacrament and struggle over its interpretation has so strongly shaped Christian history and why it continues to shape Christian practice today. It can therefore illuminate how particular practices and experiences inform religious communities and confirm identities. On some occasions and in some contexts, such experiences may well turn out to be overwhelming and saturated in the ways Marion suggests, and such excessive experience may be one of the reasons why it has become a central Christian practice. On other occasions and in other contexts, the experience may be of a lesser degree of givenness.

Yet even the instances of particularly excessive experience rely on and are made possible by important hermeneutic contexts that situate the event in such a manner that it can be experienced as saturated precisely because of the ways in which it has been prepared. Marion consistently claims that the saturated phenomenon comes to me completely without preparation and foresight. Part of what makes it so excessive is precisely the way in which it arrives as a complete surprise and comes out of nowhere—both temporally and spatially. Especially in the case of the Eucharist, this simply cannot be true in that extreme fashion, as the event is deeply grounded in the larger liturgical context in which it occurs. The bread and wine are given to me only after liturgical preparation, especially its preceding narrative that has a long history and seeks to situate and interpret the event before it even occurs. Participation in the Eucharist does not come as a complete surprise, but the first time as the culmination of catechesis and always following all those who have partaken before me (immediately and for centuries past). It can be experienced as saturated and overwhelming—even as intensely surprising and bedazzling—only because of this preparation and context. This hermeneutic context that precedes me is the condition of possibility for my experience, whether poor or overwhelming or in any number of degrees of givenness in between these extremes.

Conclusion

In this book I have examined Marion's proposal of saturated phenomena and argued that Marion focuses too exclusively on their absolute excess and almost complete lack of context. I have suggested, instead, that phenomena are given in degrees of saturation and not only in the two or three degrees Marion indicates, poverty and saturation, but instead in a whole variety and range of degrees. Phenomena are more or less saturated in many different ways, fitting not along a narrow spectrum, but occupying a wide field of diversity of appearance or givenness. Focusing entirely on absolute and total givenness, excessive saturation, as Marion does, polarizes the field of givenness unnecessarily. In order to temper this excess of his presentation, I have examined precisely the kind of phenomena that Marion describes as saturated: historical events, works of art, the human flesh, the beloved other, the gift, and religious phenomena such as prayer and the Eucharist. In each case I have tried to show that even these ostensibly saturated phenomena are not always given in as excessive and absolute a manner as Marion suggests, but these very phenomena already come in manifold degrees and levels of saturation of givenness. When they are given in less absolute or completely blinding fashion, this is not due only to the fault or incapacity of the recipient, as Marion generally maintains, but instead often shows the diversity of the phenomena. In the case of many phenomena, including the ones depicted by Marion as saturated, acknowledging a range and diversity of degrees of givenness is a more faithful presentation of the phenomena.

Historical events, whether wars or founding national events or other occurrences in history, do not come only in the most intense and overwhelming mode, but are of varying degrees of intensity and complexity. Marion speaks of historical events as saturated because they are impossible to quantify and because no cause can be assigned to them; instead, the effect determines the causes. Yet, historical events differ in their level of complexity and in the ways in which causality can be ascertained or the number of causal events that come together to bring about an occurrence. Not all events are equally complex, therefore making distinctions between levels of complexity is meaningful and useful for historical research. Furthermore, a complete refusal of understanding or of any ability to provide an account of historical events not only seems to deny the validity of historical research and the disciplines of history and historiography more generally, but it also at times constitutes an abdication of responsibility. It matters to the victims of historical events, especially of the atrocities of war and genocide, that as careful and accurate accounts as possible are provided, and that these attempt to represent the historical event truthfully and seek to distinguish at least some levels of causality and responsibility for the injustice that has occurred. I have also suggested that through such careful research our knowledge about or understanding of an event can increase, even if it can never be total. Such increase of knowledge is not a denial of the saturated nature of the phenomenon, but rather a greater exposure to it that appreciates its complexity and saturation more fully. Increase even of quantifiable knowledge need not automatically mean an assertion of control or objectification of an event.

Similarly, encounters with works of art, although they may well be overwhelming and bedazzling experiences, need not always be so absolutely bedazzling that nothing can be said about them. I have suggested that Marion's account of the work of art requires it to be exclusively the work of genius, namely the transferal of a special vision of the unseen into the realm of the visible. This ability to perceive the unseen and to "create" it as a phenomenon in the realm of the visible demands a special kind of talent and giftedness. Appreciating the great work of art, being bedazzled by its complete visibility, seems to require a similar sort of genius for Marion. His depiction and analysis here appear closely aligned with those of Kant and his romantic appropriators. I have suggested, with Gadamer, that this disregards the larger context of the phenomenon and gives no role to the community. It constitutes an utter subjectivization of art, as only for the especially gifted and talented. In Marion, this is intensified through the abolition of the subject, so that it is the receptivity of the gifted that becomes isolated and singled out in this fashion. This also again seems to make it impossible to make distinctions between works of art or degrees of saturation within them, although Marion himself consistently makes judgments about "authentic" and "inauthentic" art. Such judgment, I have argued, requires methods of distinction that are not currently provided by his work.

Marion's account of the flesh as utterly immediate and immanent and without any possibility of distanciation relies heavily on Michel Henry's phenomenology of the flesh. I have suggested that this account disregards the animality and organicity of the flesh and also does not consider its close connection to nature. More generally, phenomena of nature find no place in Marion's work and are more or less entirely ignored. I have argued that they can be experienced and described as saturated phenomena in Marion's sense, but that they also come in a range of degrees and kinds of givenness with variable levels of intensity and saturation. Less fully saturated phenomena of nature, such as a city garden, are not therefore objects. There are many intermediary positions that do not fall neatly along one line of intensification. Opening Marion's phenomenology in the direction of natural phenomena also allows some of its potential for ecological dialogue to emerge. Regarding natural phenomena as saturated, as imposing themselves in complex and dazzling fashion, helps us to respond to them in ways that are less objectifying and exploitative. A sensitivity to their saturation can hence lead to the kind of devotion or care for phenomena in the case of nature that Marion has outlined for other saturated phenomena. Finally, I have tried to show that Marion's (and Henry's) accounts of the flesh require an acknowledgement of the "naturalness" and animality of our flesh. Our passions and desires, pains and pleasures, namely the self-affectivity of the flesh Henry and Marion speak about, are natural phenomena and a fuller account of these feelings, passions, and enjoyments requires that one pay attention to this rootedness in nature.

For the phenomenon of the other I have, as Marion does, focused primarily on the saturated phenomenon of love and loving encounter. I have criticized Marion's repeated comparisons of love to war, all of which stress the absolute and total nature of love in various ways. This comparison is telling: love for Marion is an absolute and overwhelming phenomenon that becomes almost impossible to avoid or refuse. Marion maintains strongly that love must be described in univocal fashion: all love is ultimately the same, whether human or divine, whether charitable or erotic. I have argued that such a monolithic picture of love is ultimately not helpful for ascertaining and faithfully describing its many and various phenomenological manifestations. Love is displayed and experienced in a great variety of types and degrees and it is not ultimately all that useful to lump them all together in such monolithic fashion. In order to describe the phenomenon of love more faithfully and more accurately, we must pay attention to these many different manifestations and allow for a great diversity of degrees and kinds. Love is not always experienced in the kind of absolute and overwhelming fashion Marion depicts and it is rarely as completely kenotic and self-giving as he advocates. Less intense manifestations of love are not therefore necessarily deficient or poor in love.

The phenomenon of the gift has occupied French phenomenology generally and Marion especially for several decades. In *Being Given,* the gift seemed primarily employed to confirm his phenomenology of givenness more broadly. In *Certitudes négatives,* Marion considers the phenomenon of the gift more closely, especially in its relationship with the phenomena of sacrifice and of forgiveness. The phenomenon of the gift is depicted as a giving that is pure, gratuitous, selfless, and unconditioned, completely without connection to economy and reciprocity. The gift is ultimately an impossible or saturated phenomenon because its manifestation in concrete, everyday economies of gift giving would attach conditions to it. The gift cannot finally make an appearance. I suggest that such an absolute account fails to acknowledge the mundane gifts that are given in daily life. Although they are not

absolute or unconditioned, but indeed "contaminated" by commercial and economic considerations, they still deserve our phenomenological analysis and explication. Gifts come in many varieties and degrees of givenness and less saturated
gift-phenomena may well give us important insight into our culture and conduct.

Marion has written extensively about the phenomenality of prayer. His account of prayer is closely linked to his desire to protect God's name from contamination and to keep talk about God as absolute as possible. In consequence,
his account of the phenomenon of a person at prayer often tends to the excessive
and solitary. At prayer, one finds oneself individually envisioned or envisaged and
overwhelmed by the divine gaze. Prayer hence becomes a solitary and invisible
event that has very little real effect on how one lives in the world. Similarly, the
phenomenon of sainthood or sanctity is depicted by Marion as entirely invisible
and impossible to determine in any sense. I have suggested that the tradition has
instead spoken of degrees and stages of prayer. Growth in prayer is not only important to the experience of prayer, but excessive experiences are actually often
suspect and warned against. Marion's account also says very little about the communal and corporeal dimensions of prayer or the social and political implications
of sanctity, which is often phenomenologically manifested in acts of charity and
care for the poor, if not in political revolution and transformation. These are important aspects of prayer and sainthood that a phenomenological account should
not disregard.

Finally, I have considered Marion's extensive writings on the Eucharist, which
again portray it as a supremely excessive experience, the gift par excellence. I have
wondered whether depicting it as such an intensely saturated experience is ultimately the most helpful way of approaching this phenomenon. As with his accounts of prayer, his writings on the Eucharist seem to focus on individual mystical experience instead of considering more communal and corporeal dimensions.
Marion says little about the physicality of the eucharistic elements, the sacred
space within which this meal occurs, the transformative effect it has or maybe
should have on the community, and the varying degrees of intensity of its experience through the cycle of the liturgical year and its seasons, which themselves indicate different levels of intensity and focus. I have suggested that the eucharistic
experience does not only come in different types and degrees, depending on the ecclesial tradition in which it is experienced, but that it opens the space for phenomenological examination of religious experience more generally, in a way that does
not merely speculate about its possibility but is concerned with its actual manifold and varied manifestations.

Marion's most fundamental task has been to introduce the notion of the saturated phenomenon and to argue for its highest kind of intensity and excess. This
has at times led to such a starkly excessive account that it seems to disregard even

slightly less intense phenomena and overall pays little attention to mundane phenomena that are often dismissed as "poor" or "common" and unworthy of our attention. Even his more concrete depictions of saturated phenomena often give the impression that they are only manifested in the most absolute and excessive sense and that anything less is a betrayal of their excessive nature, a blindness to their mode of bedazzlement. Yet, in more sober moments, Marion acknowledges that all of phenomenality is important and that it does not manifest itself only in the intensely saturated fashion on which he focuses in his work. This is what I have tried to show here more fully, by examining precisely the phenomena Marion depicts as saturated and to explicate the ways in which even these very phenomena differ in their degrees of intensity. This opens up the realms of phenomenality to a whole variety of large fields and spectra of phenomena instead of a polarized account of only two extremes at which all phenomenality must congregate. This seems to me a more faithful account of how phenomena actually manifest themselves in our experience, something not denied by Marion's account but certainly not the primary focus of his investigation so far.

The second part of my argument has been in regard to the role of hermeneutics in Marion's phenomenology. Having been repeatedly criticized for his lack of focus on hermeneutics, he has certainly made an effort to address this particular issue. In respect to various of the saturated phenomena, especially the event and the face of the other, he now acknowledges an "endless" or "infinite" hermeneutics, which seems to mean for him that these phenomena are so excessive in meaning that they give rise to an endless number of interpretations that continue infinitely because no single interpretation can ever do justice to the phenomenon and one cannot finally ever arrive at a definitive interpretation. Unfortunately, that gives the impression that this "endless" number of interpretations is fairly arbitrary and that no meaningful distinctions can be made among them. Interpretation then really does not provide much further insight about the phenomenon and is unable not only to ascertain the meaning of the phenomenon but even to help toward any fuller understanding of it. This is closely connected to Marion's proposal of "negative certainties," which he maintains characterize saturated phenomena. In the case of these excessive phenomena, we know "certainly" that we will never understand them and that no definitive knowledge in the sense of certainty or objective comprehension is possible. Negative certainty defines them essentially.

This seems to disregard, however, that knowledge can indeed increase in regard to at least some of these phenomena. We can learn more about historical events and with more data and greater understanding come to know more fully, although we can never do complete justice to their complexity or claim to comprehend them entirely. We can learn about great works of art, and with increasing exposure to them and greater knowledge about their context and technique and focus, we can come to appreciate them more deeply, instead of thereby turning them into an object. We can learn about the complexity of natural phenomena, and in investigating them more fully we learn to experience them as saturated phenomena instead of mere resources of exploitation. Learning more about the people we love and seeking to understand them more intimately, our love can be increased instead of decimated. More consistent practice of prayer or eucharistic participation may open us more fully to the manifestation of the divine. Even in the case of saturated phenomena, then, greater knowledge or even increased understanding are not necessarily a detriment to appreciating their excess and such better understanding does not therefore objectify or trivialize them.

Marion also seems to consider hermeneutics primarily in its sense of interpretation after a phenomenon has been encountered. He thinks of the hermeneutic context or phenomenological horizon within which phenomena appear and manifest themselves primarily as limiting the self-givenness of the phenomenon. This is why he claims that saturated phenomena appear completely without a context, in surprising and blinding ways that utterly overwhelm us and sweep away all our preconceptions and expectations. Saturated phenomena hence appear without context or horizon. Any such context would lead to a predictability of and control over such a phenomenon, which ultimately would reassert the power of the subject and take away the self-givenness of the phenomenon. I have argued, instead, that a hermeneutic context in many cases enables us to appreciate the saturated manifestation of the phenomenon more fully instead of reducing it to lesser forms of givenness. The cultural context of the historical phenomenon enables us to appreciate its levels of complexity and its newness and surprising manifestation. The aesthetic context of the work of art helps us appreciate the creativity and uniqueness of the artist and the work more fully. The work of nature writers and scientists prepares us hermeneutically to encounter natural phenomena as saturated. Our particular familial, social, cultural, and religious context shapes and enables our experience and manifestations of love and indeed our recognition of it. The context in which a gift occurs or is given often enables the recipient to recognize and receive it as a gift. The spatial and temporal context in which prayer occurs is an important dimension of its phenomenality. Similarly, the corporeal and communal contexts of the eucharistic meal are essential for experiencing it as a saturated phenomenon. Ascetic and ecclesial practices prepare us for prayer and enable us to receive the gift of the Eucharist in ways less likely to diminish the divine self-givenness. These contexts cannot be abandoned, but are a significant dimension of the experience and manifestation itself. Without such a phenomenological horizon the phenomenon cannot give itself from itself, because it cannot be received. The hermeneutic context does not restrict or exercise control over the phenomenon, but designates the openness and receptivity of the one who encounters the phenomenon. A saturated phenomenon is overwhelming precisely because it is encountered within the recipient's field of experience in a different way than a less saturated one and sets a hermeneutic circle in motion that tries to respond to it and bear its impact responsibly.

This also has an important element of discernment. Hermeneutics enables discerning between fuller and lesser levels of saturation, more and less appropriate manifestations, authentic or inauthentic forms of the phenomenon. It is hermeneutics that enables us to begin the process of discernment that gauges the effect of the historical phenomenon, distinguishes a great work of art from kitsch, discerns between better and worse accounts of climate change or other nature phenomena, ascertains whether an offer of love is genuine, distinguishes a gratuitous gift from a manipulative one, depicts various levels of prayer and sanctity or the eucharistic experience in a diversity of traditions and on various occasions. Marion himself does occasionally makes such judgments about authentic and inauthentic experience, especially in regard to the work of art. Such judgment is only preserved from being completely arbitrary, if it is connected to a hermeneutic circle of discernment that is rooted in the traditions and communities relevant to the particular phenomenon under consideration.

Marion had already early on spoken of a hermeneutics of the Eucharist that proceeds from the divine and imposes itself upon the recipient. Although this particular account of hermeneutics is strongest in his writings on the Eucharist, its assumptions color his phenomenology more generally. Both his reluctance in regard to interpretation more generally and his insistence that phenomena are invented and discovered (e.g., by the artist or theologian) seek to bolster his conviction and argument that these are real and authentic phenomena, not merely arbitrary interpretations. Phenomena really are given as saturated, even when the particular recipients receive them as poor and are unable to "bear" their saturation. The "fault" lies with the recipient not with the phenomenon. Hence the "correct" interpretation is imposed by the phenomenon upon the recipient instead of the reverse. This is precisely the concern that leads to his repeated vacillation on this important issue: On the one hand, the phenomenon really is given as saturated and I am merely blind to the saturation; on the other hand, the same phenomenon might be interpreted as "poor" or "saturated" depending on the context.

This is the crucial difficulty in Marion's account that I would suggest he has not yet fully resolved. It is closely connected also to the question of the recipient, so central to Marion's work: Is the "meaning" of the phenomenon imposed, in a sort of "ready-made" fashion, on the recipient? Or is the meaning ascertained and maybe even "imposed" by the recipient on the phenomenon, which comes anonymously and must be identified by the one to whom it is given and who becomes devoted to the phenomenon? Is, in short, the recipient, "servant" or "master" of the given? If both are the case, that is, if both phenomenon and recipient are active and passive in certain important respects, what is the relationship between these elements and how can they be distinguished and described phenomenologically? These various aspects can only be held together, it seems to me, when phenomenology is recognized as essentially hermeneutic. The saturated phenomenon can be recognized as saturated only when the hermeneutic horizon of the recipient is brought up short against the phenomenal horizon and continually adjusted via open encounter and more careful description, which circles back and forth between exposure to the experience and attempt to describe it faithfully. Such a *process* of interpretation is not merely imposed on the phenomenon but holds in tension the elements of "activity" and "passivity," bearing the impact and responding to the phenomenon, being faithful to it and making it visible in some fashion, guarding its givenness or self-giving initiative and providing the "training" or preparation (or "belief") necessary to "see" it at all.

When I originally conceived this book, I intended to organize it in two parts, with a first part focusing on what Marion calls "simply saturated phenomena," such as the historical event, the idol, the flesh, the icon, and a second part focusing on his "doubly saturated phenomena" or "paradox of paradoxa," namely the phenomena of revelation. As I was writing, it became impossible to maintain that neat division. Although Marion still occasionally makes that distinction himself, his work overall tends to treat all rich phenomena as instances of the saturated phenomenon and does not consistently uphold the distinction between simple and double saturation. Yet there certainly is a sense in which the intensity of saturation increases for religious phenomena. We have also seen that all these phenomena become more and more defined in terms of each other: All phenomena are given, so the saturated phenomenon becomes the paradigm for all phenomena, even poor ones. All phenomena are ultimately given as gifts, so the gift in some way becomes the paradigm for all saturated phenomena and even for phenomenality as such. Finally, the Eucharist is the gift par excellence and becomes the paradigm for all gifts and thereby for all saturated phenomena and ultimately for all phenomena of any sort.

This raises again the question—occupying the secondary literature to an almost obsessive degree—to what extent Marion's "theology"—that is, his convictions about phenomena of revelation—influences his phenomenology more generally. Are all phenomena ultimately eucharistic gifts? And if they are, is this an adequate account of phenomena, especially when they are experienced by people who do not subscribe to the Christian tradition? Even his emphasis on the quasi-kenotic self-givenness of the phenomenon, which gives itself in complete abandon and invites similar loving abandon from the devoted recipient, appears preeminently Christian in character and impetus. Does such Christian inspiration

or Christian structure of phenomenality compromise its faithfulness to the phenomena? This has, of course, been the argument of many phenomenologists, both
preceding and following Janicaud's most well-known of such critiques.

My sense is that the place where Marion's particular Christian predispositions
become most dangerous to his philosophical account are precisely the two I have
highlighted in this book: his tendency to absolute excess in his account and his dismissal of, or at least restrained acknowledgment of, hermeneutics. These are not
solely or peculiarly Christian per se, but they do seem to me rooted in Marion's
particular conception of Christian faith and theology, which are grounded and
displayed already in his early writings on Descartes, Dionysius, and Pascal: on the
one hand, the strong emphasis on apophaticism and divine distance, and on the
other hand, the heavy stress on utter selflessness and loving kenosis. On the one
hand, we cannot approach God ourselves, but any such approach is a divine gift
enacted only in loving kenosis by and starting from the divine. On the other hand,
we cannot know anything about God, that is, any attempt at comprehension is
immediately limiting to the divine and hence blasphemous and idolatrous. God is
manifested only as utterly absolute and incomprehensible. Any self-communica-
tion of the divine, any revelation, is an overwhelming and bedazzling experience
that can never be grasped by finite creatures. These various convictions conjointly
lead to an almost exclusive focus on the most intense and most bedazzling degree
of intensity: complete and utter saturation. They also lead to a consistent refusal
of comprehension or understanding, which is conceived as limiting and controlling, as imposing illegitimate constrictions on the divine abundance given to us.
Such saturation can only be received by loving devotion. That is why an account
of degrees of givenness and of the various hermeneutic contexts, which enable
us to receive and respond to them, is essential for Marion's account. It is not a betrayal of his central insights, but a tempering of their excess, motivated by his religious convictions, that makes them more faithful and responsible to the phenomena. After focusing primarily on critique so far, let me say a few words about
why I think what I have said ultimately contributes to the overall thrust of Marion's work rather than going against it.

The insight that most deeply shapes Marion's phenomenology, as we have
seen, is that of the self-givenness of phenomena, especially of "rich" phenomena,
the way we experience them as abundant and overwhelming, as *given* to us. The
stance of the self, consequently, is one of *receptivity*. I have argued that this goes
beyond the dichotomy between simple activity and passivity usually invoked, the
question of "who" is in control—the consciousness of the "subject" or the phenomenon. At the same time, Marion's work is motivated by the desire not to
"reduce" the phenomenon—in the sense of "minimizing" it, ignoring it, or imposing arbitrary and unacceptable conditions on it, such as turning it into a meta-

physical object. My insistence on greater variety of degrees, on hermeneutic discernment, and of an account of preparatory practices or the context within which phenomena give themselves / are given to us, are not only not incompatible with these core concerns of Marion's work, but, it seems to me, are called for by it. A greater attentiveness to the many and varied levels of saturation and a greater concern with our ability to see, hear, or feel (that is, to apprehend) them as they come to us, all *enhance* both the self-givenness of the phenomena and our receptivity to or of them.

A more nuanced description of varieties and degrees of givenness might also convince some of Marion's critics that these phenomena are worth examining and give us real insight about many aspects of our experience. Such a description might alleviate the fear that his phenomenology is merely a veiled attempt to make all philosophy dependent upon the divine instead of a genuine engagement with the phenomena. Marion's work has much to offer for a variety of analysis of historical and aesthetic phenomena, for eco-phenomenology and human affectivity, for phenomena of loving and giving on many levels. And it does, finally, also (but not only) enable us to provide phenomenological descriptions of religious experiences, which are, after all (contra Burch), central to the lives of many people, past and present, and which are a forceful reality for both good and evil in the contemporary world on many personal, social, cultural, and political levels. Marion's work gives us important insight for why and how historical, aesthetic, and religious phenomena *matter* for us and the many and varied meanings they carry.

Marion generally contends that such phenomena must come entirely from themselves and that standard phenomenological horizons must be suspended, which seems diametrically opposed to the sort of hermeneutic preparation for which I have argued throughout this book. Rather than a genuine opposition, however, this disagreement might depend more on terminology.[1] I have for the most part followed the descriptions of hermeneutics given by Merold Westphal and Richard Kearney—some of it in explicit response to Marion's work—who, following Paul Ricoeur, stress the importance of hermeneutics in any phenomenological project.[2] In contrast, in his analysis of mystical experience Anthony Steinbock refuses to call his account hermeneutical. Like Marion, he insists that for the mystics their "experiences are *from* God and not only *of* God" and prefers to avoid the language of hermeneutics: "If one wants to call the spiritual practice of the 'discernment of spirits' hermeneutics, that is fine, but I think it is safe to call it by that name (discernment) rather than risk conflating practices." And he concludes—sounding very much like Marion: "I want to avoid calling religious experience hermeneutics plain and simple because this tends to make the presence of God relative to me and my powers, and this ultimately would be an expression of forcing my will on the presence of God, which is to say, to commit idolatry. The religious experience is 'absolute' in the sense described above, not dialectical or hermeneutical. . . . A hermeneutics of *religious experience* must itself be situated and relativized by religious experience, its unmistakable features made salient *by* a givenness that it is incapable of producing."[3] At the same time, he situates his project as very close to that of Kearney's descriptions of religious experiences and his subsequent analyses in the book bear out those parallels. Distancing himself from the terminology of hermeneutics clearly does not mean for Steinbock that no discernment is at work or that experiences occur entirely within a vacuum. Rather, he stresses both variety, context, and particularity of religious experiences and engages in close description of specific texts and experiences, but sees that as a primarily phenomenological endeavor.

What is required, then, is a back-and-forth between the phenomenon as it gives itself *and* one's reception and account of it, one's preparation for a phenomenon (cultivating one's ability to "see") *and* its full self-givenness. Florian Forestier, who finds such a back-and-forth missing in Marion's account, calls this the "to and fro" between "what enables the phenomenon to open us up a reality, and how the possible faces of this reality come into view according to the phenomenality that gives access to it," while I have referred to it throughout this book as engaging in a hermeneutic circle.[4] What matters, however, is not what we call this exercise but the affirmation that both the genuine givenness of the phenomenon (at whatever level of saturation) and the active receptivity of the one who phenomenalizes it must be held together. Neither should compromise the other. This requires us to be attentive in our phenomenological descriptions of the phenomena (and of their deeper structures and meaning) to how they actually gives themselves to us. Such attentiveness can and must both precede and follow the experience, as the phenomenon continually surprises and challenges us and we come up short against its givenness, while trying to be ever more prepared and more faithful in our receptivity. It is this kind of attentiveness and receptivity that saturated phenomena call for in all their manifold varieties and degrees of givenness.

NOTES

Introduction

1. See, for example, Éric Alliez, *De l'impossibilité de la phénoménologie. Sur la philosophie française contemporaine* (Paris: Vrin, 1995), 60–66; Dominique Janicaud, *Phenomenology "Wide Open": After the French Debate*, trans. Charles N. Cabral (New York: Fordham University Press, 2005), 33–40; Jocelyn Benoist, "L'écart plutôt que l'excédent," *Philosophie. Jean-Luc Marion* 78 (2003): 77–93; Marie-Andrée Ricard, "La question de la donation chez Jean-Luc Marion," *Laval théologique et philosophique* 57 (2001): 83–94. Jean Grondin also comments on this issue in his review of Marion's work (discussed in more detail in the final section of this introduction).

2. Earlier versions of two of these texts are translated as the first two chapters of *The Reason of the Gift*. The first chapter also appears as the lead article in *Quaestiones disputatae* 1.1 (2010): 3–18.

3. Benoist, "L'écart plutôt que l'excédent," 77.

4. François-David Sebbah, *Testing the Limit: Derrida, Henry, Levinas, and the Phenomenological Tradition* (Stanford, Calif.: Stanford University Press, 2012), 104–122.

5. Vincent Holzer, "Phénoménologie radicale et phénomène de révélation," *Transversalités. Revue de l'Institut catholique de Paris* 70 (1999): 55–68; Martin Gagnon, "La phénoménologie à la limite," *Eidos* 11.1–2 (1993): 111–30; Emmanuel Falque, "Phénoménologie de l'extraordinaire," *Philosophie. Jean-Luc Marion* 78 (2003): 52–76. See also Kühn's account of what he calls "radicalized phenomenology" (that of Lévinas, Derrida, and Marion) in Rolf Kühn, *Radikalisierte Phänomenologie* (Frankfurt: Peter Lang/Europäischer Verlag der Wissenschaften, 2003), 175–239. He does think that Marion remains dependent on metaphysics (198) and that his account of absolute givenness as principle of reduction is phenomenologically problematic (201). See also his article "Passivität und Zeugenschaft— oder die Verdächtigung des 'Subjekts.' Eine radikal-phänomenologische Anfrage an J.-L. Marion," in *Jean-Luc Marion. Studien zum Werk*, ed. Hanna-Barbara Gerl-Falkovitz (Dresden, Germany: Verlag Text & Dialog, 2013), 177–98, where he is even more critical of Marion.

6. For explicit critique of Marion's phenomenology as such, see Dominique Janicaud et al. in *Phenomenology and the "Theological Turn": The French Debate* (New York: Fordham University Press, 2000) and Janicaud's *Phenomenology "Wide Open"*; Sebbah, *Testing the Limit*; Shane Mackinlay, *Interpreting Excess: Jean-Luc Marion, Saturated Phenomena, and Hermeneutics* (New York: Fordham University Press, 2010), chapters 1–3; and any number of articles that criticize particular aspects of his thought (for treatment of many of these, see my *Reading Jean-Luc Marion*). For a more fundamental criticism of Marion's phenome-

nological method, see Florian Forestier, "The Phenomenon and the Transcendental: Jean-Luc Marion, Marc Richir, and the Issue of Phenomenalization," *Continental Philosophy Review* 45 (2012): 381–402, especially 387–93, and Lorenz Puntel's work who consistently dismisses Marion's phenomenology as entirely incoherent and nonsensical.

7. I have attempted to provide such an introduction in my *Reading Jean-Luc Marion: Exceeding Metaphysics* (Bloomington: Indiana University Press, 2007). See also Robyn Horner, *Jean-Luc Marion: A Theo-logical Introduction* (Hants, U.K.: Ashgate, 2005), and Mackinlay, *Interpreting Excess*. Mackinlay's work is only to some extent introductory; it also provides extensive critique. Kevin Hart's overall introduction and his particular introductions to each section of his edited collection, Jean-Luc Marion, *The Essential Writings* (New York: Fordham University Press, 2013), are also eminently useful. I have provided briefer introductions to Marion's work in "Jean-Luc Marion: On the Possibility of a Religious Phenomenon," Morny Joy, ed., *Continental Philosophy and Philosophy of Religion* (Heidelberg, London, and New York: Springer, 2011), the chapter on Marion in my *Postmodern Apologetics? Arguments for God in Contemporary Philosophy* (New York: Fordham University Press, 2012), and the second revised edition of the *Blackwell Companion to Continental Philosophy*, ed. William Schroeder (Oxford: Blackwell Publishers, forthcoming). For a French introduction to his work, see Stéphane Vinolo, *Dieu n'a que faire de l'être. Introduction à l'œuvre de Jean-Luc Marion* (Paris: Éditions Germina, 2012).

8. In a 2012 lecture he summarizes his thrust in *Reduction and Givenness* as follows: "Husserl's initial 'breakthrough' consists in recognizing not only that intuition is not limited to sensitivity (but can and should extend to the eidetic and categorial intuitions), but that intuition itself is worth something only as far as it implements a givenness, a givenness which is all the more radical as it also includes signification" (GH, 12–13, trans. mod.).

9. Marion returned to this topic of the gift in *The Reason of the Gift* and in chapters 3 and 4 of *Certitudes négatives*. Chapter 5 explores the topic of the gift in detail.

10. This has been criticized in illuminating fashion by Anthony Steinbock in his important piece on the poor phenomenon: "The Poor Phenomenon: Marion and the Problem of Givenness," in *Words of Life: New Theological Turns in French Phenomenology*, ed. Bruce Ellis Benson and Norman Wirzba (New York: Fordham University Press, 2010), 120–31. His outline of the various different ways in which a phenomenon might appear as "poor" in Marion's account (and his critique of this ambiguity and Marion's failure to explore this topic more fully) are eminently helpful. They are examined in more detail in the next section of this introduction.

11. This is especially true of the event, which is first examined in §17 as a general characteristic of all phenomena (BG, 159–73; ED, 225–44), but then becomes as historical or cultural event one of the paradigmatic cases of the saturated phenomenon. He makes the connection of these "determinations" of the given with the saturated phenomenon already within *Being Given* at the end of part 4, where he argues that his broadening of the definition of the phenomenon (to the given) has made possible the inclusion of the phenomenon of revelation into givenness or phenomenality more generally (BG, 214, 227, 246–47; ED, 299, 317, 342). He says in regard to "anamorphosis" and "fait accompli" that

they "begin with the object and the being so as to overcome them in the given as such" (BG, 176; ED, 248).

12. Similarly, the saturated phenomenon of revelation is saturated to a "second degree" and at the same time the "paradox of paradoxa."

13. This essay first appeared in French with a collection of other papers by Henry, Chrétien, and Ricoeur responding to Janicaud's claim, and later translated by Jeffrey Kosky in Dominique Janicaud et al., *Phenomenology and the "Theological Turn,"* 176–216. Its first English translation appeared (after having been presented as a keynote address at the Society for Phenomenology and Existential Philosophy annual meeting in 1995) in the SPEP Supplement of *Philosophy Today* 40.1 (Spring 1996): 103–124, translated by Thomas Carlson. The essay is retranslated as chapter 2 in *The Visible and the Revealed* (VR, 18–48; VeR, 35–74).

14. Saturated phenomena are therefore events that escape causality: "phenomena as such, namely as given, not only do not satisfy this demand [being understood as effects of a cause], but far from paying for their refusal with their unintelligibility, appear and let themselves be understood all the better as they slip from the sway of cause and the status of effect. The less they let themselves be inscribed in causality, the more they show themselves and render themselves intelligible as such" (BG, 162; ED, 229).

15. He explicates the notion of "counter-experience" in more detail in section 6 of "The Banality of Saturation" (VR, 136–39; VeR, 170–75). Counter-experience turns intentionality back on itself and thus "measures the range of my disappointed vision." It can be detected in the way in which it "alters" the aim of intentionality (VR, 137; VeR, 172). It is also "marked by the saturation of every concept by intuition" and thus a kind of disappointment of the original aim of intentionality (VR, 138; VeR, 172). Finally, it is an experience of excess that cannot be grasped but whose effect can be felt. Thus, "counter-experience is an issue of the obstinate resistance of what refuses itself to knowledge that is transparent without remainder, of what withdraws into its obscure origin" (VR, 138; 173). This is taken up again in the conclusion of *Certitudes négatives.* Counter-experience attests to the saturation of the phenomenon (CN, 314).

16. This is first outlined in *Being Given* (BG, 225–47; ED, 314–42) and then examined in more detail in the following study, *In Excess*, which devotes a chapter to each of the saturated phenomena. For discussions of Marion's use of Kant, see Claudia Serban, "Jean-Luc Marion als Leser Kants," in Gerl-Falkovitz, *Jean-Luc Marion*, 199–215; Claudia Serban, "Résonances kantiennes et renouveau phénoménologique dans *Certitudes négatives* de Jean-Luc Marion," *Symposium* 15 (2011): 190–99; Carla Canullo, *La fenomenologia rovesciata. Percorsi tentati in Jean-Luc Marion, Michel Henry e Jean-Louis Chrétien* (Torino, Italy: Rosenberg & Sellier, 2004).

17. Marion repeatedly insists that these give everything to visibility at once on their bedazzling surface that there is no "back" to them. Thus it would be much harder to show how sculptures or music might serve as examples for this type of phenomenon.

18. For this important distinction, see *Being Given* (BG, 367, note 90; ED, 329). Marion tries to mark the difference between the mere phenomenological possibility of revelation and the actuality of Revelation accessed only by theology by capitalizing only the latter.

Several commentators (beginning with Thomas Carlson in his translator's introduction to *Idol and Distance* and most recently Mackinlay in *Interpreting Excess*) have argued that this distinction cannot be maintained as cleanly as Marion suggests.

19. He provides an analysis of Christ's transfiguration as an illustration of saturation in all four respects. See BG, 234–45; ED, 325–40.

20. This is a claim Marion later seems to qualify to some extent. See his essay on "The Banality of Saturation," discussed in more detail below.

21. Marion draws heavily on his previous analyses of the saturated phenomenon in his work on *The Erotic Phenomenon*, although he does not identify it explicitly as a saturated phenomenon.

22. For the most detailed such essay, which establishes an explicit relationship between the Eucharist and the phenomenology of givenness, see "The Phenomenality of the Sacrament—Being and Givenness," in Benson and Wirzba, *Words of Life*, 89–102. The final chapter of this book examines Marion's work on the Eucharist in detail.

23. See chapters 3 and 4 of *Certitudes négatives.*

24. Yet, he does briefly reiterate the four types of saturated phenomena in the conclusion (CN, 312–13), thus suggesting that despite his analyses of other saturated phenomena within the book, such as those of the gift and of sacrifice, he has not rescinded the earlier account in terms of the four types of saturation. The phenomenon of revelation is not mentioned in this context.

25. And to some small extent this may even be true of all phenomena to some degree, as Marion claims that givenness determines all of phenomenality, not just rich phenomena.

26. Even Kant recognizes that we can never treat the other *only* as an end, although he stresses that we should never treat others *only* as means. That seems an important distinction.

27. Steinbock, "Poor Phenomenon," 124.

28. Ibid., 127.

29. See my critique of this language and imagery in chapter 4 on love.

30. It also seems interesting that the completely passive and self-sacrificial love is illustrated by (rather mistreated) women, while the gift of paternity can only be accomplished by the father (see chapter 5 on the gift). The gendered nature of many of Marion's examples is troubling. For his analysis of Clélia in *The Charterhouse of Parma*, see chapter 6 in *The Visible and the Revealed*.

31. Marion returns to this point in his analysis of art where he argues for the artist as one most able to bear the excess of the invisible and best able to portray it. See chapter 2 on art.

32. Steinbock, "Poor Phenomenon," 129, 128.

33. "What, then, does the eye without gaze see? It sees the superabundance of intuitive givenness; or rather, it does not see it clearly and precisely as such since its excess renders it irregardable and difficult to master. The intuition of the phenomenon is nevertheless seen, but as blurred by the too narrow aperture, the too short lens, the too cramped frame, that receives it—or rather that cannot receive it as such. The eye no longer apper-

ceives the apparition of the saturated phenomenon so much as it apperceives the perturbation that it in person produces within the ordinary conditions of experience . . . the eye does not see an exterior spectacle so much as it sees the reified traces of its own power- lessness to constitute whatever it might be into an object" (BG, 215–16; ED, 301).

34. That interpretation, however, ends up playing a role in the account of certainty. See the final section of this introduction.

35. In fact, although the concept of "negative certainty" provides the title to the book, the idea is more proposed than examined in detail in this book. Its most extensive discussion happens in preface and conclusion of the book, as most of the chapters are revised versions of much earlier essays. Presumably Marion will pursue this proposal more fully in the future.

36. This is a question of degree different from the one raised above. One worry concerns the ability to recognize the difference between "poor" and "saturated" phenomena (which Marion claims is a difference of degree), the other concerns the possibility of degrees of *saturation,* thus that "knowledge" about a saturated phenomenon might increase or that some saturated phenomena might be "more saturated" than others.

37. Although the epistemological and hermeneutic dimensions are indeed connected, they are not identical. Stephen Lewis draws a subtle but important distinction between them in his introduction to *The Reason of the Gift* (RoG, 15).

38. Jean Greisch, "L'herméneutique dans la 'phénoménologie comme telle.' Trois questions à propos de Réduction et Donation," *Revue de métaphysique et de morale* 96.1 (1991): 43–63.

39. Jean Grondin, "La tension de la donation ultime et de la pensée herméneutique de l'application chez Jean-Luc Marion," *Dialogue* 38.3 (1999): 547–59.

40. In the same piece, Grondin also objects to Marion's ambivalent use of the term *Gegebenheit* and argues that the gift, the given, and donation (or givenness) must remain distinct (553–54).

41. Richard Kearney, *Debates in Continental Philosophy: Conversations with Contemporary Thinkers* (New York: Fordham University Press, 2004), 15–32.

42. Ibid., 18.

43. In contrast, Merold Westphal describes Marion's phenomenology as hermeneutic and judges it a good framework for exploring religious phenomena. "Vision and Voice: Phenomenology and Theology in the Work of Jean-Luc Marion," *International Journal of Philosophy of Religion* 60 (2006): 117–37.

44. Marion refers to both Grondin's and Greisch's criticisms in footnote 3 to chapter 2 (IE, 33; DS, 39, note 1).

45. IE, 33; DS, 39 (the event) and IE, 123–27; DS, 148–53 (for the icon).

46. The final chapter of *In Excess* actually examines less a phenomenon of revelation than the possibility of mystical theology, that is, appropriate language about the divine. Despite all of Marion's reluctance about hermeneutics, he actually has quite a bit to say about language. See also chapter 6, "What Cannot Be Said: Apophasis and the Discourse of Love," in *The Visible and the Revealed.*

47. Kearney, *Debates in Continental Philosophy,* 16–18.

48. Mackinlay, *Interpreting Excess*, 36.

49. Tamsin Jones, *A Genealogy of Marion's Philosophy of Religion: Apparent Darkness* (Bloomington: Indiana University Press, 2011), 109.

50. Ibid., 115, 117.

51. Ibid., 156, 157.

52. Stephen E. Lewis, "The Phenomenological Concept of Givenness and the 'Myth of the Given,'" (introduction to RoG, 15, 16).

53. Ibid., 17.

54. Marion here explicitly identifies the human being as a saturated phenomenon (CN, 83).

55. This is the final line of part 5 (on the devoted recipient of the saturated phenomenon) of *Being Given* (BG, 319; ED, 438). It is striking that Mackinlay, who accuses Marion of collapsing this tension in favor of the phenomenon and making the recipient entirely passive, does not cite this phrase, which clearly maintains the paradoxical tension. While Mackinlay is right to criticize the lack of hermeneutics in Marion, I think he is wrong in his claim that Marion never considers a more active role for the recipient.

56. "Gives itself," or "is given"—in the French, *se donne* can indicate both the reflexive and the passive.

57. Marion uses this and similar imagery in his first depiction of the *adonné* (BG, 264–65, 283–90; ED, 364–65, 391–400).

58. Mackinlay, *Interpreting Excess*, 33; Joeri Schrijvers, "Ontotheological Turnings? Marion, Lacoste and Levinas on the Decentring of Modern Subjectivity," *Modern Theology* 22.2 (2006): 226, 227. See also his "In (the) Place of the Self: A Critical Study of Jean-Luc Marion's 'Au lieu de soi. L'approche de saint Augustin,'" *Modern Theology* 25.4 (2009): 661–86. He argues in the latter piece that "an 'active' and metaphysical 'I' is needed here to pave the way for a passivity towards the other" and "that we have yet to surpass a metaphysics that cannot see in human finitude but a failure and a defect to be overcome. This has not at all been countered in Marion's latest work" (672, 681).

59. Mackinlay, *Interpreting Excess*, 30; Schrijvers, "Ontotheological Turnings?," 227.

60. *In Excess* describes this role of the recipient in terms of resistance (49–53). This is also the terminology used in "Banality."

61. Marlène Zarader, "Phenomenality and Transcendence," in *Transcendence in Philosophy and Religion,* ed. James Faulconer (Bloomington: Indiana University Press, 2003), 114. John Milbank often makes similar claims. See, for example, his *Being Reconciled: Ontology and Pardon* (New York: Routledge, 2003), 156. For a refutation of Zarader's argument against Marion, see Westphal, "Vision and Voice," 123–25.

62. Derek Morrow focuses heavily on Marion's elucidation of this concept in Descartes in his "The Cartesian Metaphorization of Capax/Capacitas," *Quaestiones disputatae* 1.1 (2010): 72–98, while Stephen Lewis shows how this category is central to Marion's analysis of the erotic phenomenon: "The Lover's Capacity," *Quaestiones disputatae* 1.1 (2010): 226–44. Daniel J. Dwyer argues that already in Husserl the dative self admits of both passivity and receptivity as an active openness to the given. Daniel J. Dwyer, "Husserl and Marion on the Transcendental I," *Quaestiones disputatae* 1.1 (2010): 39–55.

63. In fact, in a couple of instances Marion depicts this as the opening of a world: "The event thus attests its nonconstitutability by constituting me, myself, its effect. Whence the third surprise: the event that comes forward with this pleasure is not summed up in it. At issue is the remembrance of the narrator's entire past, not only a reactivation of his memory (secondary retention), but the return of the living present in and through present retention of a past that, at the moment it was lived, was not even remembered or perceived. The event announced by this pleasure provokes, immeasurably beyond, the arising of a world, the world. The event prompts not only the memory of an individual (the narrator), nor just the work in which this past would again become a living present . . . but precisely the total world of history" (BG, 170; ED, 239–40). He contends that events open horizons (BG, 172; ED, 242).

64. Marion often employs the expression of a telling silence. In fact, the final chapter of *In Excess* explicitly considers how silence in the face of the divine is the context for proper speech about God and itself gives rise to it (IE, 162; DS, 195).

65. Hart, *Essential Writings*, 30. Marion explains this also in his interview with Richard Kearney: "In fact, belief is also to commit yourself, and in that case it is also, perhaps, a theoretical attitude. Because by committing yourself to somebody else, you open a field of experience. And so it's not only a substitute for not knowing; it is an act which makes a new kind of experience possible. It is because I believe that I will see, and not as a compensation. It's the very fact that you believe which makes you see new things, which would not be seen if you did not believe. It's the *credo ut intelligam*. So all this makes clear that what is at stake with the end of metaphysics, and with phenomenology, is that the distinction between the theoretical attitude and the practical attitude should be questioned." Kearney, *Debates in Continental Philosophy*, 29.

66. This is the aforementioned "counter-experience" (VR, 134; VeR, 167).

67. This goes back to a claim that Marion made early on. In an early essay exploring the possibility of a "Christian philosophy" (an identification he usually rejects because of its Thomistic connotations), he is rather dismissive of hermeneutics, which he considers a mere interpretation after the fact that renders such interpretation utterly relative and therefore ultimately meaningless. Instead he suggests Christian philosophy should be "heuristic" in character in that it would discover previously unseen phenomena (found in the realm of theology), formulate them philosophically (presumably via phenomenology), and then "abandon" them to strictly philosophical investigation. Marion's "'Christian Philosophy': Hermeneutic or Heuristic?" originally appeared in *The Question of Christian Philosophy Today*, ed. Francis J. Ambrosio (New York: Fordham University Press, 1999), and is retranslated as chapter 4 of *The Visible and the Revealed*. Marion makes similar claims about the role of the artist in chapter 3 of *In Excess*. In fact, Marion presents the idea that the artist makes visible what was previously unseen fairly consistently in his writings on art. He also speaks of the recipient more generally as receiving the "unseen" (via resistance to it) throughout *In Excess* to the point that this becomes the primary function of the *adonné* in this book. I return to this in chapter 2.

1. Historical Events and Historical Research

1. See especially EP, 219–20; PE, 337–39.

2. Mackinlay, *Interpreting Excess,* 80. For a detailed study of Marion's concept of event, especially its relation to Heidegger's notion of *Ereignis,* see Lasma Pirktina, *Ereignis, Phänomen und Sprache: Die Philosophie des Ereignisses bei Martin Heidegger und Jean-Luc Marion* (Nordhausen, Germany: Verlag Traugott Bautz, 2012). Pirktina does not discuss the connection between the phenomenological category of event and a historical phenomenon, but focuses more on its connections with *Ereignis* more generally. In the only context when she does briefly discuss a historical phenomenon, she comments that "it is immediately obvious that the aspect of quantity does not stand at the center of Marion's interest" (81). This is a striking claim that may well be true, but Pirktina does not go on to explain or justify this. One would wish that this point had been explored more fully. See also her discussion of Ereignis in "Das Ereignis in der Philosophie von Martin Heidegger und Jean-Luc Marion," in *Jean-Luc Marion. Studien zum Werk,* ed. Hanna-Barbara Gerl-Falkovitz (Dresden, Germany: Verlag Text & Dialog, 2013), 323–43.

3. I have developed this fully in *Reading Jean-Luc Marion* and will hence not reiterate this Cartesian basis here. Suffice it to say that Descartes continues to remain a crucial dialogue partner for Marion and that the concern to overcome the particular kind of metaphysics that defined modernity always grounds and frames Marion's arguments. Familiarity with Marion's work on Descartes is essential for fully appreciating his phenomenological work. See especially part 1 of *Reading Jean-Luc Marion.* Thomas Alferi also sees significant parallels between Marion's phenomenological projects and his work on Descartes, although he evaluates these links more critically, seeing Marion's reading of Descartes compromised by his phenomenological commitments or presuppositions. See Thomas Alferi, "Entmündigt die Gabe / die 'donation' das Ich? Versuch einer Vermittlung zwischen Jean-Luc Marion und Hansjürgen Verweyen," *Phänomenologische Forschungen* (2004): 317–41. See also his *"Worüber hinaus Größeres nicht 'gegeben' werden kann . . .": Phänomenologie und Offenbarung nach Jean-Luc Marion* (Freiburg / München: Alber, 2007).

4. Ludmilla Jordanova, *History in Practice* (London: Arnold, 2000), 108–109, 110. For two extremes, see John Vincent, who thinks that "causes do not exist" and that the category of causality is a mistaken one in historical research (to be replaced with "explanation"), versus Aviezer Tucker, whose use of "historiographic explanation" moves fairly close to scientific accuracy and who seeks to recover a strong account of historical agency. John Vincent, *An Intelligent Person's Guide to History* (London: Duckworth, 1995), especially 45–50; Aviezer Tucker, *Our Knowledge of the Past: A Philosophy of Historiography* (Cambridge: Cambridge University Press, 2004), especially 185–253.

5. Most accounts of historical research or historiography mention this. See, for example, Jordanova, *History in Practice,* 100–103. Even Tucker insists "most of history has left no lasting information-carrying effects after it. Therefore, most of history is and always will be unknown and unknowable" (*Our Knowledge of the Past,* 258).

6. Jordanova, *History in Practice,* 100.

7. In responding to constructivist understandings and various other critics, Tucker argues:

If historiography is the best explanation of the historical evidence, it does
not imply that it is a representation of the past, it could be wrong, it is fal-
lible. . . . Yet, the theories and methods of historiography are shared by
a large heterogeneous and uncoerced community of historians, as well
as by textual critics, philologists, detectives, and judges. I have argued . . .
that when historians reach an uncoerced, uniquely heterogeneous and
large consensus on historiography, the best explanation is that they possess knowledge of the past. When one historiographic common cause hypothesis is clearly superior to all its alternatives, when it increases the likeli-
hood of a broad scope of evidence, it generates a sufficient degree of belief
in it, similar to that we have in everyday facts. . . . Constructionism fails to
offer a convincing explanation of the historiographic consensus on theories and methods for interpreting the evidence that has determined historiographic consensus on beliefs for two centuries. (*Our Knowledge of the
Past,* 257)

8. This refers to Proust's description of eating a morsel of madeleine on a cold
winter day: "At the very instant when the warm liquid, and the crumbs with it, touched
my palate, a shudder ran through my whole body, and I stopped, intent upon the extraordinary happening going its own way inside me. An exquisite pleasure had invaded
my senses, but individual, detached, with no suggestion of its cause. And at once the vi-
cissitudes of life had become indifferent to me, its disasters innocuous, its brevity illu-
sory—this new sensation having had on me the effect which love has of filling me with a
precious essence; or rather, this essence was not in me; it was myself." Marcel Proust, *Remembrance of Things Past* (as cited in *Being Given,* 169).

9. The terminology of "world," which Marion presumably appropriates from Heidegger, is striking in this context, because it is central to both Ricoeur's and Derrida's
treatments in different ways. For Ricoeur, poetic interpretation gives rise to a world
which it posits before us and invites us to inhabit. Marion here seems to suggest something similar in regard to events. Derrida speaks of "world" more in terms of experience
of the other. When a friend dies, a whole world dies. Indeed, in some ways *the* world
comes to an end. Death is indeed one of the examples Marion will later give of an event.
Mackinlay finds that "ascribing the opening of a world to an event in this way is a significant modification of Heidegger's account" (*Interpreting Excess,* 91).

10. Pirktina thinks that defining 9/11 as an event is possible on Marion's (though not
on Heidegger's) terms, but that this raises problems for Marion's account because it
seems to indicate that practically all experienced phenomena could become events (Pirktina, *Ereignis, Phänomen und Sprache,* 112–13). She concludes: "If consequently all experiences—the fragrance of the rose, the taste of bread, the understanding of Being, the
grace of God, the absurd (in Camus's sense)—are events, then there are no events. And
Marion admits this." Pirktina, *Ereignis, Phänomen und Sprache,* 114. It is not clear to me either why it follows that there are no events, or how Marion would "admit" this. If Pirktina is calling for more careful distinctions between events, I think she is on the right
track, however, she seems to be getting at something more fundamental, namely that

the call of the event is not phenomenalized. She says: "It is thus claimed [by Marion] that the call calls and the I hears *without any phenomenal experience*. And that is *speculation*. The only phenomenologically correct solution in this case would be to add: When the experience is already there, then what gives itself *appears* as something that was already there previously and called. Speculation about processes in the depths of consciousness cannot be justified phenomenologically." Pirktina, *Ereignis, Phänomen und Sprache,* 106, original emphasis. It is worth pointing out that Pirktina is following Dalferth's criticism of Marion's account of the gift in this. See note 18 in chapter 5.

11. That Marion employs the terminology of "reduction" for a "reduction" of the event to an object is particularly confusing. This is not a phenomenological reduction that sets aside certain presuppositions in order to allow something to appear more clearly, but rather it is a simplistic reduction that is reductionistic by missing what really matters. A saturated phenomenon is here reduced to a common phenomenon that appears in full objectivity (IE, 35).

12. Mackinlay, *Interpreting Excess,* 98.

13. Ibid., 75. Mackinlay criticizes Marion's position on the event primarily in terms of Romano's discussion of phenomenological eventmentality. See *Interpreting Excess,* 47–54 and 112–16.

14. Marion hence sides with Heidegger against Lévinas and Derrida here, although he makes a brief reference to the Derridian "gift of death."

15. Mackinlay, *Interpreting Excess,* 108–109.

16. Historian Alan Munslow puts this in terms of a "story space": "None of this has anything to do with the events of the past *per se,* but everything to do with the decisions that went into creating a fresh story space within which the past can be put to new uses." *Narrative and History: Theory and History* (London: Palgrave, 2007), 19.

17. Jordanova speaks of this in terms of "trust" and reliability (instead of "truth"). *History in Practice,* 93–94.

18. Ricoeur is maybe the one to explore this tension the most fully in his monumental work *Memory, History, Forgetting,* trans. Kathleen Blamey and David Pellauer (Chicago: University of Chicago Press, 2004).

19. *Écraser* actually means to crush or squash; something *écrasant* is overwhelming, burdensome, or unbearable. *Écran* can also be a shield that protects against the weight or blow coming toward it.

20. He suggests that this includes the examination of miracles, although "theological virtues" are required for such an examination (IE, 53).

21. Marion capitalizes Revelation here, which is somewhat inconsistent with his earlier distinction in *Being Given* that only theology can speak of the actuality of "Revelation," while philosophy examines merely the possibility of "phenomena of revelation."

22. An English translation of an earlier version of the final chapter of *Certitudes négatives* can be found as "Phenomenon and Event" in *Graduate Faculty Philosophy Journal* 26.1 (2005): 147–59. One should point out, however, that the later version in *Certitudes négatives* is considerably longer and more fully developed. The reference to hermeneutics (CN, 246–47), for example, is much shorter in the earlier version, where hermeneutics itself is qualified as "imprecise" (148).

23. In fact, throughout this section he refers to Cartesian terminology, such as the *intuitus,* the *mathesis universalis,* and so forth. As indicated in note 3, the important Cartesian context of Marion's thought is my main argument in *Reading Jean-Luc Marion,* which I do not reiterate here but continue to consider essential for understanding Marion's work.

24. While in general the French text is much longer and more fully developed than the earlier English version, Marion has actually removed a discussion of the battle of Waterloo from the text here ("Phenomenon and Event," 154). While the discussion is more or less a reiteration of the same analysis in *Being Given,* it is curious that Marion would choose to remove the only full reference to history in his chapter on the event. Although he maintains that the historical event is one of the four kinds of saturated phenomena (CN, 312), the chapter on the event examines almost exclusively the more general event-like character of *all* saturated phenomena.

25. This claim and his distinction between the two types of knowing are also grounded in his analysis of Descartes and (even more) Pascal. See my discussion in *Reading Jean-Luc Marion* and section 2 of my "Marion and Negative Certainty: Epistemological Dimensions of the Phenomenology of Givenness," *Philosophy Today* 56.3 (2012), where I show how his proposal of "negative certainties" is grounded in his earlier work and has important connections with it.

26. Marion, "Phenomenon and Event," 158.

27. Tucker questions any notion of uniqueness in historical research. He also draws a distinction between events that may well be "unique" and their description, which necessary appeals to general structures or common means of understanding. *Our Knowledge of the Past,* 240–53. Ricoeur specifically addresses the discussions surrounding the Shoah and questions any uncritical claims to uniqueness even in this context. Instead, he suggests the category of a moral idea of "exemplary singularity" and rejects the idea of historical "incomparability" or uniqueness. *Memory, History, Forgetting,* 326–33. It is interesting that Marion never engages with the extensive French discussion of the immemorial and the imprescriptible. He does mention it once in his analysis of sacrifice in *Certitudes négatives* but never engages it in his various writings on the event.

28. As indicated earlier (note 17), Jordanova questions the use of the term "truth" in this context and instead opts for something like "trust" and "reliability." *History in Practice,* 92–94.

29. Tucker, who admittedly seeks to establish history on firm scientific foundations that are diametrically opposed to Marion's project, argues that "even if we found a system that is currently too complex for our contemporary scientific tools, it does not imply that it must be so for all eternity" (*Our Knowledge of the Past,* 218).

30. The French discussion surrounding the Armenian genocide in Turkey may be a helpful example here.

31. Richard Kearney, *Strangers, Gods, and Monsters: Interpreting Otherness* (London and New York: Routledge, 2003), 181.

32. For an evaluation of both the overlap and some of the important distinctions between literary and historical accounts, see Richard Kearney, *On Stories* (London and New York: Routledge, 2002). He explicitly discusses the issue of history and fiction in regard to the Shoah in chapters 4 and 5. See also his explanation of why narrative matters in the final chapter.

33. Carolyn Forché, *Against Forgetting: Twentieth-Century Poetry of Witness* (New York: W. W. Norton, 1993).

34. Ibid., 31.

35. Ibid., 32, 33.

36. Ibid., 42. Forché also tries to maintain the balance between "evidence" and "fragmentation" by providing historical introductions to each period and poet she includes in the collection.

37. See Ricoeur's analysis of testimony in *Memory, History, Forgetting*, 161–66, and his much more extensive discussion of the overlaps and distinctions between fictional and historical narrative in his three-volume work, *Time and Narrative*.

38. These are obviously only two brief examples. Most of Morrison's novels examine particular historical realities from a new perspective by placing themselves imaginatively within them in the form of fictive and yet believable characters. This is, of course, a characteristic of all historical fiction and even to some extent of fiction that does not purport to be primarily historical. One should also note that Morrison's writings are not strictly speaking historical fiction, in the sense that she does not usually treat specific historical events but evokes and helps us imaginatively enter certain historical periods by placing her characters within them.

39. Kearney, *Strangers, Gods, and Monsters*, 185.

40. See especially Kearney's analysis of Marion's work in *The God Who May Be*. I summarize his charge of Marion's tendency to excess and lack of hermeneutics in *Reading Jean-Luc Marion*, 97–101, 169–71.

41. Kearney, *Strangers, Gods and Monsters*, 187.

42. Ibid., 190. See also Kearney's *On Stories*, 134–37.

43. Mackinlay points also to the forestructure of understanding that precedes the event: "Although an event has the power to unforeseeably upend my world, it has that power because of the hermeneutic structure in which that world already has meaning and possibility *for me*. . . . the richness of these possibilities depends on their being part of the hermeneutic structure of human understanding and projection" (*Interpreting Excess*, 115, original emphasis). We make sense of an event from within a particular horizon.

44. Marion actually seems to acknowledge this once in a very brief statement. The final sentence of his first exposition of the event as first type of saturated phenomenon refers to the historical community that examines a historical event: "The hermeneutic of the (saturated because historical) event is enough to produce a historical community, and, through its very inachievability, to render communication possible" (BG, 229; ED, 319). In a footnote to this sentence, he praises Ricoeur's work in *Time and Narrative* as an example of this. Interestingly enough, he nowhere refers to Ricoeur's major work on history and historiography, *Memory, History, Forgetting*. Unfortunately, Marion never returns to this brief suggestion and also does not explain how the "inachievable" hermeneutic of the community communicates or how that might enlighten the historical event. Katharina Bauer suggests that Marion's account of the historical event actually requires a communal dimension because it cannot be analyzed from the perspective of any single individual. Katharina Bauer, "Von der *Donation* zur *Interdonation*. Interpersonale Beziehungen in der Phänomenologie Jean-Luc Marions," in Gerl-Falkovitz, *Jean-Luc Marion*, 220.

45. I am obviously informed here by Richard Kearney's work on diacritical hermeneutics in order to avoid "the inhospitable extremities of vertiginous heights and abyssal depths," which he suggests is often implied in the postmodern obsession with utter alterity and ultimately constitutes an abandonment of discernment. *Strangers, Gods, and Monsters,* 11.

46. Tucker, who has almost as little use for hermeneutics as Marion (albeit for different reasons), points out that "hermeneutics in historiography is not about a reader, a text, or the relationship between them, but about a community of interpreters, their theories, and sets of documents. The world is not a text, but it can be interpreted as texts." *Our Knowledge of the Past,* 259–60.

47. Pirktina also points to Marion's account of the witness in stressing that his notion of the self is not merely passive. Pirktina, "Das Ereignis in der Philosophie von Martin Heidegger und Jean-Luc Marion," 341.

48. Tucker points to the importance of historical knowledge for identity and conduct: "What we know, do not know, can and cannot know, what we should and should not believe about the past matters for our temporal orientation, personal identity, and, consequently, conduct in the presence." *Our Knowledge of the Past,* 262.

2. Art and the Artist

1. One exception is Peter Joseph Fritz, who compares some of Marion's and Henry's writings on aesthetics in his "Black Holes and Revelations: Michel Henry and Jean-Luc Marion on the Aesthetics of the Invisible," *Modern Theology* 25.3 (2009): 415–40. For a German treatment, see László Tengelyi, "Jean-Luc Marion," in *Bildtheorien aus Frankreich,* ed. K. Busch and I. Därmann (München, 2010), 289–98.

2. Marion also speaks of the icon as determining all four types, so there is a sense in which each type also serves as a characteristic of all given phenomena.

3. Marion, *Courbet ou la peinture à l'œil* (Paris: Flammarion, 2014). Unfortunately, the book appeared too late to be considered in this chapter. Marion discusses his interest in Courbet briefly in his interview with Dan Arbib (RC, 246–49).

4. See BG, 215; ED, 300–301. Throughout his writing about the saturated phenomenon, Marion repeatedly uses terminology taken from the realm of photography.

5. In the first lines of the book, he speaks of the idol as "the splendor of the visible" and the icon as "the brilliance of the visible" (GWB, 7; DSL, 15).

6. Marion distinguishes the religious gaze from the artistic "production" in this case: "The gaze, by freezing, marks the place where the first visible bursts in its splendor; art attempts, then, to consign materially, on a second level, and by what one habitually calls an idol, the brilliance of the god" (GWB, 15; DSL, 25).

7. Marion is insistent in this treatment that the icon has nothing to do with aesthetics (GWB, 20; DSL, 33). He does, however, speak of it in terms of appearance and (in)visibility. His treatments after *Being Given* make a fuller distinction between idol (as work of art) and icon (as face of the other).

8. He will also apply the language of relief to the relationship between phenomenology and theology, inasmuch as phenomenology provides "relief" to theology (see

chapter 3 of *The Visible and the Revealed*, originally published in 1993). In that context also, several senses of that term must be heard.

9. As in the case of the historical event, Marion also mentions here again the creation of a world (CV, 6; CdV, 20). Similarly: "The opening of a world should not be confused with the production of spectacles, even if it makes them possible" (CV, 22; CdV, 44).

10. For this point, see my entry on Jean-Luc Marion in *The International Encyclopedia of Ethics*, ed. Hugh LaFollette (Oxford: Blackwell, 2013).

11. Marion often uses the French idiomatic expression "ce que cela donne" when discussing painting. Literally, this means "what this gives," but it refers to the effect something has or even its "payoff."

12. Marion here, in going back to the original mediocre painting, again emphasizes the play of light (BG, 51; ED, 75). He had focused on light in his analysis of Monet in *The Crossing of the Visible*. Visibility is again central to his analysis here.

13. It is noteworthy that in the final chapter, Marion speaks of the saturated phenomenon as appearing *first* in terms of quality. When we cannot bear this quality, we faint (BG, 314–15; ED, 432). The saturated phenomenon is unbearable and too heavy for us, and so we often faint under its weight.

14. See, for example, his comments in "The Banality of Saturation" on listening to an opera diva. In *Being Given* he had written of paintings as having a "melody" (*mélodie*) or their colors "singing" (*chantent*)—a French idiomatic expression for the harmonious play of color (BG, 48–49; ED, 73).

15. One wonders what this means about portrait painting in general or, maybe more specifically, about Rembrandt's famous self-portraits? Marion does make a dismissive comment about Dürer's self-portrait in *The Crossing of the Visible* (CV, 23; CdV, 46). But surely he would not dismiss all paintings of faces in the tradition?

16. Marion at least twice considers chapels decorated by artists in his discussions—Matisse's Chapelle du Rosaire and Cocteau's Chapelle St. Pierre, in *The Crossing of the Visible*, and Rothko's Houston Chapel, in *In Excess*.

17. Although this is the first explicit discussion of the painter or artist, it parallels the claim in *God without Being* that the maker of idols creates a particular vision of the divine, namely by introducing into visibility for the first time his or her specific vision of the divine unseen (e.g., GWB, 27; DSL, 41–42).

18. In his more theologically oriented writings, Marion repeatedly prefers this "productive" function of phenomenology over a merely "interpretive" function of hermeneutics. See, for example, chapter 4 in *The Visible and the Revealed*, which distinguishes between "heuristic" and "hermeneutic" functions for Christian philosophy. Marion elevates the first and rejects the second in fairly strong language. I return to this parallel at the end of the chapter.

19. Note that the existing English translation renders "trivialité" as "banality," but this is not the "banalité" of "The Banality of Saturation," which is employed positively of the saturated phenomenon.

20. It is noteworthy that Marion here employs the term of the imprescriptible, while he does not speak of it in the context of his discussion of historical events and does not

engage in the popular French debate about that issue in light of Jankélévitch's claims in *Le pardon* and "L'Imprescriptible," texts with which Derrida engages heavily in his discussions of forgiveness. Marion also refers to this discussion briefly when treating of forgiveness in the chapter on the gift and sacrifice in *Certitudes négatives* (see my discussion of this in chapter 5).

21. Again, judgment is made about what is "truly creative" and "real" art.

22. This is also what Shane Mackinlay finds: "The appearing of idols and paintings depends not only on what they give, but also on the way they are seen, and in at least some instances, their appearing is literally a reflection of the way in which a viewer looks at them" (*Interpreting Excess*, 129). He comes to that conclusion in a rather different way, though, and seems confused about several aspects of Marion's treatment of aesthetics.

23. Jean-Luc Marion, "What We See and What Appears," in *Idol Anxiety*, ed. Josh Ellenbogen and Aaron Tugendhaft (Stanford, Calif.: Stanford University Press, 2011), 152–68. In my original translation of this piece, I translated "tableau" as "picture" instead of as "painting" in order to employ a wider, more inclusive term and to be able to distinguish it from "peinture," which Marion also uses in the article. I now think that "painting" would have been a better translation, as that is the primary focus of Marion's discussion. *Tableau* can mean a board or screen, a painting or picture, a list or table, a (theatrical) scene or performance, or even a sight or visual arrangement. Marion is clearly discussing the realm of aesthetics in the essay but is drawing various connections to visibility more generally.

24. Marion, "What We See," 162, trans. mod.

25. Ibid., 163, trans. mod.

26. Ibid., 164, trans. mod. Presumably Marion's forthcoming book on Courbet will explore this much more fully.

27. Marion, "What We See," 164.

28. Ibid., 167, trans. mod.

29. Ibid., 168.

30. Ibid., 165, trans. mod.

31. Ibid., 168.

32. In fact, Marion suggests a parallel between painting and literature in the essay on art just examined (ibid., 164).

33. For Kant's discussion of the artistic genius, see §§46–50 of *The Critique of Judgment*.

34. The Hebrew word for "glory" also means "weight."

35. See Hans-Georg Gadamer, *Truth and Method*, trans. Joel Weinsheimer and Donald G. Marshall (London and New York: Continuum, 2004), part 1.2.1.

36. Gadamer, *Truth and Method*, 52. The next section (1.1.2.B) is a discussion of the history of the term *Erlebnis* (experience).

37. Gadamer, *Truth and Method*, 61.

38. Ibid., 68.

39. Ibid., 70.

40. This is also part of Gadamer's critique of Romantic aesthetics. See *Truth and Method*, 1.1.3.

41. Jeffrey L. Kosky, "Philosophy of Religion and Return to Phenomenology in Jean-Luc Marion: From *God without Being* to *Being Given*," *American Catholic Philosophical Quarterly* 78.4 (2004): 639.

42. Marion, "What We See," 163, trans. mod.

43. In the interview with Arbib, Marion says that he has always been most interested in things or texts he did not understand and everything else bored him. Therefore, "it has always seemed to me that philosophy consists in showing (or understanding) things that at first glance one does not see—paradoxa" (RC, 160). He points to Heidegger, for whom phenomenology is about showing the things that "most of the time do not show themselves" and attributes his own fascination with theology to the fact that it is concerned with paradoxa and with what remains at first glance invisible. What merits our attention, he claims, is "not what we see, but that which, within what we see, we do not understand but must understand in order to see what we see" (RC 160).

44. Of course, in some sense it is no longer the same phenomenon if it is experienced by different people or even the same person at different times. Yet in order for us to communicate about phenomena, they must be identifiable in some sense. And Marion often speaks of the same phenomenon being experienced in different fashion (e.g., God or the stone at the end of *Certitudes négatives* or the diva in "Banality").

45. The first performances of the New York Philharmonic and of the New York Metropolitan Opera that season were dedicated to the victims in the twin towers and to the firefighters who perished trying to rescue them. Countless artistic creations tried to express people's emotions in the wake of the tragedy, to commemorate and console. For one example, see Lisa Radakovich Holsberg, *Race for the Sky: Songs for New York and 9/11* (2005) and her accompanying website, www.raceforthesky.org. The December 2001 performance of Händel's *Messiah* in Trinity Church, a church that faces Ground Zero and was heavily involved in the relief efforts surrounding the tragedy, is still transmitted on WQXR (the New York classical radio station) several times each year during the Christmas season. Similar responses have met other tragedies, such as the shooting at Sandy Hook Elementary School in Newtown, Connecticut, in December 2012.

3. Nature and Flesh

1. An early version of this chapter profited greatly from a yearlong electronic discussion on environmental hermeneutics, organized by Brian Treanor and Forrest Clingerman. The papers of the other participants have also influenced my thinking. (This is far more evident in the version of this chapter included in the volume based on the discussion, but as I cannot assume that a reader of this book would have read that other volume, I have here removed the references to its other chapters and instead referred to more widely known sources.) Forrest Clingerman et al., eds., *Interpreting Nature: The Emerging Field of Environmental Hermeneutics* (New York: Fordham University Press, 2013).

2. Mark Manolopoulos examines the possibility that creation might be conceived as a "gift," drawing on Derrida's and Marion's phenomenological accounts of the gift. He tries to develop what he calls an "oscillational eco-ethos" by suggesting that a "double movement of acceptance and return" can get beyond the aporia of the gift or at least hold it in continual tension. In that sense all of "what-is" can be conceived as a gift that

should be loved. Mark Manolopoulos, *If Creation Is a Gift* (Albany: State University of New York Press, 2009).

3. All these saturated phenomena are either human creations or they describe human activities, thus they are all clearly connected to the human in some way (including the excessive phenomenon of revelation, which is a *human* experience of the divine). Although Marion claims that they come to us from the "unseen," they are made "visible" by the human recipient.

4. I am here evoking the progression in which ethical consideration tends to be extended: first to so-called "higher" animals (especially those most like us like the great apes), then to other animals, then to plants or all living things (biocentrism), and finally to entire ecosystems (ecocentrism and deep ecology). H. Peter Steeves makes a rare attempt to extend ethical consideration even further in "Mars Attacked! Interplanetary Environmental Ethics and the Science of Life," chapter 7 of his *The Things Themselves: Phenomenology and the Return to the Everyday* (Albany: State University of New York Press, 2006), 126–45.

5. Katharina Bauer, *Einander zu erkennen geben. Das Selbst zwischen Erkenntnis und Gabe* (Freiburg/München: Alber, 2012), 453. She makes a similar comment in her "Von der Donation zur Interdonation," 220. This is not the primary concern of her discussions, which focus on Marion's phenomenology of the gift and on mutual recognition. I return to her treatment in *Einander zu erkennen geben* in more detail in chapter 5 on the gift.

6. Marion briefly suggests at the end of *Certitudes négatives* that a stone might appear to us as a saturated phenomenon once it is incorporated into a cultural building. I return to this later in the chapter.

7. It should also be noted that Marion designates Kant's notion of the sublime, or of the "aesthetic idea" more generally, as a precedent for his analysis of the saturated phenomenon, focusing solely on its sense of being overwhelming and impossible to be conceptualized (VR, 33, 46–47; VeR, 56, 72–73; BG, 219–20; ED, 305–309). Yet most of Kant's examples for the sublime (at least in the Third Critique) are natural phenomena: imposing mountains, great thunderstorms, and so forth. (Furthermore, Kant's analysis seems to imply that we actually perceive ourselves as greater than the phenomenon in the experience of the sublime, while Marion clearly implies the opposite.)

8. Bernd Heinrich, *A Year in the Maine Woods* (Reading, Mass.: Addison-Wesley, 1994), *The Trees in My Forest* (New York: Cliff Street Books, 1997), *Mind of the Raven* (New York: Cliff Street Books, 1999), *One Man's Owl* (Princeton, N.J.: Princeton University Press, 1987), and various other texts.

9. Edward Abbey, *Desert Solitaire* (New York: Touchstone, 1990); *The Journey Home* (New York: Plume, 1991).

10. John Muir, *The Wilderness World of John Muir* (Boston: Houghton Mifflin, 1976); *Our National Parks* (Madison: University of Wisconsin Press, 1981); *The Yosemite* (Madison: University of Wisconsin Press, 1986); *Nature Writings* (New York: Library of America, 1997), and others.

11. In fact, Leopold's "A Land Ethic," in *A Sand County Almanac: With Other Essays on Conservation from Round River* (New York: Oxford University Press, 1949), is convincing precisely because of the detailed descriptions with which the book as a whole has moved

us. Some commentators argue that "A Land Ethic," the final chapter of *A Sand County Almanac* (the only one that is usually read in environmental ethics classes), only makes sense within and because of those prior descriptions of the book.

12. Annie Dillard, *Pilgrim at Tinker Creek* (New York: HarperCollins, 1974), 35–36. If this does not qualify as an experience of a saturated phenomenon, I'm not sure what would!

13. Something similar could be said of the writings of Thoreau and those of other transcendentalists.

14. In careful reading one discovers, however, that most of these nature writers do not romanticize nature, but often also depict its more violent side in vivid detail. To remain with the same example, Dillard's book is set up as a sort of kataphatic and apophatic dialogue: the first part shows the beauty and abundance of nature, while the second its horror and meaninglessness. It certainly is not a purely romanticized account.

15. It is noteworthy that although Marion generally uses very "positive" examples for the saturated phenomenon in his writings, he gives a couple of "negative" ones in the interview with Dan Arbib (RC, 145, 271, both referring to the 9/11 attacks) and actually twice mentions the ecological crisis and the need to take it seriously (RC, 262, 269–70). He does express some doubt about whether the heating of the planet is due to human activity and whether it constitutes a real danger (RC, 267–68).

16. Scientists have repeatedly been surprised by the extent of melting in Antarctica or Greenland—far more extensive than anticipated by even some of the most dire prognoses. While there is strong consensus in the scientific community that climate change is a reality and that human-produced carbon dioxide is changing the atmosphere in a detrimental way, there is far less consensus about the precise degree and intensity of anticipated repercussions of the warming trend. See the reports of the Intergovernmental Panel on Climate Change (IPCC, www.ipcc.ch), updated every five years, and the various responses to it.

17. Even the human release of carbon dioxide and methane into the atmosphere, which is now generally acknowledged as a major contributor to global climate change, was only identified as a *cause* of climate change in light of the warming *effect*. It hence fits precisely the reversed sequence of effect and cause that Marion outlines in *Being Given*.

18. This has become a large and rich field. For one example, see the extensive work of Sandra Harding on this issue, such as *Whose Science? Whose Knowledge? Thinking from Women's Lives* (Ithaca, N.Y.: Cornell University Press, 1991); *The Science Question in Feminism* (Ithaca, N.Y.: Cornell University Press, 1986); *Sciences from Below: Feminisms, Postcolonialisms, and Modernities* (Durham, N.C.: Duke University Press, 2008). Barbara McClintock's scientific work has at times been taken to highlight the "involved" nature of scientific research (e.g., in Evelyn Fox Keller's *A Feeling for the Organisms: The Life and Work of Barbara McClintock* [San Francisco: W. H. Freeman, 1983]). For a summary and rather strident criticism of this position, see Alan Soble, "Keller on Gender, Science, and McClintock: A Feeling for the Organism," in *Scrutinizing Feminist Epistemology: An Examination of Gender in Science,* ed. Cassandra L. Pinnick, Noretta Koertge, and Robert F. Almeder (New Brunswick, N.J.: Rutgers University Press, 2003), 65–101.

19. I am reminded of one occasion when I gave students in environmental ethics the assignment to "dig in the dirt" and then journal about their experience. My assumption was that they would do some gardening, maybe plant some flowers or vegetables. Most of them, however, merely poked a stick an inch into the ground and obviously discovered nothing particularly exciting by doing so.

20. For an example of a more "saturated" account of encounters with rocks, see the chapter on Mars by Steeves, *The Things Themselves*.

21. This dimension is particularly strong in Ricoeur's and Kearney's hermeneutics, but to some extent it is also true even of Caputo's more radical appropriation of Derrida. Although Caputo eschews anything that might limit the flux of interpretation, he certainly does not counsel irresponsibility or complete relativism.

22. See James Garvey's discussion of supposed technological fixes of the climate crisis in *The Ethics of Climate Change: Right and Wrong in a Warming World* (London: Continuum, 2008), 101–106.

23. This also highlights again that nature is not a technical object (despite Marion's conflation of the two in the example of the tree) and thus may justifiably be regarded as a saturated phenomenon.

24. The distinction between the "design" of technical objects and the witness to the saturated phenomenon is found in "The Banality of Saturation" (VR, 143; VeR, 180). He explores it also in more detail in the article on aesthetic visibility, "What We See and What Appears."

25. He is also very much influenced by Heidegger on this point. See, for example, his analysis in *Being Given*, which engages heavily with the "ready-to-hand" in the context of the analysis of "anamorphosis" (BG, 126–30; ED, 179–82; see also VR, 150; CpV, 23).

26. Derrida has done interesting work on this question in *The Animal That Therefore I Am*, trans. David Wills (New York: Fordham University Press, 2008). Emmanuel Falque has begun to explore this question to some extent in *Les noces de l'agneau. Essai sur le corps et l'eucharistie* (Paris: Cerf, 2011). For a discussion of the treatment of the animal in the texts of various philosophers, see Kelly Oliver, *Animal Lessons: How They Teach Us to Be Human* (New York: Columbia University Press, 2009).

27. This desire to "extend" Lévinas's account of the face to animals is obviously not unproblematic, as it grounds ethical consideration in similarity to the human (animals must have a face like the human in order to be worthy of consideration—just as earlier animal-rights activists argued that animals suffer like us or have interests like us and are therefore worthy of dignity and moral treatment). Many "environmental" discussions of Lévinas grapple with this problem. See, for example, Matthew Calarco, "Faced by Animals," in *Radicalizing Levinas*, ed. Peter Atterton and Matthew Calarco (New York: State University of New York Press, 2010), 113–33; and John Llewelyn, *The Middle Voice of Ecological Conscience* (New York: St. Martin's Press, 1991). Other important sources in eco-phenomenology grapple with similar questions. See David Macauley, *Elemental Philosophy: Earth, Air, Fire, and Water as Environmental Ideas* (Albany: State University of New York Press, 2011); Charles S. Brown and Ted Toadvine, eds., *Eco-Phenomenology: Back to the Earth Itself* (Albany: State University of New York Press, 2003); and Bruce V. Foltz and

Robert Frodeman, eds., *Rethinking Nature: Essays in Environmental Philosophy* (Bloomington: Indiana University Press, 2004).

28. Note in this context that Henry's phenomenology of the flesh (and his philosophy of Christianity) has occasionally been condemned as "pantheistic," precisely because he equates Life and the divine.

29. In his *Sur la pensée passive de Descartes,* Marion suggests that even the Cartesian self is not the independent subject that the tradition has usually supposed, but has a passive dimension to it that is attentive to the flesh and its passions. See especially his chapters 2 and 4.

30. Steeves, *The Things Themselves,* 62.

31. It is striking, however, that in the interview with Arbib, Marion asserts that "the flesh establishes the very type of the saturated phenomenon" (RC, 150).

32. Mackinlay argues that the idea that the flesh is an "absolute" phenomenon cannot be maintained consistently (*Interpreting Excess,* 142–58). Although Marion certainly identifies this as the way in which the third type of saturated phenomenon turns the Kantian category of relation on its head, overall the claim of absoluteness plays a rather small role in his account; he focuses much more extensively on immediacy and self-affectivity. Mackinlay also claims that Marion relies on a metaphysical claim about Life (via Henry), yet not only does Marion rarely explicitly appeal to Henry's notion of Life instead focusing primarily on the notion of self-affection, but he also operates with a completely different definition of metaphysics than the one Mackinlay seems to assume here. Marion should not be accused of reintroducing metaphysics without carefully engaging with his many writings on this topic, on the one hand because he operates with a precise definition of metaphysics, and on the other hand because overcoming metaphysics is the central aim of his project.

33. The idea that we have a self-consciousness of the givenness of our body in a way in which no other animals do is questionable, as many recent studies in animal ethology have shown, but that is not my main point here. I briefly return to it below.

34. Although Marion mentions the earth here, note that it is only in the context of the grounding of an electrical current.

35. Benjamin Baumann suggests, however, that Marion's account successfully overcomes these kinds of disconnects in his phenomenon of the flesh. "Jean-Luc Marion und die Überwindung der *Störung durch die Welt.* Subjekt und Welt als *gesättigte Phänomene,*" in Gerl-Falkovitz, *Jean-Luc Marion,* 308.

36. In his defense of icons (a treatise on which Marion draws extensively in other contexts), John of Damascus argues that iconoclasts denigrate the material and that the incarnation provides license for icons painted on wood because Christ's "wearing" a "material body" hallows and sanctifies matter. See John of Damascus, *Three Treatises on the Divine Images,* trans. Andrew Louth (Crestwood, N.Y.: St. Vladimir's Seminary Press, 2003), I.16, 29–30.

37. See especially chapters 2, 5, and 8 of *Les noces de l'agneau.* Falque is significantly influenced by Marion, although his account of our organic or animal nature obviously does not rely on Marion, as Marion never discusses this.

38. See my critique of Falque's position on this point in "Corporeality, Animality, Bestiality: Emmanuel Falque on Incarnate Flesh," *Analecta Hermeneutica* 4 (2012): 1–16.

39. For a trenchant account of what happens when the "flesh" breaks down, see Catherine Malabou, *Ontology of the Accident: An Essay on Destructive Plasticity*, trans. Carolyn Shread (Cambridge: Polity Press, 2012). She describes various ways in which terrible accidents, the breakdown of bodily functions, or the process of aging affect our sense of identity and of our body.

4. Love and Violence

1. "La croisée des regards" literally means "the crossing of gazes," which is how it is usually translated, but it is also the French idiomatic expression for "meeting" someone's gaze (thus Marion's frequent insistence that one must "bear up" under a gaze is to some extent implied in the French expression).

2. Marion suggests in the introduction that he speaks primarily from his personal experience (EP, 10; PE, 22). He reiterates the importance of this first-person account in his interview with Arbib (RC, 201–202). I am by no means intending to dismiss all of Marion's treatment of love, but I highlight one aspect of this discussion that seems problematic, namely its link with violence and its absolute character.

3. He had already made this claim at the end of *God without Being,* where charity serves to displace ontology (GWB, 136–38; DSL, 193–95).

4. EP, 89–97; PE, 143–55. Even a bit earlier he emphasizes that "the lover loves to love for the love of love" (*L'amant aime aimer pour l'amour de l'amour*) (EP, 87; PE, 140).

5. Especially in statements such as the following: "In fact, falling in love depends solely on me" (EP, 94, trans. mod.; PE, 150).

6. Robyn Horner, "The Weight of Love," in *Counter-Experiences: Reading Jean-Luc Marion,* ed. Kevin Hart (South Bend, Ind.: Notre Dame University Press, 2007), 241.

7. Claude Romano, "Love in Its Concept," in Hart, *Counter-Experiences,* 323.

8. It is not clear why this avoids the return of any notions of self-sufficiency or autonomy.

9. Stephen Lewis, "The Lover's Capacity," *Quaestiones disputatae* 1.1 (2010): 235. Lewis provides an analysis of Marion's article on the changing meaning of "capax" in his text. See also my discussion of this issue in *Reading Jean-Luc Marion,* 189–91.

10. Lewis argues against Milbank's misunderstanding of Marion's refusal of reciprocity in love: "Marion distinguishes between reciprocity or exchange, which have only to do with finite, limited relations framed by objective certainty and being, and assurance, which the lover hopes in precisely because it is a gift that is unconditioned, unmerited, and completely bound up with the beloved's infinite unfolding in the lover's advance." Lewis, "Lover's Capacity," 242.

11. In this, Marion is not alone. See my tracing of the strong emphasis on kenosis in writing about love in the work of many contemporary authors (besides Marion including Lacoste, Chrétien, Henry, and Falque): "The Phenomenon of Kenotic Love in Contemporary Continental Philosophy of Religion," in *Understanding Love,* ed. Diane Enns and Antonio Calcagno (forthcoming).

12. Lewis, "Lover's Capacity," 238.

13. It is troubling here that he exclusively uses the male pronoun for the lover and only occasionally (twice, on my count) switches to the feminine pronoun when speaking of the beloved, in particular when describing the need to "enter into" the beloved. In one passage he seems to realize this himself: "Il voit avec les yeux de l'amour, c'est-à-dire en s'aveuglant (la grande est majestueuse, la petite délicieuse, l'hystérique passionnée, la garce excitante, la sotte spontanée, la raisonneuse brilliante, etc.—et on peut le transposer au masculin)" (PE, 130–31); "He sees with the eyes of love, which is to say by blinding himself (the large woman is majestic, the petite, delightful; the hysterical, passionate; the bitch, arousing; the silly, spontaneous; the argumentative, brilliant, etc.—and one can easily transpose these so that they apply to men, too)" (EP, 80). It is not entirely clear to me that one could really so easily "transpose this into the masculine." See Stephen Lewis's comment on the issue of gender in the English translation (EP, 24).

14. In contrast, Kühn argues that Marion's account of love shows a "false subject" that is entirely passive in the face of love. Kühn, "Passivität und Zeugenschaft," 196. Even differently, Bauer argues that Marion succeeds in an account of "interdonation" that makes giving and receiving between lover and beloved entirely equal: "On the level of interpersonality this role is explicitly reciprocal [wechselseitig] and must consist in the crossing of the perspectives of the participants. . . . In the insoluably crossed structure of loving one another the roles—the personae—of giver and recipient cannot be distinguished, although the singularity and personality of the actors can. These roles only become visible in a reciprocal exchange [wechselseitigen Austausch]." Bauer, "Von der Donation zur Interdonation," 231.

15. For a more detailed engagement with this particular piece, its parallels to The Erotic Phenomenon, and its engagement with Lévinas, see Derek J. Morrow, "The Love 'without being' That Opens (to) Distance, Part One: Exploring the Givenness of the Erotic Phenomenon with Jean-Luc Marion," Heythrop Journal 46.3 (2005): 281–98, and "The Love 'without Being' That Opens (to) Distance, Part Two: From the Icon of Distance to the Distance of the Icon in Marion's Phenomenology of Love," Heythrop Journal 46.4 (2005): 493–511.

16. He explicates this critique of Lévinas much more fully in his article "From the Other to the Individual," Levinas Studies: An Annual Review, ed. Jeffrey Bloechl and Jeffrey L. Kosky (Pittsburgh, Pa.: Duquesne University Press, 2005), 99–117. I criticize this reading of Lévinas in "Ethics, Eros, or Caritas? Lévinas and Marion on Individuation of the Other," Philosophy Today 49.1 (2005): 78–95. Geoffrey Dierckxsens, in contrast, criticizes both Lévinas's and Marion's accounts, arguing that "Marion ultimately equates charitable love for the other with the moment of the ethical commandment, which makes him unable to give a proper account of love of neighbour." Even Marion does not sufficiently individuate the beloved other. While most of Dierckxsens's article relies on "The Intentionality of Love," he finds even The Erotic Phenomenon unsatisfying: "Unfortunately, it is not explained in The Erotic Phenomenon how erotic love must include charity in its essence and no trace is there to be found of a particular concept of charity as love for the unique other." Ultimately, he finds that Marion's earlier account is reducible to that of Lévinas,

while the later account excludes an ethical dimension altogether and fails to distinguish eros and charity. Neither manage to speak adequately of the *unique* beloved. Geoffrey Dierckxsens, "Loving Unintentionally: Charity and the Bad Conscience in the Works of Levinas and Marion," *Bijdragen: International Journal in Philosophy and Theology* 73.1 (2012): 5, 20.

17. Marion employs painting imagery and terminology throughout this section by speaking of the "field of vision," of "vanishing lines," of the "empty frame," and so forth (EP, 84; PE, 137).

18. John Milbank, "The Gift and the Mirror," in Hart, *Counter-Experiences,* 269. Kühn also thinks that Marion's account ultimately returns us to a metaphysical paradigm. "Passivität und Zeugenschaft," 179, 188, 193–96. In contrast to Milbank, however, he thinks that the subject in Marion is entirely passive; Marion merely reverses the traditional metaphysical relations (195).

19. For example, Milbank's claims about Descartes (especially "Cartesian subjectivity"), metaphysics, and reciprocity (three topics that figure prominently in his critique of Marion) more or less entirely disregard Marion's work on Descartes, on subjectivity, and on metaphysics. Overall, Milbank's tirades against Marion are usually more about his own project than about a careful reading of Marion's work.

20. He reiterates this parallel between Don Juan and God in the interview with Arbib: "The lover leaves the logic of exchange and takes the risk of loving without return. This is the position of Don Juan but also the position of God, who loves those who do not love him and, potentially, who loves what is not yet, draws it *ex nihilo*. . . . In this case, one loves without return, because there simply is no possibility of return" (RC, 194).

21. In a later passage, he suggests that the future of the erotic experience coincides with the hope of Christian eschatology (EP, 210; PE, 325). We must always love as if the first time was the last: "The lovers accomplish their oath in the *adieu*—in the passage unto God [*à Dieu*], whom they summon as their final witness, their first witness, the one who never leaves and never lies. For the first time, they say 'adieu' to one another: next year in Jerusalem—next time in God. Thinking unto God [*penser à Dieu*] can be done, erotically, in this 'adieu'" (EP, 212; PE, 326). In the interview with Arbib he refers to "the third" as either "the child" or "God" (RC, 199).

22. See especially the final chapter of *In Excess,* but also passages in *Idol and Distance* and *God without Being.*

23. He speaks of the icon here both in terms of the sign of the cross and of an actual painted icon or "type" (CV, 66–87; CdV, 119–54).

24. Beáta Tóth criticizes Marion's account of erotic speech as lacking a real consideration of "enfleshed sexual love." She asks: "What is the difference between the words of sexual love-making and those of non-sexual eroticisation? Disappointingly, Marion does not elaborate on this point in any useful detail" and concludes: "What one is given here is a curiously passionless portrayal of the phenomenon of erotic love, one that faithfully captures sense perception and physical feeling and is also insightful concerning the way love knows, yet one that is without emotion, beyond the sensation of affected flesh." She takes recourse instead to Pope John Paul II's theology of the body for a more adequate

account of enfleshment. Beáta Tóth, "Love between Embodiment and Spirituality: Jean-Luc Marion and John Paul II on Erotic Love," *Modern Theology* 29.1 (2013): 27, 28.

25. The phrases quoted in the text were the subtitles of various sections of the article when it first appeared in English as "The Unspoken: Apophasis and the Discourse of Love," *Proceedings of the American Catholic Philosophical Association* 76 (2002): 39–56. The subtitles were removed when the article was edited for *The Visible and the Revealed* to make them parallel with other chapters (and the French version), which lacked section titles.

26. Another reference, which occurs in the fifth meditation, is much less explicit and will not be explored in this context. Marion is here dealing with the issues of betrayal and veracity. In this particular section, he describes two false moves: either I advance fully but am abandoned by the other and thus fall into a void (my love is not returned), or I deceive the other by pretending to offer myself fully but hold something back. This second move is compared to capitulation in a siege: "I do not want to declare my face open, as one declares a city open because one has given up its defense and has placed it under the supposed benevolence of the victor" (EP, 169; PE, 262). In the French it is not completely clear whether the "openness" of the abandoned town is compared to the false or to the right openness of love. This reference would not be particularly problematic if it were not part of a larger pattern of such comparisons. I have only discussed some of them here.

27. This implies for him that desire for objects is excluded from the erotic reduction and thus is not love (EP, 221; PE, 335).

28. In "Love in Its Concept," Romano acknowledges, however, that "friendship, just as much as eroticism (in the narrow sense) is characterized by the advance, by the unconditional nature of the oath that inspires to the eternal" (325).

29. Jean-Luc Marion, "The Gift of a Presence," in *Prolegomena to Charity*, chapter 6 (PC, 124–52; PaC, 147–78).

30. See especially Marion's repeated references to the need for *theosis* (deification) in his theological work (e.g., ID, 160; IeD, 198; RC, 190).

31. See also his vigorous critique of Nygren in the interview with Arbib. Nygren's distinction has "no truly biblical basis" and "lacks any Christian sense" (RC, 190).

32. More positively, in the interview with Arbib, Marion says that the conviction that "nothing remains outside of God" and that "the world is found in the Trinity" or in the heart of God guided his writing of *The Erotic Phenomenon*: "The idea that there is anything outside of God has no meaning. This was really a Copernican revolution about which I have never had the least doubt. When I wrote *The Erotic Phenomenon*, it was with that conviction" (RC, 54).

33. While I find Marion's account more convincing as a theological reflection, I would surmise that the association of love with war would be equally problematic on a theological reading. There are also striking parallels between what Marion says about love here and what he says of forgiveness in his analysis in "The Impossible for Man—God," where he insists that only God can truly forgive and all sins are ultimately against God. One wonders exactly what this assertion that only God loves truly is supposed to accomplish. Is it an attempt to preserve God's ineffability and distance? Then why insist that hu-

man and divine love function in the same manner? Marion consistently claims that his phenomenological accounts can stand on their own and that they are not grounded in faith or theological claims. Passages like these, however, make his critics wonder to what extent that can be true.

34. Most of the popular discourse about homosexual love tends to emphasize its similarity or even identity to heterosexual love. Whether to treat homosexual conceptions of love as similar to or different from heterosexual ones seems fraught with the same kinds of difficulties as arguments in regard to gender. Feminists who have stressed feminine difference, such as Kristeva and Irigaray, have often been accused of essentializing women. I suspect that drawing distinctions between homosexual and heterosexual love would meet similar objections. The fact that all the phenomenological treatments of eros by French philosophers of religion (Marion, Chrétien, Lacoste, Falque) are exclusively heterosexual (and often entirely from a male standpoint) certainly deserves further exploration and critique.

35. See Milbank's long diatribe against Marion's account of love in Hart's *Counter-Experiences*.

36. Falque, *Les noces de l'agneau*, 228.

37. Romano, "Love in Its Concept," in Hart, *Counter-Experiences*, 326.

38. Ibid., 328–31.

39. Ibid., 333. To some extent, this concern is shared by Milbank, although he explicates it quite differently and seeks to return to a pre-modern, traditionally metaphysical, account of love. See his long article in the same volume.

40. Others have of course made this criticism already in the wake of the publication of *God without Being*. See, for example, Kenneth L. Schmitz's review of *God without Being*: "The God of Love," *Thomist* 57.3 (1993): 495–508; and Géry Provoust's review of *Questions cartésiennes II*: "La tension irrésolue. Les *Questions cartésiennes, II* de Jean-Luc Marion," *Revue Thomiste* 98.1 (1998): 95–102.

41. For a detailed summary of this, see my *Reading Jean-Luc Marion*, 106–113.

42. This argument becomes greatly expanded and applied to Aquinas and Heidegger in different ways in *God without Being*.

43. Like Romano, I wonder about Marion's claim that love is more important than being. When the other does not actually exist, does my love not run the danger of loving a disembodied ideal that is merely an image or figment of my own imagination? Does it not ultimately become an idol, a mirror of what I desire and worship in myself? Is not a denial of the importance of being in this context tantamount to a denial of corporeality? And are not flesh and bodies essential for love? This is linked in some way to the worry above that the lover could love completely without a beloved. That also seems disembodied, as if the lover could love a Platonic ideal. Marion claims that only love truly individuates the other, while ethics remains at the level of universality. I am not convinced that is true, especially of Lévinas's ethics, but it is also not always clear that Marion's account of love provides full individuation. If the lover can love love itself, that is, he or she can love without any return of love from the beloved, does the flesh and body of the beloved matter? Would not then any beloved do as a substitute in that context? Love of neighbor here becomes precisely the kind of universalistic paradigm that Marion describes for the Lévi-

nassian account of ethics. If one can love "for the love of love," then surely one no longer needs a particular and concretely embodied beloved.

44. For a thorough explication of this issue, including an analysis of the ways in which it is grounded in Pascal, see the final chapter and the conclusion of my *Reading Jean-Luc Marion*, 225–50. Robyn Horner also considers Marion's claims about love as a kind of knowing in her "Weight of Love," 237–44.

45. Joeri Schrijvers, "Jean-Luc Marion and the Transcendence 'par Excellence': Love," in *Looking Beyond? Shifting Views of Transcendence in Philosophy, Theology, Art, and Politics*, ed. Wessel Stoker and W. L. van der Merwe (New York and Amsterdam: Rodopi Press, 2011), 158. Schrijvers also repeatedly comments on the univocity in Marion's account of love.

46. Schrijvers, "Jean-Luc Marion and the Transcendence 'par Excellence,'" 168.

47. See Lewis, "Lover's Capacity."

48. In passing, Bauer suggests in her account of intersubjectivity in Marion that a hermeneutic perspective might be helpful and also speaks briefly of its requiring "as comprehensive and continued additions of various perspectives as possible." Bauer, "Von der Donation zur Interdonation," 233, 234.

49. This is particularly striking in *Building the Bonds of Attachment: Awakening Love in Deeply Troubled Children*, in which Daniel Hughes describes attachment therapy via the story of one specific child, Katie, in terms of early neglect, failure of the foster system, and the focused (but immensely difficult) therapy of a foster parent trained in how to build bonds with such children. This account may well be called phenomenological in its close description and attention to underlying structural issues and their meaning. The literature on reactive attachment disorder and attachment theory more generally is extensive. For readable introductions, see: Daniel A. Hughes, *Building the Bonds of Attachment: Awakening Love in Deeply Troubled Children* (Lanham, Md.: Jason Aronson, 2006); Hughes, *Attachment-Focused Family Therapy* (New York: W. W. Norton, 2007); Daniel A. Hughes and Jonathan Baylin, *Brain-Based Parenting: The Neuroscience of Caregiving for Healthy Attachment* (New York: W. W. Norton, 2012); Catherine Swanson Cain, *Attachment Disorders: Treatment Strategies for Traumatized Children* (Lanham, Md.: Jason Aronson, 2006); Vivien Prior, *Understanding Attachment and Attachment Disorder: Theory, Evidence and Practice* (London and Philadelphia: Jessica Kingston, 2006).

50. Horner, "Weight of Love," 238, 239.

51. As Horner also says: "According to the erotic reduction, the erotic phenomenon lasts for as long as the oath lasts: fidelity is what allows the phenomenon to be seen" (ibid., 242).

5. Gift and Sacrifice

1. Jean-Luc Marion, "Sketch of a Phenomenological Concept of the Gift," in *Postmodern Philosophy and Christian Thought*, ed. J. Conley and D. Poe (Bloomington: Indiana University Press, 1999), retranslated in *The Visible and the Revealed*, chapter 5. All references are to the latter version. As this chapter is included only in the English translation of the book, no references to the French are given.

2. The conference proceedings were published as *God, the Gift, and Postmodernism,* ed. John D. Caputo and Michael J. Scanlon (Bloomington: Indiana University Press, 1999); the volume includes both Marion's original presentation, the debate between Marion and Derrida at the conference (moderated by Richard Kearney), and several secondary articles reflecting on the stakes of the debate. Marion's address was later included as the final chapter of his *In Excess*. It does not actually treat the gift but rather considers the language for God of apophatic theology, arguing against Derrida that this language is not one of description, causality, or objectivity. It is examined in more detail in my chapter 6 on prayer. As not many of Marion's works had been translated at that point, the debate with Derrida in *God, the Gift, and Postmodernism* has often been the main source used for English-language writing on his philosophy (together with *God without Being*), thus giving a rather skewed version of Marion's overall thought.

3. See Robyn Horner, *Rethinking God as Gift: Marion, Derrida, and the Limits of Phenomenology* (New York: Fordham University Press, 2001), and Thomas A. Carlson, *Indiscretion: Finitude and the Naming of God* (Chicago: University of Chicago Press, 1999), especially the final chapter, and various other articles written about Marion around that time.

4. Two of the five chapters in *Certitudes négatives* (chapters 3 and 4) focus explicitly on the gift, and to some extent it also appears in the other chapters.

5. Only one of the four papers collected in *The Reason of the Gift* deals explicitly with the gift (chapter 4, which is a translation of an earlier version of chapter 4 in *Certitudes négatives*). The others focus more generally on the notion of givenness and its phenomenological precedents in Husserl, Heidegger, and Lévinas (the first three chapters respectively).

6. Marcel Mauss, *The Gift: The Form and Reason for Exchange in Archaic Societies,* trans. W. D. Halls (New York: W. W. Norton, 1990). Originally published in France in 1924.

7. Jacques Derrida, *Given Time I: Counterfeit Money,* trans. Peggy Kamuf (Chicago: University of Chicago Press, 1992).

8. Jacques Derrida, *The Gift of Death,* trans. David Willis (Chicago: University of Chicago Press, 1995).

9. Antonio Malo highlights these differences in Derrida's and Marion's treatments of economy, although he then returns to defining reciprocity as central to the gift, something both Derrida and Marion seek to avoid. "The Limits of Marion's and Derrida's Philosophy of the Gift," *International Philosophical Quarterly* 52.2 (2012): 149–68.

10. Bauer points to Marion's vacillation on this point: "In general Marion's discussions of the topic of the gift are ambivalent. On the one hand, in his more methodical phenomenological works he refuses to set it in the center of his interest, on the other hand, he interprets the treatment of the thought model of the gift as a privileged possibility to explicate the figure of givenness." Bauer, "Von der *Donation* zur *Interdonation,*" 224.

11. Marion uses this terminology later for the Eucharist. See my chapter 7.

12. See book 1 of *Being Given* (BG, 7–70; ED, 13–102).

13. "As it is given" or "as it gives itself"—the two grammatical constructions (passive and reflexive) in English are actually identical in French, which at times makes it hard to ascertain to what extent Marion either posits a giver of some sort (maybe divine?) be-

hind the given phenomenon by whom it "is given" or attributes subjectivity to the phenomenon as it "gives itself." He has been criticized for both connotations.

14. BG, 69–70; ED, 101–102. He develops this further in book 3. See especially the summary in §18 (BG, 173–78; ED, 244–50).

15. See book 2, "The Gift" (BG, 71–118; ED, 103–168).

16. In fact, his summaries at the end of sections that often relate his expositions back to earlier parts of the book curiously ignore book 2 on the gift entirely. See BG, 227 and 246–47; ED, 317, 341–42.

17. Jean-Luc Marion, "The Gift of a Presence," (PC, 129, 133, 136, 147, 151; PaC, 155, 159, 162, 172–73, 177). This was the final chapter in the French edition and is the penultimate in the English translation. See also a more recent version of this discussion in his *Le croire pour le voir* (discussed more fully in my chapter 7, on the Eucharist).

18. Ingolf Dalferth criticizes this especially in his "Alles umsonst. Zur Kunst des Schenkens und den Grenzen der Gabe," where he contends that while Derrida claims that the gift cannot become a phenomenon at all, Marion turns all phenomena into gifts. Doing so, however, not only jeopardizes the status of the gift as a special phenomenon but also makes the claim meaningless. He also recognizes (rightly, in my view) that for both Derrida and Marion the discussion revolves "less around the gift and its limits than the limits of phenomenology and their transgression: The debate about the gift as phenomenon is at its core a dispute about phenomenological method." Ingolf U. Dalferth, "Alles umsonst. Zur Kunst des Schenkens und den Grenzen der Gabe," in *Von der Ursprünglichkeit der Gabe. Jean-Luc Marions Phänomenologie in der Diskussion*, ed. Michael Gabel and Hans Joas (Freiburg/München: Verlag Karl Alber, 2007), 161, 162. Alferi also questions the relationship between the phenomena of gift and of revelation in Marion in his contribution to the same volume: Thomas Alferi, "Von der Offenbarungsfrage zu Marions Phänomenologie der Gebung," in ibid., 210–33. The entire volume revolves around the question of the gift or the given more generally. Bauer is informed by this discussion in her dissertation *Einander zu erkennen geben*. The German terms "Geschenk" and "Gabe" do not precisely map onto the French terms "le don"/"le donné" or the English "gift" and "given," as *Gabe*—the term generally employed in the German discussion—can mean both "gift" and "given." This leads to some conflation between gifts proper and the given more broadly (for example, I do not think that it can be said that Marion turns all phenomena into *gifts*, although he does speak of all *saturated* phenomena as *given* and certainly uses the gift as a "paradigm" for other "given" phenomena). This also orients the German discussion somewhat differently, making it less concerned with the dimensions of economy and exchange than the French and English debates, although both Dalferth (168–70) and Wohlmuth (253–56) refer to this discussion and several pieces mention Mauss briefly. One might also point out that most of the German appropriation of Marion's work occurs in a more explicitly theological context and is somewhat hampered by the fact that only few of his works are translated into German (several essays; *La croisée du visible* [2005, curiously translated as the "opening" of the visible]; *Le phénomène érotique* [2011]; *Dieu sans l'être* [2013, more than thirty years after its French publication]; a translation of *Étant donné* is due to appear in 2014). Note that I was able to procure the German sources only when this book was in its final stages and hence may not have given them quite the attention they deserve.

19. This is particularly striking in the final chapter, which was originally the presentation at the conference on the gift ("God, the Gift, and Postmodernism"). The chapter does not mention the gift, and the term does not appear in the index for the book.

20. These early accounts of the gift have been repeatedly criticized. See my fairly detailed review of the various criticisms in *Reading Jean-Luc Marion*, 160–77 and 222–23. More recently, Ilsup Ahn has explored the issue of debt in Marion's phenomenology in order to formulate a Christian ethics. "The Genealogy of Debt and the Phenomenology of Forgiveness: Nietzsche, Marion, and Derrida on the Meaning of the *Peculiar Phenomenon*," *Heythrop Journal* 51.3 (2010): 454–70. In contrast, Kühn criticizes what he calls Marion's "hermeneutical turn to ethics" at the end of *Being Given*, which he considers also a return to metaphysics, in "Passivität und Zeugenschaft," 193.

21. For the notion of "counter-experience" see also the section with that title in *Being Given* (BG, 215–16; ED, 300–302), "The Banality of Saturation" in *The Visible and the Revealed*, and Kevin Hart's useful introduction in his edited volume, *Counter-Experience: Reading Jean-Luc Marion* (Notre Dame, Ind.: Notre Dame University Press, 2007), 1–54.

22. An earlier version of this chapter was translated as "The Reason of the Gift" in *Givenness and God: Questions of Jean-Luc Marion*, ed. Ian Leask and Eoin Cassidy (New York: Fordham University Press, 2005), 101–134.

23. The French word *pardon* (like the English) contains the word for gift (*don*). *Pardonner* (forgiving or pardoning) derives from *donner* (giving).

24. An earlier version of this chapter is translated as "Sketch of a Phenomenological Concept of Sacrifice" in *The Reason of the Gift*, trans. Stephen E. Lewis (Charlottesville: University of Virginia Press, 2011), 69–90.

25. Marion is unambiguous that the same cannot be said of the mother or of motherhood, and that only paternity provides such a privileged example. He has already made similar claims in the "The Child and the Father" section in *Being Given* (BG, 300–302; ED, 414–17) and in his "The Voice without Name: Homage to Lévinas," in *The Face of the Other and the Trace of God: Essays on the Philosophy of Emmanuel Lévinas*, ed. Jeffrey Bloechel (New York: Fordham University Press, 2000), 224–42. (See also the section on the "third" in *The Erotic Phenomenon*.) He has also repeatedly explored the notion of God's fatherhood in *Idol and Distance*, *God without Being*, and *In Excess*. Similarly, he draws a connection to divine fatherhood in *Certitudes négatives* (CN, 169). Obviously, the privileging of fatherhood (and dismissal of motherhood) here should be questioned further.

26. Marion stresses the lack of reciprocity repeatedly and emphatically in his treatment (as he also does in earlier treatments), to some extent in response to John Milbank, who has repeatedly tried to insist otherwise and condemned in the strongest terms Marion's earlier treatments of the gift. See John Milbank, "Can a Gift Be Given? Prolegomena to a Future Trinitarian Metaphysics," *Modern Theology* 11.1 (1995): 119–58; "The Soul of Reciprocity, Part One: Reciprocity Refused," *Modern Theology* 17.3 (2001): 335–91; "The Soul of Reciprocity, Part Two: Reciprocity Regained," *Modern Theology* 17.4 (2001): 485–507; and "The Gift and the Mirror: On the Philosophy of Love," in Hart, *Counter-Experiences*, 253–317.

27. For a more detailed examination that highlights especially the connection between gift and displacement of subjectivity, see Joeri Schrijvers, *Ontotheological Turnings? The Decentering of the Modern Subject in Recent French Phenomenology* (Albany: State University of

New York Press, 2011), 51–80. Like Mackinlay, Schrijvers interprets this primarily as a "reversal" of subjectivity (73). He also stresses the apparent solipsism of Marion's account (77–78).

28. Translation taken from the English version of the article in *Givenness and God*, 133.

29. Presumably it is this claim that inspired the title of the English collection of articles, *The Reason of the Gift*. The earlier English version of this essay is, in fact, titled "The Reason of the Gift."

30. This claim is explored in more detail in the final chapter of *Certitudes négatives*, which focuses on the phenomenality of the event. In the earlier English version, Marion draws an explicit parallel here to the artist who "produces a new visible" by introducing a new phenomenon into the world of visibility (*Givenness and God*, 134). It is noteworthy that this particular sentence has been removed in the later French version in *Certitudes négatives*.

31. An earlier version of this chapter was translated by Stephen E. Lewis as chapter 4 of *The Reason of the Gift* (69–90).

32. The notion of "abandon" here was only introduced in the later version in *Certitudes négatives*. It is not yet present in the earlier version (see RoG, 84).

33. This claim is odd, not only because Isaac is in fact *not* Abraham's firstborn son but only Sarah's, and because according to the story's chronology these regulations from Exodus are given much later and therefore presumably would not apply to Abraham or be known to him.

34. The final sentence of this quotation does not appear in the earlier English version. It is also interesting in this context that the plain meaning of *redondance* actually is redundancy, not re-giving, although it contains the term *don* (gift). Marion clearly means a kind of repetition here that makes the original meaning clearer, but there is certainly also a sense in which the sacrifice is "redundant," as Abraham should have realized the gift the first time around, which would have made the demand for the sacrifice on some level unnecessary (at least in Marion's interpretation of the story).

35. The second half of this chapter, beginning with this section, is not in the English translation in *The Reason of the Gift*.

36. Several of the important words in this sentence have multiple connotations: *l'abandon* can mean both abandonment or rejection and abandon or freedom (in the sense of letting go); *le don perdu* can be the lost gift, the rejected gift, the spoiled gift, or the non-returnable gift.

37. It is noteworthy that Marion chooses to interact with Derrida's discussion of Jankélévitch here instead of with his analysis of Patočka in *The Gift of Death*. He is certainly responding to Derrida's discussion of sacrifice in that book, but he does not engage Derrida's critique of Patočka. Derrida's discussion of forgiveness and Jankélévitch can be found in his *On Cosmopolitanism and Forgiveness* (New York: Routledge, 2001).

38. This brief section, not including the discussion of the parable of the prodigal son, was originally part of chapter 2. See the earlier version of chapter 2 as "The Impossible for Man—God," in *Transcendence and Beyond: A Postmodern Inquiry*, ed. John D. Caputo and Michael J. Scanlon (Bloomington: Indiana University Press, 2007). Although the lan-

guage here is not quite as strong as that of the earlier version, it still attributes true forgiveness primarily to God.

39. Marion claims that this forgiveness has Trinitarian status: father, son, and shared gift (CN, 237).

40. Bauer, *Einander zu erkennen geben,* 416. See also the section in which she analyzes the displacement of the subject by the givenness of the phenomenon (422–57). The need to phenomenalize the incoming phenomenon via a response to its call "does not suspend the a priori of the call, but it only becomes manifest in the prism of the a posterior of the response" (447). Although the self is passive recipient "the significance of the recipient should not be underestimated. He is the filter through which phenomenality must pass in order to become manifest. He gives the response, which only articulates the call addressed to him. He is responsible for the entirety of phenomenality" (458). Her overall concern is to develop an account of giving as mutual recognition, informed by Ricoeur, Derrida, and Marion. She sees Marion as ultimately most successful in providing such an account.

41. Maybe this will confirm the fear of some early commentators that this phenomenology of givenness is actually deeply theological and depicts phenomena as gracious gifts of a divine giver. Although Marion does use biblical examples as freely as he usually does, he certainly insists that this is a phenomenological, not a theological, account. The role of these (theological) examples in his overall phenomenology warrants fuller examination.

42. Bauer expresses a similar worry, namely that Marion's account of giving is only an empty formula that conflates terminologies of giving that usually operate on different levels. She also calls for more explication of concrete phenomena of giving. Bauer, *Einander zu erkennen geben,* 539.

43. Of course this applies not just to Christmas, but also to other holidays celebrated at this time of year. But the mania of gift giving has actually "infected" those holidays, as well. Hanukkah, for example, did not originally include an exchange of gifts but increasingly does so now.

44. Something similar is true of the bridal or baby shower, where bringing a gift is an obligation. The point of the shower is to "shower" the bride or mother-to-be with gifts. Sometimes a theme for the gift is even prescribed. The gift is constrained by various sorts of considerations: its monetary value, the appropriateness for the recipient, the way it will be regarded by the other guests. Often gifts are solicited by the recipient in the form of a registry. Nothing is surprising or gratuitous about such gift giving. This does not mean that the gifts at times are not given with genuine affection for the recipient and meant to elicit merely joy, not an obligation of gratitude or return in kind, as is surely also true of many holiday gifts. Yet, the event can give us important insight about our society, just as Marcel Mauss's original explorations did actually show the ways in which gift giving functioned in a variety of societies. The economic connotations themselves are an important dimension of how gifts are experienced. Dalferth stresses this need to be attentive to how we experience gifts in real life. He says: "In order to understand the gift [*Gabe*] we must change the style, namely no longer to use the essential structure postu-

lated by the guideline of phenomenological reduction and its aporetic limit cases, but instead the giving and receiving of gifts [*Gaben*] in concrete contexts as they are lived in the world [*konreten lebensweltlichen Zusammenhängen*]." He thinks that by focusing on the way in which giving functions in various social interactions can then also provide a key to the more extreme limit cases. Social practice should not be ignored. He concludes that "we occlude our view of the phenomenon of the gift [*der Gabe*] in our daily, mundane practice [*lebensweltlichen Praxis*] and even more so in our religious contexts of life, when we do not pay attention to the onesidedness of this point of view and think the relationship between recipient and received only in one way or one image, which are sometimes but not always correct." Dalferth, "Alles umsonst," 171–72, 186. This is precisely the point I am trying to make here, although I would maintain that phenomenological analysis that is attentive to these contexts and degrees of givenness is still useful and can shed light on social praxis.

45. Dalferth also comments on this negativity, especially in regard to Derrida ("Alles umsonst," 168, 182–85). Marion himself remarks on this in his treatment in *Certitudes négatives*, where he attempts to give a more "positive" account. It is somewhat ironic, however, that the positive account is that of a father sacrificing his child and a loving daughter rejected. Neither the Abraham story nor the play *King Lear* are exactly "positive" stories.

46. This is what Marcel Hénaff attempts in *The Price of Truth: Gift, Money, and Philosophy*, trans. Jean-Louis Morhange (Stanford, Calif.: Stanford University Press, 2010). This is the sort of account I had in mind when I first wrote this chapter (at the time without having read his work). In places, Hénaff's story is too sweeping, misrepresenting or ignoring certain elements. For example, his account of the move from communal to individual giving in Seneca and early Christianity ("biblical grace," "Roman grace," "Christian grace," 242–90) is too simple and disregards the way in which the public giving of gifts in the ancient world (*euergetism* or *leitourgia*) was appropriated by early Christian communities (as "liturgy") and the way in which especially imperial Christianity attempted to shape the public imagination. (It is strange that he focuses only on the terminology of *charis/kharis*, not of *leitourgia*, and even in his account of charis does not say a word about *eucharistia*.) For a fuller philosophical account of the function of *leitourgia* in early Christianity, see Giorgio Agamben, *The Kingdom and the Glory: For a Theological Genealogy of Economy and Government*, trans. Lorenza Chiesa (Stanford, Calif.: Stanford University Press, 2011). For an excellent analysis of the ways in which early Christianity forged social bonds and sought to shape the public imagination, see John F. Baldovin, *The Urban Character of Christian Worship: The Origins, Development and Meaning of Stational Liturgy* (Rome: Pontificum Institutum Studiorum Orientalium, 1987). For a thorough (and moving) account of the ways in which early Christianity took up and transformed the tradition of "public giving," especially in its care for the poor, see Susan R. Holman, *The Hungry Are Dying: Beggars and Bishops in Roman Cappadocia* (Oxford: Oxford University Press, 2001). Despite the lacunae in Hénaff' account, I do think he is going in the right direction. Although I cannot do it in this context, this is something I would like to explore much more fully in the future.

47. This is, of course, the central problem raised by Anthony Steinbock's essay on the poor phenomenon, examined in more detail in the introduction. Steinbock, "Poor Phenomenon."

48. Thomas A. Carlson, "Blindness and the Decision to See," in Hart, *Counter-Experiences*, 168. See also Ruud Welten's analysis of the importance of "disappointment" in phenomenological reception in his "Saturation and Disappointment: Marion According to Husserl," *Tijdschrift voor Filosofie en Theologie/International Journal in Philosophy and Theology* 65.1 (2004): 79–96.

49. Bauer also hopes that a fuller story of receptivity and reply might provide a better account of the individuation of the recipient. She affirms that for this "precisely a combination of interpretation, deconstruction, and explication might be particularly fruitful methodologically in order to describe the self as crucial point in which given [*Gegebenes*], self-giving [*Sich-Geben*] of phenomenality, recognition [*Zu-erkennen-Gegebenes*], its handing on [*Weitergabe*], might meet up with one's ability to give (to recognize) [*(zu erkennen) zu geben*]." Bauer, *Einander zu erkennen geben*, 547.

6. Prayer and Sainthood

1. Theresa Sanders in "The Gift of Prayer" claims that prayer "is not a topic that has found much attention in postmodern theology; a quick glance at the indexes of deconstructive theological works shows that the word 'prayer' seldom even appears. This is true despite a large and growing body of literature concerning the relation between deconstruction and negative or apophatic theology. Since negative theology, at least in the Christian tradition, nearly always occurs in the context of prayer, it is odd that so little attention has been paid to the subject. And yet, deconstructive literature has virtually ignored it." It is considerably odder, however, that she draws only on Derrida's and Milbank's work to substantiate her claim and to develop ways in which the discussion of the gift might be helpful to understand the phenomenon of prayer, while entirely ignoring Marion's important work on this topic (she mentions him once in the discussion of Milbank's criticism). Admittedly, not all of Marion's texts on prayer were translated when the article was written, yet even *God without Being* says considerably more about prayer than she acknowledges and the discussion on the gift in which Marion articulates his account of prayer in the context of a discussion of apophatic or mystical theology had already taken place and was published. Theresa Sanders, "The Gift of Prayer," in *Secular Theology: American Radical Theological Thought*, ed. Clayton Crockett (New York: Routledge, 2001), 130–40. There are, in fact, a significant number of publications that consider Marion's treatment of "negative theology"—often in conversation with Derrida's work—in the context of the discussion of the gift, although few of them make prayer a topic of discussion per se (e.g., Benson's *Graven Ideologies*, Carlson's *Indiscretion*, Horner's *Rethinking God as Gift*, Smith's *Speech and Theology*, Specker's *Einen anderen Gott denken*, to some extent also Meessen's *L'être et le bien*).

2. Various versions and translations of this article exist. English translations can be found in: Jean-Luc Marion, "In the Name: How to Avoid Speaking of 'Negative Theology,'" in Caputo and Scanlon, *God, the Gift, and Postmodernism*, 20–53, or the final chap-

ter of *In Excess* (IE, 128–162; DS, 155–95). Marion first presented this paper in the context of the conference "God, the Gift, and Postmodernism" at Villanova in 1997. Joself Wohlmuth calls this "one of the exceptional events of philosophy at the end of the twentieth century." Wohlmuth, "Impulse für eine künftige Theologie der Gabe bei Jean-Luc Marion," in Gabel and Joas, *Von der Ursprünglichkeit der Gabe*, 253. He employs Marion's phenomenology in order to articulate a "theology of the gift" (*Theologie der Gabe*).

3. Kevin Hart also points out Marion's lack of any explicit consideration of ethics in his introduction to *The Essential Writings*, 29, 30. Two German essays appropriate Marion's phenomenology of givenness for a deliberately ethical discussion: Hans Joas, "Die Logik der Gabe und das Postulat der Menschenwürde," in Gabel and Joas, *Von der Ursprünglichkeit der Gabe*, 143–58; and Christof Mandry, "Logik der Ethik—Logik der Gabe: Theologisch-ethische Überlegungen," in Gabel and Joas, *Von der Ursprünglichkeit der Gabe*, 234–51.

4. For two comparisons of Marion's account to Eastern Orthodox discussions of iconography, see Sandro Gorgone, "Idol und Ikone. Die Phänomenologie des Unsichtbaren von J.-L. Marion," in *Jean-Luc Marion: Studien zum Werk*, ed. Hanna-Barbara Gerl-Falkovitz (Dresden, Germany: Verlag Text & Dialog, 2013), 237–53; and Martin Hähnel, "Geteilte Ansichten. Zum Problem der Perspektivität bei Jean-Luc Marion und Pawel Florenskij," in Gerl-Falkovitz, *Jean-Luc Marion*, 257–76.

5. In light of the parallel Marion establishes in *God without Being* between visual idols and icons, on the one hand, and conceptual ones, on the other, it is interesting that the Eastern tradition generally speaks of writing an icon, not of painting it, as it is not considered a work of art but is more closely linked to prayer and the auditory sense. Marion himself of course strongly stresses the visual element in this particular treatment.

6. In the earlier passages, Marion is actually analyzing the cross as a religious "type," but he repeats the same analysis for the icon (CV, 75; CdV, 133).

7. It is unfortunate that the citations from the Byzantine liturgy are not reproduced in the English translation. "The holy things for the holy" is the phrase the priest says over the chalice, when he raises it "on behalf of all and for all" immediately before communion. The response of the congregation to this phrase is "One is holy, one is the Lord, Jesus Christ, to the glory of God the Father." This interchange conveys precisely the kind of dialectic Marion continually explores: the excessive holiness that comes to us and requires our holiness, to which we can only respond by acknowledging our unworthiness and lack of sanctity. I return to this later in this chapter when discussing his article on the saint.

8. This definition does indeed correspond to the one given to the icon in *God without Being* (e.g., GWB, 17–22; DSL, 28–35).

9. See especially his analysis of God's becoming visible in the wounds we inflict upon Christ (CV, 74, 84; CdV, 131, 149). He explores a similar discussion of sin, evil, and hurt in the first chapter of *Prolegomena to Charity* (PC, 1–30; PaC, 13–42).

10. Jacques Derrida, *On the Name*, ed. Thomas Dutoit (Stanford, Calif.: Stanford University Press, 1993); Jacques Derrida, "How to Avoid Speaking: Denials," in *Derrida and Negative Theology*, ed. Harold Coward and Toby Foshay (Albany: State University of New York Press, 1992), 73–142.

11. DS, 156–57; IE, 129–30. For a consideration of both Derrida's and Marion's claims, see James K. A. Smith, "Between Predication and Silence: Augustine on how (not) to speak of God," *Heythrop Journal* 41.1 (2000): 66–86, or John Caputo, "Apostles of the Impossible: On God and the Gift in Derrida and Marion," in Caputo and Scanlon, *God, the Gift and Postmodernism*, 185–222. For a good explication of the same theme in *Idol and Distance*, see Victor Kal, "Being Unable to Speak, Seen As a Period: Difference and Distance in Jean-Luc Marion," in *Flight of the Gods*, ed. Ilse N. Bulhof and Laurens ten Kate (New York: Fordham University Press, 2002), 143–65. Tamsin Jones examines Marion's use of Dionysius (and compares it to that of Hans Urs von Balthasar) in "Dionysius in Hans Urs von Balthasar and Jean-Luc Marion," *Modern Theology* 24.4 (2008): 743–54. She judges Marion's a "richer" account than that of other contemporary theologians, but criticizes him for not distinguishing more carefully between his exposition of Dionysius and his "translation" of ideas for a new time and audience (751). Antonio Malo claims that Marion "is neither a metaphysician nor a phenomenologist, but a kind of apophatic thinker" although it is not entirely clear why one would have to exclude the other. Malo, "Marion's and Derrida's Philosophy of the Gift," 161.For a more extensive discussion of the relationship of Marion's work to that of Hans Urs von Balthasar, see Thomas Alferi, "'. . . die Unfasslichkeit der uns übersteigend-zuvorkommenden Liebe Gottes . . .' Von Balthasar als Orientierung für Marion," in Gerl-Falkovitz, *Jean-Luc Marion*, 103–125.

12. The English version of the article translates this (somewhat problematically) as "de-nomination." Caputo finds this term appropriate in his discussion of Marion because he contends that Marion is reinscribing the name of God into a higher "economy" and that Marion's work is very determined by his particular "denomination" of Roman Catholicism. See his discussion in Caputo, "Apostles of the Impossible."

13. In the interview with Arbib, he speaks of the debate with Derrida as a dispute over whether prayer is a "particular case of praise" or praise a species of prayer (RC, 278).

14. This is a movement very close to that of *God without Being*. In this book Marion also moves from a concern to protect God from blasphemy and idolatry (in favor of an iconic naming of God) to an address of God to the believer. See, for example, his chapter on the confession of faith (GWB, 183–97; DSL, 259–77).

15. See the similar account of the "unspeakability" of the word and the contention that "theological speech feeds on the silence in which, at last, it speaks correctly" in *God without Being* (GWB, 139–44, 1; DSL, 197–203, 9).

16. See also the end of the chapter (IE, 158–62; DS, 190–95). This is a movement to which Derrida understandably objects; it is not here, however, my concern to defend either Marion's reading of Derrida or Derrida's reading of Marion.

17. It is not without significance that this is the context in which Marion first explicitly articulates his notion of the saturated phenomenon, although he has later revised his stance on it in regard to revelation.

18. Marion develops the importance of the category of "distance," especially in regard to speaking of God, in detail in *The Idol and Distance*. See especially the third part, which is also an analysis of Dionysius's apophatic theology.

19. It is, of course, far from clear that prayer automatically ceases to be predicative, something Marion himself recognizes. In response to Derrida, who distinguishes be-

tween prayer and praise, Marion contests that praying can be accomplished without naming someone: "seeing as no prayer can pray without giving a name, without acknowledging an identity, even and especially an improper one. Not only does naming not contradict the invocation of the prayer, but without the invocation the prayer would be impossible—what would it mean, in fact, to praise without praising anyone, to ask without asking from anyone, to offer a sacrifice without offering it to anyone? An anonymous prayer would make no more sense than does the claim to attain the proper by an (im-)proper name" (IE, 144; DS, 173). What Marion does contest is that such naming designates a referent or predicates anything of God.

20. In fact, this final chapter follows on the four chapters exploring the "simply" saturated phenomena of event, idol, flesh, and icon and ostensibly discusses the fifth type of the phenomenon of revelation. Marion does not, however, explicitly employ that language within this particular chapter.

21. There is also an interesting parallel between this account of being named by the divine and Marion's discussion of paternity (in *Being Given*, in an essay on Lévinas, "The Voice without Name," and again in *Certitudes négatives*, as summarized in my chapter 5). Marion also (somewhat problematically) repeatedly stresses the paternity of God.

22. Jean-Luc Marion, chapter 6, "The Gift of a Presence" (PC, 124–52; PaC, 147–78).

23. See also his analysis of the priestly function in the Eucharist (GWB, 149–58; DSL, 210–22; see also CpV, 77–100). I return to this discussion of the Eucharist more fully in the next chapter.

24. Marion reflects more explicitly on the role of individual believers within the church in several essays included in *Le croire pour le voir*. In one chapter he condemns the distinction between clergy and laity and argues instead for a distinction between all baptized and the bishop who acts in *persona Christi* (CpV, 77–100). He also comments repeatedly on the link between belonging to the church (or to Christ) and love (e.g., CpV, 106).

25. Gerald McKenny and Michael Kessler criticize Marion's neglect of ethical and political questions in their respective essays in Hart, *Counter-Experience,* 339–79.

26. English translation: "The Invisibility of the Saint," *Critical Inquiry* 35.3 (2008): 703–710; reprinted in *Saints: Faith without Borders,* ed. Françoise Meltzer and Jaś Elsner (Chicago: University of Chicago Press, 2011), 355–62.

27. *Unvisable* can mean both that one cannot aim at it, but also that it cannot be envisaged or conceived; I am hence using two English words to express what is said in only one word in French. There was a misprint in the French when the English translation was first prepared, which Marion must have corrected when the earlier article was included in the book. The current English translation is therefore incorrect here.

28. In the interview with Arbib, he also links holiness and love. Sanctity is not found "in ontic perfections or coming from being, because being and its modes . . . separate us from God; but we can love him as he loves us" (RC, 190–91).

29. This is Richard Kearney's claim in much of his work, but especially in *Anatheism: Returning to God after God* (New York: Columbia University Press, 2010). He argues for a micro-eschatology that would see holiness in the littlest things and sanctity in a "cup of tea"; he concludes his treatment with an examination of the "everyday" saints, Jean Vanier, Dorothy Day, and Gandhi (152–65).

30. For an interesting discussion of prayer that does consider both its individual and its communal context and its free or scripted nature, see Jean-Louis Chrétien, "The Wounded Word" (printed both in the volume *Phenomenology and the "Theological Turn"* and in his *The Ark of Speech*).

31. Hart, introduction to Marion, *Essential Writings,* 29.

32. He himself points out that the fathers of the church function like a "talmud" for him (RC, 215). He also points to the insight gained from Louis Bouyer that "the Christian eucharistic liturgy remains unintelligible without the Jewish liturgy" (RC, 297).

33. Jones, *Genealogy of Marion's Philosophy of Religion.*

34. For a review of the standard interpretations of the passage, see Claus Westermann, *Genesis 12–36: A Commentary,* trans. J. J. Scullion (London: SPCK, 1985); and Gordon J. Wenham, *Genesis 16–50,* Word Biblical Commentary (Waco, Tex.: Word Books, 1987). For an alternative interpretation, see Yair Lorberbaum, "Yitshak and God's Separation Anxiety," *Journal of Jewish Thought and Philosophy* 21 (2013): 105–142.

35. Of course, no interpretation ever occurs completely in a vacuum. Extreme interpretations still arise out of and are informed by certain contexts.

36. In his treatment of Marion's discussion of the icon, Gorgone claims that "the contemplation of an icon also requires an extreme hermeneutic ability: to be able to read the intention or the invisible in the visible, that is, to contemplate the visible in the same way as the invisible within it looks at" us. Gorgone, "Idol und Ikone," 252.

37. For the most well-known elaboration of this, see the work of Alexander Schmemann, especially *For the Life of the World: Sacraments and Orthodoxy* (Crestwood, N.Y.: St. Vladimir's Seminary Press, 1973) and *The Eucharist: Sacrament of the Kingdom* (Crestwood, N.Y.: St. Vladimir's Seminary Press, 1987).

38. Jones, *Genealogy of Marion's Philosophy of Religion,* 156.

39. Ibid., 157.

40. For example, Metropolitan Anthony Bloom says: "Now, if we imagine that we can sustain spontaneous prayer throughout our life, we are in a childish delusion. Spontaneous prayer must gush out of our souls, we cannot simply turn on a tap and get it out. It is not there for us to draw from to use at any moment. It comes from the depths of our soul, from either wonder or distress, but it does not come from the middle situation in which we are neither overwhelmed by the divine presence nor overwhelmed by a sense of who we are and the position in which we are." *Beginning to Pray* (New York: Paulist Press, 1970), 57. Later he counsels a young person he had met at a Taizé retreat and who had attempted to pray unceasingly: "You've got indigestion. You should have used common sense in prayer, as one uses common sense in life. You cannot, having never prayed before, start with eighteen hours of dialogue and prayer with God continuously like this while you do other things. But you can easily single out one or two moments and put all your energy into them." He concludes the chapter by suggesting soberness in prayer (77, 78).

41. As my formulation of the examples indicates, however, even in these instances, interpretation of their experience differed tremendously among their contemporaries (and obviously also among subsequent interpreters).

42. Of course, Marion always stresses that we cannot control the divine presence and that there is no way of predicting God's coming, yet authentic prayer seems for him always defined by this divine encounter, which seems to make it "predictable" at least in some sense.

43. See especially the book of her life, but also her *Way of Perfection* and her various letters and other correspondence. Teresa of Avila, *The Collected Works of St. Teresa of Avila*, 3 vols., trans. Kieran Kavanaugh and Otilio Rodriguez (Washington, D.C.: ICS Publications, 1976–80). In one instance, for example, Teresa warns of "excessive love" among the sisters, because it can quickly become too exclusive and eliminate love of neighbor and God: "It seems that having excessive love among ourselves could not be evil, but such excess carries with it so much evil and so many imperfections that I don't think anyone will believe this save the one who has been an eyewitness" (Teresa of Avila, *Way of Perfection*, 4.5, in *Collected Works*, 2:54). She goes on to detail all the harm such "excessive love" does to communities. Of course, even the commitment to poverty is precisely a means to avoiding excess. For more detailed discussions of Teresa, see Anthony J. Steinbock, *Phenomenology and Mysticism: The Verticality of Religious Experience* (Bloomington: Indiana University Press, 2007), 45–65; Julia Kristeva, "Saint Teresa of Avila," in *Saints: Faith without Borders,* ed. Françoise Meltzer and Jaś Elsner (Chicago: University of Chicago Press, 2011), 321–33; Julia Kristeva, *Thérèse mon amour. Sainte Thérèse d'Avila* (Paris: Fayard, 2008).

44. Teresa of Avila, *Way of Perfection*, 7.5, in *Collected Works*, 2:68.

45. Teresa of Avila, *Way of Perfection*, 17.3, in *Collected Works*, 2:99.

46. Ibid., 2:100.

47. One elder, after being asked about two people, one who fasted strenuously and one tending to a sick person, says: "Even if the one who fasts for six days were to hang himself up by his nostrils, he could not be the equal of the one who tends the sick." John Wortley, trans., *The Book of the Elders: Sayings of the Desert Fathers: The Systematic Collection* (Collegeville, Minn.: Liturgical Press, 2012), 305.

48. Wortley, *Book of the Elders*, 310. For similar stories, see ibid., 144, 358, 372–73.

49. Wortley, *Book of the Elders*, 373–74. See also the story about the woodcutter (a "dark-skinned old man" whose prayers for rain are answered although the bishop's prayers remain unheard) that concludes the collection (375–76).

50. Abba Isidore says: "It is better for a person to eat meat than to become puffed up and boastful." Wortley, *Book of the Elders*, 153. See also the "Humility" section, which is one of the longest sections in the collection (246–88).

51. Wortley, *Book of the Elders*, 156.

52. Ibid., 116. The elders often insist that one's good works should remain hidden and that one ought to practice humility (e.g., ibid., 125, 129, 192).

53. Wortley, *Book of the Elders*, 151. There are several other stories like this (e.g., 167). The ascetic life was, indeed, often compared to the angelic life, but the elders were always quite clear that one could not only pray but needed to work and remain firmly on the earth.

54. Wortley, *Book of the Elders*, 169.

55. Ibid., 244.

56. This is the standard depiction of Elijah's encounter with the divine at Mount Horeb, where God was not in the whirlwind or the storm, but instead appeared as a whisper. Some commentators claim that it would be more correct to translate this as silence, not even a "small voice."

57. Teresa of Avila, *The Interior Castle,* 4:2 in *Collected Works,* 2:322–27. In *The Interior Castle,* she actually remarks on her fondness for water which she finds particularly "appropriate to explain some spiritual experiences" and an element that she has "observed more attentively than other things" (4.2 in 2:323).

58. Teresa of Avila, *The Book of Her Life,* in *Collected Works,* 11.6–7, 1:113. Steinbock discusses this passage in detail in *Phenomenology and Mysticism,* 55–65. He also points out that for Teresa experience progresses over time and that increased experience enables one to distinguish more easily between authentic and inauthentic experiences (124). I return to Steinbock's account of mysticism more fully at the end of this chapter.

59. Steinbock claims that each stage of prayer is "complete" and experienced as a "gift." It is seen as a somewhat "lower" level only when viewed from within the next stage. He also stresses Teresa's contention "that not everyone is led by the same path or in the same measure." Her account is meant to "attune us to such experiences as much as possible." Steinbock, *Phenomenology and Mysticism,* 55, 54. Jean-Yves Lacoste's account of liturgical "being-before-God" is also helpful here. He explicitly considers boredom as a phenomenological moment of such exposure to the divine. See his *Experience and the Absolute: Disputed Questions on the Humanity of Man,* trans. Mark Raftery-Skeban (New York: Fordham University Press, 2004), 148–49.

60. The icon for John Climacus portrays such a ladder, from which monks are being pushed off at various stages. This is clearly no linear progression and it is most decidedly not a "saturated" experience for most of the arduous and dangerous climb. For one such image, a detail from the painted exterior walls of the monastery of Suceviţa in Bukovina (Romania), see the cover of this book. There are many popular icons of John Climacus's ladder. He is liturgically commemorated in the Eastern Orthodox tradition on the fourth Sunday of Great Lent.

61. John Climacus, *The Ladder of Divine Ascent,* trans. Colm Luibheid and Norman Russell (New York: Paulist Press, 1982), 75. There are thirty steps or rungs to the ladder, corresponding to Christ's age at the time of his baptism (291).

62. Climacus, *Ladder of Divine Ascent,* 255.

63. Ibid., 275.

64. Kearney, *Anatheism,* 152–65.

65. This is both presupposed and most fully depicted in the Eastern collection of the *Philokalia,* a collection of spiritual writings covering several centuries, which gives advice on how to practice prayer and progress on the path toward sanctity.

66. See, for example, the story of Abba Poemen and Abba Dioscorus. Wortley, *Book of the Elders,* 30.

67. Ibid., 133. In fact, this entire section of the collection consists of stories warning against judging anybody (133–42).

68. Burch, "Blurred Vision: Marion on the 'possibility' of revelation," *International Journal of Philosophy of Religion* 67 (2010): 162.

69. Ibid., 164. He concludes from this that Marion's work cannot be useful for theology due to its "failure to distinguish adequately between phenomenology and theology" because "a discourse that fails to respect its own limits can only become muddled and confused" (166).

70. Steinbock, *Phenomenology and Mysticism*, 34. He stresses that religious experience has to be examined on its own terms and within its own parameters, yet "as lived, as experienced, it thereby opens itself for us to phenomenological description and investigation according to its philosophical significance" (115); "Religious experiencing constitutes its own sphere of evidence; it has its own modes of givenness that are distinct from presentation but no less genuine" (116). His conclusion states this most forcefully: "The philosophical task of this book has been to show that there are kinds of human experiencing that go beyond the presentation of empirical and ideal objects, and that although they do not conform to the way in which objects are presented, they are nonetheless modes of *human experience* that have their own modes of evidence and raise their own problems of evidence" (241, original emphasis).

71. Steinbock, *Phenomenology and Mysticism*, 119, 118.

72. Ibid., 208.

73. Ibid., 123, 139, 140.

7. Eucharist and Sacrament

1. Marion vacillates between considering *God without Being* as a philosophical or as a theological text. *God without Being* contains five chapters in the text "proper" and two chapters in a section titled "hors-texte" (outside the text), presumably a stab at Derrida's claim that there is nothing outside the text. The distinction between text proper and "hors-texte" seems to imply that the former is philosophical and the latter are theological (which is indeed one interpretation Marion has given to his own text; e.g., RC, 187). At other times, he identifies the entire text as philosophical. In the introduction to the English translation, he talks about it more as a theological text. See my discussion of this issue in *Reading Jean-Luc Marion*, 243–50.

2. "Hermeneutic of the text by the community, to be sure, thanks to the service of the theologian, but on condition that the community itself be interpreted by the Word and assimilated to the place where *theo*logical interpretation can be exercised, thanks to the liturgical service of the theologian par excellence, the bishop" (GWB, 152; DSL, 215; original emphasis). Also: "The theological teacher is not justified unless he serves charity. Otherwise, he brings death" (GWB, 154; DSL, 216). Many commentators have been critical of this statement. For one of the most thorough examinations see Peter-Ben Smit, "The Bishop and His/Her Eucharistic Community: A Critique of Jean-Luc Marion's Eucharistic Hermeneutic," *Modern Theology* 19.1 (2003): 29–40. For a fuller discussion of the various critiques, see my *Reading Jean-Luc Marion*, 89–103, 174–77.

3. "*Only the saintly person knows whereof he speaks in theology, only he that a bishop delegates knows wherefrom he speaks*" (GWB, 155; DSL, 218; original emphasis).

4. He says that theology must move from sign to referent, "*the 'progress' of theology works only to overcome the irreducible delay of the eucharistic interpretation of the text in rela-*

tion to the manifestation of the Word" (GWB, 157; DSL, 220; original emphasis). Marion rejects progress or even creativity in theology, concluding that "theology cannot aim at any other progress than its own conversion to the Word" by unfolding the "possibilities already realized in the Word but not yet in us and our words" (GWB, 158; DSL, 222). This, he claims, is "infinite freedom."

5. Kearney, *Debates in Continental Philosophy,* 21–22.

6. "The Eucharist thus becomes the test of every theological systematization, because, in gathering all, it poses the greatest challenge to thought" (GWB, 161; DSL, 225).

7. "What the consecrated host imposes, or rather permits, is the irreducible exteriority of the present that Christ makes us of himself in this thing that to him becomes sacramental body. That this exteriority, far from forbidding intimacy, renders it possible in sparing it from foundering in idolatry, can be misunderstood only by those who do not want to open themselves to *distance.* Only distance, in maintaining a distinct separation of terms (of persons), renders communion possible, and immediately mediates the relation" (GWB, 169; DSL, 239; original emphasis). He claims that such an attachment to presence is ultimately more profoundly metaphysical than the doctrine of transubstantiation (GWB, 170; DSL, 240).

8. "In the eucharistic present, all presence is deduced from the charity of the gift; all the rest in it becomes appearance for a gaze without charity. . . . The consecrated bread and wine become the ultimate aspect in which charity delivers itself body and soul" (GWB, 178; DSL, 252). This previews what Marion will say later: the Eucharist is a sign of kenotic abandon.

9. "In short, *the eucharistic present is deduced from the commitment of charity*" (GWB, 178; DSL, 252; original emphasis). One wonders how Marion gets so quickly in his text from the Eucharist as gift to the Eucharist as an instance of divine charity. Love and gift are always closely identified for Marion.

10. "In consuming this food, we do not assimilate the Christ—to our person or to our 'social body,' or whatever—like the food that finds in us its end and sole justification. On the contrary, we become assimilated through the sacramental body of the Christ to his ecclesiastical body" (GWB, 179; DSL, 253). "The bread and the wine must be consumed, to be sure, but so that our definitive union with the Father may be consummated in them, through communion with the ecclesiastical body of his Son. *The eucharistic present is deduced from the real edification of the ecclesiastical body of Christ*" (GWB, 179; DSL, 254; original emphasis).

11. Marion prepares here his later conception of blindness in face of the saturated phenomenon: "For our naturally blind gaze, the bread and wine *are* real, the consecrated bread and wine *are* real as bread and wine, sacramental ('mystical' in the ordinary sense) as Body and Blood of Christ, whereas the ecclesiastical body remains purely sacramental ('mystical body,' according to a modern acceptation). But only the inverse has a correct theological meaning" (GWB, 180; DSL, 255, original emphasis). "*The eucharistic present is deduced from theological, mystical 'reality' alone*" (GWB, 181; DSL, 256; original emphasis). Marion claims that his interpretation therefore brings together "subjective" and "objective" accounts of eucharistic presence.

12. *Prolegomena to Charity* indicates that "The Gift of a Presence" was composed in 1983.

13. "The Eucharistic sign provokes the corporeal presence of the spirit: in the institution narrative, this corporeal presence of the spirit (gift of presence) is accomplished first of all in the consecrated bread: 'This is my body' (22:19); in the story of Emmaus, it is accomplished also and in addition in the recognition of Christ—namely: the recognition of the gift of the presence of God in *this* man, because this man can give himself to the point of abandoning himself like bread is distributed, abandoning himself like bread, like *this* bread, can concentrate all his presence in a gift, whether in a fleshly body or by taking body of the bread, always without any reserve whatsoever. In blessing, Christ makes himself recognized as gift of presence; the consecrated bread incarnates the perfectly abandoned gift of a 'body given for [us]' (Luke 22:19). Thus Christ makes himself recognized—as gift of presence—ever since Easter by the sign of the blessing" (PC, 133; PaC, 158–59).

14. "That this fleshly body disappears and leaves place for the eucharistic body of bread that one eats, that one assimilates to oneself, and which, in this unique case, assimilates to itself those who assimilate it (Augustine), means: Christ becomes present, not to the senses (which cannot receive him, or even see him), but to the heart, burning from now on, and the mind, from hereafter understanding. The sensible disappearance allows the blessing to give the presence of Christ still more intimately, radically: the presence becomes still more of a gift, since it makes itself a gift communicable to the point of assimilation" (PC, 136; PaC, 162).

15. "Thus as much by the Eucharist as by the gift of the Spirit, the withdrawal of the Ascension makes the disciples come unto a perfect, though paradoxical presence in Christ. Paradoxical, for this presence no longer admits any sensible support and, for outside observers, reduces to pure and simple absence. Perfect, precisely because this presence no longer consists in seeing another, even the Christ, loving, dying, and returning to life, but oneself, like him, in him, according to him, actually loving, dying, and returning to life. Presence: not to find oneself in the presence of Christ, but to become present to him (to declare oneself present, available) in order to receive from him the present (the gift) of the Spirit who makes us, here and now (in the present), bless him like he blesses the Father—until and in order that he return. The highest presence of Christ lies in the Spirit's action of making us, with him and in him, bless the Father" (PC, 145; PaC, 171).

16. This is the penultimate chapter in *Le croire pour le voir*. It was translated by Stephen E. Lewis as "They Recognized Him; and He Became Invisible to Them," *Modern Theology* 18.2 (2002): 145–52. All references in the rest of this paragraph refer to this article, unless indicated otherwise.

17. "The opening of the meaning, and thus of the mind . . . is decided in and by 'the Scriptures', taken not as pure letters, but as the recording of significations established by God in order to constitute the intuitions of his incarnation in a full and wholly complete phenomenon of Revelation" (Lewis, "They Recognized Him," 151; CpV, 204–205). This is a forceful statement that Marion never reiterates in quite this blatant form. Usually he is careful to guard against any suggestion that somehow we could fully constitute a phe-

nomenon of revelation or could know it completely. Shane Mackinlay was right to criticize this and to insist that hermeneutics must play a much larger role in the recipient's response to the phenomenon. "Eyes Wide Shut: A Response to Jean-Luc Marion's Account of the Journey to Emmaus," *Modern Theology* 20.3 (2004): 447–56, esp. 451–54.

18. These (and other parallels) in Marion's work are pointed out by Thomas Carlson already in his introduction to the translation of *Idol and Distance,* where he suggests that Marion's theological and phenomenological accounts fit each other rather too well.

19. He talks again about Christ as the visible face of the invisible God, citing Irenaeus (CpV, 187).

20. There is an untranslatable French word play here: "L'abandon du don accompli jusqu'à l'excès de la trahison, rend désormais possible la tradition" (CpV, 189).

21. Marion indicates within the information about previous publication that the argument of this particular piece is developed further in chapter 4 of *Certitudes négatives,* which is the chapter on sacrifice and forgiveness, examined in my chapter 5. Forgiveness and sacrifice emerge as essential aspects of the gift in *Certitudes négatives.* Both, of course, are also important aspects of the eucharistic gift. One may therefore ask: Is it only the moment of the sacrifice that makes visible the Eucharist as gift? Is the forgiveness offered within the liturgical rite an important aspect of the thanksgiving ("eucharistia") of the sacrament? Marion leaves these questions unexplored. On the other hand, one may also wonder again to what extent theology here serves as the paradigm for phenomenology: if the Eucharist is the paradigm for the gift, is the perfect gift, and the gift is the paradigm for the fully given phenomenon or indeed for "all phenomenality" (CN, 181), this raises questions about the ways in which Marion's theology determines his phenomenology. The earlier chapter on the gift was translated as "The Reason of the Gift" in *Givenness and God: Questions of Jean-Luc Marion,* ed. Ian Leask and Eoin Cassidy (New York: Fordham University Press, 2005), 101–134.

22. The essay is actually on sacraments as such, not just the Eucharist. I am citing from the English translation of this piece included in *Words of Life: New Theological Turns in French Phenomenology,* ed. Bruce Ellis Benson and Norman Wirzba (New York: Fordham University Press, 2010), 89–102. All references in the rest of the section refer to this translation unless indicated otherwise.

23. He says that the "assumption of a visibility of the invisible" has "a positive consequence: since in any sacrament it is a matter of rendering visible the invisible grace of God granted to the Church in Christ, theological reflection cannot get by without a strictly phenomenological analysis" (90; CpV, 151).

24. "The phenomenon thus recovers the sovereignty of its appearance only while being phenomenalized of and for *itself,* in showing *itself* as from *itself.* Yet it attests this *self* only when the appearance engages itself in its appearing. It engages itself in and to the appearing only if it gives *itself*" (98; CpV, 160–61; original emphasis).

25. "It is a question of admitting phenomena where the excess of given intuition exceeds the range of concepts that we would have at our disposal to constitute them as objects" (100; CpV, 164). The kind of knowledge that can receive these phenomena is called "faith."

26. He wonders: "Can one not, by analogy, envision a case where what is given would give *itself* in fact so radically that it guarantees, even by this engagement with our consciousness, that itself shows effectively all that it says it will give to see—all that which is invisible that it promises to see, since it gives it? Should one not envision the hypothesis that what gives *itself* would give *itself* so definitively that all that it promises to show is *itself* really shown" (101; CpV, 165; original emphasis).

27. Marion first articulates this important distinction in note 90 of *Being Given* (BG, 367; ED, 329 note 1).

28. Cyril of Jerusalem, *Lectures on the Christian Sacraments* (Crestwood, N.Y.: St. Vladimir's Seminary Press, 1986), 23.21, 79.

29. The Roman Catholic rite admits right before reception of the elements: "Lord, I am not worthy to receive you, but only say the word and I shall be healed." In the Orthodox tradition, the priest proclaims right after reception: "As this has touched your lips, it shall take away your iniquities and cleanse you from all your sins."

30. For descriptions of the diversity of experiencing the Eucharist, see, among many other sources: Bruce Morrill, ed. *Bodies of Worship: Explorations in Theory and Practice* (Collegeville, Minn.: Liturgical Press, 1999); John Baldovin, *Worship: City, Church, and Renewal* (Washington, D.C.: Pastoral Press, 1991); Anscar Chupungco, *Cultural Adaptations of the Liturgy* (New York: Paulist Press, 1982); Martin D. Stringer, *On the Perception of Worship: The Ethnography of Worship in four Christian Congregations in Manchester* (Birmingham: Birmingham University Press, 1999) and *A Sociological History of Christian Worship* (Cambridge: Cambridge University Press, 2005).

31. Obviously, these are only brief descriptions that could and should be worked out much more fully. But they give some preliminary examples of the ways in which particular differences between traditions might be explored phenomenologically.

32. For the most detailed exploration of this, see Alexander Schmemann, *The Eucharist: Sacrament of the Kingdom* (Crestwood, N.Y.: St. Vladimir's Orthodox Theological Seminary, 1987).

33. Although Marion's student Emmanuel Falque pays far more attention to this dimension, he nevertheless may not go far enough. He insists on our animality and sees it affirmed by the Eucharist, and yet (as noted in chapter 3) he consistently draws an almost absolute distinction between human animality and the "bestiality" of other creatures.

34. "I do not venerate matter, I venerate the fashioner of matter, who became matter for my sake and accepted to dwell in matter and through matter worked my salvation, and I will not cease from reverencing matter, through which my salvation was worked. I do not reverence it as God—far from it; how can that which has come to be from nothing be God?—if the body of God has become God unchangeably through the hypostatic union, what gives anointing remains, and what was by nature flesh animated with a rational and intellectual soul is formed, it is not uncreated. Therefore I reverence the rest of matter and hold in respect that through which my salvation came, because it is filled with divine energy and grace. . . . Do not abuse matter; for it is not dishonourable; this is the view of the Manichees." John of Damascus, *Three Treatises on the Divine Images*, trans. Andrew Louth (Crestwood, N.Y.: St. Vladimir's Seminary Press, 2003), 1.16, 29–30.

35. Although I cannot explore this in fuller detail here, I think close phenomenological analysis of the fleshly and material phenomenality of the Eucharist may well provide important insights for ecological phenomenology.

36. Jacob D. Myers, however, uses Marion's phenomenology in order to give a liturgical account that is in conversation with Schmemann's liturgical theology. "Toward an Erotic Liturgical Theology: Schmemann in Conversation with Contemporary Philosophy," *Worship* 87.5 (2013): 387–413. See also Donald L. Wallenfang, "Sacramental Givenness: The Notion of Givenness in Husserl, Heidegger, and Marion, and Its Import for Interpreting the Phenomenality of the Eucharist," *Philosophy and Theology* 22.1–2 (2010): 131–54, and Wohlmuth, "Impulse für eine künftige Theologie der Gabe bei Jean-Luc Marion," 267–71.

37. This is where Michel Henry's admittedly cursory account might prove helpful, since he speaks of the "mystical body" of Christ as our communal fleshly sharing in the divine. Unfortunately, he leaves it tantalizingly unexplored. It is interesting, however, that Marion fully appropriates Henry's analysis of the flesh, yet never comments on his account of community. Even when Marion speaks of love or intersubjectivity it is always in the singular—to the point where one can be a lover without a beloved. See chapter 4 on love.

38. In his more general phenomenological account in *Being Given,* Marion consistently stresses this. See especially part 5. He seems much more careful (and more phenomenological) in his treatment there.

39. Bruce Ellis Benson, "Love Is a Given," *Christian Century* (2003): 25. Mike Kraftson-Hogue raises similar questions about Marion's account of the Eucharist in his "Predication Turning to Praise: Marion and Augustine on God and Hermeneutics—(Giver, Giving, Gift, Giving)," *Literature and Theology* 14.4 (2000): 399–411.

40. It seems to me that the recipient plays a much stronger role in Marion's more strictly phenomenological accounts. There he does stress the need for receptivity (and even naming of the anonymous phenomenon) to the point where the recipient can become the "master" of the given, while also remaining its servant. This dimension seems to be lacking in his accounts of religious phenomena.

41. Bauer draws a useful distinction between "acceptability" and "receptivity." We do not take possession or control of the given phenomenon, but we do receive it. Bauer, *Einander zu erkennen geben,* 494.

42. Hart also questions this distinction in his introduction to *The Essential Writings,* 29. In a different vein, Burch claims that Marion "implies that faith as a matter of fact grants the individual access to religious intuition, and this claim is unwarranted, because faith cannot transform a mere possibility into a matter of fact." "Blurred Vision," 167.

43. Marion does say, however, that "as philosopher I do not have to decide whether I am a believer or not, but have only to elucidate the things themselves; these things can take on the face of Revelation, of revealed phenomena, of everything that rational and religious minds can take seriously" (RC, 207).

44. This is, of course, a hermeneutic exercise of the sort Ricoeur practices in his biblical hermeneutics. Several of his essays on biblical hermeneutics are collected in *Figuring*

the Sacred: Religion, Narrative, and Imagination, trans. David Pellauer (Minneapolis, Minn.: Fortress Press, 1995).

45. See especially his analysis of the "poetic" nature of religious language in several of the essays in *Figuring the Sacred.*

Conclusion

1. Another issue of terminology concerns "preparation" versus "anticipation." Marion identifies "anticipating" a phenomenon with "metaphysical rationality" and a "transcendental attitude" (RC, 138). It hence means something like "predictability" and implies control. What I describe as "preparatory practices" is not this sort of controlling anticipation, but a deliberate openness that allows greater receptivity.

2. Generally, Westphal sees such a hermeneutics already operative in Marion's work, while Kearney tends to find it missing. See Westphal, "Vision and Voice" and "Continental Philosophy of Religion"; Kearney, *Debates in Continental Philosophy,* 15–32, and *The God Who May Be,* 31–33.

3. Steinbock, *Phenomenology and Mysticism,* 36, 37, 38, original emphasis.

4. Forestier, "The Phenomenon and the Transcendental," 391.

BIBLIOGRAPHY

Primary Sources (Marion)

Sur l'ontologie grise de Descartes. Science cartésienne et savoir aristotélicien dans les "Regulae." Paris: Vrin, 1975 (2nd ed. 1981; 3rd ed. 1992; 4th ed. 2002). Published in English as *Descartes's Grey Ontology: Cartesian Science and Aristotelian Thought in the "Regulae."* Translated by S. Donohue. South Bend, Ind.: St. Augustine's Press, forthcoming.

L'idole et la distance. Cinq études. Paris: Grasset, 1977 (2nd ed. 1989; 3rd ed. 1991). Published in English as *The Idol and Distance: Five Studies.* Translated and introduced by Thomas A. Carlson. New York: Fordham University Press, 2001.

Sur la théologie blanche de Descartes. Analogie, création des vérités éternelles, fondement. Paris: Presses Universitaires de France, 1981 (2nd ed. 1991; 3rd ed. 2009).

Dieu sans l'être. Paris: Fayard, 1982 (2nd ed. Presses Universitaires de France, "Quadrige," 1991; 3rd ed. 2002; 4th ed. 2010). Published in English as *God without Being.* Translated by Thomas A. Carlson. Chicago: University of Chicago Press, 1991 (2nd ed. 2012).

Prolégomènes à la charité. Paris: Éd. de la Différence, 1986 (2nd ed. 1991). Published in English as *Prolegomena to Charity.* Translated by Stephen E. Lewis. New York: Fordham University Press, 2002.

Sur le prisme métaphysique de Descartes. Constitution et limites de l'onto-théo-logie dans la pensée cartésienne. Paris: Presses Universitaires de France, 1986 (2nd ed. 2004). Published in English as *On Descartes' Metaphysical Prism: The Constitution and the Limits of Onto-theo-logy in Cartesian Thought.* Translated by Jeffrey L. Kosky. Chicago: University of Chicago Press, 1999.

"La fin de la fin de la métaphysique." *Laval théologique et philosophique* 42.1 (1986): 23–33. Translated as "The End of the End of Metaphysics." *Epoche* 2.2 (1994): 1–22.

"L'interloqué." *Topoi* 7 (1988): 175–80. Translated in *Who Comes After the Subject?*, edited by Eduardo Cadava, Peter Connor, and Jean-Luc Nancy, 236–45. London and New York: Routledge, 1991.

Réduction et donation. Recherches sur Husserl, Heidgger et la phénoménologie. Paris: Presses Universitaires de France, 1989 (2nd ed. 2004). Published in English as *Reduction and Givenness: Investigations of Husserl, Heidegger, and Phenomenology.* Translated by Thomas A. Carlson. Evanston, Ill.: Northwestern University Press, 1998.

La croisée du visible. Paris: Éd. de la Différence, 1991 (2nd ed. Presses Universitaires de France, 1996; 3rd ed. "Quadrige" 2007). Published in English as *The Crossing of the Visible.* Translated by James K. A. Smith. Stanford, Calif.: Stanford University Press, 2004.

Questions cartésiennes. Méthode et métaphysique. Paris: Presses Universitaires de France, 1991. Published in English as *Cartesian Questions: Method and Metaphysics.* Chicago: University of Chicago Press, 1999.

"Le sujet en dernier appel." *Revue de métaphysique et de morale* 96.1 (1991): 77–95. Translated as "The Final Appeal of the Subject." In *Deconstructive Subjectivities,* edited by Simon Critchley and Peter Dews, 85–104. Albany: State University of New York Press, 1996. Reprinted in *The Religious,* edited by John D. Caputo, 131–44. Oxford: Blackwell, 2002.

"Le phénomène saturé." In *Phénomenologie et théologie,* edited by Jean-François Courtine, 79–128. Paris: Critérion, 1992. Translated as "The Saturated Phenomenon." *Philosophy Today* 40.1–4 (1996): 103–124. Retranslated in Janicaud et al., *Phenomenology and the "Theological Turn,"* 176–216, and as chapter 2 of *Le visible et le révélé/The Visible and the Revealed.*

"Métaphysique et phénoménologie. Une relève pour la théologie." *Bulletin de littérature ecclésiastique* 94.3 (1993): 189–206. Translated as "Metaphysics and Phenomenology: A Relief for Theology." *Critical Inquiry* 20.4 (1994): 572–91. Retranslated as chapter 3 of *Le visible et le révélé/The Visible and the Revealed.*

"Esquisse d'un concept phénoménologique du don." *Archivo di Filosofia* 62.1–3 (1994): 75–94. Translated as "Sketch of a Phenomenological Concept of Gift." In *Postmodern Philosophy and Christian Thought,* edited by Merold Westphal, 122–43. Bloomington: Indiana University Press, 1999. Retranslated as chapter 5 of *The Visible and the Revealed.*

"Saint Thomas d'Aquin et l'onto-théo-logie." *Revue Thomiste* 95.1 (1995): 31–66. Translated by B. Gendreau, R. Rethty, and M. Sweeney as "Saint Thomas Aquinas and Onto-theo-logy." In *Mystic: Presence and Aporia,* edited by M. Kessler and C. Sheppard, 38–74. Chicago: Chicago University Press, 2003. Reprinted in *God without Being* (2nd rev. ed.) and in *Essential Writings.*

Questions cartésiennes II. L'ego et Dieu. Paris: Presses Universitaires de France, 1996 (2nd ed. 2004). Published partially in English as *On the Ego and on God: Further Cartesian Questions.* Translated by Christina M. Gschwandtner. New York: Fordham University Press, 2007.

Étant donné. Essai d'une phénoménologie de la donation. Paris: Presses Universitaires de France, 1997 (2nd. ed. 1998; 3rd ed. 2005). Published in English as *Being Given: Toward a Phenomenology of Givenness.* Translated by Jeffrey L. Kosky. Stanford, Calif.: Stanford University Press, 2002.

"A Note Concerning the Ontological Indifference." *Graduate Faculty Philosophy Journal* 20/21.1/2 (1998): 25–40.

"La voix sans nom." *Rue Descartes. Emmanuel Lévinas.* Paris: Collège International de philosophie, 1998. 11–26. Translated as "The Voice without Name: Homage to Levinas." In *The Face of the Other and the Trace of God: Essays on the Philosophy of Emmanuel Levinas,* edited by Jeffrey Bloechl, 224–42. New York: Fordham University Press, 2000.

"'Christian Philosophy': Hermeneutic or Heuristic?" In *The Question of Christian Philosophy Today,* edited by Francis J. Ambrosio, 247–64. New York: Fordham University

Press, 1999. Retranslated as chapter 4 of *Le visible et le révélé/The Visible and the Revealed*.

"Au nom. Comment ne pas parler de 'théologie negative.'" *Laval théologique et philosophique* 55.3 (1999): 339–63. Translated as "In the Name: How to Avoid Speaking of 'Negative Theology.'" In *God, the Gift, and Postmodernism*, edited by John D. Caputo and Michael Scanlon, 20–53. Bloomington: Indiana University Press, 1999. Revised as chapter 6 of *De surcroît/In Excess*.

"D'autrui à l'individu." In Emmanuel Lévinas, *Positivité et transcendance; suivi de Lévinas et la phénoménologie*. Paris: Presses Universitaires de France, 2000. Translated by Robyn Horner as "From the Other to the Individual." In *Transcendence: Philosophy, Literature, and Theology Approach the Beyond*, edited by Regina Schwartz, 43–59. New York and London: Routledge, 2004. Also translated by Arianne Conty. In *Levinas Studies: An Annual Review*, edited by Jeffrey Bloechl and Jeffrey L. Kosky, 99–117. Pittsburgh, Pa.: Duquesne University Press, 2005.

De surcroît. Études sur les phénomènes saturés. Paris: Presses Universitaires de France, 2001 (2nd ed. "Quadrige" 2010). Published in English as *In Excess: Studies of Saturated Phenomena*. Translated by Robyn Horner and Vincent Berraud. New York: Fordham University Press, 2002.

"Ils le reconnurent et lui-même leur devint invisible." In *Demain l'Église. Hommage au cardinal Lustiger*, edited by J. Duchesne and J. Ollier. Paris: Plon, 2001. Translated by Stephen E. Lewis as "They Recognized Him; And He Became Invisible to Them." *Modern Theology* 18.2 (2002): 145–52. Revised as penultimate chapter of *Le croire pour le voir*.

"Notes sur le phénomène et son événement." *Iris. Annales de philosophie* (Université Saint-Joseph de Beyrouth) 23 (2002), revised as "Le phénomène et l'événement." In *Questio 3, L'esistenza. L'existence. Die Existenz. Existence*, edited by C. Esposito and Vincent Carraud. Turnhout, Belgium: Brepols, and Bari, Italy: Pagina, 2003. Translated as "Phenomenon and Event." *Graduate Faculty Philosophy Journal* 26.1 (2005): 147–59. Revised as chapter 5 of *Certitudes négatives*.

"The Unspoken: Apophasis and the Discourse of Love." *Proceedings of the American Catholic Philosophical Association* 76 (2002): 39–56. Revised as chapter 5 of *Le visible et le révélé* and retranslated as chapter 6 of *The Visible and the Revealed*.

"The 'End of Metaphysics' as a Possibility." In *Religion after Metaphysics*, edited by Mark A. Wrathall, 166–89. Cambridge: Cambridge University Press, 2003.

Le phénomène érotique. Six méditations. Paris: Grasset, 2003 (2nd ed. 2004). Published in English as *The Erotic Phenomenon*. Translated by Stephen E. Lewis. Chicago: University of Chicago Press, 2003.

Le visible et le révélé. Paris: Éditions du CERF, coll. Philosophie & Théologie, 2005. Published in English as *The Visible and the Revealed*. New York: Fordham University Press, 2008.

"The Impossible for Man—God." Translated by Anne Davenport. In *Transcendence—and Beyond*, edited by John D. Caputo and Michael S. Scanlon, 17–43. Bloomington: Indiana University Press, 2007. Revised as chapter 2 of *Certitudes négatives*.

Au lieu de soi. L'approche de saint Augustin. Paris: Presses Universitaires de France, 2008. Published in English as *In the Self's Place: The Approach of Saint Augustine.* Translated by Jeffrey L. Kosky. Stanford, Calif.: Stanford University Press, 2012.

"The Invisibility of the Saint." *Critical Inquiry 35.3* (2008): 703–710. Reprinted in *Saints: Faith without Borders,* edited by Françoise Meltzer and Jaś Elsner, 355–62. Chicago: University of Chicago Press, 2011. Revised as final chapter of *Le croire pour le voir.*

"La reconnaissance du don." *Revue catholique internationale Communio 33.1* (2008): 169–82. Translated as "The Recognition of the Gift." Special issue, *Studia phaenomenologica* (2009): 15–28. Revised as chapter 10 of *Le croire pour le voir.*

"The Phenomenality of the Sacrament—Being and Givenness." In *Words of Life: New Theological Turns in French Phenomenology,* edited by Bruce Ellis Benson and Norman Wirzba, 89–102. New York: Fordham University Press, 2010. Revised as chapter 8 of *Le croire pour le voir.*

Certitudes négatives. Paris: Grasset, 2010. To be published in English as *Negative Certainties.* Translated by Stephen E. Lewis. Chicago: University of Chicago Press, forthcoming 2015.

Le croire pour le voir. Réflexions diverses sur la rationalité de la révélation et l'irrationalité de quelques croyants. Paris: Parole et Silence, coll. Communio, 2010. To be published in English as *Believing as Seeing.* New York: Fordham University Press, forthcoming 2015.

Discours de réception de Jean-Luc Marion à l'Académie française et réponse de Mgr. Claude Dagens. Paris: Grasset, 2010.

The Reason of the Gift. Edited and translated by Stephen E. Lewis. Charlottesville: University of Virginia Press, 2011.

"What We See and What Appears." In *Idol Anxiety,* edited by Josh Ellenbogen and Aaron Tugendhaft, 152–68. Stanford, Calif.: Stanford University Press, 2011.

Figures de Phénoménologie. Husserl, Heidegger, Levinas, Henry, Derrida. Paris: Vrin, 2012.

La Rigueur des choses. Entretiens avec Dan Arbib. Paris: Flammarion, 2012.

"On the Foundation of the Distinction Between Theology and Philosophy." In *Phenomenology and the Theological Turn: The Twenty-Seventh Annual Symposium of The Simon Silverman Phenomenology Center,* edited by Jeffrey McCurry and Angelle Pryor, 48–71. Pittsburgh, Pa.: Simon Silverman Phenomenology Center, 2012.

Givenness and Hermeneutics. The Père Marquette Lecture in Theology 2013. Translated by Jean-Pierre Lafouge. Milwaukee, Wisc.: Marquette University Press, 2012. Includes French text of the lecture.

The Essential Writings. Edited by Kevin Hart. New York: Fordham University Press, 2013.

Sur la pensée passive de Descartes. Paris: Presses Universitaires de France, 2013. To be published in English as *On Descartes' Passive Thought.* Chicago: University of Chicago Press, forthcoming.

Courbet ou la peinture à l'œil. Paris: Flammarion, 2014.

With Alain Benoist. *Avec ou sans Dieu? L'avenir des valeurs chrétiennes.* Carrefour des Jeunes. Paris: Beauchesne, 1970.

Secondary Sources (Marion)

Ahn, Ilsup. "The Genealogy of Debt and the Phenomenology of Forgiveness: Nietzsche, Marion, and Derrida on the Meaning of the 'Peculiar Phenomenon.'" *Heythrop Journal: A Bimonthly Review of Philosophy and Theology* 51.3 (2010): 454–70.

Alferi, Thomas. "Entmündigt die Gebung/die 'donation' das Ich? Versuch einer Vermittlung zwischen Jean-Luc Marion und Hansjürgen Verweyen." *Phänomenologische Forschungen* (2004): 317–41.

———. "Dem Sich-Gebenden nachdenken. Ein Gespräch zum philosophisch-theologischen Werk von Jean-Luc Marion." *Journal Phänomenologie* 25 (2006): 60–70.

———. "Von der Offenbarungsfrage zu Marions Phänomenologie der Gebung." In Gabel and Joas, *Von der Ursprünglichkeit der Gabe*, 210–33.

———. *"Worüber hinaus Größeres nicht 'gegeben' werden kann . . ." Phänomenologie und Offenbarung nach Jean-Luc Marion.* Freiburg/München: Alber, 2007.

———. "'. . . die Unfasslichkeit der uns übersteigend-zuvorkommenden Liebe Gottes . . .' Von Balthasar als Orientierung für Marion." In Gerl-Falkovitz, *Jean-Luc Marion*, 103–125.

Alliez, Éric. *De l'impossibilité de la phénoménologie. Sur la philosophie française contemporaine.* Paris: Vrin, 1995.

Alweiss, Lilian. "I Am, I Exist." In Leask and Cassidy, *Givenness and God*, 37–46.

Ambrosio, Francis J., ed. *The Question of Christian Philosophy Today.* New York: Fordham University Press, 1999.

Bauer, Katharina. *Einander zu erkennen geben: Das Selbst zwischen Erkenntnis und Gabe.* Freiburg/München: Alber, 2012.

———. "Von der *donation* zur *interdonation.* Interpersonale Beziehungen in der Phänomenologie Jean-Luc Marions." In Gerl-Falkovitz, *Jean-Luc Marion*, 217–36.

Bassas Vila, Javier. "Écriture phénoménologique et théologique: Fonctions du 'comme,' 'comme si' et 'en tant que' chez Jean-Luc Marion." Special issue, *Studia phaenomenologica* (2009): 135–55.

Baumann, Benjamin. "Jean-Luc Marion und die Überwindung der *Störung durch die Welt.* Subjekt und Welt als *gesättigte Phänomene.*" In Gerl-Falkovitz, *Jean-Luc Marion*, 297–321.

Bell, Jeffrey A. Review of Jean-Luc Marion, *Reduction and Givenness. International Studies in Philosophy* 35 (2003): 356–57.

Benoist, Jocelyn. "Qu'est-ce qui est donné? La pensée et l'événement." *Archives de philosophie* 59 (1996): 629–57.

———. "L'écart plutôt que l'excédent." *Philosophie. Jean-Luc Marion* 78 (2003): 77–93.

Benson, Bruce Ellis. *Graven Ideologies: Nietzsche, Derrida and Marion on Modern Idolatry.* Downers Grove, Ill.: InterVarsity Press, 2002.

———. "Love Is a Given." *Christian Century* (2003): 22–25.

———, and Norman Wirzba, eds. *Words of Life: New Theological Turns in French Phenomenology.* New York: Fordham University Press, 2010.

Bloechl, Jeffrey. "Dialectical Approaches to Retrieving God after Heidegger: Premises and Consequences (Lacoste and Marion)." *Pacifica* 13 (2000): 288–98.

Blohm, Michelle. "Releasing the Idol-Icon Dichotomy: An Exposition of Non-Conceptual Experience." *Quaestiones disputatae* 1.1 (2010): 251–57.

Blond, Phillip. "Theology and Perception." *Modern Theology* 14.4 (1998): 523–34.

Bossche, Stijn van den. "God Does Appear in Immanence After All: Jean-Luc Marion's Phenomenology as a New First Philosophy for Theology." In *Sacramental Presence in a Postmodern Context*, edited by L. Boeve and L. Leijssen, 325–46. Leuven, Belgium: Leuven University Press, 2001.

Bovell, Carlos R. "Phenomenology and the Search for the Infinite God." *Quaestiones disputatae* 1.1 (2010): 133–43.

Bradley, Arthur. "God *sans* Being: Derrida, Marion and 'A Paradoxical Writing of the Word *Without*.'" *Literature and Theology* 14.3 (2000): 299–312.

Burch, Matthew I. "Blurred Vision: Marion on the 'Possibility' of Revelation." *International Journal for Philosophy of Religion* 67.3 (2010): 157–71.

Camilleri, Sylvain. "Phénoménologie, théologie et Écritures." In Camilleri and Takács, *Jean-Luc Marion*, 139–61.

———, and Ádám Takács, eds. *Jean-Luc Marion. Cartésianisme, phénoménologie, théologie. Actes du colloque international organisé les 19 et 20 mars 2010 à Budapest.* Paris: Archives Karéline, 2012.

Canullo, Carla. *La fenomenologia rovesciata. Percorsi tentati in Jean-Luc Marion, Michel Henry e Jean-Louis Chrétien.* Torino, Italy: Rosenberg & Sellier, 2004.

Caputo, John D. "How to Avoid Speaking of God: The Violence of Natural Theology." In *Prospects for Natural Theology*, edited by Eugene Thomas Long, 128–50. Washington, D.C.: Catholic University of America Press, 1992.

———. "God Is Wholly Other—Almost: 'Difference' and the Hyperbolic Alterity of God." In *The Otherness of God*, edited by Orrin F. Summerell, 190–205. Charlottesville: University Press of Virginia, 1998.

———. "Apostles of the Impossible: On God and the Gift in Derrida and Marion." In Caputo and Scanlon, *God, the Gift, and Postmodernism*, 185–222.

———. "The Poetics of the Impossible and the Kingdom of God." In *Rethinking Philosophy of Religion: Approaches from Continental Philosophy*, edited by Philip Goodchild, 42–58. New York: Fordham University Press, 2002.

———. "The Hyperbolization of Phenomenology: Two Possibilities for Religion in Recent Continental Philosophy." In Hart, *Counter-Experiences*, 67–93.

———, and Michael J. Scanlon, eds. *God, the Gift, and Postmodernism.* Bloomington: Indiana University Press, 1999.

Carew, Joseph. "The Threat of Givenness in Jean-Luc Marion: Toward a New Phenomenology of Psychosis." *Symposium: Canadian Journal of Continental Philosophy* 13.2 (2009): 97–115.

Carlson, Thomas A. *Indiscretion: Finitude and the Naming of God.* Chicago: University of Chicago Press, 1999.

———. "Converting the Given into the Seen: Introductory Remarks on Theological and Phenomenological Vision." In Jean-Luc Marion, *The Idol and Distance: Five Studies*, xi–xxxi. New York: Fordham University Press, 2001.

———. "Blindness and the Decision to See: On Revelation and Reception in Jean-Luc Marion." In Hart, *Counter-Experiences*, 153–79.

Cassidy, Eoin. "*Le phénomène érotique:* Augustinian Resonances in Marion's Phenomenology of Love." In Leask and Cassidy, *Givenness and God,* 201–219.

Chicoine, Glenn. "The Intuition of Meaning-Acts in Jean-Luc Marion: The Sign, Gift and Word of God." *Quaestiones disputatae* 1.1 (2010): 144–62.

Ciocan, Cristian. "Philosophical Concepts and Religious Metaphors: New Perspectives on Phenomenology and Theology." Special issue, *Studia phaenomenologica* (2009): 7–13.

———. "Entre visible et invisible. Les paradigmes de l'image chez Jean-Luc Marion." In Camilleri and Takács, *Jean-Luc Marion,* 93–113.

Ciomoş, Virgil. "Phénoménologie de l'inapparent et apophatisme chrétien." In Camilleri and Takács, *Jean-Luc Marion,* 163–81.

Cooke, Alexander. "What Saturates? Jean-Luc Marion's Phenomenological Theology." *Philosophy Today* 48.2 (2004): 179–87.

Costello, Peter R. "Towards a Phenomenology of Gratitude—a Response to Jean-Luc Marion." *Balkan Journal of Philosophy* 1.2 (2009): 77–82.

Crosby, John F. "A Question About Marion's 'Principle of Insufficient Reason.'" *Quaestiones disputatae* 1.1 (2010): 245–50.

Dalferth, Ingolf U. "Alles umsonst. Zur Kunst des Schenkens und den Grenzen der Gabe." In Gabel and Joas, *Von der Ursprünglichkeit der Gabe,* 159–91.

Depraz, Natalie. "Gibt es eine Gebung des Unendlichen?" In *Perspektiven der Philosophie,* edited by Rudolph Berlinger, 111–55. Amsterdam: Rodopi, 1997.

———. "The Return of Phenomenology in Recent French Moral Philosophy." In *Phenomenological Approaches to Moral Philosophy,* edited by John J. Drummond and Lester Embree, 517–32. Dordrecht, Netherlands: Kluwer Academic Publishers, 2002.

Diekhans, Jonas. "Das saturierte Phänomen. Über das Unbehagen an der Grenze der Erkenntnis." In Gerl-Falkovitz, *Jean-Luc Marion,* 277–96.

Dierckxsens, Geoffrey. "Loving Unintentionally: Charity and the Bad Conscience in the Works of Levinas and Marion." *Bijdragen: Tijdschrift voor Filosofie en Theologie* 73.1 (2012): 3–27.

Dodd, James. "Marion and Phenomenology." *Graduate Faculty Philosophy Journal* 25.1 (2004): 161–84.

Dooley, Mark. "Marion's Ambition of Transcendence." In Leask and Cassidy, *Givenness and God,* 190–98.

Drabinski, John E. "Sense and Icon: The Problem of *Sinngebung* in Levinas and Marion." *Philosophy Today* 42 suppl. (1998): 47–58.

Duquesne, Marcel. "A propos d'un livre récent. Jean-Luc Marion 'Dieu sans l'être.'" *Mélanges de science religieuse* 42.2 (1985): 57–75; 42.3 (1985): 127–39.

Dwyer, Daniel J. "Husserl and Marion on the Transcendental I." *Quaestiones disputatae* 1.1 (2010): 39–55.

Elliott, Brian. "Reduced Phenomena and Unreserved Debts in Marion's Reading of Heidegger." In Leask and Cassidy, *Givenness and God,* 87–97.

Falque, Emmanuel. "Phénoménologie de l'extraordinaire." *Philosophie. Jean-Luc Marion* 78 (2003): 52–76.

———. "*Larvatus pro Deo:* Jean-Luc Marion's Phenomenology and Theology." In Hart, *Counter-Experiences,* 181–99.

Faulconer, James E., ed. *Transcendence in Philosophy and Religion*. Bloomington: Indiana University Press, 2003.

――――. "Theological and Philosophical Transcendence: Bodily Excess; the Word Made Flesh." Special issue, *Studia phaenomenologica* (2009): 223–35.

Finegan, Thomas. "Is the Compatibility of Jean-Luc Marion's Philosophy with Husserlian Phenomenology a Matter of Faith?" *Yearbook of the Irish Philosophical Society: Voices of Irish Philosophy* (2009): 133–49.

Forestier, Florian. "The Phenomenon and the Transcendental: Jean-Luc Marion, Marc Richir, and the Issue of Phenomenalization." *Continental Philosophy Review* 45.3 (2012): 381–402.

Fritz, Peter Joseph. "Black Holes and Revelations: Michel Henry and Jean-Luc Marion on the Aesthetics of the Invisible." *Modern Theology* 25.3 (2009): 415–40.

Gabel, Michael. "Hingegebener Blick und Selbstgegebenheit." In Gabel and Joas, *Von der Ursprünglichkeit der Gabe*, 192–209.

――――, and Hans Joas, eds. *Von der Ursprünglichkeit der Gabe*. Freiburg/München: Alber, 2007.

Gabellieri, Emmanuel. "De la métaphysique à la phénoménology. Une 'relève'?" *Revue philosophique de Louvain* 94.4 (1996): 625–45.

Gagnon, Martin. "La phénoménologie à la limite." *Eidos* 11.1–2 (1993): 111–30.

Gerl-Falkovitz, Hanna-Barbara, ed. *Jean-Luc Marion: Studien zum Werk*. Dresden, Germany: Verlag Text & Dialog, 2013.

Gilbert, Paul. "Substance et présence. Derrida et Marion, critiques de Husserl." *Gregorianum* 75.1 (1994): 95–133.

Godzieba, Anthony J. "Ontotheology to Excess: Imagining God without Being." *Theological Studies* 56.1 (1995): 3–20.

Gondek, Hans-Dieter, and László Tengelyi. *Neue Phänomenologie in Frankreich*. Berlin: Suhrkamp, 2011.

Goodchild, Philip, ed. *Rethinking Philosophy of Religion: Approaches from Continental Philosophy*. New York: Fordham University Press, 2002.

Gorgone, Sandro. "Idol und Ikone. Die Phänomenologie des Unsichtbaren von Jean-Luc Marion." In Gerl-Falkovitz, *Jean-Luc Marion*, 237–53.

Greisch, Jean. "L'herméneutique dans la 'phénoménologie comme telle.' Trois questions à propos de Réduction et Donation." *Revue de métaphysique et de morale* 96.1 (1991): 43–63.

――――. "Index sui et non dati. Les paradoxes d'une phénoménologie de la donation." *Transversalités. Revue de l'Institut catholique de Paris* 70 (1999): 27–54.

Grondin, Jean. "La tension de la donation ultime et de la pensée herméneutique de l'application chez Jean-Luc Marion." *Dialogue* 38.3 (1999): 547–59.

Gschwandtner, Christina M. "Ethics, Eros, or Caritas? Levinas and Marion on Individuation of the Other." *Philosophy Today* 49.1 (2005): 70–87.

――――. "A New 'Apologia': The Relationship between Theology and Philosophy in the Work of Jean-Luc Marion." *Heythrop Journal: A Bimonthly Review of Philosophy and Theology* 46 (2005): 299–313.

———. "Praise—Pure and Personal? Jean-Luc Marion's Phenomenologies of Prayer." In *The Phenomenology of Prayer,* edited by Bruce Ellis Benson and Norman Wirzba, 168–81. New York: Fordham University Press, 2005.

———. "Love as a Declaration of War? On the Absolute Nature of Love in Jean-Luc Marion's Phenomenology of Eros." In *Transforming Philosophy and Religion: Love's Wisdom,* edited by Bruce Ellis Benson and Norman Wirzba, 185–98. Bloomington: Indiana University Press, 2007.

———. "The Neighbor and the Infinite: Marion and Levinas on the Encounter Between Self, Human Other, and God." *Continental Philosophy Review* 40 (2007): 231–49.

———. *Reading Jean-Luc Marion: Exceeding Metaphysics.* Bloomington: Indiana University Press, 2007.

———. "*À Dieu* or from the *Logos*? Emmanuel Lévinas and Jean-Luc Marion: Prophets of the Infinite." *Philosophy and Theology: Marquette University Quarterly* 22.1–2 (2010): 177–203.

———. "The Excess of the Gift in Jean-Luc Marion." In *Gift and Economy: Ethics, Hospitality, and the Market,* edited by Eric R. Severson, 20–32. Newcastle upon Tyne: Cambridge Scholars Publishing, 2011.

———. "Jean-Luc Marion: On the Possibility of a Religious Phenomenon." In *Continental Philosophy and Philosophy of Religion,* edited by Morny Joy, 165–86. Heidelberg, London, and New York: Springer, 2011.

———. "Marion and Negative Certainty: Epistemological Dimensions of the Phenomenology of Givenness." *Philosophy Today* 56.3 (2012): 363–70.

———. *Postmodern Apologetics? Arguments for God in Contemporary Philosophy.* New York: Fordham University Press, 2012.

———. "Jean-Luc Marion." In *The International Encyclopedia of Ethics,* edited by Hugh LaFollette. Oxford: Blackwell, 2013.

———. "Might Nature Be Interpreted as Saturated Phenomenon?" In *Interpreting Nature: The Emerging Field of Environmental Hermeneutics,* edited by Forrest Clingerman et al., 82–108. New York: Fordham University Press, 2013.

Hähnel, Martin. "Geteilte Ansichten. Zum Problem der Perspektivität bei Jean-Luc Marion und Pawel Florenskij." In Gerl-Falkovitz, *Jean-Luc Marion,* 257–76.

Halloran, Nathan W. "A Study of Woman as Saturated Phenomenon in Marion and Irigaray." *Quaestiones disputatae* 1.1 (2010): 190–205.

Han, Béatrice. "Transcendence and the Hermeneutic Circle: Some Thoughts on Marion and Heidegger." In Faulconer, *Transcendence in Philosophy and Religion,* 120–44.

Hanson, J. A. "Jean-Luc Marion and the Possibility of a Post-Modern Theology." *Mars Hill Review* 12 (1998): 93–104.

Harding, Brian. "Saturating the Phenomenon: Marion and Buber." *Sophia: International Journal for Philosophy of Religion, Metaphysical Theology and Ethics* 52.2 (2013): 295–313.

Harold, Philip J. "Givenness and Inspiration: Levinassian Responses to Marion." *Quaestiones disputatae* 1.1 (2010): 207–225.

Hart, Kevin, ed. *Counter-Experiences: Reading Jean-Luc Marion.* South Bend, Ind.: Notre Dame University Press, 2007.

———. "Introduction." In Jean-Luc Marion, *The Essential Writings*, 1–38. New York: Fordham University Press, 2013.

Henry, Michel. "Quatre Principes de la phénoménolgie. A propos de *Réduction et donation* de Jean-Luc Marion." *Revue de métaphysique et de morale* 96.1 (1991): 3–26.

Holzer, Vincent. "Phénoménologie radicale et phénomène de révélation." *Transversalités. Revue de l'Institut catholique de Paris* 70 (1999): 55–68.

Horner, Robyn. *Rethinking God as Gift: Derrida, Marion, and the Limits of Phenomenology.* New York: Fordham University Press, 2001.

———. "Problème du mal et péché des origines." *Recherches de science religieuse* 90.1 (2002): 63–86.

———. "The Betrayal of Transcendence." In *Transcendence: Philosophy, Literature, and Theology Approach the Beyond,* edited by Regina Schwartz, 61–79. New York and London: Routledge, 2004.

———. "The Face as Icon: A Phenomenology of the Invisible." *Australasian Catholic Record* 82 (2005): 19–28.

———. *Jean-Luc Marion: A Theo-logical Introduction.* Hants, U.K.: Ashgate, 2005.

———. "The Weight of Love." In Hart, *Counter-Experiences,* 235–51.

Janicaud, Dominique, Jean-François Courtine, Jean-Louis Chrétien, Michel Henry, Jean-Luc Marion, and Paul Ricœur. *Phenomenology and the "Theological Turn": The French Debate.* New York: Fordham University Press, 2000.

Janicaud, Dominique. *Phenomenology "Wide Open": After the French Debate.* Translated by Charles N. Cabral. New York: Fordham University Press, 2005.

Joas, Hans. "Die Logik der Gabe und das Postulat der Menschenwürde." In Gabel and Joas, *Von der Ursprünglichkeit der Gabe,* 143–58.

Jones, Tamsin. "Dionysius in Hans Urs von Balthasar and Jean-Luc Marion." *Modern Theology* 24.4 (2008): 743–54.

———. *A Genealogy of Marion's Philosophy of Religion: Apparent Darkness.* Bloomington: Indiana University Press, 2011.

Kal, Victor. "Being Unable to Speak, Seen as a Period: Difference and Distance in Jean-Luc Marion." In *Flight of the Gods,* edited by Ilse N. Bulhof and Laurens ten Kate, 143–65. New York: Fordham University Press, 2000.

Kaufmann, René. "Das Böse in Person. Zu Jean-Luc Marions Hermeneutik des *Mysterium iniquitatis.*" In Gerl-Falkovitz, *Jean-Luc Marion,* 345–55.

Kearney, Richard. *Debates in Continental Philosophy: Conversations with Contemporary Thinkers.* New York: Fordham University Press, 2004.

Komanski, Andrew. "A Transcendental Phenomenology that Leads out of Transcendental Phenomenology: Using Climacus' Paradox to Explain Marion's Being Given." *Quaestiones disputatae* 1.1 (2010): 114–32.

Kosky, Jeffrey L. "Philosophy of Religion and Return to Phenomenology in Jean-Luc Marion: From *God without Being* to *Being Given.*" *American Catholic Philosophical Quarterly* 78.4 (2004): 629–47.

———. "The Human in Question: Augustinian Dimensions in Jean-Luc Marion." In Benson and Wirzba, *Words of Life,* 103–119.

Kraftson-Hogue, Mike. "Predication Turning to Praise: Marion and Augustine on God and Hermeneutics—(Giver, Giving, Gift, Giving)." *Literature and Theology* 14.4 (2000): 399–411.

Kühn, Rolf. "Intentionale und Materiale Phänomenologie." *Tijdschift voor Filosofie* 54.4 (1992): 693–714.

———. "'Sättigung' als absolutes Phänomen, Zur Kritik der klassischen Phänomenalität (Kant, Husserl) bei Jean-Luc Marion." *Zeitschrift für philosophischen Ost-West-Dialog* 3 (1994): 337–45.

———. "Langeweile und Anruf: Eine Heidegger- und Husserl-Revision mit dem Problemhintergrund 'absoluter Phänomene' bei Jean-Luc Marion." *Philosophisches Jahrbuch* 102 (1995): 144–55.

———. *Radikalisierte Phänomenologie.* Frankfurt am Main: Peter Lang/Europäischer Verlag der Wissenschaften, 2003.

———. "Passivität und Zeugenschaft—oder die Verdächtigung des 'Subjekts.'. Eine radikal-phänomenologische Anfrage an Jean-Luc Marion." In Gerl-Falkovitz, *Jean-Luc Marion,* 177–98.

Lacoste, Jean-Yves. "Penser à Dieu en l'aimant. Philosophie et théologie de J.-L. Marion." *Archives de philosophie* 50 (1987): 245–270.

Larulle, François. "L'Appel et le phénomène." *Revue de métaphysique et de morale* 96.1 (1991): 27–41.

Lawell, Declan. "God without Being? St. Thomas Aquinas and Jean-Luc Marion on Naming God." *Yearbook of the Irish Philosophical Society: Voices of Irish Philosophy* (2004): 27–39.

———. "Thomas Aquinas, Jean-Luc Marion, and an Alleged Category Mistake Involving God and Being." *American Catholic Philosophical Quarterly* 83.1 (2009): 23–50.

Leask, Ian. "The Dative Subject (and the 'Principle of Principles')." In Leask and Cassidy, *Givenness and God,* 182–89.

———, and Eoin Cassidy, eds. *Givenness and God: Questions of Jean-Luc Marion.* New York: Fordham University Press, 2005.

Lewis Allport, Bryne. "'Behold the Maidservant of the Lord': Reading the Annunciation in Terms of Abundance and Absence in Marion's Witness." *Quaestiones disputatae* 1.1 (2010): 99–113.

Lewis, Stephen E. "The Lover's Capacity in Jean-Luc Marion's *The Erotic Phenomenon.*" *Quaestiones disputatae* 1.1 (2010): 226–44.

———. "The Phenomenological Concept of Givenness and the 'Myth of the Given.'" In Marion, *The Reason of the Gift,* 1–17.

Llewelyn, John. "Meanings Reserved, Re-served, and Reduced." *Southern Journal of Philosophy* 32 suppl. (1994): 27–54.

Lock, Charles. "Against Being: An Introduction to the Thought of Jean-Luc Marion." *St. Vladimir's Theological Quarterly* 37.4 (1993): 370–80.

Loughead, Tanya. "The *Happy Idiot* in El Salvador: Jean-Luc Marion's Phenomenology of Self-Love." *Quaestiones disputatae* 1.1 (2010): 163–73.

Mackinlay, Shane. "Eyes Wide Shut: A Response to Jean-Luc Marion's Account of the Journey to Emmaus." *Modern Theology* 20.3 (2004): 447–56.

———. "Phenomenality in the Middle: Marion, Romano, and the Hermeneutics of the Event." In Leask and Cassidy, *Givenness and God*, 167–61.

———. *Interpreting Excess: Jean-Luc Marion, Saturated Phenomena, and Hermeneutics*. New York: Fordham University Press, 2010.

Macquarrie, John. "Postmodernism in Philosophy of Religion and Theology." *International Journal for Philosophy of Religion* 50 (2001): 9–27.

Malo, Antonio. "The Limits of Marion's and Derrida's Philosophy of the Gift." *International Philosophical Quarterly* 52.2 (2012): 149–68.

Mandry, Christof. "Logik der Ethik—Logik der Gabe. Theologisch-ethische Überlegungen." In Gabel and Joas, *Von der Ursprünglichkeit der Gabe*, 234–51.

Manolopoulos, Mark. *If Creation Is a Gift*. Albany: State University of New York Press, 2009.

Manoussakis, John P. "The Phenomenon of God: From Husserl to Marion." *American Catholic Philosophical Quarterly* 78.1 (2004): 53–68.

———. "Thinking at the Limits: Jacques Derrida and Jean-Luc Marion in Dialogue with Richard Kearney." *Philosophy Today* 48.1 (2004): 3–26.

———. *God After Metaphysics: A Theological Aesthetic*. Bloomington: Indiana University Press, 2007.

McKenny, Gerald. "(Re)placing Ethics: Jean-Luc Marion and the Horizon of Modern Morality." In Hart, *Counter-Experiences*, 339–55.

Meessen, Yves. *L'être et le bien. Relecture phénoménologique*. Paris: Les Éditions du Cerf, 2011.

Milbank, John. "Can a Gift Be Given? Prolegomena to a Future Trinitarian Metaphysic." *Modern Theology* 11.1 (1995): 119–58.

———. *The Word Made Strange: Theology, Language, Culture*. Oxford: Blackwell Publishers, 1997.

———. "The Soul of Reciprocity, Part One: Reciprocity Refused." *Modern Theology* 17.3 (2001): 335–91.

———. "The Soul of Reciprocity, Part Two: Reciprocity Granted." *Modern Theology* 17.4 (2001): 485–507.

———. *Being Reconciled: Ontology and Pardon*. New York: Routledge, 2003.

———. "The Gift and the Mirror: On the Philosophy of Love." In Hart, *Counter-Experiences*, 253–317.

Miller, Adam S. "Reduction or Subtraction: Jean-Luc Marion, Alain Badiou, and the Recuperation of Truth." *Philosophy Today* 51 suppl. (2007): 23–32.

———. *Badiou, Marion and St. Paul: Immanent Grace*. London: Continuum, 2008.

Mooney, Timothy. "Hubris and Humility: Husserl's Reduction and Givenness." In Leask and Cassidy, *Givenness and God*, 47–68.

Moore, Jason. "Beyond Metaphysics: Jean-Luc Marion's Phenomenology of Givenness." *Dialogue: Journal of Phi Sigma Tau* 54.1 (2011): 23–35.

Morrow, Derek J. "The Conceptual Idolatry of Descartes's Gray Ontology: An Epistemology 'without Being.'" In Leask and Cassidy, *Givenness and God*, 11–36.

———. "The Love 'without Being' that Opens (to) Distance, Part One: Exploring the Givenness of the Erotic Phenomenon with Jean-Luc Marion." *Heythrop Journal: A Bimonthly Review of Philosophy and Theology* 46.3 (2005): 281–98.

———. "The Love 'without Being' that Opens (to) Distance, Part Two: From the Icon of Distance to the Distance of the Icon in Marion's Phenomenology of Love." *Heythrop Journal: A Bimonthly Review of Philosophy and Theology* 46.4 (2005): 493–511.

———. "Aquinas According to the Horizon of Distance: Jean-Luc Marion's Phenomenological reading of Thomistic Analogy." *International Philosophical Quarterly* 47.1 (2007): 59–77.

———. "From Divinization to Domination: The Cartesian Metaphorization of *Capax/ Capacitas*." *Quaestiones disputatae* 1.1 (2010): 72–98.

Murchadha, Felix Ó. "Glory, Idolatry, Kairos: Revelation and the Ontological Difference in Marion." In Leask and Cassidy, *Givenness and God,* 69–86.

Myers, Jacob D. "Toward an Erotic Liturgical Theology: Schmemann in Conversation with Contemporary Philosophy." *Worship* 87.5 (2013): 387–413.

O'Donohue, John. "The Absent Threshold: An Eckhartian Afterword." In Leask and Cassidy, *Givenness and God,* 258–85.

O'Leary, Joseph S. "The Gift: A Trojan Horse in the Citadel of Phenomenology?" In Leask and Cassidy, *Givenness and God,* 135–66.

O'Regan, Cyril. "Jean-Luc Marion: Crossing Hegel." In Hart, *Counter-Experiences,* 95–150.

Pavlovits, Tamás. "Jean-Luc Marion lecteur de Pascal." In Camilleri and Takács, *Jean-Luc Marion,* 33–51.

Pirktina, Lasma. *Ereignis, Phänomen und Sprache: Die Philosophie des Ereignisses bei Martin Heidegger und Jean-Luc Marion.* Nordhausen, Germany: Verlag Traugott Bautz, 2012.

———. "Das Ereignis in der Philosophie von Martin Heidegger und Jean-Luc Marion." In Gerl-Falkovitz, *Jean-Luc Marion,* 323–43.

Prouvost, Géry. "La tension irrésolue. Les *Questions cartésiennes, II* de Jean-Luc Marion." *Revue thomiste* 98.1 (1998): 95–102.

Puntel, Lorenz B. *Sein und Gott. Ein systematischer Ansatz in Auseinandersetung mit M. Heidegger, E. Lévinas und J.-L. Marion.* Tübingen: Mohr Siebeck, 2010. Published in English as *Being and God: A Systematic Approach in Confrontation with Martin Heidegger, Emmanuel Levinas, and Jean-Luc Marion.* Translated by Alan White. Evanston, Ill.: Northwestern University Press, 2011.

———. "Eine fundamentale und umfassende Kritik der Denkrichtung Jean-Luc Marions." In Gerl-Falkovitz, *Jean-Luc Marion,* 47–101.

Purcell, Michael. "The Ethical Signification of the Sacraments." *Gregorianum* 79.2 (1998): 323–43.

———. "Sacramental Signification and Ecclesial Exteriority: Derrida and Marion on Sign." Special issue, *Studia phaenomenologica* (2009): 115–33.

Ricard, Marie-Andrée. "La question de la donation chez Jean-Luc Marion." *Laval théologique et philosophique* 57 (2001): 83–94.

Richard, Gildas. "La phénoménologie de la donation et ses limites. Étude sur la pensée de Jean-Luc Marion." http://philo.pourtous.free.fr/Articles/Gildas/surMarion.htm.

Rölli, Marc. *Ereignis auf Französisch*. München: Fink, 2004.

Romano, Claude. "Love in Its Concept: Jean-Luc Marion's *The Erotic Phenomemon*." In Hart, *Counter-Experiences*, 319–35.

Rottenberg, Ian. "Fine Art as a Preparation for Christian Love." *Journal of Religious Ethics* 42.2 (2014): 243–62.

Sanders, Theresa. "The Gift of Prayer." In *Secular Theology: American Radical Theological Thought*, edited by Clayton Crockett, 130–40. New York and London: Routledge, 2001.

Saunders, Bret. "The Distance of Friendship: Reading Augustine's *Confessions* with Jean-Luc Marion." *Quaestiones disputatae* 1.1 (2010): 3–38.

Schmitz, Kenneth L. "The God of Love." Review of *God without Being*. *Thomist* 57.3 (1993): 495–508.

Schrijvers, Joeri. "Ontotheological Turnings? Marion, Lacoste and Levinas on the Decentring of Modern Subjectivity." *Modern Theology* 22.2 (2006): 221–53.

———. "In (the) Place of the Self: A Critical Study of Jean-Luc Marion's 'Au Lieu de soi. L'approche de Saint Augustin.'" *Modern Theology* 25.4 (2009): 661–86.

———. "Jean-Luc Marion and the Transcendence 'par Excellence': Love." In *Looking Beyond? Shifting Views of Transcendence in Philosophy, Theology, Art, and Politics*, edited by Wessel Stoker and W. L. van der Merwe. New York and Amsterdam: Rodopi, 2011.

———. *Ontotheological Turnings? The Decentering of the Modern Subject in Recent French Phenomenology*. Albany: State University of New York Press, 2011.

Sebbah, François-David. *Testing the Limit: Derrida, Henry, Levinas, and the Phenomenological Tradition*. Translated by Stephen Barker. Stanford, Calif.: Stanford University Press, 2012.

Serban, Claudia. "Résonances kantiennes et renouveau phénoménologique dans *Certitudes négatives* de Jean-Luc Marion." *Symposium* 15 (2011): 190–99.

———. "L'impossible et la phénoménologie, à partir des *Certitudes négatives*." In Camilleri and Takács, *Jean-Luc Marion*, 75–92.

———. "La méthode phénoménologique, entre réduction et herméneutique." *Les Études philosophique* (2012): 81–100.

———. "Jean-Luc Marion als Leser Kants." In Gerl-Falkovitz, *Jean-Luc Marion*, 199–215.

Seubert, Harald. "Gott und das Sein. Zu einer religionsphilosophischen Grunddifferenz zwischen Jean-Luc Marion und Lorenz B. Puntel." In Gerl-Falkovitz, *Jean-Luc Marion*, 127–56.

Smit, Peter-Ben. "The Bishop and His / Her Eucharistic Community: A Critique of Jean-Luc Marion's Eucharistic Hermeneutic." *Modern Theology* 19.1 (2003): 29–40.

Smith, James K. A. "Respect and Donation: A Critique of Marion's Critique of Husserl." *American Catholic Philosophical Quarterly* 71.4 (1997): 523–38.

———. "Liberating Religion from Theology: Marion and Heidegger on the Possibility of a Phenomenology of Religion." *International Journal for Philosophy of Religion* 46.1 (1999): 17–33.

———. "Between Predication and Silence: Augustine on How (Not) to Speak of God." *Heythrop Journal* 41.1 (2000): 66–86.

———. "How (Not) to Tell a Secret: Interiority and the Strategy of 'Confession.'" *American Catholic Philosophical Quarterly* 74.1 (2000): 135–51.

———. *Speech and Theology: Language and the Logic of Incarnation.* London and New York: Routledge, 2002.

———. "The Call as Gift: The Subject's Donation in Marion and Levinas." In *The Hermeneutics of Charity: Interpretation, Selfhood, and Postmodern Faith,* edited by James K. A. Smith and Henry Venema. Grand Rapids, Mich.: Brazos Press, 2004.

Specker, Tobias. *Einen anderen Gott denken? Zum Verständnis der Alterität Gottes bei Jean-Luc Marion.* Frankfurt am Main: Verlag Josef Knecht, 2002.

Stapleton, Charles Matthew. "The Derrida-Marion Debate: Performative Language and Mystical Theology." *Kinesis* 31.2 (2004): 4–17.

Staron, Andrew. "Moral Action and the Pragmatic As If: Gerald McKenny's Critique of Jean-Luc Marion's Privileging of Love." *Quaestiones disputatae* 1.1 (2010): 56–71.

Starzyński, Wojciech. "La phénoménologie de Jean-Luc Marion est-elle cartésienne?" In Camilleri and Takács, *Jean-Luc Marion,* 17–32.

Steinbock, Anthony. "The Poor Phenomenon: Marion and the Problem of Givenness." In Benson and Wirzba, *Words of Life,* 120–31.

Sturdevant, Molly. "The Necessity of Concepts, and Possibly Ontology: Jean-Luc Marion on Ontological Arguments." *Quaestiones disputatae* 1.1 (2010): 174–89.

Takács, Ádám. "L'idée de corrélation et la phénoménologie de l'objet chez Jean-Luc Marion." In Camilleri and Takács, *Jean-Luc Marion,* 53–73.

Tanner, Kathryn. "Theology at the Limits of Phenomenology." In Hart, *Counter-Experiences,* 201–231.

Tengelyi, László. "Jean-Luc Marion." In *Bildtheorien aus Frankreich. Ein Handbuch,* edited by Kathrin Busch and Iris Därmann, 289–98. München: Wilhelm Fink Verlag, 2011.

Tilliette, Xavier. "Phénoménologies autonomes: Michel Henry & Jean-Luc Marion." *Revista Portuguesa de Filosofia* 60.2 (2004): 473–84.

Tóth, Beáta. "Gift as God—God as Gift? Notes Towards Rethinking the Gift of Theology." Special issue, *Studia phaenomenologica* (2009): 255–67.

———. "Love between Embodiment and Spirituality: Jean-Luc Marion and John Paul II on Erotic Love." *Modern Theology* 29.1 (2013): 18–47.

Tracy, David. "Jean-Luc Marion: Phenomenology, Hermeneutics, Theology." In Hart, *Counter-Experiences,* 57–65.

Vető, Miklós. "Approches de Dieu chez Jean-Luc Marion." In Camilleri and Takács, *Jean-Luc Marion,* 115–38.

Vinolo, Stéphane. *Dieu n'a que faire de l'être. Introduction à l'œuvre de Jean-Luc Marion.* Paris: Éditions Germina, 2012.

Wallenfang, Donald L. "Sacramental Givenness: The Notion of Givenness in Husserl, Heidegger, and Marion, and Its Import for Interpreting the Phenomenality of the Eucharist." *Philosophy and Theology: Marquette University Quarterly* 22.1–2 (2010): 131–54.

Ward, Graham. "The Theological Project of Jean-Luc Marion." In *Post-secular Philosophy: Between Philosophy and Theology,* edited by Phillip Blond. New York and London: Routledge, 1998.

Wardley, Kenneth Jason. "'A Desire unto Death': The Deconstructive Thanatology of Jean-Luc Marion." *Heythrop Journal: A Bimonthly Review of Philosophy and Theology* 49.1 (2008): 79–96.

Webb, Stephen H. *The Gifting God: A Trinitarian Ethics of Excess.* Oxford: Oxford University Press, 1996.

Welten, Ruud. "Het andere ego van Descartes." *Tijdschrift voor Filosofie* 60.3 (1998): 572–79.

———, ed. *God en het Denken: Over de filosofie van Jean-Luc Marion.* Nijmegen, Netherlands: Valkhof Pers, 2000.

———. *Fenomenologie en beeldverbod bij Emmanuel Levinas en Jean-Luc Marion.* Budel, Netherlands: Damon, 2001.

———. "Saturation and Disappointment: Marion According to Husserl." *Tijdschrift voor Filosofie en Theologie/International Journal in Philosophy and Theology* 65.1 (2004): 79–96.

———. "The Paradox of God's Appearance: On Jean-Luc Marion." In *God in France: Eight Contemporary French Thinkers on God,* edited by Peter Jonkers and Ruud Welten, 186–206. Leuven, Belgium: Peeters, 2005.

———. *Phénoménologie du Dieu invisible. Essais et Études sur Emmanuel Lévinas, Michel Henry et Jean-Luc Marion.* Paris: L'Harmattan, 2011.

Westphal, Merold, ed. *Postmodern Philosophy and Christian Thought.* Bloomington: Indiana University Press, 1999.

———. "Transfiguration as Saturated Phenomenon." *Philosophy and Scripture* 1.1 (2003): 1–10.

———. "Continental Philosophy of Religion." In *The Oxford Handbook of Philosophy of Religion,* edited by William J. Wainwright, 472–93. Oxford: Oxford University Press, 2005.

———. "Vision and Voice: Phenomenology and Theology in the Work of Jean-Luc Marion." *International Journal for Philosophy of Religion* 60.1–3 (2006): 117–37.

Wohlmuth, Josef, ed. *Ruf und Gabe: Zum Verhältnis von Phänomenologie und Theologie.* Bonn: Borengässer, 2000.

Wohlmuth, Josef. "Impulse für eine künftige Theologie der Gabe bei Jean-Luc Marion." In Gabel and Joas, *Von der Ursprünglichkeit der Gabe,* 252–72.

Wolf, Kurt. *Religionsphilosophie in Frankreich: Der 'ganz Andere' und die personale Struktur der Welt.* München: Wilhelm Fink Verlag, 1999.

———. *Philosophie der Gabe. Meditationen über die Liebe in der französischen Gegenwartsphilosophie.* Stuttgart, Germany: Kohlhammer, 2006.

Zarader, Marlène. "Phenomenality and Transcendence." In Faulconer, *Transcendence in Philosophy and Religion,* 106–119.

Other Sources Cited and Consulted

Abbey, Edward. *Desert Solitaire.* New York: Touchstone, 1990.

———. *The Journey Home.* New York: Plume, 1991.

Agamben, Giorgio. *The Kingdom and the Glory: For a Theological Genealogy of Economy and Government.* Translated by Lorenzo Chiesa. Stanford, Calif.: Stanford University Press, 2011.

Baldovin, John. *The Urban Character of Christian Worship: The Origins, Development and Meaning of Stational Liturgy.* Rome: Pontificum Institutum Studiorum Orientalium, 1987.

———. *Worship: City, Church, and Renewal.* Washington, D.C.: Pastoral Press, 1991.

Bloom, Anthony. *Beginning to Pray.* New York: Paulist Press, 1970.

Brown, Charles S., and Ted Toadvine, eds. *Eco-Phenomenology: Back to the Earth Itself.* Albany: State University of New York Press, 2003.

Cain, Catherine Swanson. *Attachment Disorders: Treatment Strategies for Traumatized Children.* Lanham, Md.: Jason Aronson, 2006.

Calarco, Matthew. "Faced by Animals." In *Radicalizing Levinas,* edited by Peter Atterton and Matthew Calarco, 113–33. Albany: State University of New York Press, 2010.

Chrétien, Jean-Louis. *The Ark of Speech.* Translated by Andrew Brown. London and New York: Routledge, 2004.

Chupungco, Anscar. *Cultural Adaptations of the Liturgy.* New York: Paulist Press, 1982.

Clingerman, Forrest, Brian Treanor, Martin Drenthen, and David Utsler, eds. *Interpreting Nature: The Emerging Field of Environmental Hermeneutics.* New York: Fordham University Press, 2013.

Cyril of Jerusalem. *Lectures on the Christian Sacraments.* Crestwood, N.Y.: St. Vladimir's Seminary Press, 1986.

Derrida, Jacques. *Given Time I: Counterfeit Money.* Translated by Peggy Kamuf. Chicago: University of Chicago Press, 1992.

———. "How to Avoid Speaking: Denials." In *Derrida and Negative Theology,* edited by Harold Coward and Toby Foshay, 73–142. Albany: State University of New York Press, 1992.

———. *On the Name.* Edited by Thomas Dutoit. Stanford, Calif.: Stanford University Press, 1995.

———. *The Gift of Death.* Translated by David Wills. Chicago: University of Chicago Press, 1999.

———. *On Cosmopolitanism and Forgiveness.* New York: Routledge, 2001.

———. *The Animal That Therefore I Am.* Translated by David Wills. New York: Fordham University Press, 2008.

Dillard, Annie. *Pilgrim at Tinker Creek.* New York: HarperCollins, 1974.

Falque, Emmanuel. *Les noces de l'agneau. Essai philosophique sur le corps et l'eucharistie.* Paris: Les Éditions du Cerf, 2011.

Foltz, Bruce V., and Robert Frodeman, eds. *Rethinking Nature: Essays in Environmental Philosophy.* Bloomington: Indiana University Press, 2004.

Forché, Carolyn. *Against Forgetting: Twentieth-Century Poetry of Witness.* New York: W. W. Norton, 1993.

Gadamer, Hans-Georg. *Truth and Method.* Translated by Joel Weinsheimer and Donald G. Marshall. London and New York: Continuum, 2006.

Garvey, James. *The Ethics of Climate Change: Right and Wrong in a Warming World*. London: Continuum, 2008.

Harding, Sandra. *The Science Question in Feminism*. Ithaca, N.Y.: Cornell University Press, 1986.

———. *Whose Science? Whose Knowledge? Thinking From Women's Lives*. Ithaca, N.Y.: Cornell University Press, 1991.

———. *Sciences from Below: Feminisms, Postcolonialisms, and Modernities*. Durham, N.C.: Duke University Press, 2008.

Heinrich, Bernd. *One Man's Owl*. Princeton, N.J.: Princeton University Press, 1987.

———. *A Year in the Maine Woods*. Reading, Mass.: Addison-Wesley, 1994.

———. *The Trees in My Forest*. New York: Cliff Street Books, 1997.

———. *Mind of the Raven*. New York: Cliff Street Books, 1999.

Hénaff, Marcel. *The Price of Truth: Gift, Money, and Philosophy*. Translated by Jean-Louis Morhange. Stanford, Calif.: Stanford University Press, 2010.

Holman, Susan R. *The Hungry Are Dying: Beggars and Bishops in Roman Cappadocia*. Oxford: Oxford University Press, 2001.

Holsberg, Lisa Radakovich. *Race for the Sky: Songs for New York and 9/11*. Lisa Radakovich Holsberg (soprano), LeAnn Overton (piano), Katie Kresek (violin), Karla Moe (piccolo). Recorded in New York, 2005, compact disc.

Hughes, Daniel A. *Building the Bonds of Attachment: Awakening Love in Deeply Troubled Children*. Lanham, Md.: Jason Aronson, 2006.

———. *Attachment-Focused Family Therapy*. New York: W. W. Norton, 2007.

———, and Jonathan Baylin. *Brain-Based Parenting: The Neuroscience of Caregiving for Healthy Attachment*. New York: W. W. Norton, 2012.

John Climacus. *The Ladder of Divine Ascent*. Translated by Colm Luibheid and Norman Russell. New York and Toronto: Paulist Press, 1982.

John of Damascus. *Three Treatises on the Divine Images*. Translated by Andrew Louth. Crestwood, N.Y.: St. Vladimir's Seminary Press, 2003.

Jordanova, Ludmilla. *History in Practice*. London: Arnold, 2000.

Kant, Immanuel. *Critique of the Power of Judgment*. Translated by Paul Guyer and Eric Matthews. Cambridge: Cambridge University Press, 2000.

Kearney, Richard. *The God Who May Be: A Hermeneutics of Religion*. Bloomington: Indiana University Press, 2001.

———. *On Stories*. London and New York: Routledge, 2002.

———. *Strangers, Gods, and Monsters: Interpreting Otherness*. London and New York: Routledge, 2003.

———. *Anatheism: Returning to God after God*. New York: Columbia University Press, 2010.

Keller, Evelyn Fox. *A Feeling for the Organism: The Life and Work of Barbara McClintock*. San Francisco: W. H. Freeman, 1983.

Kristeva, Julia. *Thérèse mon amour. Sainte Thérèse d'Avila*. Paris: Fayard, 2008.

———. "Saint Teresa of Avila." In *Saints: Faith without Borders*, edited by Françoise Meltzer and Jaś Elsner, 321–33. Chicago: University of Chicago Press, 2011.

Lacoste, Jean-Yves. *Experience and the Absolute: Disputed Questions on the Humanity of Man.* Translated by Mark Raftery-Skeban. New York: Fordham University Press, 2004.

Leopold, Aldo. *A Sand County Almanac: With Other Essays on Conservation from Round River.* New York: Oxford University Press, 1949.

Llewelyn, John. *The Middle Voice of Ecological Conscience.* New York: St. Martin's Press, 1991.

Lorberbaum, Yair. "Yitshak and God's Separation Anxiety." *Journal of Jewish Thought and Philosophy* 21 (2013): 105–142.

Macauley, David. *Elemental Philosophy: Earth, Air, Fire, and Water as Environmental Ideas.* Albany: State University of New York Press, 2011.

Malabou, Catherine. *Ontology of the Accident: An Essay on Destructive Plasticity.* Translated by Carolyn Shread. Cambridge: Polity Press, 2012.

Mauss, Marcel. *The Gift: The Form and Reason for Exchange in Archaic Societies.* Translated by W. D. Halls. New York: W. W. Norton, 1990.

Morrill, Bruce, ed. *Bodies of Worship: Explorations in Theory and Practice.* Collegeville, Minn.: Liturgical Press, 1999.

Morrison, Toni. *Sula.* New York: Alfred A. Knopf, 2002.

———. *Beloved.* New York: Vintage, 2004.

———. *A Mercy.* New York: Alfred A. Knopf, 2008.

———. *Home.* New York: Alfred A. Knopf, 2012.

Muir, John. *The Wilderness World of John Muir.* Boston: Houghton Mifflin, 1976.

———. *Our National Parks.* Madison: University of Wisconsin Press, 1981.

———. *The Yosemite.* Madison: University of Wisconsin Press, 1986.

———. *Nature Writings.* New York: Library of America, 1997.

Munslow, Alan. *Narrative and History: Theory and History.* London: Palgrave, 2007.

Oliver, Kelly. *Animal Lessons: How They Teach Us to Be Human.* New York: Columbia University Press, 2009.

Prior, Vivien. *Understanding Attachment and Attachment Disorder: Theory, Evidence and Practice.* London and Philadelphia: Jessica Kingston, 2006.

Ricoeur, Paul. *Time and Narrative.* Translated by Kathleen Blamey and David Pellauer. 3 vols. Chicago: University of Chicago Press, 1984–88.

———. *Figuring the Sacred: Religion, Narrative, and Imagination.* Translated by David Pellauer. Minneapolis: Fortress Press, 1995.

———. *Memory, History, Forgetting.* Translated by Kathleen Blamey and David Pellauer. Chicago: University of Chicago Press, 2004.

Schmemann, Alexander. *For the Life of the World: Sacraments and Orthodoxy.* Crestwood, N.Y.: St. Vladimir's Orthodox Theological Seminary, 1973.

———. *The Eucharist: Sacrament of the Kingdom.* Crestwood, N.Y.: St. Vladimir's Orthodox Theological Seminary, 1987.

Soble, Alan. "Keller on Gender, Science, and McClintock: A Feeling for the Organism." In *Scrutinizing Feminist Epistemology: An Examination of Gender in Science,* edited by Cassandra L. Pinnick, Noretta Koertge, and Robert F. Almeder, 65–101. New Brunswick, N.J.: Rutgers University Press, 2003.

Steeves, H. Peter. *The Things Themselves: Phenomenology and the Return to the Everyday.* Albany: State University of New York Press, 2006.

Steinbock, Anthony J. *Phenomenology and Mysticism: The Verticality of Religious Experience.* Bloomington: Indiana University Press, 2007.

Stringer, Martin D. *On the Perception of Worship: The Ethnography of Worship in four Christian Congregations in Manchester.* Birmingham: Birmingham University Press, 1999.

———. *A Sociological History of Christian Worship.* Cambridge: Cambridge University Press, 2005.

Teresa of Avila. *The Collected Works of St. Teresa of Avila.* 3 vols. Translated by Kieran Kavanaugh and Otilio Rodriguez. Washington, D.C.: ICS Publications, 1976–80.

Tucker, Aviezer. *Our Knowledge of the Past: A Philosophy of Historiography.* Cambridge: Cambridge University Press, 2004.

Vincent, John. *An Intelligent Person's Guide to History.* London: Duckworth, 1995.

Wenham, Gordon J. *Genesis 16–50.* Word Biblical Commentary. Waco, Tex.: Word Books, 1987.

Westermann, Claus. *Genesis 12–36: A Commentary.* Translated by J. J. Scullion. London: SPCK, 1985.

Wortley, John, trans. *The Book of the Elders: Sayings of the Desert Fathers: The Systematic Collection.* Collegeville, Minn.: Liturgical Press, 2012.

INDEX

CHRISTINA M. GSCHWANDTNER is Associate Professor of Philosophy at Fordham University. She is the author of *Reading Jean-Luc Marion: Exceeding Metaphysics* (IUP, 2007) and *Postmodern Apologetics? Arguments for God in Contemporary Philosophy* (2012). She has also translated Jean-Luc Marion's *The Visible and the Revealed, On the Ego and on God,* and Michel Henry's *Words of Christ.* Her translations of Marion's *Le croire pour le voir* and *Sur la pensée passive de Descartes* are forthcoming.